WAY UP NORTH IN LOUISVILLE

The John Hope Franklin Series in
African American History and Culture
Waldo E. Martin Jr. and Patricia Sullivan, editors

WAY UP NORTH IN
Louisville

AFRICAN AMERICAN MIGRATION IN THE
URBAN SOUTH, 1930–1970

LUTHER ADAMS

The University of North Carolina Press

Chapel Hill

Library of Congress Cataloging-in-Publication Data
Adams, Luther.
Way up north in Louisville: African American migration in the urban South, 1930–1970 / Luther Adams.
p. cm.—(The John Hope Franklin series in African American history and culture)
Includes bibliographical references and index.
ISBN 978-0-8078-3422-0 (cloth : alk. paper)
1. African Americans—Kentucky—Louisville—History—20th century. 2. African Americans—Kentucky—Louisville—Social conditions—20th century. 3. African Americans—Civil rights—Kentucky—Louisville—History—20th century. 4. Civil rights movements—Kentucky—Louisville—History—20th century. 5. Civil rights movements—Southern States—History—20th century. 6. African Americans—Migrations—History—20th century. 7. Migration, Internal—Southern States—History—20th century. 8. Rural-urban migration—Southern States—History—20th century. I. Title.
F459.L89N427 2010   307.2089′96073076944—dc22   2010023647

"One-Way Ticket" from *The Collected Poems of Langston Hughes* by Langston Hughes, edited by Arnold Rampersad with David Roessel, Associate Editor, copyright © 1994 by the Estate of Langston Hughes. Used by permission of Alfred A. Knopf, a division of Random House, Inc., and Harold Ober Associates.

Portions of the text have previously been published as "Headed to Louisville: Rethinking Rural to Urban Migration in the South, 1930–1950," *Journal of Social History* 40, no. 2 (Winter 2006): 407–30; "It Was North of Tennessee: African American Migration and the Meaning of the South," *Ohio Valley History* 3, no. 3 (Fall 2003): 37–52; and "African American Migration to Louisville in the Mid-Twentieth Century," *Register of the Kentucky Historical Society* 99, no. 4 (Autumn 2001): 363–84. Used with permission.

cloth 14 13 12 11 10   5 4 3 2 1

My Mother

ARNETTA F. ADAMS

1949–1997

and

My Father

LUTHER T. ADAMS

1944–1995

CONTENTS

ILLUSTRATIONS, MAPS, AND TABLES

ILLUSTRATIONS

MAPS

TABLES

ACKNOWLEDGMENTS

My family has lived in Kentucky for over 150 years, with the earliest arrivals coming as slaves from Virginia in the 1830s. For generations, there have been Markses, Adamses, Overstreets, Govers, and Grays who have worked, raised families, fellowshipped at churches, and watched basketball with a passion. In doing so they made Kentucky their own. Collectively, they taught me the importance and the power of place. Across the years, some family members have left and returned, while some just left and others never left at all. For some, there was too much racism and too little opportunity. Yet, for all of us, Kentucky has always been home. This book is dedicated to my family, and to my mother and father.

As a graduate student at the University of Pennsylvania, I had the good fortune to be surrounded by a supportive and nurturing community of students and faculty. To my fellow students and friends—Jacqueline Akins, Ed Baptist, Deborah Broadnax, Stephanie Camp, Shefali Chandra, Edda Fields, Rhonda Frederick, Kali Gross, Leticia Hernandez, Carmen Higgins, James Peterson, Hayley Thomas, Butch Ware, Monique Williams, Rhonda Y. Williams, and Raphael Zapata—thank you all for your camaraderie. As faculty, Mary Frances Berry, Barbara Savage, Farah Griffin, Drew Faust, Walter Licht, Robert Engs, Herman Beavers, Tom Sugrue, Lee Cassanelli, and Sumathi Ramaswamy provided guidance and help at an early stage in this project. I especially thank Drew Faust, for teaching me so much about teaching the history of the South; Farah Griffin, for her kindness and aid with music and migration; Barbara Savage, for her generosity and guidance; and, above all, Mary Frances Berry for her insight and wisdom.

I would also like to give special thanks to John Cumbler, Mary Hawkesworth, and Blaine Hudson, who, as faculty at the University of Louisville, helped broaden my horizons as an undergraduate student. I thank George C. Wright, whose work on blacks in Kentucky made studies like mine possible;

also for his interest in my work and his willingness to review it over the years. I also thank Francille Wilson for all her sage advice since I first met her as a graduate student at the University of Pennsylvania. At the University of Washington–Seattle I would like to thank Quintard Taylor for his aid and my colleagues at the University of Washington–Tacoma.

In 2006 and 2007 I spent a year at Carnegie Mellon University (CMU) as an African American Urban Studies Fellow at the Center for African American Urban Studies and the Economy. Not only did the fellowship allow me the time to make substantial progress toward completing this book, but also the warmth and wisdom of Joe Trotter, Tera Hunter, and Stephanie Batiste made my time at CMU an invaluable experience both personally and professionally. In addition, I was aided by the University of Washington–Tacoma's Faculty Scholarship Support Award. My work also greatly benefited from participating in the Harvard University, NEH (National Endowment for the Humanities) Summer Institute on African American Civil Rights, organized by Patricia Sullivan and Waldo Martin, whose stellar cast of faculty, activists, and facilitators helped refine my thinking on civil rights movements in the twentieth century. I thank Cheryl Hicks and Tiyi Morris for making the summer institute and that time in the Boston area both edifying and enjoyable.

I extend my deepest thanks to the numerous librarians and archivists who helped me along the way; without their assistance this book would have been impossible. I thank the entire staff at the University of Louisville Archives and Records Center, including Tom Owen and Professor John Anderson, who graciously donated his maps of Louisville for my use. I would like to express my appreciation to Carrie Daniels, Beth Shields, and Charlene Smith at the Kentucky Historical Society. The entire staff at the City Archives of Louisville (now the Louisville Metro Archives) provided indispensable support. In particular, Agnie Griffin helped locate urban renewal maps and put me in contact with Paul Vissman, who shared his knowledge of urban renewal in Louisville. Amy Inskeep at the *Louisville Courier-Journal*'s Photographic Archives helped track down many of the images used in the book. Talal Abugabal helped locate numerous reports of the Kentucky Commission on Human Rights. I also thank the Louisville Chamber of Commerce and the staffs of the Library of Congress, Louisville Free Public Library, Van Pelt Library at the University of Pennsylvania, Suzzulo/Allen Library at the University of Washington, and Hunt Library at Carnegie Mellon University. At the University of North Carolina Press, I thank Chuck Grench, Paul Betz, and Katy O'Brien for their editorial support; Stevie Champion for her careful attention to detail as a copyeditor; and three anonymous readers for their suggestions which have made this a better book.

I have been blessed with the laughter, understanding, patience, and good cooking of my family and friends during the time it has taken to write this book. As this project has grown over the years, I would like to think that I have too. Neither my own growth nor that of this book would have been possible without my family. A host of Adamses, Markses, Overstreets, and Grays have given me love, wisdom, insight, and occasional aggravation, all of which somehow made this a better book. This project would not have been possible without my grandparents, Elizabeth and James K. Marks and Lou Ida and Henry Gray; my aunts and uncles, June and Joyce Marks, Lee Ernest and Savola Marks, Artemsia and Bythewood Adams, Nell Frierson, Bonnie Smith, Mildred Carr, Bill Marks, Charlotte and Greg Taylor; and all of my cousins. I also thank the more recent additions to my family in Seattle, Solomon and Carolyn Williams.

Jackie Akins and Cheryl Hicks deserve special thanks, not only for being such good friends, but also for discussing and reading my work too many times to count. Jackie has given enough wisdom and insight for a lifetime. Shefali Chandra and Butch and Kaaronica Ware, as well as their entire family, were not only a great source of intellectual inspiration but also opened their homes and hearts to me. In Philadelphia, Angel Del Villar, Vincent Henry, Phil Ting, and I forged lasting friendships over our love of basketball and trash talking at Gimbel. In Seattle, William Gill, Gillian Harkins, and Elaine Waller-Rose all brought a bit of sunshine to "Rain City." I also thank Mt. Zion Baptist Church, Karita Randall, Tanya Thomas, and Ronald Johnson for helping me find a home away from home. I would like to thank Rashamel Jones for always making me laugh, Ginni and Keith Wakefield for their friendship and constant reminder that, in the end, this book is about the complex lives of black people in Louisville. I thank my uncle William G. Marks for allowing me to interview him and for making me smile.

For my brother, Shontelle Adams, no words can express my gratitude and admiration. Thanks for everything you have done to give me the support and strength to continue forward. Thanks to Brenda Adams for enduring my long and frequent visits with grace. And a special thanks to my nieces, Devin Adams, Amanda Adams, and Aleena Adams, who I like to think take after me as much as their parents and who keep me focused on the important things in life—like monopoly, cheerleading, soccer, and horror books. I thank my wife and friend, Mynique, who in addition to her wit, humor, kindness, and passion for books has brought peace, love, magic, and happiness.

Lastly, I hope this book does justice to the real struggles, triumphs, strength, and endurance of black people in Louisville. This book is a tribute to their monumental efforts to make Louisville a better place.

WAY UP NORTH IN LOUISVILLE

INTRODUCTION

Surrounded by hate, yet I love home.
—COMMON, "Respiration," *Mos Def & Talib Kweli Are Black Star* (1998)

This is a book about "Home." It is a book about the South and how some African Americans chose to stay in the South hoping to transform it economically, politically, and socially to suit their needs at a time when roughly half the black population left the South moving north and west. Their commitment to making the South a safe space for African Americans points to an intersection of migration, civil rights, and southern identity that is largely unexplored. Yet black in-migration is crucial to understanding black southern mobility and agency, and to understanding the transformation of the postwar urban landscape. By examining African American migration through the lens of Home, it becomes clear that persistent patterns of class and racial inequality did not rob black people of their capacity to act in their own interests.

African American migrants in Louisville, Kentucky, viewed the South as Home, as both a symbolic and a real location. Infused with meaning by collective memory, Home encompassed conflict and contradiction. It was at once a site of violence and oppression, and at the same time a source of raced and gendered agency. For many of these migrants, the decision to stay in the South was linked to their desire to combat oppression. In this light, migration within the South takes on new meaning as an act of resistance. Migrants went to Louisville with the resolve to improve the social, economic, and racial climate for African Americans in the South. As much as blacks defined the South as a site of oppression, it was also their Home and held a long tradition of resistance. African Americans throughout the South proved more than willing to stay and battle for freedom. At a time when roughly half the black population left the South seeking greater opportunity and freedom in the North and the West, that same desire was often a catalyst for some blacks to remain in the South. The decision *not* to migrate north or west but to fight for freedom in the South points to an intersection of migration, civil rights, and southern identity that has thus far been overlooked.

Although African Americans defined the South as sites of both oppression and resistance, these were not its only meanings. Fixating solely on oppression and resistance fails to shift historical attention away from whites. More importantly, both definitions of the South obscure the agency black migrants demonstrated throughout their lives and fail to capture the complexity of how African Americans viewed the South. As much as the South was defined by oppression and resistance, it was also *Home*.

In its focus on blacks who chose to remain in the South, *Way Up North in Louisville* offers a powerful reinterpretation of the modern civil rights movement within the interrelated contexts of migration, urban renewal, and the fight against residential segregation and economic inequality in the postwar metropolis. The urban America that emerged from the postwar era was a product of the aspirations and agency of African Americans as much as it was of the action of the state, the vision of urban planners, or white resistance. While blacks in Louisville may not have wielded power in equal amounts, they were by no means powerless. Time after time, they acted to reshape the urban landscape to meet their own visions of equality. In the end, this book is foremost about African American migrants like Goldie Winstead-Beckett and William G. Marks, who, though settling in Louisville decades apart, were equally driven by the desire to make their hopes and dreams of a better life, a better South, a reality.

Born in Hopkins County, Kentucky, on April 6, 1914, Goldie Winstead-Beckett was the only daughter and the second of four children in a family of farmers. While she was still a young girl, the Winsteads fell on hard times after her father and oldest brother were killed in a car wreck. Although the Winsteads were poor, Goldie's mother was determined that her children would receive an education at the little school six miles away. After graduating from Roosevelt High School in Madisonville, Goldie Winstead went on to what was then called Kentucky State College for Negroes, in Frankfort, one of the few colleges in Kentucky that admitted black students.

In a sense, Goldie Winstead was more fortunate than her brothers and most other black children in Hopkins County, or, for that matter, anywhere else in the South; few blacks—male or female—completed high school, and even fewer had a chance to attend college. Like most African Americans who did go on to college, Goldie worked throughout the school year and in the summer to pay for her tuition. Despite her job in the business office at Kentucky State, she graduated in three and a half years with a degree in home economics. Goldie then moved to Owensboro, Kentucky, and taught at Western High School for three years.

During this time Goldie met William Washington Beckett, a native of Baltimore. In 1936 William finished mortuary school in St. Louis and bought the A. B. Riddley Funeral Home in Louisville. Two years later, in 1938, Goldie and William were married. Thus, at the age of twenty-four, Goldie quit her job in Owensboro, packed her bags, and headed for Louisville to begin a new life.[1] She and her new husband were among the many African American women and men who chose to migrate to a more familiar southern city in search of a brighter future rather than moving north or west. Like many black migrants, Goldie and William arrived in Louisville after having experienced life in cities of various sizes during stops along the way.

In the twenty-six years Goldie Winstead-Beckett lived in Louisville, African Americans instituted remarkable changes in the cultural, socioeconomic, and political landscape of a city where they successfully fought for political power and against segregation. In the 1950s, they gained a foothold in numerous facilities, including all branches of the public library, the University of Louisville, the Greyhound Bus Station, and municipal parks and public schools. Between 1951 and 1961, William Beckett won election and reelection to the city's Board of Aldermen, becoming the second black to ever hold that position.[2]

While her husband served multiple terms on the Board of Aldermen, Goldie Winstead-Beckett was busy raising their three children, Patricia, Jacqueline, and William Jr., keeping their house in order, and running the family business.[3] Yet, according to Goldie, the biggest change for blacks in Louisville was not increased political power or access to public accommodations; it was urban renewal. In her eyes, urban renewal "tore the heart out of the black community" in the process of destroying the Walnut Street business district.[4] Walnut Street was the center of the African American community; it housed black churches, businesses, restaurants, and nightspots. But more than a business district, it was a "haven" for blacks in Louisville—a place where they could escape the harsh realities of life in a southern city. For Goldie Winstead-Beckett, Walnut Street was a place where she and her family were "respected."[5]

Ultimately, a new expressway, government buildings, and a small number of new homes replaced the Walnut Street business district. For many of Louisville's black residents, the new construction also marked the creation of a ghetto. But for Goldie Winstead-Beckett, urban renewal compounded the death of her husband William in 1963 by forcing her to sell her family business and tearing down her home of twenty-six years at 1024–26 Walnut Street. After almost thirty years in Louisville, Goldie reached the conclusion that it was time to move on. In January 1965 she gathered her belongings and left Kentucky, establishing a new residence at 108 East Sedgwick Street in Philadelphia.[6]

The year after she departed, Reverend William G. Marks and his wife Rose arrived in the River City. Marks, who was recently called to preach, thought it would be in the best interests of his ministry to attend Louisville's Simmons Bible College. Initially, he drove back and forth between their home in Lexington, some seventy-odd miles away, and the college as a part-time student. However, on discovering that the commute cost too much, Rose and William loaded their belongings into his 1955 Chevy and moved to Louisville in the fall of 1966.

William was no stranger to the city. As early as 1962, he and his younger sister Arnetta would visit Louisville for three or four days at a time as delegates from Bethel Baptist Church in Lexington. During Baptist district association conventions, they became close friends with Reverend A. J. Elmore and his family, who were themselves migrants from Alabama. They stayed at Sister Sadie Elmore's home anytime they went to Louisville on church business.

It was not long before William and Arnetta Marks began to make special trips to the city just to visit the Elmores or to (enjoy) fellowship with them on Sunday at Oakland Baptist Church. Between his contacts at Simmons Bible College and Oakland Baptist Church, William fashioned an extensive network of friends that helped ease his transition to a new city.[7] Moreover, in Louisville his prior experiences with urbanization were far more common among black migrants than not. His network of family and friends helped him get his first good job in Louisville, as custodian at General Electric. Like Marks, many migrants arrived in the city with a range of strategies and networks to help them negotiate the urban landscape. In his words, "If hadn't been for Simmons Bible College and the ministers that treated me well, I don't know if I'da stuck it out here."[8]

Though largely overlooked by historians, the experiences of Goldie Winstead-Beckett and Reverend William Marks point to the range of blacks who chose to remain in the South. Goldie Beckett was a college-educated woman from rural Kentucky; if we can speak of a black middle class during this era, then she was definitely a member. Her business generated an annual income in excess of $5,000, a sum few blacks earned over a number of years. Reverend Marks, on the other hand, was a man from what was then the second largest city in Kentucky. Even though he moved to Louisville to attend Bible College, he had little more than an eighth-grade education. Yet both Beckett and Marks chose to remain in the South with the hope of making a better life in Louisville. Not all migrants came from within the state, but whether they were from Kentucky, Tennessee, Mississippi, Louisiana, or Alabama, their narratives of relocation within the South were equally complex.

In some ways the Louisville encountered by Marks in 1966 was a different city from the one Beckett had entered in 1938. Life for Louisville's African Americans was somewhat paradoxical. Segregation was no longer legal, but Walnut Street—the old business and social center of black Louisville—was on its deathbed. Politically blacks gained more power than at any other time in the city, yet in the minds of many African Americans, the construction of a ghetto was well under way. And, as always during the period, African Americans struggled to find decent jobs that paid decent wages. Although some aspects of Louisville changed, it would be a mistake to think the city made a great break from its past.

According to Reverend Marks, "racial tensions" still ran high throughout the city. He perceptively pointed out that just because African Americans had the legal right to use a public park did not mean they would be safe there. Nor were their housing problems solved. Indeed, blacks organized and initiated campaigns for the right to live where they chose as early as 1914, when they formed a local branch of the NAACP to challenge an ordinance requiring residential segregation. When Marks entered the city more than fifty years later, the struggle against residential segregation and for open housing continued. Nor had the economic conditions most blacks faced in the city radically altered during those five decades. Throughout the period African Americans mostly worked in menial jobs as domestics or casual laborers. Indeed, as late as 1967, one of the city's largest businesses—General Electric—employed 14,374 workers, of whom only 35 nonwhites were skilled, while 784 were unskilled.[9] Or as Marks put it, most blacks in Louisville remained "on the broom."[10]

Although William Marks and Goldie Winstead-Beckett were part of the largest African American migration in U.S. history, neither the Second Great Migration (1940–70) nor black relocation within the South has received much attention from historians. We have all heard of the Great Migration (1915–21), the mass exodus from the South by over a million blacks moving north and west in search of a better life. Many left during the era of World War I and even more during World War II. During the Second Great Migration the South lost more than half of its black population, comprising 5.5

million people. At the same time, however, other African Americans stayed, and not because they lacked the resources or the motivation to move. They stayed, often relocating within the South, because it was Home. They acted on their belief that equality must be secured at home, in the South, before anywhere else. Although a historic site of black oppression and resistance, the region, for many African Americans, remained a source of connection, of identity weaving history, family, and place together in a single word: Home.

Way Up North in Louisville: African American Migration in Louisville, Kentucky, 1930–1970 challenges our historical understanding of black migration and postwar American history. It examines relocation during the era of the Second Great Migration, which as yet remains largely unexplored. Indeed, few scholars have given this second, and larger, migration the attention generated by the first Great Migration. Moreover, in their zeal to understand black migration in the urban North, historians seemingly overlook the fact that while more than five million African Americans abandoned the South during this period, an equally large number chose to remain, often relocating to southern cities.[11] Millions moved from rural areas and small towns to cities like Memphis, New Orleans, Atlanta, and Louisville. The lives of African Americans, like the more than 17,000 migrants who made Louisville their home between 1930 and 1970, have not drawn the interest of historians.

Nonetheless, *Way Up North in Louisville* builds on the work of scholars of prior black migrations. Though the histories of these earlier movements were substantially different, they offer insights that shape any study of black migration in the United States.[12] At a time when most historians only examined relocation from the rural South to the urban North, with its emphasis on terrorism and poverty, Nell Painter's *Exodusters* suggests that the complexity of black mobility cannot be captured in one rural-to-urban migration narrative.[13] Whereas *Exodusters* points to the need to study migration outside of the North-South paradigm, other works emphasize the importance of culture and what Darlene Clark Hine calls "non-economic" motives for migration.[14]

Through its focus on Louisville, Kentucky, this project also deepens our understanding of southern history. The importance that James Grossman and Earl Lewis place on the role of southern culture illuminates the process of migration and acclamation to the urban landscape in a way few other scholars do.[15] Ultimately, their emphasis on southern culture has revolutionized our understanding of the experiences of black migrants in Cleveland, Washington, D.C., and Oakland's East Bay.[16] Yet, despite the attention given its role in the transformation of American culture, the part southern culture played in southern migration is left unexplored. Indeed, this inattention to the South is mirrored by the lack of regard to the Second Great Migration as a whole. Outside of the handful of studies that examine black mobility in the West, few scholars have deemed migration within the South a topic of interest. Yet, without a clear understanding of black migration within the region, our understanding of the civil rights movement and postwar urban America is incomplete.

Recently, a number of scholars have explored the importance of the South and southern culture to migration. James N. Gregory's *The Southern Diaspora* and Glenda Gilmore's *Defying Dixie* consider the role of southern migrants in transforming American culture.[17] However, Gregory analyzes how southern migration influenced the transformation of culture and politics outside the South, and Gilmore is concerned with the role of southern expatriates in transforming the South from afar. Drawing on the work of earlier scholars of African American migration who examined southern culture in the North, Gregory's study of black and white mobility to the North and West makes an invaluable contribution to our understanding of relocation patterns, but it neglects migration within the South itself. Similarly, Gilmore's work excavates the role of southern "refugees" in directing attention to the ongoing injustices in the South during the pre–civil rights era, arguing that the "brightest minds and most beautiful spirits" were chased from the South.[18] While retaining their focus on southern culture, *Way Up North in Louisville* departs from the previous scholarship by examining how African American migrants who *stayed* in the South transformed the culture and politics of the South from *within* the South.

Like *Way Up North in Louisville*, Laurie Green's *Battling the Plantation Mentality* probes African American migration within the context of the urban South. Green's brilliant illumination of black Memphis during the civil rights era "explores how working-class African Americans thought about freedom, how they conceived of their own activism, and how these perceptions reflected their historically specific experiences in the changing postwar urban South."[19] In doing so, she directs much-needed attention to the centrality of African American efforts in the shaping of the postwar urban landscape. Moreover, her study signals the importance of examining the convergence of work, culture, and politics in the civil rights movement.

At the same time, Green's emphasis on the "plantation mentality" is problematic at best. According to Green, the "plantation mentality" refers both to "white racist attitudes that promoted white domination and black subservience" and an ethic of "fear and dependency" fostered among blacks in

Memphis by the cultural memories of slavery.[20] Although the term "plantation mentality" did not come into vogue until the 1960s, African Americans used it to describe "contemporary urban power relations between whites and blacks as ones of master/slave."[21] Green's notion of the "plantation mentality" invokes theories such as the "culture of poverty" and the "slave mentality" but is closest to the findings of sociologist Charles S. Johnson in his *Shadow of the Plantation*. Published in 1934, Johnson's work argues that "the tradition of slavery; in the survival of the plantation" was observed in the daily life of African Americans in some parts of the South.[22] For Johnson, these traditions were evident in "patterns of life, social codes, as well as social attitudes" that were set in the political economy of slavery and transmitted from one generation to the next.[23] Yet, unlike Green, Johnson maintains that these traditions were broken by migration from the isolated places where such traditions endured. Given that as early as 1935–40 most black migrants in southern cities such as Charlotte, Birmingham, Atlanta, Nashville, New Orleans, and Louisville were originally from urban areas, it is unclear whether the "plantation mentality" offers an analytic tool that is applicable across the urban South.[24]

Undoubtedly, for both blacks and whites across the nation, the legacy of slavery was, and remains, powerful. Yet Green's work suggests that African Americans' own plantation mentality was as much an impediment to achieving freedom and equality as white supremacy. For Green, "both the white man and the black man maintained, 'mental reservations' emanating from slavery that needed to be eradicated for different race relations to be achieved."[25] Thus, blacks first needed to challenge their own "cultural memories of slavery" as much as contemporary racism. While surely there were some African Americans who internalized the racism passed down from generation to generation, it is less clear whether the so-called plantation mentality existed in rhetoric or reality since black people could seldom speak or act freely without reprisal.[26] Unlike blacks in Memphis, blacks in Louisville were less concerned with battling a plantation mentality than confronting the racist actions of whites that inscribed white supremacy in economics, housing, education, and the urban landscape itself.

Despite the limitations of the plantation mentality, Green's work points to the importance of examining African American migration in the South. Though much has been written about Muhammad Ali, substantially less has been written about the community that produced him. Until recently, our understanding of the history of African Americans in Louisville has rested mainly on the work of George C. Wright.[27] Once known as the "Gateway to the South," Louisville is significant not only because it held the largest concentration of African Americans in Kentucky, but also because the history of black migration to Louisville suggests the need to forge a more complex understanding of African Americans' relationship to the South as well as of their southern identities. Black migrants in Louisville consciously chose to remain in the South because they viewed it as Home. Their initiatives, whether political, social, or economic, illustrate the ways in which they claimed the South and "the city" as their own, while acting on their hopes and dreams of making Louisville and the South a better place for African Americans to live in.

Just as *Way Up North in Louisville* deepens our understanding of southern history, by combining the disparate histories of migration, civil rights, and urban renewal it also offers a more complicated but more accurate view of postwar urban America. Much of what we know about that era has been dominated by discussions of the "origins of the urban crisis" and the "making of the second ghetto," which have illuminated the complex relationship between the state, urban planning, and white supremacy in shaping the urban landscape. While many of these studies point directly to the impact of race and racism on the urban landscape, few examine in adequate detail the lives of black people or their attempts to shape the cities of postwar America to suit their own interests. Clearly, the importance of state institutions, the changing dynamics of postindustrial capitalism, and white violence cannot be dismissed, but African Americans were no less historical actors in this period.[28]

The scholarship stemming from the "making of the second ghetto" and the "urban crisis" paved the way for whiteness studies on the politics of school integration, modern conservatism, urban policy, and state, municipal, and neighborhood activism. Urban scholars such as Thomas Sugrue and Heather Thompson have expressed concern about the lack of "African American voices" in the history of the "making of the second ghetto," suggesting that it "gave too much power to the process of ghettoization and too little to blacks themselves." On the other hand, Arnold Hirsch is more ambivalent.[29] He argues that his inattention to African Americans in Chicago was purposeful since there was an "asymmetrical distribution of power," and that he devoted "primary attention to whites, because that's where the power was."[30] Moreover, his focus is the "making of the second ghetto not the ghetto itself."[31] In doing so, he implies that African Americans had no role in the making of the second ghetto, when in large measure much of what white urbanities did— whether in fleeing to the suburbs or engaging in massive resistance—was in response to black activism. Though blacks were not omnipotent, they were by no means powerless. Their hopes, dreams, and actions are no less an integral part of understanding the postwar urban landscape than the resistance of whites or the state.

The histories of the "second ghetto" are reminiscent of the scholarship on the process of ghettoization during the era of the first Great Migration. Historians of that event in Harlem, Chicago, and Cleveland emphasized relocation as an agent in the creation of large, segregated African American communities within urban environments. Though these studies were often heroic in their exposé of patterns of urban housing and institutional segregation in northern cities, they often neglected the agency and internal lives of black migrants in the face of larger economic forces.[32] Collectively, this literature has made an important contribution to our understanding of the larger structural forces that led to the spatial isolation of blacks in American cities across the nation. Yet, in exposing the conditions that made the first or second ghettos, or what Sugrue calls the "urban crisis," historians have revealed more about the anxieties of white urbanites and suburbanites than they have about the lives of black folk. Given the centrality of migration, urbanization, and the struggle for equality across urban landscapes, both northern and southern, the actions and aspirations of black people are an integral part of the narrative of postwar urban history. Only recently have historians began to devote serious attention to black lives during this period.[33]

Way Up North in Louisville shifts our understanding of African Americans in postwar urban America, even as it suggests the need for more attention to the urban South. Black southern history is rightly dominated by the ongoing civil rights movements in the postwar era; however, few of those studies attempt to discuss civil rights in the context of the urban South that gives some of those movements meaning.[34] *Way Up North in Louisville* points to the interconnectedness of black migration, civil rights, and the struggle to shape the urban landscape in postwar America. Without an examination of migration and urban renewal, the struggle against residential segregation loses much of the significance and urgency it held for blacks at the time. This book shifts historical attention to black lives in postwar America by placing our understanding of civil rights at the crossroads of the histories of black migration and the transformation of the urban landscape.

THE FIRST TWO CHAPTERS, "Headed for Louisville" and "Way Up North in Louisville," work in tandem to analyze the political economy and different meanings that migration held for African Americans. Access to defense industries lured a diverse pool of professional and working-class blacks to the River City. "Headed for Louisville" focuses on the economic motives involved in African American migration and reconsiders the explanatory power of the rural-to-urban migration motif. During the 1940s the origin of black migration was in the *urban* South. In terms of pace and scale, Louisville may have represented a somewhat different urban environment, but *the city* itself was not necessarily an unknown entity.

"Way Up North in Louisville" considers the different ways African American migrants defined the South and their own southernness. Blacks characterized Louisville in terms of oppression, resistance, and Home. Though it was described as a "progressive city" in the South, blues singer Clara Smith pointed out that it was in Louisville that the South began. Her 1925 "L. & N. Blues" claimed that the region was defined not so much geographically as it was culturally or by its politics of oppression. Activist and scholar Angela Davis argues that "'Home' is evocatively and metaphorically represented as the South, conceptualized as the territorial location of historical sites of resistance to white supremacy."[35] In defining the South as Home, black migrants demonstrated that neither their lives nor their conceptions of the South were wholly defined by racial oppression or their resistance to it; rather, they infused the South with a meaning all their own.[36]

Chapter 3, "I Never Jim Crowed Myself," shifts our attention to the strategies migrants deployed to adjust to the urban landscape in Louisville. In doing so, this study highlights the nature of Jim Crow in the city. Whereas traditional migration narratives describe African Americans as unprepared to cope with life in the city, *Way Up North in Louisville* demonstrates that migrants arrived in Louisville equipped with a network of family and friends, a range of experiences with urban life, and a "cultural arsenal" that they deployed to successfully navigate the urban landscape.[37] At the same time migrants used an array of strategies to deal with Jim Crow, the limited housing stock, and incidences of violence, including dissemblance, passing or refusing to pass, and declining to patronize segregated businesses whenever possible. In doing so, blacks demonstrated that although they were forced to defer to Jim Crow in practice, they would not do so in principle.

Chapter 4, "No Room for Possum or Crawfish," centers on the range of political activism migrants engaged in between 1930 and the early 1950s in an effort to remake Louisville as Home. Here "Home" is defined as a "safe place, where there is no need to explain oneself to outsiders; it stands for community; more problematically it can elicit a nostalgia . . . that elides exclusion, power relations, and difference."[38] However, the nature of segregation and inequality made it impossible for blacks to elide power or view Louisville as a safe place. Migrants initiated campaigns to desegregate the public libraries and state universities, to gain access to better employment opportunities through economic boycotts, to make the local Republican and Democratic parties responsive to black voters, and to make the city a safer place. In doing so, they shaped the nature of both the postwar civil rights movements in the city and the city itself.

Chapters 5 and 6, "Behold the Land" and "Upon This Rock," direct attention to the decade of the 1960s. "Behold the Land" argues that many African Americans arrived in Louisville highly politicized and, like blacks throughout the region, brought with them a tradition of fighting for equality within the South. They stayed in the South, demonstrating a commitment to freedom that combined a desire to make the South a safer place and the belief that they could not "run away" from its problems. Through a variety of strategies civil rights activists, often led by migrants, struggled to desegregate public accommodations and secure equal access to employment.

"Upon This Rock" weaves together the histories of migration and the struggle for open housing with the history of urban renewal and white flight to the suburbs. As migrants continued to arrive, urban renewal tore out the heart of Louisville's black community, the Walnut Street business district, thrusting the issue of residential segregation to the forefront of the civil rights struggle. While many scholars have identified this as the era of the "making of the second ghetto," it was also a time in which African Americans fought to make their vision of an urban landscape—shaped to meet blacks' needs—a reality. Thus, the hopes, dreams, and desires of blacks were as much a part of the shaping of postwar urban America as urban planning, white flight, and ghettoization.

Migration was central to the civil rights movement—both in terms of the presence of large numbers of migrants and as a contributing factor in creating the crisis that made open housing imperative. Though migration exacerbated the housing crisis, the limited housing options available to blacks were the result of urban renewal and an enduring commitment to residential segregation. Without placing the histories of migration, urban renewal, and suburbanization in dialogue, the struggle for open housing loses much of its meaning. Moreover, by emphasizing the "making of the second ghetto" or the "origins of the urban crisis," we neglect the degree to which African Americans themselves attempted to shape the urban landscape to suit their own interests. In doing so we should be reminded that the unacceptable conditions many cities confront in the twenty-first century were not inevitable. Rather, they are a product of competing visions of the urban landscape that shaped postwar urban America.

HEADED FOR LOUISVILLE

AFRICAN AMERICAN MIGRATION WITHIN THE SOUTH

Roughly 140 miles southwest of Louisville, a Confederate flag flew over the center of the small town of Russellville. The son of sharecroppers and the grandchild of slaves, James Wright was seventeen and recently married. Like many other Americans in 1936, he struggled to find a job. While his wife Gladys worked as a cook in a white home, James alternately cut corn, worked at a Civilian Conservation Corps camp, and washed cars at the local Chevrolet dealership in an attempt to make ends meet. Of the latter job he recalled, "You worked like a dog" and the owners, Henry and George Page, "called you nigger."[1] Over the next few years Wright made no less than three trips to Louisville to find work but returned to Russellville each time without success.

But the Wrights did not give up. As James Wright recalled, "I left Russellville on the first day of September 1941, and I never went back no more. I said, "I'm going to stay in Louisville if I have to dig ditches, get put in jail, steal somebody, rob, cut their head off.' So I stayed." According to historian Toni Gilpin, Wright worked a number of odd jobs in Louisville, carrying cross ties for the railroad and doing menial labor for a moving company before he was hired by a construction company owned by DuPont. With the growth of defense industries in the area, he was employed briefly by the Vultee Aircraft factory prior to being drafted and sent to Burma. In 1946 Wright chose to return to Louisville, where he found a job with International Harvester and settled into his new environment.[2]

Like Wright, Rebecca Smith was one of the many African Americans nationwide who acquired their first industrial work experience by migration. The oldest of four children, Smith was a twenty-eight-year-old single mother when she arrived in Louisville in 1945 looking for work.[3] Though born in

Cumberland County, Kentucky, in 1917, she had lived in Toledo, Ohio, then returned to Cumberland County before moving to Louisville. Told by her cousin she could find work at the Louisville and Nashville (L & N) Railroad for the duration of the war, she quit her job as a domestic but returned home once again in disappointment before learning she had secured a job at the L & N on a rivet gang. Indeed, even with the labor shortages caused by World War II, the L & N seldom hired black women as anything other than cleaners, sweepers, material handlers, or rivet catchers. Smith was not so much motivated by patriotism, or the desire to support the war effort, as she was by the necessity of supporting her family. She often worked seven days a week without overtime or sick days for sixty cents an hour doing manual labor. The work was dirty and dangerous but ultimately rewarding. Although the L & N continued to employ nearly 100 black women after the war, that figure was less than the 237 employed in 1943, and 98 percent of those remaining worked as unskilled laborers.[4] By 1967, Smith was one of 40 blacks in the L & N workforce of 2,027.[5] Unlike many African American women, who were the "last hired and the first fired," she retained her job at the end of the war.[6]

Nearly ten years after the process that brought James Wright to Louisville began and one year after Smith was hired by the L & N, Dr. Maurice Rabb and his family arrived from Shelbyville, a small Kentucky town thirty miles away. A native of Columbus, Mississippi, Rabb had studied medicine at Meharry Medical College, in Nashville, Tennessee, one of the few medical schools in the South open to African Americans. By the time Rabb landed in the River City, he had lived in Nashville; Kansas City, Missouri; and Frankfort and Shelbyville, Kentucky.

During the Great Depression, Rabb was the only black physician treating people of color in Shelbyville. The Depression was a difficult era not only for agriculturalists and industrial workers, but also for the doctors and lawyers who served them. Reliant on these impoverished communities, black doctors and lawyers struggled to support their own families. For Rabb, the "depression was rough" since his patients could seldom afford to pay him in cash; one family settled its debts each year by razing a hog. In fact, Rabb recalled, he was most often paid with "chicken eggs, fish, frog legs, [or] duck. . . . We could eat, but we didn't make a lot of money."[7] The opportunity to provide a bit of economic security for his family helped propel the Rabbs toward Louisville.

The personal histories of James Wright, Rebecca Smith, and Maurice Rabb contain a number of threads that can be woven into a larger narrative of African American migration within the South during the Second Great Migration. Between 1930 and 1970 more than 17,000 migrants moved to Louisville in ever-increasing numbers, hoping to find a better life or at least better jobs.[8] The experiences of Louisville migrants like Wright, Smith, and Rabb raise a number of critical questions concerning our understanding of the origins and periodization of black migration as a whole and of the historical emphasis on rural-to-urban migration in particular. African American relocation in Louisville challenges us to rethink the centrality of rural-to-urban migration narratives during the Second Great Migration.

While the literature on the first Great Migration (1915–21) is voluminous, scant attention is paid to African American migration during the World War II era. Except for a handful of excellent studies of migration to the West Coast, few scholars consider black relocation during this period. Not one focuses solely on African American migration within the South. Louis M. Kyriakoudes examines black and white migration in Nashville but only between 1890 and 1930.[9] And while historians such as James Grossman, Peter Gottlieb, and Jacqueline Jones make mention of seasonal or "step-wise" migration patterns in the early twentieth century, they give little consideration to the distinctive patterns of migration within the South during the Second Great Migration.[10] For scholars like Gottlieb and Grossman, migration to southern cities was simply part of the rural migration that eventually led to the urban North. African Americans either "tarried" or were stranded in southern cities.[11]

Too often our understanding of the Great Migration to the urban North substitutes for a sustained analysis of the Second Great Migration (1940–70). Though some migrants regarded the city as only a temporary stop on their way north, for many African Americans between 1930 and 1950 Louisville was their final destination. A number of black migrant streams pooled in the River City, including those from the Deep South who were displaced by changing New Deal policies, those in the Upper South who were involved in urban-to-urban migration, and professionals reliant on the concentrations of blacks in Louisville. These different streams combined with more well-known groups of black migrants spurred by World War II and the access to defense industry employment provided by Executive Order 8802 in many southern cities. (Executive order 8802, issued by President Franklin D. Roosevelt in 1941, established the Fair Employment Practices Commission to facilitate the "full participation in the defense program by all persons, regardless of race, creed, color or national origin.")[12] African American migration to Louisville demonstrates the distinctiveness of the Second Great Migration and thus the importance of black mobility within the South.

For many blacks, the economic wheels of this migration were set in motion during the era of the Great Depression and the New Deal. The financial hardships produced by the Depression fueled African American migration as a whole regardless of class. During the decade of 1930–40, the New Deal's Agricultural Adjustment Administration (AAA) as well as the National Recovery Administration (NRA) displaced large numbers of African Americans, who for the most part had no outlet until World War II. Both programs directly and indirectly created the economic conditions that drove African American migration within the South. During the life of the AAA there were two high points of tenant and sharecropper eviction. The first was between 1933 and 1934, and the second lasted from 1935 to 1937 during the second life of the AAA.[13] As early as the winter of 1933, the year the AAA was set in motion, widespread tenant evictions were already under way.[14]

By 1934, the first full year of its operation, landowners began to evict entire families of sharecroppers and tenant farmers as a means of reducing crop acreage. The idea behind the AAA was to raise the price of staple crops, including corn, cotton, and tobacco, by limiting production. To induce landowners to decrease production, the government offered planters "parity payments" *not* to produce crops in order to raise their income to the amount they would have earned if they had brought those crops to market.[15] The necessity of producing fewer crops and the nature of the parity payments caused planters to cut the number of tenants and sharecroppers. According to Raymond Wolters, a historian of African Americans during the Great Depression, landowners found that one of the easiest and most economical ways to lower production was to evict sharecroppers. The rate of tenant and sharecropper evictions were highest between 1935 and 1937.[16]

Indirectly, and perhaps unintentionally, the AAA's parity payments infused the South with cash, facilitating the mechanization of southern agriculture. Increasingly, landowners began to replace whole families of sharecroppers and tenants with tractors.[17] Between 1930 and 1939 the number of tractors in the United States nearly doubled to more than 1,626,000. In the cotton-producing southern states alone, 111,399 tractors displaced between 100,000 and 500,000 families or from one-half million to two million people.[18] In 1941, the U.S. Department of Agriculture reported that "nearly every one of these tractors has pushed a few tenants, sharecroppers, or hired hands out of jobs."[19] Unlike the Great Migration in the earlier part of the twentieth century, during the 1930s *planters* themselves fueled black migration through widespread evictions.

Once evicted, African Americans had few options. The majority either stayed on or around the farms they previously worked as wage or seasonal labor, or they moved to urban areas within the South.[20] As Alan Brinkley observes, "The exodus of sharecroppers from the land was responsible, too, for a major increase in the black population of southern cities."[21] Atlanta, Birmingham, New Orleans, Memphis, Norfolk, and Louisville were some of the southern cities that absorbed African Americans who were displaced from southern agriculture.

African Americans who sought employment in these cities after losing their homes and jobs in the rural South were often disappointed. At the same time, many urban blacks throughout the United States faced similar problems. Just as the actions of the AAA uprooted countless blacks in rural areas of the South, so the NRA facilitated the displacement of African Americans in many southern cities as well as nationally.

The NRA fueled this displacement in several ways. First, many employers reasoned that if they were required to pay blacks and whites an equal wage, then there was no real reason to keep black workers, since blacks were often hired precisely because they could be paid less than whites.[22] Second, over a hundred NRA codes allowed southern employers to pay a lower minimum wage than anywhere else in the country. Many African Americans were denied the same minimum wage whites received. Lastly, the NRA failed to account for the way the economic problems of blacks were intertwined with race.[23]

For African Americans, the NRA's program, which was intended to boost employment and increase the wages of the "average" American, had the reverse effect. Instead of achieving either of these goals, it simply encouraged many employers to fire blacks. In one widely publicized case, a maitre d'hôtel in Louisville boasted that he would never pay African Americans code wages. Instead, he intended to fire his entire staff of black waiters and replace them with whites, whom he would gladly pay code wages.[24] The frequency of incidents such as this led African Americans to supply the NRA acronym with their own meaning: "Negro Run Around," "Negroes Ruined Again," "Negroes Robbed Again," and, most significantly, the "Negro Removal Act."[25]

Although the NRA's program displaced fewer African Americans than the AAA's, they converged to create a large pool of potential migrants. Many of the economic conditions that fueled black migration were established during the Great Depression and the New Deal, giving large numbers of African Americans no place to go. The migration of southern whites highlights the importance of the Depression as an impetus to mobility. According to Chad Berry, historian of the "Great White Migration," the only prospect for countless Americans "if they wanted to stay fed and alive" was to move.[26] Yet racial discrimination in employment circumscribed the job prospects of African Americans, effectively short-circuiting their potential mobility.

On the other hand, by 1930 southern whites had already arrived in cities such as Chicago, Detroit, Akron, Dayton, and Cincinnati looking for jobs. A 1938 report of the Works Progress Administration (WPA) found more than 200,000 families already on the move, representing over 700,000 people. It characterized the growing movement of whites within and from the South as "a migration of depression-stricken families."[27] Unfortunately, complete information on in-migration and out-migration rates for the entire era of the Second Great Migration does not exist. The surveys that do exist suggest that historians have yet to give attention to the large numbers of migrants within the South moving from one urban location to another. Despite the high rates of out-migration from the South, many southerners migrated to southern cities.

Although historians have often focused on rural-to-urban narratives, in 1940 many of the migrants to the largest southern cities were from the *urban* (rather than the rural) South. In that year the U.S. Census found that over half of all in-migrants to Charlotte, Birmingham, Memphis, Atlanta, Nashville, New Orleans, and Louisville had lived in an urban community five years before. For instance, in Birmingham there were 38,008 out-migrants and 31,223 in-migrants, 15,925 of whom had lived in a location defined as urban in 1935.[28]

The Leightons were among those white families driven into migration by the Depression and recorded in *Case Studies of Unemployment*. Having been laid off due to "business depression" in Texas, Leighton "piled" his wife and six children into the family Ford and headed for Louisville, hoping to secure employment. Although he initially found work at the Arctic Ice Company and later at a box factory, after he lost both jobs the family faced the difficult decision of remaining in Louisville or moving on to Detroit or Akron.[29] Whether the Leightons stayed or moved on is not recorded, but their case reflects the way many white southerners used migration to ameliorate the economic hardships of the Depression.

While many white southerners migrated during the Depression, smaller numbers of blacks began to relocate within the South prior to World War II. Although net migration rates suggest far more out-migrants from southern cities, these rates obscure the numbers of black in-migrants to southern cities and the desire of many African Americans to remain in the South. Despite the exodus of African Americans, Atlanta, Birmingham, Charlotte, Louisville, Memphis, and New Orleans all witnessed a substantial influx of blacks. Atlanta, Charlotte, Memphis, and New Orleans saw nearly half as many in-migrants as out-migrants, while Birmingham and Louisville made small gains in their migrant population between 1935 and 1940.

Not only did the largest southern cities witness an influx of blacks, but also many of them originated in the urban, not rural, South. In Charlotte, Louisville, and New Orleans, over half the black migrants relocated from an-other southern city. By contrast, barely 25 percent of the migrants in Mem-phis had moved there from the urban South. In Birmingham, however, nearly 37 percent of black men and almost 40 percent of black women had migrated from cities. Significantly, the Sixteenth Census indicates that many of the mi-grants to these cities had come from communities of over 100,000 residents. Whether they had moved from large or small cities, it is clear that numerous blacks migrated to Birmingham, New Orleans, Charlotte, or Louisville from the urban South. Many of them moved between 1935 and 1940, before the largest waves of African American migration were facilitated by the need for labor in the defense industries during the war. But the influx of black mi-grants from the urban South may indicate that during the Second Great Mi-gration rural-to-urban migration was not the only pathway to the city.

The stream of working-class blacks displaced by New Deal policies was joined by smaller numbers of professional blacks flowing into the urban South. Southern cities provided an ideal setting to ply their trade. In 1940, 77 percent of African Americans in the United States still lived below the Mason-Dixon Line. While few cities in the North contained black populations above 10 percent, the proportion in any number of southern cities ranged from 25 to 50 percent. In Louisville, as in Memphis, Atlanta, and Richmond, the black community existed almost as a "city within a city," a segregated "separate city," served by black businesses and professionals. As Christopher Silver and John Moeser observe, in spite of a narrow economic base blacks "served their own community in matters such as financing, insurance, jobs, personal ser-vices and patronage, as well as offering a social life that rivaled that of the white world in its depth and diversity."[30]

For a black lawyer, physician, or dentist, those concentrations of Afri-can Americans represented potential customers. A 1942 study of business and employment in Louisville found that only 616 blacks worked for white-owned establishments. Nearly 50,000 blacks spent more than $4.6 million in the city's retail businesses, and they often patronized black-owned and -operated establishments. The majority of Louisville's 654 black businesses were located within an area two blocks wide centered on West Walnut Street extending from Sixth to Eighteenth streets. According to the study, "If a business conducted by Negroes in Louisville is not on West Walnut or West Chestnut Street, between the boundaries of 6th and 18th, it is either not in existence, or is located in a Negro neighborhood."[31]

Although black-owned businesses ranged in size from the massive Mammoth Life Insurance Company to individual "peddlers," the African American establishments in Louisville were best characterized as "small businesses." The majority were either service oriented or "food stores," taverns, restaurants, or lunch counters "selling groceries, meats, poultry, and vegetables and fruits, or selling those items processed."[32] Taverns generated over half the income of black businesses in the River City. While proprietors of restaurants, funeral homes, and transfer companies tended to fit the mold of the average black entrepreneur (over forty-four years in age with limited training and born in Kentucky, although not necessarily Louisville), slightly less than half the black grocers, barbers, and ice, wood, or junk peddlers were migrants. According to the 1942 survey, many of the black enterprises in Louisville were owned by migrants who had gained their business skills elsewhere. Junk, ice, and fuel peddling all seemed particularly inviting to older migrants who were "unable to find any other place in the economic life of the city."[33]

Similarly, a 1947 study of black migration found that although some college-educated men and women migrated north to secure employment, "most of them find jobs among people of their own race and these, of course, reside principally in the South."[34] Indeed, many of the cities with the largest black populations such as Atlanta, Memphis, New Orleans, and Richmond were in the South. At that time the black population in Louisville was more sizable than that of Los Angeles, Oakland, San Francisco, and Norfolk.[35] Like the experience of many professional black migrants, the 1947 study concluded that "economic security" could be found by remaining in the South.

Many of the most prominent black law firms in the River City had migrants at the helm. C. Ewbank Tucker was born in Baltimore, became a pastor in the African Methodist Episcopal (AME) Zion Church in Arlington, Virginia, and was first admitted to the bar in West Virginia before setting up shop in Louisville in 1929. A native of Spartanburg, South Carolina, James Crumlin attended Howard University and the Terrell School of Law in Washington, D.C.; in 1944 he headed to Louisville, where he and Alfred Carroll formed the firm of Carroll and Crumlin. Washington, D.C., proved common ground for many of Louisville's lawyers.[36] Originally from Frankfort, Kentucky, Charles W. Anderson also received his degree at Howard. In 1932, during the height of the Depression, he relocated in Louisville and cofounded the firm of Williams and Anderson, Attorney and Counsel at Law, located at 614 West Walnut Street.[37]

Tucker, Crumlin, and Anderson are significant not just because they chose to migrate to a southern city, or because they built businesses founded on the large concentrations of African Americans located in the South, but also because they brought a wealth of experience with urbanization to Louisville. Though southerners, they were not the ignorant, uncouth, or unsophisticated people their northern cousins and historians' portrayals often suggest. A migrant's class or personal history often helped determine how he or she adapted to Louisville.

For instance, Lyman T. Johnson hailed from a middle-class household in Columbia, Tennessee. His family owned land, retained the ability to vote, and was on the whole educated. By the time he arrived in Louisville, he was well traveled and well educated.[38] For Johnson, culturally and educationally, Louisville had far less to offer African Americans than other southern cities. The point here is not that he initially thought Louisville's cultural life was lacking, but that he was one of a number of migrants with extensive experience in the urban South before moving to Louisville. More importantly, this experience helped ameliorate his adjustment to the city's particular urban environment.

Considering the limited higher education available to African Americans in Louisville, as well as in Kentucky as a whole, many of the black medical professionals in the city—twenty-eight doctors, forty-five nurses, and fourteen dentists—were apt to be migrants.[39] At Red Cross Hospital for African Americans, the majority of the doctors on call, including Milton Young, Maurice Rabb, Jessie Bell, and Houston Baker Sr., were migrants. This was also true of the faculty at Louisville Municipal College for Negroes—from its president on down to the librarian, Ms. Atkins. In fact, before Dr. Rufus E. Clement, president of Municipal College, arrived in Louisville, he had lived in North Carolina and then in Atlanta.[40] As a whole, professionals like Clement were apt to have spent time in a number of towns or cities prior to their arrival in the River City.

Given the limits of higher education for African Americans throughout the South, the choice to become a doctor, teacher, or lawyer often required them to migrate. The concentrations of African Americans in Louisville played a central role in the decision of college-educated blacks to relocate in Louisville. Although their number was admittedly small, their actions demonstrate that they were no more immune to the hardships of the Depression than members of the black working class or agricultural workers. These differing classes of black migrants combined to make Louisville and its environs one of the few areas in the state to increase its black population through migration.[41]

Between 1930 and 1950 Louisville gained 7,994 African American migrants. The 4,053 black women represented a slight majority, indicative of the migratory pattern during the period as a whole. According to Goldie Winstead-Beckett, who moved from Clarksville, Tennessee, to Louisville in 1938, the city functioned as a kind of way station, where migrants stopped for a time before continuing on to the North.[42] Some migrants were native Louisvillians or Kentuckians who used the "Falls City" as their jumping off point to the North. For instance, Harry S. McAlpin, who arrived in the late 1940s, became deeply involved in the community, participating in civil rights struggles, before moving to California nearly a decade later.[43] Yet for many others, whether they were from the Deep South or Kentucky, Louisville was their terminus.

A survey of 491 migrant households in the Southwick neighborhood, compiled from the city's Urban Renewal Relocation Files between 1960 and 1965, revealed that the average tenure in Louisville was 18.18 years at the time the interviews were conducted. It seems safe to say that migrants were committed to staying in Louisville when they arrived.[44] According to this survey, many African Americans came to Louisville prior to the establishment of the Fair Employment Practices Commission (FEPC). However, it is no coincidence that migration peaked in 1943, the first year Executive Order 8802 was widely "enforced." The same survey revealed that there were more migrant women (462) than men (367). On average, both women and men were likely to be roughly twenty-four years old on their arrival in the River City. Nor did they live in the city alone. The household survey found that migrants lived with between one and ten relatives. Whether or not they entered the city alone, migrants generally lived with 1.9 family members in addition to their spouse. Roy Bennett, a single migrant from another part of Kentucky, resided with two sisters, a nephew, and his mother. Georgia native Lula Mae Holmer rented four rooms with her brother Wilmer, while the widower Leo Jackson cared for his two nieces, Jessie and Carrie Wade, from Mississippi.[45]

Many African Americans who relocated in Louisville had experienced life in numerous other places first; in fact, it appears that few blacks migrated directly to Louisville. W. L. Holmes, for example, reached Louisville after "many *unpleasant* stops." Born in Orville, Alabama, on April 13, 1913, Holmes moved to Louisville just after World War II. He first left home at the age of eighteen, when he "ran away" to attend the Prairie Normal and Industrial

School some twenty-two miles away. Interestingly, his parents allowed him to remain there only after family friends in the area checked on him to make sure he was safe.

Holmes was at the school for a year. As he recalled, there was not much to eat and he "stayed hungry an awful lot."[46] He then headed to Birmingham, where his mother, Elizabeth, lived and worked as a domestic for three dollars a week. Holmes found a job as a laborer in concrete construction for five dollars a week. He lingered in Birmingham a while before deciding to move again. He wrote to his aunt who lived in Jenkins, Kentucky, to obtain information about working in the coal mines. Once assured he could get a job there and had a place to stay, he moved. For the next five or six years Holmes labored as a coal miner and attended the local WPA school at night until he joined the army during World War II. After the war Holmes returned to Kentucky, but this time he chose to settle in Louisville, where he obtained work changing treads at a tractor company.[47] By now, Holmes had lived in no less than five cities or towns and was nearly thirty years removed from the eighteen-year-old who had left Orville, Alabama, for the first time.

Nor was Holmes alone. In fact, numerous African Americans who relocated to Louisville had already visited or lived in other cities. Rebecca Smith had followed an indirect path to the city. Born in Cumberland County, Kentucky, Smith arrived in the River City in 1945 *after* living in Toledo, Ohio, and returning to her prior home.[48] Indeed, many blacks migrated from smaller towns in Kentucky to Louisville, which offered a variety of economic and social opportunities that did not exist elsewhere in the state. Amelia B. Ray was born in Clarksville, Tennessee, and had been "in and out" of Kentucky any number of times before deciding in 1934 to make her home in Louisville, which she had visited thirteen years earlier.[49] Goldie Winstead-Beckett may have been brought into the world in Hopkins County, Kentucky, but by the time she settled in Louisville she had lived in no less that four other places. Her husband William, though born in Baltimore, lived in Nashville and St. Louis before relocating to Louisville in 1936.[50]

The majority of the 491 migrant families surveyed in Louisville's Urban Renewal Relocation Files came from within Kentucky as well as from Tennessee, Alabama, Georgia, Louisiana, and Mississippi, in descending order. The story of African American relocation to Louisville is largely one of urban-to-urban rather than rural-to-urban migration. Many black migrants in the River City came from small towns of the urban South. Although more than 44 percent of Kentucky's population was rural, its African Americans were chiefly city and town dwellers. The census definition of 2,500 may hardly seem "urban" by many standards, but by that same definition nearly 70 percent of African Americans in the South lived in rural settings in 1932.[51] That only 19 percent of Kentucky's blacks (Louisville's primary migrant pool) lived on rural farms stood in stark contrast with much of the South, although African Americans in Tennessee, Alabama, Florida, and North Carolina were also predominantly urban.[52]

Some came by car, while others sat for hours in the back of a Greyhound or Consolidated Coach Lines bus, stopping in Birmingham, Chattanooga, and Nashville before finally pulling into Louisville's segregated bus station. Still others, like young A. J. Elmore and his family, road the rails in the colored section of an L & N car all the way from Gadsden, Alabama.[53] Mabel and Richard Anderson came to Louisville from Christian County, Kentucky, a community of more than 10,000 blacks, instead of some backwoods "holler." Similarly, James and Lillian Edmondson were natives of Middlesboro, Tennessee.[54] Like the Andersons and Edmondsons, the majority of black migrants from Kentucky and Tennessee—the two leading contributors to black migration in Louisville—tended to be urbanites.

By 1941 there were 15,000 migrant workers in the River City, only 3 percent of whom were African American. Although there was a net gain of 799 African Americans in the 1930s, in large measure the situation created by AAA and NRA policies during the Depression did not change until World War II.[55] The war led to a labor shortage as the country stepped up the production of materiel to support the conflict and large numbers of white men left their jobs to serve in the armed forces in Africa, Asia, and Europe. In response to African Americans' March on Washington movement to demand defense industry employment, Franklin D. Roosevelt issued Executive Order 8802 to take advantage of all available workers.[56] The FEPC, in conjunction with the labor shortages and the absence of white male workers, created a window of economic opportunity for African Americans.

During the war African Americans seized the openings created by defense firms no matter where these jobs existed. While many blacks chose to migrate to war-boom cities such as Detroit, San Francisco, and Los Angeles, others chose to go to southern cities that were closer. Although approximately 2.8 million migrants left the South during the war years, the U.S. Census Bureau reported that there were roughly 4.3 million intrastate migrants and 2.1 million interstate migrants in the South.[57] These figures show that southern blacks were far more likely to relocate in industrial cities of the South than to move to the urban North.

Large numbers of African Americans living in rural areas of the South packed up their belongings and proceeded to southern industrial centers. According to Ira Reid's 1947 study of "Special Problems of Negro Migration during the War," more than 100,000 rural blacks moved to these industrial centers, and at least another 300,000 African Americans from the Deep South relocated in border states.[58] Cities like Norfolk, Charleston, and Mobile all drew blacks from throughout the South to fill jobs created by the defense industries located there. Indeed, the African American population in defense centers such as Birmingham, Atlanta, and Mobile, and Hampton Roads, Virginia, grew far more rapidly than Louisville as a result of their greater industrialization. Between 1940 and 1944, for example, more than 22,000 African Americans migrated to Norfolk and more than 6,000 to Charleston County in the hope of finding employment.[59] Between 1940 and 1946 Louisville's black population grew from 47,158 to 56,154.[60] Clearly, not all African Americans chose to go north; in the 1930s and 1940s many began to make their way to a number of southern cities.

So many industries were located in Louisville that it rapidly became one of the most important defense centers in the nation.[61] According to George Yater, "The massive industrial development around Louisville that had been generated by the national defense program made the area a vital part of the American role as the arsenal of democracy."[62] Defense firms in the Louisville area began in earnest early in 1940, when the E. I. Du Pont de Nemours Company announced plans to build a smokeless powder plant in Charlestown, Indiana. In 1941, the first full year of operation, more than 32,000 workers converged on the $30 million facility each day. The Du Pont plant was soon followed by the Hoosier Ordinance Works, also in Charlestown, and the Quartermasters Depot in Jeffersonville.[63]

Although all three of these plants were located in Indiana, the majority of their employees lived in Louisville. For instance, Tom Jones lived in Nashville, then Memphis, before moving to the River City to work as a hod carrier in the Charlestown powder plant. Called "Little Tom" for his less-than-towering height, he was later joined by his family once his wife Mattie settled their affairs in Tennessee. The Joneses remained in Louisville after the war.[64]

Not all defense industries were located outside the city. By 1941 Louisville defense employment was estimated at 38,000, and more plants to support the war effort were yet to be built, while other industrial jobs had increased by 18 percent. Between March and September 1941 three new plants were built in the same section of Louisville devoted to the production of synthetic rubber. Together, the plants operated by Du Pont, the B. F. Goodrich Company, and the National Synthetic Rubber Company made Louisville the world's largest producer of synthetic rubber. In 1942 the federal government expanded production. The plants quadrupled their output thanks largely to the Louisville distilleries that produced industrial alcohol. A necessary ingredient in butadiene, industrial alcohol was essential to the manufacture of synthetic rubber by both Goodrich and National Synthetic Rubber. By 1944, the highpoint of wartime production, these plants had turned out 195,000 tons of synthetic rubber, prompting Louisvillians to rename that section of the city "Rubbertown."[65]

Synthetic rubber was not Louisville's only defense-related enterprise. With two airports, Bowman Air Field and the slightly larger Standiford Field, as well as an established woodworking industry, the city was an ideal location for the production of newly designed wooden cargo planes. The C-76 Caravans were constructed in a $12 million factory built by the federal government and operated by Curtiss-Wright Corporation. When the wooden Caravans proved unsuccessful—the first plane crashed during a test flight over Jefferson County, killing its three-man crew—Curtiss-Wright continued to operate in Louisville by shifting production from the C-76 to the more conventional C-46 cargo plane.[66] Washington's decision to lease Standiford Field in 1943, expanding the airport by constructing four full-sized runways, presented the city with yet another benefit of the wartime economy.[67]

Yet, there were more advantages to war related-production than just runways in Louisville. The Army Air Corps leased the smaller Bowman Air Field, where the 46th Bombardment Squadron established its headquarters. The war saw the erection of more than 122 buildings, including barracks, mess halls, administration buildings, storehouses, and recreation halls.[68] Located on a 135-acre site on the outskirts of Louisville, the U.S. Naval Ordinance Plant produced the weaponry used to fight the war in the Atlantic and Pacific oceans. In 1941 the federal government spent more than $4.5 million expanding the plant to meet the increasing needs dictated by war. In April 1942 the army began constructing the more than $300 million Nichols General Hospital. The hospital covered over 120 acres, spread between 150 temporary buildings; its 1,000 beds made it the largest hospital in Louisville. The building of Nichols General coincided with the establishment of the Louisville Medical Depot on a 575-acre site that later served as the Louisville Industrial Center. At the same time, a number of locally owned and operated businesses played a seminal role in the war industry. For instance, when Curtiss-Wright began to produce the C-46 cargo plane, it was primarily composed of parts supplied by the locally owned Reynolds Metals and American Air Filter companies. As previously mentioned, the production of synthetic rubber was made possible by Louisville's distilleries.[69] The federal government relied on a number of companies such as Goodrich and National Synthetic Rubber to meet the demands of war.

Whereas Louisville's distilleries and businesses like Reynolds Metals were drawn into war production under direct government control, they were soon joined by a number of locally operated businesses. The Ford Motor Company retooled and converted to the production of military jeeps. The city's woodworking industry produced glider parts for military service planes, while Hillerich and Brach transformed the baseball bats they made prior to the war into gunstocks. Companies like Tube Turn and the Henry Vogt Machine Company manufactured artillery shell parts. In the 1940s World War II became the driving force behind Louisville's economy. As early as the spring of 1941, defense industries were estimated to employ more than 38,000 war workers; by 1944, the influx of war workers peaked at more than 80,000. Industrial employment in the River City had increased by more than 18 percent and continued to grow for the duration of the war.[70] According to Yater, "hardly a single Louisville industry . . . was not touched by war's demands."[71] The *Louisville Courier-Journal* reflected with some astonishment that the city was "the biggest, busiest industrial community that it has been in the last 163 years"; so many migrants had flocked to the city to fill the jobs created by war that housing was "bursting out at the seams."[72]

In spite of the demand for labor, employment opportunities did not simply open before African Americans like the Red Sea before Moses. In fact, jobs were slow in coming and ultimately short-lived. Even after Roosevelt established the FEPC, the Louisville Urban League reported that the city's industrialists had made "little or no effort to comply with the President's Executive Order."[73] The report asserted that blacks who applied for skilled positions were invariably informed by foremen that "there is no point in referring Negroes to those departments as they would not be accepted because of race."[74] Nevertheless, by 1943 the combination of the FEPC and the growing need to take advantage of all available labor eventually overcame the resistance of white Louisvillians, opening the door to blacks' first widespread industrial experience.

At the Naval Ordinance plant and the Hoosier Ordinance Works in Charlestown, Indiana, African Americans were hired as production workers, machine operators, foremen, and assistant chemists. For the first time blacks in the Louisville area worked as shipbuilders. The navy-owned Howard Ship Yards in nearby Jeffersonville, Indiana, hired blacks as buffers, painters, and welders in the production of landing craft to carry tanks and infantry. The synthetic rubber plants—central to the local war effort—began to employ African Americans in every phase of the production process.[75] Women like Gladys Bussey, a migrant from Alabama, became power machine operators. Others, such as Mildred Bradley, Rebecca Smith, and Annie Ruth Laid, migrants from Upton and Cumberland County, Kentucky, and Giles, Tennessee, respectively, all found defense-related work on the L & N Railroad.[76] Layfayette Brown was one of the many migrants from rural Kentucky to secure a wartime job; in 1943 he made his way to Louisville and began working for the E. I. Du Pont Company as a common laborer.[77] African American employment soared, and for the first time blacks in Louisville were hired for a wide range of manufacturing positions that had previously been closed to them.

James Glass was one such African American. He had been born and raised in Jenkins, Kentucky, where he had lived for most of his life. Life was not easy in Jenkins, but working in its coal mines did provide some semblance of economic security. At the age of fifteen Glass quit school and joined his father in the mines of the Consolidated Coal Company. He often arrived at the mine around five in the morning and "would not come out until 6 and 7 at night."[78] Initially, Glass, like many other African Americans, sought to join the war effort as a soldier but was rejected when his physical examiner discovered his six fingers and toes. Glass remained in Jenkins until 1942, when he decided to follow his father to Louisville. He loaded up his new convertible and traveled 167 miles to the city, hoping to find a better job. Like many blacks looking for work that year, he was disappointed. In Louisville the best job he could find paid $100 every two weeks, compared to the $200 to $300 he brought home over the same period working in the coal mine. Despite the FEPC and the labor shortages created by war, blacks were seldom hired in Louisville in 1942. Faced with grim employment prospects, Glass went back to the coal mines.

He stayed there until 1944, when his father "got after [him] about coming on back down."[79] Glass did so with the understanding that if did not find a suitable job, he would not stay. Glass returned to Louisville not only to improve his work situation but also because of the close bond with his father. With a bit of luck he landed a job at the Louisville Gas and Electric Company (LG & E), where he was one of the 291 blacks on the 2,224-person labor force.[80] The majority of these workers, both during and after the war, were employed as common laborers; of the 291 African Americans hired, there were only 10 semiskilled workers and 2 foremen. Nonetheless, Glass liked his job, bought a home on South Forty-second Street, and chose to stay in Louisville.

The arrival of so many migrants in the city soon created a shortage of living accommodations for war workers. Two newly constructed housing projects, Sheppard Square and Parkway Place, were accustomed to housing defense employees rather than the public for which they were originally intended. Migrants also represented a substantial number of the families in public housing generally. In the city's black housing projects, migrants occupied more than a third of all available apartments. In Sheppard Square, 94 of the 291 families who lived there were migrants; in the smaller College Court, 51 of 125 families were new to the city; in Beecher Terrace, the largest black housing project in the city, more than 270 of its dwelling units were inhabited by migrants.[81] As Lillian Hudson, migrant and employee at the Tenant Selection Office recalled, "People just flocked here from the south and just filled up these projects."[82] Although similar information does not exist for white migrants, there is no reason to doubt that their presence was any less in the white housing projects. The numbers of migrant *families* also indicates that Louisville was swelled not only by the large numbers of women and men who came seeking employment, but also by the families who accompanied them. These figures suggest as well the large numbers of African Americans who were lured to Louisville during the war by the hint of opportunity.

As part of the U.S. Senate Hearings on National Defense Migration, the federal government conducted a survey through the Public Employment Office on defense employment in May 1941, which suggested many of the black workers employed in war production may have migrated from other urban centers. The survey was based on roughly 20 percent of the applications and referrals received by defense industries. Of the 8,619 applications considered, 6,392 were from referrals obtained in response to employers' demands and the remaining 2,227 were drawn from active files (walk-ins); 13 percent of the referrals and 10 percent of the active files were obtained from migrants. Of the 8,619 war workers employed in Louisville, 1,028 had recently moved to the city—the majority of whom were from elsewhere in Kentucky.[83] The rest, roughly 42 percent, had relocated to Louisville from a neighboring state and were mostly likely from an urban, rather than a rural, setting.[84]

According to the survey, 83 percent of all applicants were male and 17 percent were female; however, women failed to secure employment at the same rate as men. Only 8 percent of the women who applied were hired, whereas more than 93 percent of the male applicants obtained a job. Clearly, defense industries preferred to employ men rather than women. Although the majority of workers in this applicant pool were either unskilled or semiskilled, less than 41 percent claimed industrial skills of any sort; only 30 percent were employed as unskilled labor.[85] Between 1940 and 1941 most of them were hired as construction workers.

Louisville's defense industries valued prior work experience; however, experience alone did not determine one's employment prospects. The importance of gender and race in obtaining wartime employment was made visible when it came to hiring African Americans. Although blacks represented more than 22 percent of all applications in May 1941 alone, they made up no more than 3 percent of all defense employees that year.[86] Given that the majority of whites hired as skilled laborers had no previous experience in such work, the fact that blacks did not either cannot account for their lack of employment. Quite simply, despite the emergency of war, white employers rarely hired blacks in large numbers. In somewhat of an understatement, one migrant from Jenkins said as for blacks getting defense jobs, "there were not too many back then."[87]

Nor were there many industrial jobs for blacks before World War II. A "tradition" of not hiring blacks for anything but the most menial positions existed before and continued well into the war. The majority of African Americans nationwide were employed as service workers, domestics, or unskilled laborers. In Louisville, more than 75 percent of all African Americans held those occupations. By contrast, only 16 percent of whites held those occupations. Although blacks constituted only 14.8 percent of Louisville's entire population, more than 40.0 percent of the "lower classes" were black. In 1940, 30.5 percent of all black workers were employed strictly as domestics, while another 24.3 percent were employed as service workers.[88] Only 276 African American women in the entire city held industrial jobs. In 1940, more than 11,748 women in Louisville were employed as clerical, sales, and kindred personnel, but only 136 of them were black. For African American women, there seems to have been few job opportunities outside the domestic arena; 78.6 percent of all black women who worked were domestics. In fact, of the 6,959 domestics in the city as a whole, more than 5,000 of them were African American women.[89]

The situation was not that different for African American men. Only 8 percent of all employed black men performed skilled or semiskilled work. The vast majority—more than 74 percent—were employed as unskilled labor. Their most common occupations were in service or domestic work, which employed 30.5 percent of all black men in Louisville; unspecified labor represented another 32 percent.[90] Given that 67 percent of migrants worked as unskilled labor, it seems safe to say that migrants were only slightly more skilled than native Louisvillians. For blacks in Louisville, whether male or female, migrant or native Louisvillian, proletarianization was more rumor than reality.

African Americans worked as domestics, porters, service workers, and unskilled laborers because even though there were no other jobs to choose from, most blacks preferred hard work at low pay over crime or unemployment. The labor shortages brought on by the war began to erode many of the artificial barriers that limited the employment opportunities for black women and men. According to an Urban League survey conducted in Louisville shortly after the war, before blacks were hired, "top management, labor union officials, and workers had to be relieved of doubts of the feasibility of Negroes and whites working together even to meet a common danger."[91] Yet the only doubts about the "feasibility" of blacks performing industrial labor existed in the minds of whites and in large measure stemmed from their own racist traditions. Prior to World War II, whites in Louisville, as elsewhere, created and maintained a custom of not hiring black labor in any form outside of menial work, a pattern that continued well after the war ended.

The Urban League's survey found that white Louisvillians so closely adhered to these traditions that the exclusion of African Americans workers had become "a fetish and symbol which was highly regarded by both employer and employee."[92] Until as late as 1951, the city listed jobs as "white only" or "colored only." Robert Douglass only held his job as an artist in a print shop for one day after his boss realized that "the guys in the shop refuse to work in a shop where a Negro has a professional job up in the front office."[93] The words of the Urban League survey echoed those of W. E. B. Du Bois. In Black Reconstruction, he argued that the exclusion of black workers was less about their ability to perform certain tasks as it was about competition for jobs and whiteness. The collective act of forcing African Americans into poor-paying jobs that primarily served whites functioned as a "psychological wage."[94] Although some whites were not much better off than blacks, "they were given public deference and titles of courtesy because they were white. Public functions, public parks, and the best schools all freely admitted with all classes of white people."[95] African Americans, on the other hand, were "subject to public insult."[96]

It would be a mistake to say that this "psychological wage" alone was responsible for circumscribing African Americans in a world of menial work. However, it is an important key in understanding why, even during the worst labor shortages, whites were reluctant to hire blacks as anything more than service workers. Poor whites especially valued its benefits as a way to distance themselves from African Americans and the economic hardships they often shared. More recently, David Roediger has demonstrated the value of "psychological wages" to Irish immigrants during the antebellum and Civil War eras.[97] Although World War II and the defense industries that it spawned provided many African Americans with their first industrial experience, the prevalence before and after the war of refusing to hire blacks as anything but menial labor suggests white workers may have collected such a psychological wage in Louisville, as elsewhere in the nation.

Despite the hard work and long hours they had contributed to America's "arsenal of democracy," by 1944 African Americans began to realize that the employment opportunities they enjoyed during the war would not last after it ended. The Kentucky Commission on Negro Affairs warned that before long African Americans would face harsh employment prospects. The commission asserted: "It is obvious that with the readjustment to peacetime production, many of these [black] workers, if not most of them, will be displaced, for this is the most marginal of labor, and the group which is utilized only in emergency."[98] Their words were prophetic; as rapidly as African Americans were mobilized for the war effort, just as quickly they found themselves unemployed.

According to the Urban League, the loss of jobs for African Americans resulted from a combination of factors. First was the availability of white workers; as large numbers of white men returned from the war, most employers no longer found it necessary or desirable to employ blacks. Second was the "influence of prejudiced white workers" who refused to work with African Americans or to see them employed in anything but the most menial labor. Third was the "effect of the local general social pattern," which was a fancy way of saying that now that the war was over, segregation was back in force throughout Louisville's industries. Fourth was the fact that the vast majority of labor unions in the city restricted their membership to whites. Thus, even if a given employer would have hired African Americans, unions ensured that a factory could only employ whites. Lastly was the lack of training to facilitate the presence of a skilled black labor force, even though African Americans had shown during the war that if given the chance they could perform as well as, if not better than, whites.[99]

The Urban League also demonstrated that, despite the exigencies of war, a number of Louisville's industries still refused to hire blacks as skilled labor regardless of their qualifications. These industries included aluminum manufacturing, automobile assembly, distilled liquor, furniture and finished lumber products, aircraft manufacturing, machine shops, electrical machinery, sheet metal, public communications systems, and public utilities. When any

of them did hire African Americans, it was principally as common laborers.[100]
As the war ended, "normalcy" returned to Louisville with a vengeance, as
large numbers of blacks were either jobless or working in the same positions
they had been restricted to before Pearl Harbor.

Despite the claims of the personnel director of one public utility that
his experience in the navy led him to believe "no distinction or comparison
should or can be made between the two groups, ["colored" and white] when
satisfactorily performing identical jobs," the hiring practices at Louisville Gas
and Electric and the Louisville Railway Company remained as exclusionary
as they were before the war.[101] Three years after the war, African Americans
comprised 342 of the total workforce at both corporations. Only 51 of the
Louisville Railway Company's 1,256 employees were black. All but 9 of them
worked as janitors, car cleaners, and laborers; there were no blacks in clerical
or skilled positions. At LG & E, the proportion of blacks employed—13 percent—was more indicative of the African American population in Louisville
as a whole. However, blacks were still limited to working as semiskilled or
common laborers.[102]

Nor were these companies alone in their view of blacks as little more than
menial labor. Of the 750 African American employees of the L & N Railroad
Company, 98 percent were common laborers. While the U.S. Post Office
offered some relief from this pattern, it was the only government employer
in the city that did. Black postal employees had the good fortune to be evenly
distributed throughout the workforce, as more than 50 percent of them were
clerks and mail carriers. In fact, 23.5 percent of the Post Office's workforce
was black; the Urban League claimed that its pool of 248 African American
workers was larger than that of any other southern city.

But this radical departure from the usual pattern of black employment
was not the product of some egalitarian impulse. Rather, it resulted from the
"strict adherence to civil service rating" required by the federal government.
No such counterpart existed on the state or local level in Kentucky. Consequently, blacks' job prospects within city government were far less promising. The Urban League found that the majority of blacks working for the city
were elevator operators, common laborers, or women like Juanita Sanders,
a migrant from within Kentucky who began working as a custodian at City
Hall in 1944.[103] As the Urban League dryly noted, "Negroes are conspicuously
absent from clerical positions in the city's administrative offices."[104] Whether
in the public or private sector, white employers in Louisville refused to hire
blacks in anything but the lowest, most physically taxing, and worst paid
positions.

African Americans' lack of access to skilled positions was exacerbated by their relationship with labor unions. The American Federation of Labor (AFL) was the largest and most influential group of unions in the city. In 1948, more than 40,000 workers belonged to unions affiliated with the AFL; however, no figures for the exact number of African Americans in the AFL exist. According to the Urban League, the "liberal policy and pronouncements in behalf of Negroes [was] ineffective in breaking down racial barriers." While a few unions—the Tobacco Workers, Building and Construction Workers, and Teachers unions—were integrated, on the whole a "general exclusion policy" flourished. For instance, the Metal Polishers (Local 248), Machinists (Locals 830, 1344, 1390, and 1704), Pipe Fitters, Carpenters, Painters, and Office Employees, containing over 2,180 workers, were "all-white" unions.[105] Under the umbrella of the AFL, roughly 875 blacks were organized as Tobacco Workers, Tobacco Handlers, Musicians, Cement Finishers, and Hod Carriers in completely segregated unions. Gus Shelby, a native of Alabama, was one of 300 blacks working as a hod carrier in the city. He arrived in Louisville in 1943 and parlayed fifteen years of skilled work into a Buick and a house on West Walnut Street.[106]

In contrast to the AFL's "general exclusion policy," the Congress of Industrial Organizations (CIO) embraced nondiscrimination from its inception. Blacks in the CIO held positions as shop stewards, officials, and delegates, an opportunity few African Americans enjoyed with the AFL. But compared to the number of workers in the AFL and the total number of black workers in Louisville as a whole, CIO membership was small. In 1948 it had 12,000 members, roughly 900 of whom were African American. A glance at the membership of the CIO's unions suggests that its ability to ameliorate blacks' exclusion from skilled employment was small. Despite the efforts of the CIO, employment prospects for African Americans after World War II were grim at best.

This was especially true for African American women. According to Karen Tucker Anderson, during World War II black women were the "last hired, first fired [and] . . . whatever the hierarchy of preference . . . black women could always be found at the bottom."[107] This national trend was no less evident in Louisville. In 1948 the Urban League reported that, for black women, "with the coming of V-J Day many of the new found job opportunities were short lived."[108] As a whole, African American women entered the industrial labor force at the lowest rungs; primarily hired as service workers or unskilled laborers, they had little hope of upward mobility. Although the war did not afford them the same economic opportunities available to black men and white women, it did offer many the chance to experience the possibilities found in an urban economy. Anderson demonstrates that since white male workers quickly replaced black women workers at the end of the war, African American women remained in virtually the same position in the U.S. economy as before the war.[109]

Although the war did not change the employment prospects for Louisville's African Americans in any lasting way, it did fuel black migration by creating a window of opportunity, of which many blacks took advantage. African Americans left their homes in Kentucky, Tennessee, and throughout the Deep South with the hope of creating a better future for themselves and their families in Louisville. Between 1940 and 1946, the city's black population grew from 47,158 to 56,154.[110] During the 1940s as a whole, more than 7,195 African Americans chose to make Louisville their home.[111] While new births account for some of the growth in black population, much of the increase was a result of black migration from the urban South.

The urban-to-urban migration pattern in Louisville and in some other southern cities suggests that more attention needs to be given to African American relocation within in the South during the era of the Second Great Migration. The black urban population in much of the Upper South and the high percentage of urban migrants between 1935 and 1940 in Birmingham, Charlotte, New Orleans, Atlanta, and Louisville suggest that multiple migration patterns existed in the South. It also indicates that our historical preoccupation with migration to the North and West cannot substitute for sustained historical inquiry into African American migration as a whole.

Examining urban-to-urban migration patterns not only offers a more complex view of black migration, it also provides a more nuanced view of the process of black urbanization. The majority of migration narratives, both literary and historical, fail to account for urban-to-urban migration or the number of steps migrants took before they reached their final destination. In the past African Americans have often been portrayed as completely unprepared to migrate, yet few of them found Louisville a totally alien environment, and more often than not they came prepared to cope with that environment.[112] No doubt, these black migrants experienced fear and confusion in varying degrees, although those were not their only emotions on their arrival. As the narrative of the migrant and state legislator Mae Street Kidd suggests, as much as migrants may have felt fear or confusion, their arrival in the River City was also marked by a sense of anticipation, excitement, and joy. Southern black migrants were far from unprepared to enter a new urban environment. Clearly, they brought with them a wide range of experiences, from Kidd's somewhat limited travels in the neighboring counties; to Dr. Maurice Rabb's familiarity with cities as large as, if not larger than, Louisville; to the adventures of first-timers like A. J. Elmore, who moved to Louisville as an adolescent from Gadsden, Alabama.[113] Many migrants in Louisville had prior experiences that smoothed the way for life in the city.

More importantly, the origin of many African American migrants in Louisville was the urban South.[114] In terms of pace or scale, Louisville may have represented a somewhat different urban environment from what migrants might have encountered before, but *the city* itself was not necessarily an unknown entity. Although it did take time to adjust to a new environment, they were by no means babes in the wilderness. Rather, black migrants arrived with a number of tools to help them begin the work of making Louisville Home.

2

WAY UP NORTH IN LOUISVILLE

MIGRATION AND THE MEANING OF THE SOUTH

In 1925 Clara Smith recorded a song called "The L & N Blues," which referred to the railway that ran between Nashville and Louisville and on up into the North. As she sang the following lyrics, she suggested one way many African Americans conceived of the South:

> I'm a ramblin' woman, I've got a ramblin' mind
> I'm a ramblin' woman, I've got a ramblin' mind
> I'm gonna buy me a ticket and ease on down the line
>
> Mason-Dixon line is down where the South begins
> Mason-Dixon line is down where the South begins
> Gonna leave a Pullman and ride the L & N.[1]

The "L & N Blues" directs our attention to the need to examine the way African Americans conceived of the South and their own southernness. In this case, let us consider how some of the more than 17,000 migrants who relocated in Louisville between 1930 and 1970 defined the South.[2]

Clara Smith's "L & N Blues" show us that the South was a region that was not so much defined geographically as it was culturally or by its politics of oppression. Although the boundary between North and South was not geographical, it was no less real. For many blacks like Clara Smith, the South was defined by oppression, by segregation in the form of Jim Crow. Her blues tell us it was a boundary that, in part, began in Kentucky—not so much because one crossed the Mason-Dixon Line there, but because it was where black passengers riding the L & N Railroad were forced from first-class seating in Pullman cars into segregated seating. In the minds of many African Americans, what made the South distinct was Jim Crow.

Clara Smith's blues direct attention to how some blacks thought of the South, but at the same time it obscures the differences that existed within the South. Kentucky held a peculiar position in the Upper South as a border state. For most migrants in Louisville, the South they encountered in Kentucky was somewhat different from the South they had known before. Unlike most southern states, Kentucky never officially succeeded from the Union during the Civil War. It never endured the "hardship" of Reconstruction, as did its sister states. Kentucky also walked a different path economically. Whereas cotton was king throughout much of the South, Kentucky's economy was more diverse. Tobacco, coal mining, and commerce and industry—rather than cotton—supported Louisville's economy.[3]

Perhaps the most significant difference between Kentucky and the rest of the South was the ability to vote. Unlike African Americans throughout most of the South who did not regain the right to vote until 1965, blacks in Kentucky, for the most part, retained the franchise after Reconstruction. Nevertheless, until the mid-1940s many blacks in Kentucky viewed their ability to vote as a "privilege," not as a right.[4] This was no semantic difference; rather, calling the right to vote a "privilege" reflected how tenuous was their ability to vote in any part of the state. It also reflected the dependency of African Americans on whites' willingness to allow them to exercise that "right" no matter how much blacks may have agitated for it.

In the 1870s Democratic legislators drafted a bill to strip blacks of the right to vote. The text of the proposed measure read: "Be it enacted by the Legislature of the commonwealth of Kentucky: That no person shall be an elector in this commonwealth who has wool or kinky hair on his scalp. That any person who shaves or otherwise removes the wool or hair from his head, so as to deceive the judges of the election, and shall cast his vote in disregard of this act, may be indicted by a grand jury, and punished as is now provided by law for fraudulent voting."[5] Although the bill did not mention African Americans specifically, the "woolly-headed" citizens it sought to disfranchise obviously were black. Although this proposal was never brought before the state legislature, whites in Paris and Danville, Kentucky, found other equally disingenuous ways to disenfranchise blacks.[6] Despite these early attempts to remove them from the electorate, African Americans in Kentucky maintained and consistently exercised their voting "privileges."

As a border state Kentucky was somewhat different from the Deep South, but it would be a mistake to think it was wholly different. According to

Omer Carmichael and Weldon Johnson's *The Louisville Story*, "Louisville, like Kentucky, seceded after Appomattox," and since 1865 the city faced South.[7] Kentucky did not have an extensive set of Jim Crow laws or Black Codes, yet segregation was maintained and enforced by tradition as much as any laws enacted in the Deep South. One of the few Jim Crow laws Kentucky did have was the Day Law. Enacted in 1904, the Day Law prohibited integrated education throughout the state and set a fine of one thousand dollars for any institution that did not segregate its students.[8]

In Kentucky, as in much of the South, racialized violence cast its shadow over everyday life. Blacks in the state faced more than their fair share of whitecapping and lynching; Edward Ayers has argued that there were more lynchings in Kentucky than anywhere else in the Upper South.[9] Similarly, George C. Wright revealed that between 1890 and 1940 there were more than 353 documented lynchings in the state.[10] Nor could Kentucky blacks expect much redress from the legal system. According to Wright, whether in Louisville, Lexington, or some small mountain community, racial discrimination often meant that to be black and accused of a crime was the same thing as being guilty. Not until the 1938 Supreme Court case *Hale v. Kentucky* were African Americans even included in a pool of potential jurors for a trial.[11] These commonalities between Kentucky and the rest of the South led one migrant, Lyman T. Johnson, to declare, "As a whole Kentucky was a hell of a place when I came here."[12]

Kentucky was indeed a hell of a place when Lyman Johnson arrived from Columbia, Tennessee, in 1930, but interestingly he continued to maintain that "I break Kentucky into two parts, Louisville and the rest of the state. Louisville is oriented to the North, culturally and commercially. The rest of Kentucky looks to the South."[13] Though many in the city would hesitate to go so far as to say that Louisville looked to the North culturally, Johnson's comments were indicative of its peculiar position in the South. During much of the late nineteenth and twentieth centuries, Louisville was labeled one of the South's most "liberal" or "progressive" cities on race relations as well as a city with "southern racial traditions and a northern class dynamic."[14] Its "progressive" reputation was accurate only when measured by the standard set by the rest of the South.

Blacks in Louisville had limited access to a small number of segregated facilities, including a hospital, the Louisville Municipal College for Negroes (a branch of the University of Louisville created specifically for African Americans), two small branches of the public library (they were denied access to all other branches of the Louisville Free Public Library), and public transportation that most African Americans in the South did not enjoy. Louisville also had more black police officers than any other southern city, although they could only work in black districts.[15] For many whites, blacks' uneven access to these small, second-rate facilities allowed them to maintain their "progressive" view of themselves and their city.

In fact, the ability of white residents to promote a "progressive" self-image was based on "polite racism" and the actions of the blacks themselves. In his groundbreaking study on blacks in Louisville, *Life Behind a Veil*, George Wright argued that what existed in Louisville was "racism in a polite form; it would remain polite as long as Afro-Americans willingly accepted 'their place,' which, of course, was at the bottom."[16] According to Wright, polite racism often allowed both whites and blacks to believe real progress was being made in the realm of race relations. But polite racism also served as a reminder that race relations could quickly become harsher should blacks refuse to "accept" their place.[17]

Although most whites attributed Louisville's "progressivism" to themselves, in reality African Americans had far more to do with moving forward than whites were willing to admit. Nor does it seem that African Americans were as willing to accept their "place" as Wright's conception of "polite racism" would have us believe. For instance, whites often pointed to the fact that blacks were not segregated in public transportation as a sign of the city's progressivism. Yet the lack of segregation resulted from protests before the turn of the century involving the entire black community that were eventually settled in district court.[18] Even after African Americans won the legal right to ride anywhere they chose on a bus or streetcar, whites often expected them to sit in the back out of deference and custom.

Similarly, whites proudly pointed to the Louisville Municipal College for Negroes as testament to their own "progressiveness"; in their minds, the fact that there even was such a school, while many other southern cities had no black institutions of higher learning, confirmed that image of themselves. In doing so, however, they obscured the role of blacks in establishing the school. Louisville Municipal College existed only because African Americans had flexed their political muscle. In 1920 the University of Louisville brought a million-dollar bond issue before the city in an effort to expand its campus. While the university gained support from the majority of Louisville's civic groups, African Americans were reluctant to vote for the expansion since it made no provision for black higher education; their tax dollars would be used to help finance white institutions they could not even use. At a private meeting of university trustees and members of the Louisville Urban League and Interracial Commission, the trustees declared that "no provision could be made for Negro students."[19]

Black Louisvillians were not impressed by the trustees' vague promises to "take care of Negroes" and through the use of a bloc vote ensured that the university did not receive the two-thirds majority it needed to pass the bond issue. Thus when the matter was revisited in 1925, the University of Louisville was more willing to make concrete provisions for higher black education in the city. In return for African Americans' support of the bond, the university agreed to establish the Louisville Municipal College for Negroes.[20] While the founding of Louisville's first full-fledged black college was an important triumph for African Americans, as a segregated institution it perpetuated white supremacy. While white Louisvillians celebrated the "progressivism" of the River City, they dismissed the part blacks had played to make it so. Whites could afford to be "liberal" as long as blacks did not step too far outside of their place.

Despite this "progressive" reputation, more often than not black Louisvillians confronted segregation throughout the city. A 1948 Urban League survey discovered that most of the traditional race relations existing in the Deep South could also be found in Louisville.[21] The difference was that in Louisville southern traditions of racial discrimination and segregation were more often maintained by custom rather than by law. Nevertheless, blacks in Louisville still faced limited employment and housing opportunities.

Residential segregation was maintained by the resistance of white civic associations, the inclusion of restrictive clauses in leases prohibiting the sale or lease of houses or apartments to "undesirable tenants," mutual agreements among property owners, and violence.[22] Yet even as African Americans grappled with residential segregation throughout the city, there was no single black ghetto in Louisville. In 1940 African Americans were largely concentrated in an area known as "downtown," extending from Seventh and Fourteenth streets between Broadway and Jefferson. In the two census tracts comprising the downtown area, over 80 percent of the population was African American. Only one other census tract in the city had a similar concentration of African Americans.[23]

The vast majority of blacks lived in four distinct clusters: Downtown, California, Parkland (also known as "Little Africa"), and "Smoketown." Parkland, an area south of Broadway and west of Twenty-eighth Street, reputedly had been settled predominantly by "Deep South Negroes."[24] Smoketown, bounded by Broadway and Kentucky, and by Shelby to First Street, was one of the few large black enclaves located east of the central business district,

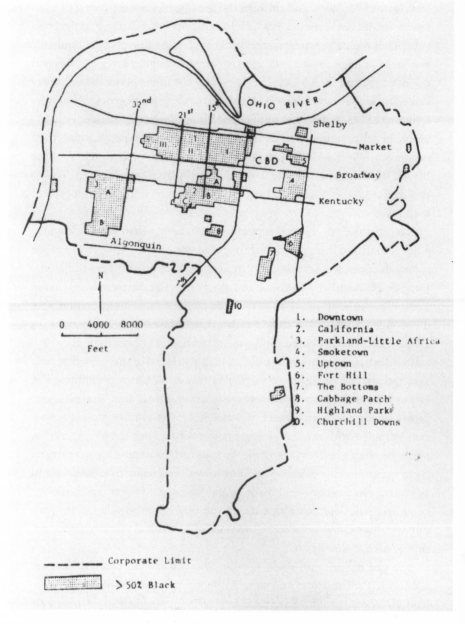

MAJOR BLACK RESIDENTIAL AREAS
LOUISVILLE, KENTUCKY, 1950

OHIO RIVER

Shelby
Market
C B D
Broadway
Kentucky

32nd
21st
15th

Algonquin

N

0   4000   8000

Feet

1. Downtown
2. California
3. Parkland-Little Africa
4. Smoketown
5. Uptown
6. Fort Hill
7. The Bottoms
8. Cabbage Patch
9. Highland Park
10. Churchill Downs

— — — Corporate Limit

⟩ 50% Black

MAP 1 Black Population, 1950. Until the 1960s there was no single black neighborhood; rather, blacks were distributed across the city in a "checkerboard" pattern. Courtesy of John L. Anderson and the University of Louisville Archives and Records Center.

outside of the West End. Although the majority of African Americans were clustered in these four areas, blacks could also be found in fewer numbers in Uptown, Fort Hill, The Bottoms, Cabbage Patch, and Highland Park, and Churchill Downs. According to the "Real Property Survey" published in the *Louisville Defender*, more than 75 percent of African Americans lived in substandard housing.[25] Black neighborhoods were characterized by inadequate sanitation, deteriorating property, cheap rents, and dense population.[26] They were also the places where migrants were most likely to live due to the constraints of Louisville's racialized housing market.

In fact, more than 50 percent of the African American residents in Louisville were crowded within ten census tracts; 80 percent of the total black population lived within twenty total census tracts. Not only did these census tracts house the majority of blacks in the city, but also their population density was twice that of whites in Louisville.[27] Black neighborhoods were overcrowded and tended to be old or run-down. The majority of African Americans in Louisville lived in housing stock built in 1899 or earlier. Their houses were not just old but often needed major repair. Blacks lived in the "oldest and most dilapidated" houses in the city.[28] The Urban League characterized many of the houses in Parkland as little more than "shacks."[29]

In 1948 there were 12,030 African American tenant-occupied dwelling units in the city, 11,375 of them in need of major repairs. Only 2,174 of the apartments rented by blacks had a private bath and a flush toilet; the vast majority were lucky just to have running water inside their home. Urban League investigators described these living conditions as nothing less than "deplorable."[30] When Georgia Davis arrived in Louisville in 1953, things had not changed much. She moved into the area known as "Little Africa" to whites and Parkland to blacks. Its unpaved streets extended south from Virginia Avenue and west from Thirty-sixth Street; as she recalled, the streets were little more than alleys, and African Americans raised chickens and hogs within the city limits.[31]

African Americans did not live in shoddy neighborhoods because they wanted to, but because they had no other choice. Blacks in Louisville faced a severe housing shortage in terms of both quality and quantity. This problem was particularly acute between 1944 and 1947 as migrants and returning veterans converged on the city, doubling the number of requests for living space.[32] Although blacks earned less money than whites, income alone did not determine where African Americans chose to live. Despite the fact that most blacks lived in areas where rents ranged between seven and fifteen dollars per month, many were both willing and able to pay more for better housing.[33]

No matter where blacks lived in Louisville's segregated housing, their homes were generally of poor quality. African Americans' homes were often rat-infested, with broken steps or whole porches missing and plumbing so poor that drinking water was located in an outside toilet. When an indoor toilet existed, it was frequently not "fit for use"; in some instances, the only available restroom was shared by as many as eight families. Blacks paid to live in houses where broken plaster hung above their heads and from the walls, or where there was no heat or there were leaking gas pipes.[34] In 1948 more than 18,000 black families shared housing accommodations. In one case, the Urban League reported:

> A mother and six children (ages ten, eight, five, four and one) [sic] occupy one room on Magazine Street. There is no direct ventilation in the room. Gas leaks from the hot water heater and stove but there are so many holes in the room it does not seem to have affected their family. A toilet in the back yard is used in common by thirty-five other persons and others who may drift in from the street. . . . Twenty people were reported living in two rooms, and in another case fourteen people occupied four rooms. When the cases were investigated some of the occupants were found sleeping in shifts.[35]

An earlier WPA study on property and sanitation pointed out that such conditions adversely affected the health of the residents, as reflected by the morbidity and mortality rates of the black population.[36] Between 1942 and 1946, the death rate among African Americans was "far out of proportion to their total in the population," greatly exceeding that of whites throughout the period.[37] Pneumonia and tuberculosis were among the leading causes of death. Although African Americans comprised 14.8 percent of Louisville's population in 1946, they accounted for 40 percent of tuberculosis deaths. With the influx of migrants in Louisville, housing conditions only worsened, increasing the danger of communicable diseases. Between 1937 and 1944, a period of high migration, chicken pox, influenza, measles, and other infectious diseases were three to four times more prevalent in black neighborhoods. As they became more common, there was a marked increase in maternal deaths as well. According to the Urban League, the increase in maternal deaths was partially due to housing conditions and the migration of African American women from "areas where they had not been exposed to pre-natal and post-partum care."[38]

Just as segregation forced African Americans to live in unhealthy conditions, it also limited access to adequate medical care. The Urban League pointed out that "the majority of the voluntary hospitals in Louisville is [*sic*] sponsored by religious groups where it would be expected the brotherhood of man . . . would include Negroes as well as whites."[39] Despite their religious leanings, neither St. Mary and Elizabeth's, St. Joseph's, St. Anthony's, nor Jewish Hospital, nor Baptist Hospital opened their doors to ailing African Americans. Red Cross Hospital and General Hospital, the only two full-service medical institutions that did not bar African Americans, maintained only 256 beds for a population in excess of 50,000. Although Red Cross was an all-black, segregated facility, only those "who could afford to pay" were treated within its walls. For most blacks the Central Louisville Health Center, which was little more than a clinic located down in the projects, was the "hub of all health activities."[40] Blacks lived in unhealthy neighborhoods, with limited access to medical facilities, not because they wanted to but because they had no choice.

On January 15, 1948, the Louisville Real Estate Board reported that of 2,427 residential units either available or under construction, none were open to "Negro occupancy."[41] The board maintained that, except for public housing, less than 200 houses built within the last twenty-five years could immediately be occupied by African Americans.[42] The housing shortage encountered by blacks was not due to a lack funds; rather, it was a product of racism. African Americans often had the resources to pay for better housing; it simply was not made available to them.

Even public housing, the one source of new housing for blacks in the city, reinforced patterns of residential segregation. Between 1937 and 1940 seven housing projects were built in Louisville. Four of them—Clarksdale, Parkway, La Salle, and Bowman—were erected specifically for white tenants and contained 2,088 units. The remaining three projects—College Court, Sheppard Square, and Beecher Terrace—were constructed to house African Americans and had 1,376 units. Nonetheless, it would be a mistake to disregard the electricity, running water, linoleum floors, heat, and functional toilets provided in public housing as a real improvement over the conditions in which most blacks lived. The relatively high rents at College Court, Sheppard Square, and Beecher Terrace reflected that segment of the black population it was mostly likely to serve.

The availability of quality housing was a concern for *all* African Americans in Louisville. At a time when the majority of their rents averaged around $11.00 per month, the figure for public housing was between $14.25 and $16.75.[43] Despite the higher-than-average rents, the Municipal Housing Commission's Tenant Selection Office consistently conducted far more interviews and received many more applications than they had vacancies. During 1944 and 1947, perhaps the height of Louisville's housing crisis for African Americans, the Tenant Selection Office received 7,224 requests for only 416 vacancies. In 1947 alone, 2,992 black families hoped to be lucky enough to obtain even 1 of the 109 vacancies in public housing.[44]

The influx of black migrants to Louisville only exacerbated these housing pressures. As more and more African Americans crowded into the city, less housing was available and what was available was often more segregated. At the same time, a number of homes in black neighborhoods were torn down to "make way" for new businesses and parking lots.[45] Blacks were increasingly segregated in terms of housing; in 1940 Louisville's segregation index stood at 70.0, but by 1970 it rose to 89.2.[46] Although restrictive residential covenants were declared unconstitutional in the 1917 Supreme Court case *Buchanan v. Warley*, Louisville's "unspoken restrictive covenant" remained well into the 1960s.[47]

Since segregation was maintained by custom in Louisville, such exclusion could be uneven, allowing for interaction between blacks and whites at some times but not at others. For many African Americans, such constantly shifting patterns of separation could be unsettling. Blacks might be allowed to eat at a restaurant one day but be forced to leave the next if whites complained or simply chose not to serve them. In the 1920s, most department stores established a new policy that prohibited African Americans from trying on clothes or shoes they wanted to purchase or from eating at the lunch counters that had previously served them. When blacks were allowed to attend white theaters, they were forced to use entrances located in dark alleys. At one Louisville theater, the entrance for blacks was in an alley behind the theater nearly half a block from the street and led to a segregated balcony on the second floor.[48]

Perhaps it was a combination of these shifting patterns of segregation, "polite racism," and the city's "progressive" reputation that shaped black Louisvillians' understanding of the South and their city. According to George Wright, the city's so-called progressivism "lulled" some blacks into "believing that Louisville's racial situation was eminently better than elsewhere."[49] African Americans clearly saw themselves and their city as southern; however, their perceptions of migrants in Louisville demonstrate their different conceptions of the Deep South. For some Louisvillians, migrants were not from Mississippi, Alabama, or Tennessee; they were all from "down home." Although blacks in Louisville never viewed migrants from "down home" as harshly as did blacks in the North, at times they too held negative views of migrants. Black migrants in Louisville were often thought of as "ignorant" or always making "noise" on the streets.[50] One mother told her son that people who spoke poorly "act like they are from the South."[51]

Perhaps the most common perception of African American migrants in Louisville was that they went "wild" on arrival in the city. According to some blacks, migrants simply could not get used to the "privileges" or freedoms African Americans enjoyed there. As one native Louisvillian said in a 1938 interview, "They ain't never been free and they can't get used to it. They come up here and go wild. Down Home they can't even walk on the streets with white people."[52] As if for emphasis he reiterated, "Down South they didn't have any privileges, but as soon as they get here they go wild."[53] While there may be some truth to these statements, they tell us more about black Louisvillians' opinion of themselves than they do about migrants.

Such comments reveal the desire of some African Americans to believe the racial discrimination and segregation that defined the South for many blacks was less evident in Louisville. They wanted to believe that their city, their South, was more free. For them, Louisville was one of the better places in the South. After returning from a visit to Nashville, where he found segregated streetcars, a lifelong Louisvillian exclaimed, "I thought Louisville was pretty bad, but I was really glad to get back from Nashville."[54] It is important to emphasize that blacks did not believe their city was free; rather, they believed it was *more* free. They also expressed the notion that the farther south one went, the worse race relations became.[55]

Ironically, black migrants shared this notion and headed to Louisville with the expectation that it would offer them greater possibilities and less racial oppression.[56] Migration was a way to escape the lack of opportunity white supremacy engendered in their former homes. Like blacks in Louisville, migrants believed that the closer to the North they were, the better life would be for them as African Americans. According to Tennessee migrant Lyman Johnson: "Negroes used to think it was such a blessing to get out of Alabama and Mississippi. If they couldn't make it all the way North, they'd try to get to Memphis or Nashville or Knoxville. To them even Tennessee was glory land! But I was from Tennessee, and used to think, 'If I could only get to Kentucky, it would be heaven.' When I was a boy I didn't know much about Kentucky, but I knew it was north of Tennessee and that was a good direction."[57]

On arrival most migrants did find that Louisville offered more opportunities for African Americans, yet it was far from heaven. Migration was a way to escape the oppression that existed in their daily lives. For instance, "Maria Walter's" family migrated from a small town just below Atlanta solely because of the better opportunities they believed existed in Louisville. In her words, "Down South they couldn't make any money and educational facilities were bad."[58] Surely, life was somewhat better for migrants in Louisville; otherwise, they would not have chosen to stay.

But the "Walters" quickly discovered that the city's "progressivism," which many black residents so proudly believed set them apart from the rest of the South, was limited at best. While Louisville's "polite racism" may have made for better race relations on the surface, migrants learned the fact that blacks were legally allowed to shop in department stores and ride streetcars with whites did not mean the whites were any less racist. According to "Maria Walters," whites often "acted funny," as if they did not want to serve or sit by African Americans.[59] Columbus, Mississippi, native Dr. Maurice Rabb encountered similar attitudes at a local Taylor's Drugstore. Although whites at Taylor's Drugs were more than willing to fill his patients' prescriptions, those same whites refused to serve his wife Jewel a bottle of Coca-Cola.[60] Earl Dearing, a Virginian by birth, faced the heartache of telling his seven-year-old son that blacks were not allowed at a theater showing *Bambi*.[61] Reverend William G. Marks, who migrated to Louisville in 1966, discovered firsthand that African Americans using city parks desegregated in the 1950s could still be subjected to hail storms of rocks and eggs.[62]

Needless to say, migrants were not always impressed by the city's "progressive" reputation. In response to the boast of black residents that things were so much better in Louisville that they were practically northern, migrants from "down home" would say, "'Hell, so you're from up North? You didn't even get as far as Indianapolis!' In those days Indianapolis was no paradise for Negroes. We caught hell when we tried to sleep in their hotels and eat in their restaurants. So we'd say, 'If you really want to claim you're from up North, you'd better move on up to Detroit or Chicago.'"[63] Clearly migrants saw Louisville as a southern city based on their own Jim Crow definitions of the South. Migrants who moved to Louisville expecting to find the Promised Land were surely disappointed. Whether or not Louisville met their expectations of a better, safer life depended in part on their life before moving to the River City.

In his classic study *Blues People*, Le Roi Jones argued that African American music reveals the fundamental nature of black people's experiences in the United States.[64] Similarly, in *Blues Fell This Morning*, Paul Oliver asserted:

In the blues were found the major catastrophes both personal and national, the triumphs and miseries that were shared by all, yet private to one. In the blues were reflected the family disputes, the upheavals caused by poverty and migration, the violence and bitterness, the tears and the happiness of all. In the blues an unsettled, unwanted people during these periods of social unrest found the security, the unity and the strength that it so desperately desired.[65]

Jones's and Oliver's insights have been echoed by many scholars, including Leon Litwack, who maintained that African Americans used "folk beliefs, proverbs, humor, sermons, gospel songs, hollers, work songs, the blues and jazz" to express their "deepest feelings," their hopes, fears, and frustrations, as well as their aspirations and expectations.[66] In her study of African American migration in Richmond, California, Shirley Ann Wilson Moore noted that music was an indicator of the "state of mind and conditions of the black community" and that during the World War II era, African Americans transported blues traditions with them.[67] The blues thus offer a unique tool for understanding the meaning of migration.

Although the events of a particular song may not necessarily be "true," blues are dedicated to "candid realism."[68] According to Lorenzo Thomas, blues served as "cautionary tales" that offered "a crash course in urban survival."[69] As "cautionary tales," blues exposed the problems migrants faced in the city; the genre "includes an important body of literature that explicitly confronts the situation of the migrants and—in fact—functions as an ameliorative agency in the transition from rural to urban lifestyles."[70] Through their lyrical content, blues tell us directly how some blacks understood the experiences of migration.

Blues lyrics not only shed light on the different motives for male and female migration, they also direct attention to patterns of migration largely overlooked by historians. For instance, the sentiments expressed in Langston Hughes's blues-inspired poem, "One-Way Ticket," are familiar:

I am fed up
With Jim Crow laws,
People who are cruel
And afraid,
Who lynch and run,
Who are scared of me
And I of them.

I pick up my life
And take it away
On a one-way ticket—
Gone up North,
Gone out West,
Gone![71]

But "One-Way Ticket" only tells half the story. In his 1966 study *The Meaning of the Blues*, Paul Oliver observed that the "startling growth" of cities in the North was mirrored by an "internal circulation within the South [that] has been no less spectacular."[72] The lyrics of many blues songs suggest that migration was not always a one-way process, nor was the North always the final destination. Songs such as Charles "Cow Cow" Davenport's "Jim Crow Blues," Buddy Guy's "Stone Crazy," and Roosevelt Sykes's "Southern Blues" captured sentiments shared by many African Americans in the period. While Davenport's "Jim Crow Blues" highlights the role of Jim Crow in fueling black migration, it also suggests that the South remained a viable option for many migrants if conditions in the North were unsatisfactory. Davenport, himself a migrant from Anniston, Alabama, sang:

I'm tired of being Jim Crowed, gonna leave this Jim Crow town,
Doggone my black soul, I'm sweet Chicago bound,
Yes, Sir, I'm leavin' here, from this ole Jim Crow town.
I'm going up North, where they think money grows on trees,
I don't give a doggone, if ma black soul should freeze
I'm goin' where I don't need no B.V.D.s.

Lord well, If I get up there—weather don't suit—
Well, I don't find no brown; got to tell that bossman of mine
Lord I'm ready to come back to my Jim Crow town.[73]

Similarly, Guy's "Stone Crazy" reiterated the experiences of many migrants who chose to return to the South after living in the North:

Lord I believe I'm going back down South
Where the weather suits my clothes
Yes I believe I'm going back down South
People where the weather suits my clothes
Yes you know that I've played around in these big cities so long man
Ohh, 'til I'm almost done froze.[74]

Recorded in 1948, Sykes's "Southern Blues" conveyed feelings that were common among African Americans when he sang:

I'm going back South,
Where men are men, and women are glad of it.

Ooooh—I've got those Southern blues
Ooooh—I've got those Southern blues
Cotton prices going higher, an' I ain't got no time to lose.

Chicago and Detroit. Folks have you heard the news?
Chicago and Detroit. Folks have you heard the news?
Old Dixieland is jumping—I've got the Southern blues.[75]

Collectively, these blues lyrics suggest that while many African Americans sought to escape Jim Crow by moving North, their decision to migrate balanced a host of factors: companionship and community, the weather and economics. Moreover, they indicate that many blacks, like Lyman Johnson, and Georgia Davis Powers, who moved to Louisville after living in the North, had the "Southern Blues."

Not only do blues lyrics capture the life experiences that compelled many African Americans to remain in or return to the South, they also illustrate that many black women experienced migration in ways black men did not. In her essay, "Black Migration to the Urban Midwest," Darlene Clark Hine points out that women used migration as a tool to escape sexual exploitation or domestic violence. She rightly argues that a rarely explored "push" factor in their migration was "the desire for freedom from sexual exploitation, especially at the hands of white men, and to escape from domestic abuse within their own families."[76]

For these women, their homes and the communities that allowed domestic violence to occur offered no shelter from the racism and inequality that white supremacy fostered outside their own front door. Migration served as a means to escape the alcoholism, violence, and dysfunction present within some homes. Such women had the strength and courage to leave an abusive situation at home as well as in their part of the South, with hopes of creating a better life for themselves. Ida Cox's "Worn Out Daddy Blues" and Lottie Beaman's "Goin' Away Blues" express the sentiments of some black women who turned to migration. Fox wrote:

Time has come for us to part,
I ain't goin' to cry, it won't break my heart,
Cause I'm through with you and I hope you don't feel hurt.

You're like an old horseshoe that's had its day,
You ain't got no money, you're down and broke,
You're just an old has-been like a worn-out joke,
So I'm through with you and I hope you don't feel hurt.[77]

Beaman sang:

I'm going away, it won't be long
I know you'll miss me for singing this lonesome song
I'm going away, it won't be long
Then you'll know you must have done me wrong . . .

My heart aches so, I can't be satisfied
I believe I'll take a train and ride
I believe I'll take a train and ride.[78]

Among the women who chose to migrate rather than stay in an unhealthy relationship was Anna Moore. At the age of twenty-four and recently separated, Moore arrived in Louisville in 1946 with six children in tow.[79]

In addition to the different reasons for migrating, the process of migration varied as well. For instance, both men and women would relocate out of a desire to improve their families' economic condition or to escape the specter Jim Crow cast over their everyday lives, but what that meant and the responsibilities it entailed often differed. Within families men would often arrive in Louisville well before women to establish a toehold in their new environment, while the women remained behind to care for any children and prepare for the move by settling debts and selling furnishings and livestock, as well as deciding what would be of use in their new home. Once the men found stable employment and housing, the women would join them.

This was the case for Ruth Bryant. More so than her husband, she wanted to move from Oklahoma to Kentucky. As she recalled, "something kept pulling me to Kentucky." She sent her husband on ahead to secure employment and housing, while she settled all the "loose-ends" in Oklahoma. After riding more than fifteen hours in the front seat of her husband's car, she was "pregnant and miserable," uncertain of what they would encounter in Louisville. As they drove into the city on a rainy morning, her husband warned her that their housing arrangements would be "tiny." But in her view the neighborhood was "substandard"—people kept pigs in their backyards and the only toilet or running water in sight was located outdoors. There were four clean rooms, but to Ruth Bryant the house was little more than a "hut."[80] Bryant's situation highlights the different roles men and women might play during the migration process. Whether they fulfilled their responsibilities was another matter entirely.

The different ways migrants viewed the educational opportunities Louisville offered provides a window on how a migrant's class or personal history helped determine whether the city met their expectations. For instance, Lyman Johnson's family in Columbia, Tennessee, raised crops on land it owned throughout town. His mother had attended high school, and his father was a college graduate who taught mathematics and was principal in the local "colored" school system for more than forty years. Unlike African Americans in much of the South, his family had maintained the right to vote by paying poll taxes since Reconstruction.[81] By the time he arrived in Louisville in 1930, Johnson had earned A.B. and M.A. degrees from Virginia Union University and the University of Michigan, respectively, and had completed a number of courses toward a Ph.D. at the University of Wisconsin.[82]

In Johnson's mind, Louisville had far less to offer than other southern cities. Whereas Nashville was known as the "Athens of the South," Louisville had few comparable institutions or cultural outlets and no college "worthy of the name." Louisville Municipal College was little more than a "starving public school," and Simmons University was a struggling seminary blacks would attend only if they had no other choice.[83] Yet for a number of migrants, those very schools offered a quality education they could not receive elsewhere. For people such as Reverend William G. Marks or Celia Cox, the schools in Louisville compared quite favorably with the ones in their former homes.[84]

Celia Cox, like Lyman Johnson, also arrived in Louisville in 1930 but from Florence, Alabama. She regarded Louisville Municipal College as the best school in the state, and it offered everything she desired.[85] For others, it presented an opportunity to achieve lifelong dreams. W. L. Holmes grew up in Orville, Alabama, and attended school in a system that went no further than the sixth grade for blacks. His sole reason for leaving Alabama at the age of eighteen was to further his education: "I left home because of that, I came here to Louisville because of that."[86] That desire led him from Orville to Birmingham, to the coal mines of Jenkins, Kentucky, and eventually to Louisville, where he finally completed high school by attending night classes given by the Works Progress Administration (WPA). He proudly began the next phase of his education at Louisville Municipal College.[87]

Jessie Bell recalled that in his native Louisiana, the school year for black students lasted only from December to February.[88] African Americans in Amelia B. Ray's former home of Clarksville, Tennessee, were forced to attend a "so-called" high school that only went to the ninth grade. She said that despite the efforts of dedicated teachers, the education she received was less than satisfactory. When she arrived in Louisville in 1934, she immediately began to attend the WPA night school. In 1938, at the age of thirty-eight, Ray began the first of five years at Louisville Municipal College. As she remembered, "I was a fossil at that time."[89]

The fact that Ray remained in school and earned her degree while working and raising a family was a testament to the intense desire for an education she shared with many migrants. Migrants' attitudes toward the educational opportunities offered in Louisville were also indicative of their expectations for a better life in their new environment. Class as well as prior educational experiences in the South inflected migrants' outlook. As Lyman Johnson pointed out, black education in Louisville suffered from a number of deficiencies; it was segregated, underfunded, and of a lesser quality when compared to the opportunities offered to its white counterpart. But relative to the dim prospects many African Americans faced before they migrated, even these second-rate facilities were an improvement. This was true not just in education, but in housing, employment, and race relations as well.

While black migrants often anticipated that life would be better in Louisville, at no time did they expect it not to be southern. In other words, migrants were well aware of the fact that there would be racial discrimination in their new environment. Most of them, in selecting Louisville, had made a conscious decision to remain in the South. Reverend Marks, for example, could easily have followed his numerous aunts, uncles, and cousins who left Lexington, Kentucky, to begin new lives in Dayton, Ohio. Instead, he moved to Louisville because Kentucky and the South were *Home*.[90]

Others, like Georgia Davis Powers or Lyman Johnson, chose to live in the South after they had either visited or lived in the North. Powers was originally from Jim Crow Town, Kentucky, but after working for a number of years in New York while living in New Jersey she longed to return to the South. On one hand, she found the pace of life too fast in the Northeast and, on the other, she missed the sense of community and hospitality that existed in the South. On departing the North in 1956 and moving to Louisville, she vowed never to leave Home again.[91] By the time Johnson's sister Cornelia invited him to Louisville, he had already decided he did not want to live in a northern city. During a visit to Detroit in 1930, the same year he arrived in Louisville, he saw with his own eyes that the North was no Promised Land. Not only was it too cold and too expensive, but also African Americans lived "trapped" in poverty. Such migrants chose Louisville—in the South—because it was Home. As E. Deedom Alston, from Norfolk, Virginia, put it, "I am a Virginian by birth, but a Louisvillian by inclination."[92]

By examining African American migration within the South, another way blacks defined the region soon emerges. At a time when more than half the black population abandoned the South, these migrants chose to stay because it was their home. Migration within the South demonstrates that, in and of itself, the region was not a bad place and for many African Americans it was and remained their home. When blacks left the South they were not fleeing the South per se, they were fleeing the racism, violence, and lack of opportunity white supremacy engendered there. African Americans who relocated in Louisville were well aware of the fact that racism and a lack of opportunity would be part of life in their new environment, but by staying in the South, these migrants effectively claimed the South as their own.

For black migrants in Louisville, as Home, the South was both a symbolic and an actual place. The South represented a site infused with meaning by collective memory as well as a "safe place." Through collective memory, sights, sounds, smells, and history all converged as a vehicle of "ethnic identity."[93] According to black feminist scholar Barbara Smith, African Americans conceived of Home as fluid and conditional, encompassing conflict and contradiction.[94] In her work on the production of Home in Asian American theater, Dorinne Kondo asserts that Home "stands for a safe place, where there is no need to explain oneself to outsiders; it stands for community."[95] Yet, for "people on the margins," Home can also be a site of violence and oppression that is "rarely, if ever safe."[96] African Americans who relocated in Louisville often viewed the South contextually; as Home, the South limited race and gender agency even while it offered a site for such agency.

In *Blues Legacies and Black Feminism*, Angela Davis points to the role of collective memory in African Americans' definition of the South as Home. According to Davis, "'Home' is evocatively and metaphorically represented as the South, conceptualized as the territorial location of historical sites of resistance to white supremacy."[97] For many migrants, the decision to stay in the South was linked to their desire to combat oppression. In this light, migration within the South takes on a new meaning, as an act of resistance. Migrants in Louisville like E. Deedom Alston, Lyman Johnson, W. L. Holmes, Ruth Bryant, and Georgia Davis Powers were involved in efforts to improve housing, education, and race relations and to gain equal access throughout the city. By choosing to remain in the South, migrants demonstrated their resolve to improve the social, economic, and racial climate for African Americans in the region. As much as they defined the South as a site of oppression, it was also their home and held a long tradition of resistance. In the words of Lyman Johnson, "I'm glad I didn't tuck tail and run like most of my kinpeople. To them I say: 'You ran away from the problem.'"[98] In staying and fighting to make the South a better place for African Americans, migrants challenged the notion that the South was entirely a land of oppression; their actions demonstrated that they also defined the South as a land of resistance.

But oppression and resistance were not the only meanings the South held for African Americans. The notion that they defined the region only in those terms is problematic at best. These definitions fail to shift conceptions of power as well as historical attention away from whites, for they view blacks either as objects that defined the South by the actions of whites or as subjects who acted only in response to white oppression. Both definitions obscure the amount of agency African Americans, migrant or otherwise, demonstrated throughout their lives.

More importantly, they fail to capture the complexity of how African Americans viewed the South. African Americans did not only construe the region in relationship to whites; they also infused it with their own meaning, on their own terms. In their work on black extended families, Elmer P. Martin and Joanne Mitchell Martin offer insight into the way African Americans defined the South as Home. As one migrant in their study eloquently explained,

> When a brother is asked where home is, he is likely to answer promptly: "Montgomery, Alabama," even if he has lived in Cleveland, Ohio, for the past forty-seven years. Home is where the land was, where one's people are. The answer might be further refined with the explanation: "Montgomery is my home, but all my people are in Birmingham." Where my people are is a part of my essential self, and where I first dug my fingers into soil is a vital part of me. Geography is thus part of the extended identity as is the extended family.[99]

This conception of the South was no less true in Cleveland than it was in Louisville; no matter where they lived, African Americans maintained their connection to the South. For many blacks, migrant or otherwise, as much as the South was defined by oppression or resistance, it was also defined as Home—the place where one's family and friends, tradition and culture, came from. It was the place where many blacks were born and raised, a place from which many drew their sense of identity. It was a place they had as much claim to as any white southerner.

African Americans' relationship to the South cannot be defined by oppression and resistance alone. A focus only on the two obscures the full complexity of African American life. Oppression may have circumscribed black life, but it would be a mistake to think that oppression or resistance wholly defined black lives. Their migration to Louisville and the meanings the South held for them demonstrate that, for African Americans, the South quite simply, defined in their own terms, was Home.

For Georgia Davis Powers, migration meant an opportunity to maintain her connection to the South; migration meant she would never have to leave Home again. While Louisville became home to many black migrants, they never lost their connection to the places they had come from. Reverend William G. Marks continued to visit his family in Lexington even though he had lived in Louisville for thirty-three years.[100] Migration held many meanings for African Americans; it provided an opportunity to escape some of the oppression that existed in their daily lives; it served as a tool to resist that oppression even as it offered a way to maintain their connection to the South. Blacks chose to move to Louisville because it *was* the South.

What emerges from this analysis is the need for historians to reconceptualize the relationship of African Americans to the South. Too often scholars view the region as if it were the source of oppression in the lives of African Americans; however, a close reading of migration within the South demonstrates that in and of itself it was not a bad place. Although it was a site of oppression, it was also a site of resistance, but, more importantly, for many blacks it was Home. As such, it served as a source from which many blacks drew their sense of identity. Moreover, African Americans' southernness is frequently examined only in the context of the North. Finally, historians discuss southerners as though they were only white. The different ways African Americans conceived of their own southernness, whether they were "down home" or "way up north in Louisville," in large measure remains unexplored. Yet, for many of the more than 17,000 black migrants who moved to Louisville between 1930 and 1970, the desire to remain in the South was very much linked to their self-identification as southerners. These migrants were more than willing to stay and fight to change the living conditions of blacks in the region. In choosing to relocate in Louisville, African Americans claimed the South as their own.

3

I NEVER JIM CROWED MYSELF

NAVIGATING THE BOUNDARIES OF RACE IN THE RIVER CITY

At the age of twenty-one, Miss Minnie Mae Jones waited on the platform of the Louisville and Nashville (L & N) train station in Millersburg, Kentucky. Her mother Anna Belle stood at her side; her clothes were packed in a brand-new trunk her mother had bought for the occasion. As Mae recalled, a lot of tears were shed that day; she was leaving Millersburg "for good." In her own words, "The time had come and sooner or later [I] would have to leave."[1]

As she waited for the train that would carry her six miles south through Paris, twelve miles to Lexington, and finally north and west another eighty miles to Louisville, her final destination, a number of thoughts raced through her mind. On one hand, she had already begun to miss the "comfortable home" located across the street from the "colored" Methodist church she had grown up in and, most of all, her family. On the other hand, in her heart of hearts she knew it was time to go, and the mere thought of the prospects awaiting her in Louisville were nothing if not "exciting."[2] Perhaps the train tracks that lay between Millersburg and Louisville represented something of a continuum between the heartache of leaving her family behind and the anticipation of a new life ahead.

Although Mae Jones, later Mae Street Kidd, had spent most of her life in Millersburg, at the time of her migration, she had some familiarity with life outside her hometown. Since the black school in Millersburg did not go beyond the eighth grade, her mother sent her to the Lincoln Institute in Shelbyville, Kentucky, where Mae spent two years in a "place of love and harmony and hard work."[3] When her family could no longer afford the minimal cost of the institute, she returned home and found a job as an insurance agent for the black-owned Mammoth Life Accident and Insurance Company. Over the next four years, her work took her throughout Millersburg, into Carlisle, and to a little town in Nicholas County selling insurance policies and collecting weekly industrial premiums at thirty-five or fifty cents apiece.[4] During this period, she learned to adapt to a variety of new environments through her numerous experiences traveling between different towns.

As she boarded the L & N bound for Louisville, Mae carried these experiences with her like the clothes packed in her trunk. Along with these experiences, she had developed a number of resources that helped familiarize her with the city once she got there. Perhaps the most important resource was her friend Lucille Fitzpatrick. Mae had met Lucille at a Mammoth Life meeting in Louisville years before she made the city her home. When she decided to move there, she arranged to live with Fitzpatrick and her adoptive parents, the Wrights. While Mae stayed with them on Magazine Street, she was treated like "a member of the family." It was her friend Lucille Fitzpatrick who was at least partly responsible for getting Mae her first job in Louisville as a file clerk for Mammoth Life, earning twenty-one dollars a week, five dollars of which she always sent home to her mother.[5] Not only did Lucille help her obtain housing and employment; she was also the one who "introduced" her to Louisville. As Mae remembered, "When I arrived in Louisville as a single black woman, my first concern was survival."[6]

Mae Street Kidd's migration is suggestive of the survival strategies black southern migrants developed and deployed in their new urban environment. In terms of pace or scale, Louisville may have been somewhat different from the cities they had known before, and it would take them time to adjust to their new surroundings. Yet these migrants arrived with a number of tools in hand which they used as they set about making Louisville their home. African Americans both challenged and were challenged by the city's racial dynamics. However, many historians neglect the array of skills migrants brought to the city. If we are to believe the traditional migration narrative, blacks' initial "confrontation" with the urban landscape was characterized by extreme fear and confusion.

In this view, migrants were simply unprepared to cope with their new urban environment. But *the city* itself was not necessarily an unknown entity to them; they were by no means babes in the wilderness. No doubt, black migrants in Louisville did experience some fear and confusion, but those were not their only emotions. As Kidd's narrative suggests, their arrival was also marked by a sense of anticipation, excitement, and joy. African American migrants did not find Louisville to be totally alien territory; more often than not, they were prepared to cope with their new surroundings.

Black migrants Amelia B. Ray, Goldie Winstead-Beckett, and Dr. Maurice Rabb had also lived in various places before moving to Louisville. A native of Clarksville, Tennessee, Ray had been "in and out" of Kentucky any number of times before deciding to make Louisville her home in 1934. Indeed, she had first visited the city thirteen years earlier.[7] Goldie Winstead-Beckett may have entered the world in Hopkins County, Kentucky, but by the time she settled in Louisville she had lived in four other places. Her husband William was born in Baltimore but lived in Nashville and St. Louis before taking up residence in Louisville in 1936.[8] By the time Dr. Rabb, a native of Columbia, Mississippi, landed in the River City, he had lived in Nashville, Tennessee; Kansas City, Missouri; and Frankfort and Shelbyville, Kentucky.

If we pause to consider this aspect of migration, it becomes clear that southern black migrants were far from unprepared to cope with another urban environment. Clearly, they brought a wide range of experiences with them—from Mae Street Kidd's somewhat limited travels in the neighboring counties, to Dr. Rabb's residence in cities as large as, if not larger than, Louisville, to A. J. Elmore's first relocation experience as an adolescent from Gadsden, Alabama.[9] Many African Americans—among them, W. L. Holmes and Mae Street Kidd—turned to networks of family and friends in Louisville to facilitate their movement and transition to life in the city. Such networks represented an infrastructure of family and friends held together by social institutions and individual initiative. Before migrants even left their homes, these networks provided them with specific information about housing, what jobs were available, how much they would earn, what kind of schooling was available, and the overall racial climate of the city. After migration, they often served to acclimate migrants to the subtleties of life in their new urban environment.

When Dr. Rabb and his family migrated from Shelbyville to Louisville during the height of the Depression, they were invited into the home of physician Dr. Milton Young, a migrant from Nashville. The Rabbs lived with Young until they found a place of their own. Young also helped Maurice Rabb obtain a position at the all-black Red Cross Hospital and allowed Rabb to see patients in his private practice.[10] George D. Wilson was invited to join the faculty of Louisville Municipal College for Negroes in 1935 by an old friend and earlier migrant, Dr. Rufus E. Clement, who was president of the college. On his arrival, Wilson already knew five other professors as well as the librarian. Before they bought a home at 3530 Grand Avenue, near the heart of the black business district, Wilson's family lived with Dr. John A. Lattimore, who was known to offer a number of African American migrants a place to stay when they first came to Louisville.[11] Although Lattimore housed the Wilson family for free, a number of African Americans supplemented their income by taking in migrants as boarders. Throughout the period and well into the 1960s, blacks provided migrants with room and board on either a long- or short-term basis. Since few hotels allowed African Americans to eat in their dining rooms, much less spend the night, blacks passing through Louisville were forced to rely on the hospitality of their own networks for accommodations.[12] At the same time, numerous migrants found renting rooms to be a viable housing option. Mae Street Kidd was one of the many who rented an upstairs room from the Widow Mahin when she first moved out on her own.[13] The networks that assisted migrants made a huge difference in their lives. By 1936 the Wilsons had joined Plymouth Congregational Church and "now thought of Louisville as home and our trips to Ohio were trips to where we used to live."[14]

These networks were no less powerful for migrants leaving Louisville. In the winter of 1939, nineteen-year-old "Juanita Green" went to Chicago for the first time. During her visit she lived with her aunt, earning $8.50 a week doing seasonal work at the Chicago Stadium. She arrived in Louisville after the holidays invigorated by the prospect of beginning a new life in the Windy City. In the course of her brief sojourn in the North, she acquired vital information; on her return, she knew where she would live, where she would work, and how much money she would earn. For instance, she knew that she could "easily" get work as a maid for as much as ten dollars a week, and that finding affordable housing would be her most difficult task. Yet, pointing to the importance of the networks she had forged, she said, "I got relatives in Chicago and that will make it easy for me to stay."[15] Though the record is silent on whether she actually migrated to Chicago, what does exist is a reminder of the instrumental role networks played in facilitating movement to or from the River City.

Although migrants seem to have depended primarily on individual relationships, a number of organizations offered them support. Ironically, the Urban League, which viewed helping recent arrivals to the city as its central mission during the era of the Great Migration, only assisted 119 African Americans in Louisville by 1948.[16] Rather than depending on the Urban League, during the Second Great Migration migrants relied on their own networks or organizations of their own devise. Bates Baptist Church, for example, was instrumental in easing the transition of A. J. Elmore and his family. Not only did the church help transport the household from Gadsden, Alabama, but it also helped the Elmores obtain housing.[17] In churches like the Fifteenth

Street Memorial African Methodist Episcopal (AME) Church, migrants organized state or county clubs, such as the Paducah County Club, which offered migrants from the same geographic region a space in which they could sit, talk, worship, and interact with people from "down home."[18] The clubs also furnished vital information on housing or employment, as well as eased the transition to life in Louisville by providing newcomers a local connection to their previous homes. By giving migrants a "sense of belonging," such organizations did more than arrange for housing or employment; they also made the city itself more livable.[19]

On their arrival, it was imperative that migrants learn to navigate many of the hidden boundaries that existed throughout the city. As Grace Hale suggests in *Making Whiteness*, race was locally inscribed through segregation in "spatially grounded signifiers of black difference and white belonging."[20] For Hale, space was a "theater of racial representation" where the quality of "cross-race contact" literally "spelled out the racial hierarchy." Quoting white southern journalist Lillian Smith, Hale notes that throughout the South "there are invisible lines that turn and bend and cut the town into segments. Invisible, but electrically charged with taboo."[21] In their groundbreaking work on black Richmond, Elsa Barkely Brown and Gregg D. Kimball argue that within cities, space exists as "more than merely fixed residential and work patterns mapped on linear blocks; we see city space as an amalgam of fluid public spaces and institutions culturally defined by the inhabitants."[22]

In Louisville, like Richmond, urban space existed as a social construction in the minds of its residents. Space was constantly being infused and reinfused with meaning by both blacks and whites. Any number of overlapping boundaries existed throughout the city. One of Mae Street Kidd's first challenges was learning to navigate these racial boundaries. As she recalled, "Louisville was a southern city and we had some Jim Crow laws, but most of us blacks knew what the boundaries were and more or less we observed them. What were those boundaries? I couldn't use the main public library. I couldn't go to the first-run movie shows on Fourth Street. I had to attend the 'colored' theaters like the Lyric and the Grand. I couldn't stay or eat in the Brown Hotel. As long as we kept within those boundaries, we never had any problems."[23] Confronted with such racial barriers, Kidd drew on a number of strategies she had brought with her from "down home." Foremost among them was to avoid any place that was "off limits" to African Americans. Once she realized that, despite Louisville's progressive reputation, none of the "first-rate" hotels, restaurants or cafeterias along Fourth Street served blacks, she never tried to go in them even though she could have easily "passed" for white. In her words, "I never wanted to put myself in an embarrassing situation."[24]

Following the 1917 Supreme Court decision that ruled Louisville's residential segregation laws unconstitutional, local whites encoded these racial boundaries by changing the names of several streets to distinguish between their black and white residents. In the West End, the boundaries of black and white neighborhoods were spatially defined: Walnut Street became Michigan, Chestnut became River Park, Madison became Vermont, and Jefferson became Lockwood as one moved from black to white space. The shift in street names reflected the broader sentiments of white homeowners' associations; at least one white resident urged his neighbors to make "a Negro living on the West End . . . as comfortable as if he were living in Hell."[25] A 1939 editorial in the *Louisville Leader* described Louisville as a city where "invisible signs were put out . . . which read 'Negroes and Dogs not allowed.'"[26] Thus, a migrant's ability to survive was often predicated upon her or his ability to successfully negotiate many of the pitfalls throughout Louisville.

Violence and crime were among the many challenges that migrants faced in the city. Migrants' networks played a pivotal role in shielding newcomers from insult or injury. These networks could point out potential sites of danger or provide vital information that would allow migrants to avoid a volatile situation. Within the black community, migrants' safety was based on their skill in maneuvering across, around, or through urban boundaries. Inattention to these boundaries could lead to a robbery, a beating, or even death. Since Louisville's black neighborhoods were centers of crime throughout this period, successfully navigating these boundaries could literally be a matter of life or death.

Before the turn of the century, most of Louisville's houses of prostitution, including the red-light district, were located in the downtown area near or in black neighborhoods. According to George C. Wright, this location was not accidental; the "police department was directly involved in virtually all of the city's illegal activities."[27] In the early 1900s the city made some halfhearted attempts to curtail vice and crime by going after "black shadies," drug pushers, numbers runners, gamblers, pimps, and prostitutes. However, this crackdown on crime did not extend to the "undesirable whites" who frequented the black district in search of illicit services, and it ultimately failed.[28]

African Americans in Louisville continued to complain about the amount of crime and vice in their neighborhoods, as well as the apparent apathy of city officials toward the problem. In 1927 the Colored Citizens of Louisville released a statement to the press proclaiming that "bootlegging, gambling and prostitution are openly carried on and fighting, stealing, blasphemy and obscenity are matters of everyday occurrences" in the black district between Seventh Street to Fourteenth Street and from Jefferson to Broadway. They pointed out that a large number of "undesirable whites" came into their communities because police ignored them.[29] Although this statement did garner some attention, it was relatively short-lived and crime remained problematic in black neighborhoods. Indeed, less than ten years later, an editorial in the *Louisville Leader* captured the frustration of many black residents when it argued that a "vortex of vice and crime . . . is allowed to run unchecked" while police and civic leaders turned "a cold shoulder of indifference."[30] Black newcomers entered a community where vice and violence had been fostered since the turn of the century through a policy of benign neglect.[31]

For migrants arriving in Louisville, physical safety was as important as housing and employment. Homicides among African Americans exceeded the death rate for the city as a whole. While violence was a chronic problem, it intensified during the 1940s, particularly for migrants. A survey conducted by sociologist Ruth Russell revealed the nature of the violence in the black community. Between 1936 and 1945, a period encompassing the New Deal and World War II, which inspired migration, there were 498 homicides within the city limits.[32]

Of this number, only 60 were native Louisvillians. Clearly, migrants were at greater risk. Of the 438 migrants murdered, the vast majority—203—had been born in Kentucky. The next closest state of origin, Tennessee, was a distant second with 60 deaths. If migrants were more likely to find themselves the targets of violence, then African Americans had even more to worry about. Twenty-seven-year-old Silas Smith was one of the 401 black victims of homicide in the River City.[33] Although men were more apt to be killed, women suffered more than their fair share of the homicides. In fact, the 97 women murdered in the city comprised a substantial number of the total deaths. Russell's study found that many of these migrant women worked as maids, laundresses, and waitresses. As a whole, roughly 65 percent of all those murdered were laborers of some kind, suggesting many of the victims were migrants who may have been drawn to the city in search of employment. Since the majority of casualties came by way of gunshot, it seems safe to say that firearms were the weapons of choice. Yet stabbing, skull fractures, strangulation, and burning were only less popular means of murder. Regardless of the method used, African American migrants in Louisville were more inclined to be on the wrong end of a fist, knife, or revolver.[34]

In the 1930s and 1940s, hardly a week passed without black newspapers such as the *Louisville Leader* recounting at least one murder, often at the hands of another African American. Blacks arriving in Louisville soon became familiar with headlines declaring "Husband Stabbed to Death by Wife" or "Tavern Shot Up, Two Wounded."[35] The latter issue of the *Leader* reported that "Jimmy's Place, 1118 West Madison, tasted the lead from the revolver of an unknown assailant as he blasted forth Sunday."[36] Obituaries often contained the result of such encounters: "Bradley Hayden, 39, gunshot wound" or "Maty A. Johnson, 32, died, stab wound of chest."[37] An evening of good music and good company at Charlie Moore's Café, The Moonglow Café, or Jimmy's Place, all of which were murder scenes during the period, could turn ugly if African Americans went to the wrong place at the wrong time.[38]

Thomas Harris, a migrant passing through Louisville on his way to Chicago, learned that lesson the hard way. He and his girlfriend, Elizabeth Miller, were in town to visit his aunt. On the evening of May 27, 1932, they stopped in a "joint" on or near 1326 West Jefferson for an evening of music, dancing, and perhaps a little drinking or gambling, a combination that proved toxic on this particular night. The trouble began when Harris lost ten cents "throwing dice" to Ben Pate, a "bad fellow" known to "shoot men and kick women."[39] Pate called Harris "all kinds of dirty names," attempted to pocket an additional forty-five cents of his money, and eventually attacked him with a hatchet as he was leaving the "joint." Harris managed to escape, went back to his aunt's, and returned with a gun in his pocket. Despite a growing crowd, he shot Pate in the forehead in what he believed to be an act of self-defense, for which he received fifteen years in prison.[40]

It would be a mistake to think that most African Americans, migrant or otherwise, either participated in or condoned the violence endemic in black Louisville. However, violence can be understood as an outgrowth of migrants' need to learn the boundaries within black neighborhoods, as well as the strategies some adopted to negotiate them. For many African Americans who were denied traditional outlets to attain status, respect could offer standing within a community as well as protection from insult or injury. Some chose to project an image, or a reality, of toughness to avoid being cheated, robbed, or physically attacked while gaining a certain amount of prestige. As Victoria Wolcott observes, "To be 'respectable' is an identity that any African American could embrace, whatever his or her economic standing," though class and gender surely shaped the definition and extension of respect.[41]

Yet respect had to be established and constantly maintained. For migrants new to the city, this meant constantly being tested and testing the boundaries of respect. Thus, for Harris the issue at hand was not just forty-five cents, but more importantly his standing in this new environment. In the eyes of many, to walk away would have been a sign of maturity, but for others it would have made him susceptible to being cheated, robbed, or disrespected. Here respect was not only a shield, it was also a commodity to be valued and guarded at all costs. Respect, and the violence it sometimes engendered, was a powerful tool in the hands of migrants attempting to navigate often hidden boundaries in Louisville.

While it is not altogether clear how violent migrants actually were, among native black Louisvillians, migrants were *believed* to be more violent. One lifelong resident claimed migrants were readily visible in the city since they all carried a "trademark which says 'Down Home,' I mean they all have cuts on them." Others maintained that migrants liked to "see fights, cut throats and [would] shoot a man for nothing."[42] Indeed, in 1947 the *Louisville Leader* continued to lament "race 'passion' homicides" as the "No. 1 headache of city officials."[43] Whether or not these perceptions were true, they do speak to the fact that some migrants chose to deal with the violence they encountered in kind.

One case, in the autumn of 1945, demonstrates both the importance of learning how to navigate the racial boundaries in Louisville and the frequency of white violence directed against African Americans. George Cook, a white motorman, returned home from work to discover three black adolescents "fooling" with a car owned by his next-door neighbor. Cook got a rifle from his house and shot one of the boys, John P. Gilbert, in the head, killing him. Although Gilbert was only seventeen and made no attempt to run, Cook was released on a "murderer's bond" set at just five hundred dollars. Adding insult to injury, John's father, Reverend C. F. Gilbert, was forced to hire a lawyer, since the Commonwealth of Kentucky refused to provide one to prosecute Cook. Young Gilbert's death illustrates the importance of learning where boundaries existed in Louisville, a city where "fooling" with a white man's *neighbor's* car could be fatal. It also highlights the impunity with which whites could deal with blacks who transgressed those boundaries.[44]

Nor could African Americans turn to law enforcement for protection. Rather, in the pages of the local black press incidents of police brutality appeared as frequently as did violence within the black community. According to George Wright, such abuse had a long history in Louisville, dating back at least to the 1890s. During the Republican administrations of the 1920s, police brutality directed against Louisville's black community continued, if not increased.[45] Wright notes that "James Bond, the director of the CIC [Commission on Interracial Cooperation] and a person usually given to viewing white actions in the most positive light, explained, 'The fact is that the beating and shooting up of Negroes by police seems to have become so common under the present administration in Louisville that is has evolved into a kind of sport or pastime and is written up by the reporting in much the same way that a chase of a rabbit through the city would be written up.'"[46]

Nonetheless, city officials typically ignored complaints of mistreatment. A letter sent to the *Louisville Courier-Journal* claimed that policemen killed no less than seventeen blacks during the 1920s alone.[47] In 1932, an NAACP press release stated that Leroy Cunningham was the eighteenth victim of police brutality in the last few years. On September 9, police officers arrived at Cunningham's home in response to a report of excessive noise. Without a search warrant, they entered the house, unleashed a "tear-gas bomb," and dragged the eighteen-year-old outside. While they did so, Cunningham "lurched into a cop, bumping him off the porch." According to the NAACP, the policeman "aimed deliberately and fired," killing Cunningham. As usual, the medical examiner found the death within the "performance of duty"; however, in this rare instance he refused to call the shooting justified.[48] While the number of deaths cannot be substantiated, it is obvious that some cases of outright murder did occur at the hands of Louisville police.

In one instance, Officer Charles Hazel killed an unarmed man, James Emery, as he exited a stolen car. According to witnesses, although Emery made no attempt to resist arrest, Hazel shot him as he emerged from the vehicle. Another report indicated that the evening of October 15, 1925, was a particularly busy one for Officer W. E. Pemberton. First he killed a black youth who ran away from a dice game, and later he shot another African American for leaving a shop with stolen property. In the few cases that did make it to court, all of the policemen pleaded self-defense and all were exonerated.[49] Throughout the period, Louisville's courts demonstrated an unwillingness to indict white police officers for the murder of African Americans, and police brutality continued unabated.

During the spring of 1938, yet another African American was killed by a policeman, in this instance for stealing four quarts of liquor. According to the *Louisville Leader*, Lieutenant Edward Metcalf "made up his mind that that regulation pistol . . . stipulated by the heads of the department, did not offer him enough protection, so he rigged up a gun of his own, a twelve-gauge shotgun, loaded with buckshot—intending perhaps to try it out on the first Negro he ran across as he cruised about the city."[50] Metcalf used this weapon to shoot Robert Gray in the back. Nor were African American women any safer than men from the bullets, fists, or nightsticks of Louisville police.

The Democratic 'Old Deal' To Negro Citizens of Louisville

THIS CAN HAPPEN TO YOU

SHE PAID

A

$5.00

FINE

FOR BEING
BEATEN IN
HER OWN
HOME

———

IT HAPPENED
UNDER THE

DEMOCRATS

IN 1927

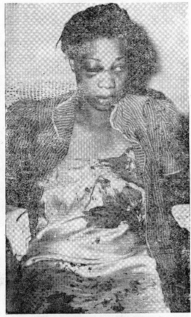

IT HAPPENED
AGAIN IN

1943

NEXT TIME IT
MAY BE

Your Home

Your Wife

or

Your Child

MRS. JULIA WOODS

who was dragged from her Home on Chestnut Street, and brutally and unmercifully beaten by two WHITE DEMOCRATIC POLICE OFFICERS under the PRESENT DEMOCRATIC CITY ADMINISTRATION and then given a $5.00 Fine by a Democratic Police Judge for DISORDERLY CONDUCT in her OWN HOME.

Insure Yourself, Your Wife, Your Children and Your Home Against Police Brutality

ITS TIME TO CHANGE

VOTE THE STRAIGHT REPUBLICAN TICKET

Next Tuesday, November 2nd

ITS YOUR DUTY

Blacks in Louisville faced the constant threat of police brutality, as demonstrated in this political flier. By 1943, it became a central issue by which the Democratic and Republican parties were evaluated. Courtesy of the Kentucky Historical Society.

On the evening of June 1, 1939, the same night Jimmy's Place was shot up and barely a year after Robert Gray was gunned down, two sisters—Beatrice and Catherine Brookins—were severely beaten by two white policemen. As the sisters were leaving Charlie Moore's Café, Officers E. Joseph and C. Sacksteder called the women over to their squad car, then arrested them for disorderly conduct when one of the sisters ran. Beatrice stated that, en route to the police station, "we were beaten like dogs because we refused to tell our names. Several times police billies were used on us." Although neither woman put up any resistance, they were pummeled, "stomped in their privates, and despite blood loss and loss of consciousness, refused medical attention for more than six hours."[51] Officer Joseph was said to have been the most "brutal and inhuman" of the two, sneering, "We ought to let them . . . bleed to death."[52] Referring to Joseph, Sacksteder, and the entire Louisville Police Department as "pseudo officers," black reporter Fletcher P. Martin observed that white women would never be treated in this manner. He rightly argued that "no matter the crime, wouldn't they have regarded her first as a woman, then a prisoner?"[53] In 1947 the *Louisville Leader*, pointing to the ongoing abuse of African Americans at the hands of police, accused Patrolman Marvin Almon of mistreating blacks on multiple occasions. According to eyewitnesses, Almon arrested Grace Miller and her fourteen-year-old daughter at gunpoint, saying "You d—d N—s are trying to run this town."[54] Despite Louisville's progressive reputation, Fletcher Martin, like many blacks in the city, regarded the police "not as public benefactors, but as public enemies."[55]

According to a Louisville police manual published in 1950, the tension between the African American community and law enforcement, as well as the excessive violence within the black community, resulted from the "maladjustment" of migrants. As "fully adjusted" whites moved out of the city and into the suburbs, rural African Americans—"unprepared" for life in the city—replaced them:

> They bring with them their rural folkways and mores, and often
> some of these conflict with the urban legal code. The rural folkways
> have permitted issues to be settled on the basis of personal combat;
> in the city personal combat would result in the apprehension of the
> adversaries on a charge of disorderly conduct. Because of low income
> and maladjustment to city life, the degree of tension among the in-
> migrants is very high. . . . A middle and upper class white group which
> is essentially law-abiding moves to the outskirts; a group of rural
> migrants in which the incidence of crime is likely to be high moves

into the city. The newcomers to the city come into conflict with the law because they are maladjusted to city life.[56]

However, given the fact that many African American migrants, including Mae Street Kidd, W. L. Holmes, and Maurice Rabb, were quite familiar with urban landscapes, "maladjustment" does not seem to fully account for the amount of crime and violence in black neighborhoods.

In her survey of murders in Louisville, Ruth Russell viewed the soaring homicide rate within the black community as a reflection of the conditions in which African Americans lived. The Haymarket area, followed by areas in the central business district and the adjacent neighborhoods just west of the business district between Seventh and Fourteenth and Broadway and Jefferson, had the highest incidence of homicide and crime in general. These were areas characterized by inadequate sanitation, "deteriorated property, undesirable institutions, cheap rents, no organized facilities, and dense population."[57] They were also the areas in which migrants were concentrated due to residential segregation.

African Americans attempting to buy homes outside the black district ran a gamut of obstacles, including the objections of civic improvement associations, racially restrictive covenants, mutual agreements among property owners not to sell to blacks, inclusion clauses in leases that prohibited leasing or subleasing of houses or apartments to "undesirable tenants," and violence. By 1940, black Louisvillians commonly believed they were "carefully contained by what seems to be an overall plan to limit Negro housing to an extension of the Central area going toward the West End." For many, this "containment policy" was so effective that "there was no hope of buying a single house outside the established pattern."[58]

The few African Americans lucky enough to escape the boundaries of the black district faced the resentment of their white neighbors. The municipal publication, *The Principles of Police Work with Minority Groups*, stressed the amount of hostility directed toward blacks who did not remain within these boundaries: "Recently a Negro bought a house in a white neighborhood. The evening of the day the white family moved out an attempt was made to set fire to the house. The Negro owner discovered the attempt when he came to inspect his new property."[59] Nor was this the only violence directed toward African Americans who transgressed Louisville's racial boundaries. When Dentist P. O. Sweeny purchased a home in the East End, a Ku Klux Klan cross was burned on his front lawn. One of the two youths involved claimed that "Negroes were about to take over St. Matthew's and he decided to do something about it."[60] African Americans like Sweeny, who did not respect the existing racial boundaries, were none too subtly reminded of them.

Given the nature of residential segregation in Louisville, African Americans had little choice but to live within the confines of the black community, areas near or within the city's red-light district. While the members of Louisville's small black middle class had the opportunity to live on upscale streets like Chestnut Street or Grand Avenue, this did not free them from the residential segregation faced by African Americans as a whole. Since blacks had little choice in housing, *how* they lived became as important as where they lived.

For Mae Street Kidd, how and where she chose to live, as well as how she chose to protect herself as a single woman living in a community where violence and crime were everyday occurrences, were all determined by strategies she brought with her from Millersburg. By the time she first set foot in the River City, Kidd had already learned how to "to survive on my own as a single black woman with a limited education." It was no accident that she never lived on her own until the day she was married. In Louisville, she initially lived with the Wrights in their Magazine Street home, then shared an apartment with Lucille Fitzpatrick in the Mammoth Life Building. As soon as she began to feel "crowded" by a third roommate, she rented an upstairs room in the Widow Mahin's Chestnut Street home. Kidd purposely chose to live with one family after another until she married James Meredith Kidd; as she pointed out, in those days it was not "proper" for young single women to live alone. Nor was it an accident that she made her home with families on Magazine and Chestnut streets, which were known to house the "best and brightest" among Louisville's black population.[61]

The combination of prior experiences and life lessons taught by her family and community, "prepared" Kidd for "the biggest move of her life." As she left for Louisville, her mother advised her that the "best people are in church."[62] Before her second Sunday in the River City passed, Kidd had joined the Colored Methodist Episcopal Church, a house of worship that was similar to the one across the street from her former home in Millersburg. Other black migrant women, such as Juanita Johnson from Nashville, did so as well. Kidd was careful to avoid "jook joints," and on the rare occasions when she did go, she seldom drank anything stronger than ginger ale.[63] In effect, by associating themselves with the "best people," or paying close attention to their public image, black migrant women hoped to demonstrate that they were respectable. The desire to be perceived as a respectable lady within the black community was not a sign of vanity or of mere middle-class pretensions; rather, it was one strategy of survival.

Historians such as Evelyn Higginbotham have discussed African American respectability as a middle-class dialogue with white society. As such, an inherently assimilationist respectability functions as a weapon against racist stereotypes or as a "bridge discourse" with white reformers. Although it often operated in this manner, the ability to claim and use respectability in black communities was not the exclusive domain of the middle class. Nor were black notions of propriety always forged through a dialogue with whites.[64] In African American communities, competing notions of respect and respectability were formed by both middle-class and working-class blacks. As folklorist Roger Abrams pointed out, "Firm distinctions are maintained between being respectable and being uppity, dicty or saddity. The former calls for maintaining self-respect through the willful imposition of order in a monitoring behavior; the latter involves setting oneself above others through a mistaken social sense."[65] Respect must be constantly earned, and anyone can possess it so long as they project the proper public image.

Not everyone had access to the best housing or the best jobs or education, but by carrying themselves in the proper manner, belonging to the right church, associating with the "best people," or at least living in the "right" situation (Mae Street Kidd only rented an upstairs room after all), migrants could be viewed as respectable. By not frequenting "jook joints," or only drinking ginger ale if they did, many black migrant women cloaked themselves in respectability. Keeping their clothes clean no matter how old they might be, maintaining a neat home, doorstep, and yard, "staying out of trouble," or simply carrying themselves with dignity were all markers of respect working-class blacks recognized within their own communities. For some black men, the desire for "respect" could lead to violence; for others, "respect" was epitomized by hard work and a dignified manner. As seen by black women, "manners and morals" served as a shield against sexual insult or assault.[66] Respectability offered a way to mediate an environment they often could not control or escape.

Migrants encountered a variety of boundaries within their community and relied on a diverse set of strategies to cope with them. Newcomers may not have had much choice in terms of where they could live, the amount of crime or violence in their neighborhoods, or even their treatment at the hands of police. However, the strategies they transported from their previous homes allowed them to navigate or survive within the racial boundaries that circumscribed their new world. These boundaries existed not only within their own communities, but also in the city as a whole.

It was important that black migrants create a mental map of segregation in Louisville generally: where they could and could not go; whether they should enter a place by the front door, the back door, or not at all; whether they could buy clothes at a given store, whether they could try them on first, or neither. Black parents had the onerous task of teaching their children to observe such boundaries. Eleanor Jordan recalled the pain her parents felt telling her that she was not allowed at Fountain Ferry. She remembered, as a child,

> riding past that amusement park and hearing the sounds of children laughing and screaming on the roller coaster, and smelling that cotton candy and the hot dogs and the popcorn. And, and—you know, you see the lights, the big Ferris wheel that had green lights on it. And we would always ask the same question, "Can we go?" And my mother and father would almost . . . simultaneously say, "No, you can't go." And we'd kind of sit there and then this deafening silence in the car. And . . . my mother always, her eyes would fill up with tears, and my father would just kind of look away, . . . and we knew something was wrong. And eventually she'd turn around and she'd say, "Well, one day we'll be able to go."[67]

Ironically, what superficially appears to have been accommodation, but was in fact reasonable caution, ultimately directed people like Jordan to future activism. Knowing the boundaries that existed throughout the city could save a migrant from encountering a potentially explosive situation at worse or an embarrassing one at best.

In the process of creating mental maps of segregation, migrants' networks played an invaluable role. While these newcomers could learn the racial boundaries on their own, the networks of family and friends often prevented them from floundering upon the rocks and shoals of racism in the River City. The *Louisville Leader*, owned and operated by I. Willis Cole, himself a migrant, continuously reminded African Americans where they could, and should, shop and be treated with respect. In a 1935 editorial, he advised them to purchase their shoes at Nettleton's, saying: "Colored people should at all times buy from those persons who appreciate their business and especially when they get what they want and at a good price." He went on to recommend two other stores open to blacks: Stephen and Koenig's and the Edwin Claspp, Cantilever Boot Shop.[68] In another editorial, he emphasized that blacks should only shop where they were "appreciated and where they are treated with courtesies due them as patrons."[69] Although this was more explicitly a political stance that blacks should not patronize businesses that "Jim Crowed" them, it also warned unknowing migrants of the kind of reception they could expect to receive in a given establishment.

Because segregation in Louisville was more a matter of custom than law, these mental maps, like segregation itself, could shift as subtly as sand underfoot. As much as racial boundaries were based on tradition, they also rested on the authority of individual whites. It was the white bus driver, waiter or waitress, usher or ticket taker, the man or woman behind counters and registers who enforced segregation. Because of this, no African American could ever be entirely sure of how they would be treated in any business. An incident during World War II highlights the nature of segregation in Louisville. Private First Class Gerald Dean, having presented his ticket to a performance of the Cincinnati Symphony Orchestra at Memorial Auditorium, was ushered from one balcony to another. Finally, he was taken to the box office, where his ticket was refunded and he was told that the concert was for "white people only . . . maybe [blacks] in 100 years but not now."[70] Dean had recently attended a number of performances at the same auditorium, including the Don Cosack Chorus and Roland Hayes, but on this particular night neither the attendant nor the manager was willing to "seat one Negro among all those white people."[71]

While Dean's case attracted widespread attention, such experiences were the norm for African Americans in Louisville and often passed with little notice outside the black community. Jewel Rabb found that Taylor's Drug Store refused to serve her a bottle of Coca-Cola but willingly filled the prescriptions of her husband's patients.[72] Stores that had allowed Murray A. Walls to shop freely when she visited Louisville refused to serve her when she settled there for good.[73] Though they were common, confronting such racial barriers could be perplexing if not downright confusing for newcomers. While migrants' networks were central in revealing the subtly shifting racial patterns in the River City, the way in which migrants dealt with those patterns was based almost entirely on their prior understanding of how to survive in a segregated society. African Americans brought a number of cultural tools to cope with, and ultimately ease, their transition to the new environment.

One of their most important tools was the ability to manipulate the seemingly all-encompassing racial boundaries. Public discourse would have us believe that there were sharp distinctions between blackness and whiteness—the supposedly concrete racial categories that Louisville's Jim Crow barriers were based on. Yet the actions of some migrants reveal a different understanding of the concept of race, or at least of the black/white binary on which segregation was founded. A number of migrants appeared to be especially adept at manipulating white Louisvillians' expectations of black inferiority, as well as the fluidity of "race" itself. A number of scholars have deconstructed "race" as an ideology, arguing that race is more a social construction than a biological fact. Many have gone on to suggest that the construction of race as an essential or biological fact masks the diversity existing within, as well as between, such categories.[74] While migrants may not have articulated their behavior in such a manner, their actions clearly demonstrated such an understanding of "race."

African American migrants skillfully exploited whites' assumptions of black inferiority. Among migrants, it was known as putting on your "monkeyshine," the "coon act," or "playing the game"; among scholars, it has been called the "art" or "culture" of dissemblance. No matter the name, the game was essentially the same. Darlene Clark Hine has offered one of the more nuanced explanations of this culture: "By dissemblance I mean the behavior and attitude of black women that created the appearance of openness and disclosure but actually shielded the truth of their inner lives and selves from their oppressors." For Hine, black migrants' use of dissemblance both relied on and was a response to whites' "unwillingness to discard tired and worn stereotypes."[75] It is important that Hine's discussion of the culture of dissemblance not be separated from the specific context in which she situates it—as a response by African American women to class, racial, and gendered forms of oppression, such as rape and domestic violence, directed at them by both black and white men. However, a number of students of black culture have identified the use of dissemblance among African Americans as a whole. For instance, James Baldwin, John Roberts, John Blassingame, Richard Wright, and Malcolm X have all discussed the use of dissemblance by women and men.[76]

More importantly, migrants themselves recognized dissemblance as a survival strategy used by many African Americans irrespective of gender. As one migrant put it, "All the way back to slavery days, blacks have been playing Bre'r Rabbit for their own benefit."[77] Lyman T. Johnson described how a fellow waiter in Tennessee tried to teach him the art of dissemblance:

My waiter friend said: "Now watch me. I'm going to show you how to get some money. Follow me and stay close enough to see." . . . As the white people passed by, he'd mumble in "darky" dialect: "You white folks sho' is mean. You the cheapest ol' no good white people I ever did see. You ain't got no sense at all!" About then a white man said, "Nigger, what you mumbling about. . . . Oh, quit your griping." He reached into his pocket and handed him a ten-dollar bill. A ten-dollar bill! And the waiter had done nothing for him. The white man said: "Now, take this money on home. Don't drink it up. Don't gamble it up. Take it home and give it to your woman." And the waiter said: "Yassuh, I will, Mr. Charley. Some of you sho' got good sense. You are right, yassuh. I'm gonna give every penny ob dis money to my ol' woman. Yassuh, every cent!" The white man said, "Just be sure you do," reached into his pocket, handed him another five dollars and said, "All right, this is for you." And as the white man left, fifteen dollars lighter, the waiter was still muttering, "Yassuh, yassuh. . . ." When the white man was out of sight, he turned to me and said, "See if you can make fifteen dollars that fast."[78]

A. J. Elmore had learned to "play the game" as a child in Alabama. His father, a pastor of the local church and a teacher at the local school, instructed him mainly to speak in "broken" English, show deference to whites, and tell them what they wanted to hear.[79]

For many migrants, dissemblance was little more than an act performed in front of white people. African Americans who played "the role" whites expected of them were often rewarded with economic gain. Dissemblance also served to protect blacks in a volatile environment, where the wrong word, gesture, or look could have grave consequences. Although dissemblance did not negate the existence of the racial boundaries that circumscribed black life in Louisville, for some migrants it was one way to deal with the "unwritten restraints" all blacks lived under.[80] And though dissemblance did not subvert the racial boundaries, it did afford African Americans a modicum of protection while helping to foster an "atmosphere inimical to realizing equal opportunity."[81] So long as they continued to act deferentially and outwardly acquiesce to the racist status quo, whites were never forced to challenge their own construction of black inferiority. Nor did they have to examine their role in breathing life into their own imaginations.

According to at least one migrant, dissemblance was not always voluntary; African Americans were "made to play the role of the master's servant." Whereas some migrants embraced dissemblance, others were taught to reject it entirely. Lyman Johnson, despite the prodding of his fellow waiters, simply "couldn't do it." Although he recognized dissemblance as a "technique of survival," for him survival would be gained at the cost of his dignity and worth as a human being. Johnson's refusal to dissemble reflected the values his family instilled in him "down home" in Clarksville, Tennessee. His father, especially, would not allow any of his children to compromise their belief in their own self-worth. "I didn't raise any of my sons to be a lackey . . . I didn't bring you in to this world to be a slave," he told young Johnson and his brothers.[82] For some migrants, dissemblance was little more than selling your "dignity and self-respect for pocket change."[83]

Dissemblance was not the only strategy migrants deployed to cope with whites' attempts to deny them full access to equality and safe mobility in the city. While dissemblance played upon racist expectations of black inferiority, passing played upon the construction of race itself. The ability of African American migrants to pass through or around the racial boundaries imposed on them was only possible because "race" was not a pure, secure, or reliable category. In her work on passing, Gayle Wald observed: "Arbitrarily ascribing race in accordance with the changing needs and interests of white supremacy, the color line has long served a variety of specific 'territorializing' functions through its ability to impose and regulate social inequality."[84] Passing as an act of transgression offered migrants a way to negotiate cultural boundaries established by social custom and legitimated by law. According to literary scholar Elaine Ginsberg, in crossing exclusionary or oppressive social and economic boundaries, passing creates a space for agency.[85] Through passing, migrants manipulated the arbitrariness of racial classifications for their own personal benefit.

Mae Street Kidd began slipping in and out of whiteness long before she stepped off the L & N in Louisville. From her home in Millersburg, she would travel to nearby Paris or Lexington where she shopped, ate, and was treated with the respect only whites received. Despite the fact that Kidd was "almost ninety percent" white and viewed herself as "a person of mixed blood who happens to be mostly white," the "one drop rule" meant that in Kentucky she was classified as black.[86] While she intermittently or strategically chose to pass, she never considered passing into whiteness permanently. In her mind, that would have been a rejection of her mother—something she would not do.

For Kidd, passing was less a rejection of blackness as it was an unwillingness to "accept second-class citizenship." She never passed within her own community or when she was in contact with other African Americans whom she knew. But, she recalled, "when I was off by myself, I lived like a first-class American citizen."[87] On her own, Kidd easily crossed the boundaries that circumscribed the lives of darker-skinned African Americans. She would simply go where she wanted under the assumption that no one would doubt her authenticity; by remaining silent she allowed herself to be passed into whiteness. For instance, in clothing stores she passed because "the clerks may have assumed I was white. I never raised the issue and it never came up."[88]

Apparently, Kidd was so convincing that she was seldom questioned about her racial identity. She spent a year working in Portland, Maine, at the lily-white United Seaman's Service Club, where neither blacks nor whites seemed to suspect she was African American. Ironically, she most often experienced "uncomfortable situations" traveling with her family or friends. On one such occasion during World War II, when she and her darker-skinned half brother, Webster, were traveling by train from Washington, D.C., to Kentucky, the conductor attempted no less than three times to force Mae to move to the "white coach." Although she would not tell the conductor why, she refused to move; "I was determined not to deny or embarrass my brother by leaving him alone in the colored coach. He was much darker than I was, so there was no question about his race. But he was my brother, and I was not going to leave him."[89] In the end, her connection to family and community was more important than the benefits of passing into whiteness.

Passing was not just a means for individual migrants to negotiate Louisville's racial boundaries. In at least one instance, passing was used by the local NAACP to challenge segregation in the River City—the ingenious idea of Harry S. McAlpin, the local branch president. Throughout the era, blacks were excluded from using the majority of Louisville's public parks, swimming pools, tennis courts, and amusement parks. But in what could only be viewed as a sincere gesture of "benevolence," the city made an exception in 1953. On the occasion of the play "The Tall Kentuckian" about the life of Abraham Lincoln, African Americans were allowed entry to the amphitheater in Iroquois Park between June 15 and July 4.[90] Prior to June 15, Mrs. Hyburnia Moorman purchased a ticket to a different play, while two black men were refused service that same evening. Moorman had light skin and "white" features: brown hair and blue eyes. Though she classified herself as African American and lived in the black section of town, while alone she had been ejected from the segregated "black" Chickasaw Park as a "white" woman. By contrast, in the company of African Americans with darker skin, she had been ejected from all-white Central Park as "black." On June 13 Hyburnia Moorman filed suit in Jefferson County Court, arguing that the segregation law should be repealed since it was "arbitrary, unenforceable and vague."[91] Though the NAACP won this case, the ruling in regard to the Iroquois Park amphitheater was not applied to public parks in the city as a whole. Yet the NAACP's strategy did reveal the paradox of Louisville's policy of racial exclusion and most likely led to a closer monitoring of theatergoers at Iroquois Park.

Whether used by individuals for personal gain or by organizations such as the NAACP, passing was not only a way for migrants to negotiate the city's racial boundaries, but also placed these boundaries themselves in question. According to Elaine Ginsberg, passing "embodies the anxieties and contradictions of a racially stratified society."[92] Since the ability to pass was almost entirely based on color, few African Americans had access to this particular form of agency. Yet "the specter of race passing"—that is, the *possibility* of passing itself, threatened white identity on both an individual and a societal level. Passing destabilized the "grounds of privilege founded upon racial identity."[93] In other words, passing demonstrated that the boundaries imposed on African Americans, in the form of Jim Crow, were a product of power and white insecurity rather than of some inherent inferiority. Thus, passing not only tempered the effect of Jim Crow; it also provided a few migrants with a kind of agency.

The amount of power passing offered, however, was limited by the very nature of passing itself. Despite the shadow cast by "the specter of racial passing," only the smallest number of migrants could exercise that option. The fact that passing was most effective when it was least visible has led one scholar to challenge the degree to which it may be viewed as resistance. For Carole Anne Tyler, at best passing is "not quite not resistance," since passing disguises difference rather than affirming it.[94] While passing did reveal the arbitrary basis of Louisville's boundaries, it did so in a way that was not highly visible. Passing may have destabilized the city's racial boundaries theoretically and ideologically, but in their appearance and operation they remained virtually unchanged.

If passing can be viewed as "not quite not resistance," then a migrant's refusal to pass can be seen as a kind of resistance that displayed blackness as a positive difference. Amelia B. Ray, like Mae Street Kidd, realized that if your "skin was light enough, you got the benefit of the doubt."[95] As long as she was not with other, darker blacks, she was able to go wherever she pleased. But refused to do so. Her unwillingness to pass, despite the rewards whiteness offered, was nothing less than an affirmation of black identity. Ray's actions offer a powerful critique of many whites' belief that, given the chance, African Americans would want to be white. As Gayle Wald suggests, the refusal to pass asserts that "African Americans, as a racially defined group, need not accommodate themselves to the needs, interests, and social definitions of the white majority, but may legitimately pursue their own interests and institutions."[96] Or as Amelia Ray herself put it: "There's one black woman in Louisville that don't want nothing if she can't come in and try it. . . . I was not going to stoop down."[97]

In refusing to pass, Ray rejected the notion of inferiority and difference on which Louisville's racial boundaries were based. For her, passing was not so much an indication of envy or the desire to be white, as it was a conscious recognition that the economic advantages and freedoms whites enjoyed were a product of power rather than some inherent characteristic of whiteness itself. Many migrants like Ray made a clear distinction between the privileges bestowed on whites and whiteness itself. She certainly wanted the freedom only whites in Louisville could access; however, it was also plain that she was not making an argument for forced social integration by saying, "Most black people don't want to come to your house if you don't invite them."[98]

Although not everyone had the option to pass, many migrants in Louisville seemed to share these same sentiments. One migrant echoed Ray, saying on one hand she did not want "social privileges" with whites, but on the other she did want "things as swell as whites." Another migrant, interviewed by sociologist Charles Parrish, declared: "If they would just let me have the same privileges a white person has. I don't mean going to their homes and things like that, I mean jobs and better breaks."[99] In other words, migrants like Amelia Ray argued for *equal treatment* regardless of race but had no real desire to interact with whites personally. Although the refusal to pass may have been no more visible than passing as a form of resistance to Louisville's racial boundaries, it offered a direct and powerful critique of those boundaries. In a society grounded in black inferiority, it affirmed racial pride and blackness itself. At the same time, it directly challenged whiteness as the standard of citizenship.

The refusal to pass was not the only means Ray had at her disposal to deal with the racial boundaries she encountered in Louisville. Throughout her life she had been puzzled by what she called the "inconsistencies" of race; nonetheless, in her former home of Clarksville, Tennessee, she became adept at manipulating these inconsistencies long before she arrived in Louisville. One incident illustrates how her methods could be more direct and overt than passing, though no less based on an understanding of race as a construction.

During the early 1940s Ray worked in the alterations department of a local department store. The store manager made the unfortunate decision to move her to the lounge to cover for a sick employee. In doing so, he placed her in the paradoxical situation of enforcing Jim Crow by keeping other African

Americans from entering the lounge. As he left he gave her this final instruction, "You are not to let Negroes in here." She cagily responded that she could not distinguish who was a Negro and who was white since "some are dark but are white, some are white but are black." In the week she worked there, the lounge was desegregated. In effect, she put the store manager in an ideological bind of either having to acknowledge that the racial boundaries drawn throughout Louisville were arbitrary, as one could not always easily distinguish between races, or he would have to allow Ray to desegregate the lounge, both of which directly challenged the construction of white supremacy. While such victories were few and far between, not to mention short-lived, Ray's manipulation of the "inconsistencies" of race presented an open challenge to the prevailing racial ideology as well as to Jim Crow itself. African Americans' manipulation of the "inconsistencies" inherent in the construction of race, whether in the form of dissemblance, passing, or the refusal to do either all proved to be effective methods of negotiating the racial boundaries encountered in Louisville.[100]

More often, black migrants responded to segregation by saying "I never Jim Crowed myself." By this they meant they would not go where they would not be served or treated with respect. By conceiving of Jim Crow as a verb rather than a noun, African Americans emphasized whites' active participation in maintaining segregation. Whenever possible, migrants avoided any business or institution that segregated or discriminated, often going well out of their way in terms of time, distance, or money to do so. On her arrival at the Louisville Greyhound Bus Station, an African American woman quickly realized the benefits of such avoidance when a Greyhound driver called a Yellow Cab to "haul a load of coal."[101] Amelia Ray discovered that at the five-and-dime stores along Fourth Street, blacks "couldn't get milk, cause you couldn't drink from a glass, [and that] if you got a sandwich you got an invitation to eat it on the street." But the same stores would gladly allow you to buy a bottle of Coca-Cola to drink *outside*. Ray refused to buy anything there. As she said, "I never Jim Crowed myself."[102]

Murray Walls remembered that down on Fourth Street, "I couldn't try on the dresses at Stewarts'. I couldn't try on one at Stillman's. Bycks' was the only place where Negro women could go and freely try on clothes. Most of us bought our things from Bycks' or we went to Cincinnati or Indianapolis."[103] Lyman Johnson took his whole family on a disappointing trip to Cincinnati for the opportunity to see *Gone with the Wind* in a first-run, desegregated movie theater.[104] Although only a few African Americans in Louisville could afford to travel to Indianapolis or Cincinnati to see a film, it was a common practice among those few blacks who had the money to do so.

In the River City, however, wealth offered no refuge to middle-class black migrants, who, as all other African Americans, were limited to the choice of shopping at a few stores such as Nettleton Shoes or at the larger, segregated Kaufman's Department Store. While not everyone could travel to Cincinnati to shop, working-class blacks found other ways to express their displeasure with second-class treatment in the stores Jim Crow forced them to patronize. In May 1938, for example, the predominantly working-class neighborhood surrounding Nineteenth and Walnut streets erupted in a protest centering on the inferior quality of goods and the mistreatment of African Americans by grocery store owner Harry Goldberg. His brutal assault of Miss Mary Golson for attempting to return a loaf of stale bread touched off nearly a month-long campaign of picketing, boycotting, and glass breaking by the "indignant citizens of the all colored community."[105] While the middle-class residents of Teachers' Row may have expressed their dissent in a different manner, both were essentially an expression of the refusal to be "Jim Crowed."

I. Willis Cole captured the sentiments of many a migrant who refused to be "Jim Crowed" when he warned "visitors" that "Stewart Dry Goods Co. located at Fourth and West Walnut Street does not want the business of Negroes. . . . Stewart Dry Goods Co. does not want Negro business, and Negroes who know that and then continue to spend their hard earned money there are bigger fools than we thought they were."[106] At times the refusal to be "Jim Crowed"—or, as Cole might say, to not be a "fool"—could be widespread. In the summer of 1946, more than 2,500 African Americans demanded refunds or refused to attend the performance of "Sugar Chile" Robinson, a black pianist child prodigy, at the Armory saying, "They were not aware that they would be segregated when they bought the tickets."[107] Clearly, whenever it was within their means African Americans went to amazing lengths to escape "Jim Crow."

Black migrants' refusal to participate in their own racial oppression, their refusal to be "Jim Crowed," represented an act of protest against white supremacy. In doing so, they rejected notions of their own inferiority. Their view of Jim Crow as an agentival process, as something being done to them, indicates that they rejected the popular discourse that segregation was a product of their own inferiority, rather than the power whites wielded. The construction of Louisville's "invisible" racial boundaries made Jim Crow a reality that all African Americans confronted. Yet, whenever feasible, many migrants refused to acquiesce to segregation or to actively take part in their own subjugation. Although they may have been forced to defer to segrega-tion in practice, their refusal to be "Jim Crowed" suggests that they did not participate in principle.

Segregation dramatized the striking differences in accommodation and treatment between blacks and whites by humiliating blacks and publicly pro-claiming their supposed inferiority. To this end, racial barriers were erected in Louisville for whites as much as for blacks. For whites, these restrictions were meant to function as a public symbol of African American inferiority. That any white could deny service or access at will inflated the value of white-ness, even as it served to keep blacks in their place. Yet, in refusing to be "Jim Crowed," blacks infused segregation with their own meaning. In the minds of many migrants, Jim Crow was a symbol of the inconsistencies in racial ide-ology and its power to shape Louisville's urban landscape. In effect, African Americans asserted their right to equal treatment and respect on their own terms.

The range of strategies people like Mae Street Kidd brought to Louisville is evidence that historians have underestimated the ability of African Ameri-cans to initially cope with the urban landscape to which they had migrated. The notion that they were unsophisticated, or unprepared to handle life in a city, overlooks the number of cities and towns migrants often passed through or lived in before they settled in Louisville. In the form of networks or strate-gies of dealing with the city's racial boundaries, these newcomers drew on a number of cultural tools they had brought with them that ultimately eased their transition to life in Louisville. Black migrants arrived equipped with an arsenal of strategies for their survival. To suggest otherwise robs them of the agency they demonstrated throughout their lives.

NO ROOM FOR POSSUM OR CRAWFISH

AFRICAN AMERICAN MIGRANTS' CHALLENGE TO JIM CROW

In April 1935 a migrant from Memphis, Tennessee, I. Willis Cole, in an editorial appearing in his *Louisville Leader*, encouraged African Americans in the city to engage in political action. Under the banner, "Negroes Urged to Play Politics Like the White Man," he argued that it was time "to take advantage of the moment, to think independently, and in terms of Negroes, first, last and always."[1] Realizing that this was not the time for inaction or for blacks to lose the few gains they had made in Louisville, he concluded there was "no room for possum or crawfish."

Cole's commentary was a call to arms, signaling the need for a newfound sense of militancy among blacks as well as the shifting political climate in Louisville. At the same time he anticipated, or at least hoped for, a radical change that would transform the city itself—by tearing down the walls of segregation. Although the local NAACP was the premier civil rights organization in the River City, it was not the only vehicle migrants used to address their civil rights concerns. Migrants existed within a broad spectrum of activism from Republican to Democrat and from strategies of negotiation to direct action calling for an immediate end to Jim Crow. At times they worked in primarily black organizations like the NAACP; in other instances their efforts relied on interracialism and the support of liberal whites. Migrants often worked independently, or in multiple civil rights organizations at the same time. In the end, however, there was no greater advocate for black equality than African Americans themselves.

It was not necessarily evident by the mid-1930s that the increasing influx of blacks migrants, or the almost imperceptible shift away from overwhelming black support of the Republican Party, would provide the catalyst for desegregation in Louisville. In fact, by 1921 African Americans constituted 45 percent of all registered Republicans in the city, although they only accounted for 17.1 percent of the population.[2] Not only did blacks comprise a disproportionate number of Republican voters, but they were also overwhelmingly Republican. There were only 57 African Americans registered as Democrats in the entire city.[3] By 1927, the city registry showed 34,150 black Republicans and 223 registered Democrats.[4] Between 1870 and 1921, then, the Republican Party—the party of Abraham Lincoln and Thaddeus Stevens—seemingly relied on the votes of African Americans without question or much regard for their interests.

Regardless of the fact that black voters consistently played a seminal role in the election of Republican mayors, aldermen, and state representatives, their concerns and desires were often neglected. African Americans in Louisville increasingly viewed the failure of the Republican Party to either recognize or reward them for their support as a sign of ingratitude. Despite the large number of black Republicans, no African Americans had been nominated for public office in Louisville.[5] Moreover, according to George C. Wright, many of the city's most prominent Republicans, policemen, and government employees were openly members of the Ku Klux Klan.[6] A growing number of African Americans began to seek alternatives to the Republican Party in Louisville.

In 1921, dissatisfaction with the Republicans' refusal to allow an African American to run for a seat in the city council coalesced in the formation of the Lincoln Independent Party.[7] At one of its first meetings, funeral home owner A. D. Porter argued that blacks in Louisville were little more than "political slaves" to the Republican Party, saying, "This condition of political slavery has placed us in the unenviable position of being owned by the Republican Party and hated by the Democrats."[8] The Lincoln Independent Party nominated candidates for every open office in Louisville and the surrounding county of Jefferson during the November 1921 campaign.

Its candidates ran on a platform that was an indictment of both Republicans and Democrats:

1 [We demand] absolute equality of opportunity.
2 [We demand] racial representation at the forum where laws are made to tax our property.
3 [We demand] our proportional share in the emoluments of official preferment.

4 We owe absolute allegiance to neither political party.

5 We can neither be bought nor bluffed.[9]

As the campaign progressed, the Lincoln Independent Party denounced the Republicans more and more forcefully. At one point, a spokesman described the Republican Party as an "apostate party, so changed in its policies and practices that Lincoln with all his native acumen would not recognize it."[10]

Although the Lincoln Independent Party represented the sentiments of many African Americans in Louisville, it failed to secure a single office for one of its candidates. Instead, the Republicans swept all city and county offices. The vote in the mayoral contest was indicative of the November elections as a whole. The Republican candidate, Huston Quin, won 63,332 votes, compared to 56,199 for the Democratic candidate and 271 for A. D. Porter, the Lincoln Independent Party candidate.[11] While many blacks were distressed by the "ungrateful" attitude of the Republican Party, the majority were unwilling to quit it.

The unwillingness of black Louisvillians to abandon the Republican Party was not a sign of loyalty, but rather of the lack of other viable options. Louisville Democrats were closely allied with white supremacy. According to George Wright, they won a number of elections by brazenly appealing to the racist fears of white voters. For instance, mayoral candidate W. O. Harris solicited white votes by claiming that ultimately local blacks wanted political domination over whites.[12]

As one historian of black political behavior in Louisville noted, "From 1921 to 1932, some of the Negroes indicated a willingness to 'take a walk' out of the Republican Party, but had no place to go."[13] African Americans continued to support Republicans, albeit less enthusiastically. In 1931, the distribution of black voters remained virtually unchanged: 25,760 Republicans, 545 Lincoln Independents, and 129 Democrats.[14] The Democratic Party as a whole remained contemptuous of African American voters. The *Louisville Leader* captured the thinking of many black Louisvillians when it declared: "It is the opinion of the *Leader*, that this is no time for Negroes to allow themselves to support a party which neither desires, invites, nor in many states accepts the Negro vote, as a protest against the Republican Party."[15]

The election of Franklin D. Roosevelt to the presidency in 1932 began a process of transformation in River City politics. For the first time blacks in Louisville and across the country viewed the Democratic Party with something other than complete skepticism. Between 1932 and 1936, the increasing numbers of black delegates at the Democratic National Convention and the economic impact of Roosevelt's' New Deal led blacks nationwide to re-evaluate the Democratic stand on black equality.[16] In 1935, however, African Americans argued in the *Louisville Defender* that "in a real sense he [FDR] has forgotten us. We believe Roosevelt is not against us, but certainly he is not for us."[17]

By 1936 the economic incentives of Roosevelt's New Deal were as readily apparent to African Americans in Louisville as they were to blacks nation-wide. Although there were still disparities in the amount of aid they obtained during the Depression, FDR's consideration of the needs of black people rep-resented a radical departure from past policies. Blacks in Louisville became less hesitant to embrace a Democratic candidate. According to the *Louis-ville Defender* in 1940, "That the Negro has shared some of the benefits of the New Deal is because he is so integrated with American life that it would be impossible to emerge from any economic dilemma without reasonable con-sideration of our largest minority group. The Negro has been denied a fair chance in American life for so long, that he is eager to show his appreciation for whatever rightful consideration is directed toward him."[18]

Not only were African Americans now willing to consider the Democratic Party, the party also became willing to consider them. Increasingly, blacks in Louisville became "Roosevelt Republicans," voting Democratic in national elections but overwhelmingly Republican at the local level. Looking to make their own foothold among black voters at home, Democrats began serious efforts to lure African Americans away from the Republican Party. By 1944 their campaign had escalated exponentially from their prior days of neglect. In a paid advertisement directed to black voters, Democrats asserted: "The first, last, and only Republican who honestly tried to do anything for the American Negro was Abraham Lincoln. Lincoln has been dead for 79 years. Ever since the Civil War the Republicans have been cashing in on Lincoln. They have been long on promises and short on performance. The Democratic Party and Roosevelt have done more for the Negro than all the Republican presidents put together."[19] Nor was the Democratic Party alone in its assess-ment of Republicans in Louisville. The *Louisville Leader* claimed that blacks received "nothing but promises and hard times" from Republicans.[20]

Throughout the 1940s local Democrats continued to capitalize on the pol-icies of Roosevelt and Harry S. Truman. Democratic endorsements claimed that both presidents had done more for "Negro Bread winners" than any Re-publican administration.[21] Truman's civil rights platform especially appealed to black voters in Louisville. The report, *To Secure These Rights*, a blueprint for ameliorating racism in America, combined with executive orders desegregating the military and civil service, led a number of African Americans to look at Democrats in a new light. The *Louisville Defender* captured the perspective of many blacks when it announced: "President Truman has demonstrated that he pilots a New Deal party dedicated to the principle of liberty. He is the most outspoken champion of civil rights to occupy the White House."[22]

Ironically, in 1948 New Dealer Henry A. Wallace, perhaps the most outspoken presidential candidate on civil rights, did not obtain much support from Louisville blacks. While black journalists recognized that his campaign forced both Democrats and Republicans to address civil rights, they refused to endorse him because they believed he could not win. Or as William Beckett, an African American candidate for city council in 1945, put it, "Wallace is not going to cut any ice with the Negro voters."[23] The issue was not so much how blacks viewed Wallace or Truman, or even Thomas E. Dewey for that matter, but that by forcing the two major parties to court their vote, African Americans in Louisville substantially increased their political bargaining power.

In a city with nearly equal numbers of white Democrats and Republicans, black votes often proved to be the difference between victory and defeat. As the pace of migration accelerated, the sheer numbers of potential black voters was sufficiently large to tip the balance of political power. Between 1930 and 1970 more than 17,000 migrants arrived in Louisville, mostly of voting age.[24] If either Democrats or Republicans were to acquire blacks' votes, they had to acknowledge and respect, or at least pay lip service to, the needs of African Americans. As the *Louisville Defender* suggested, African Americans were no longer "content to cast their votes, and [be] turned away from the polls to be satisfied with a slap on the back and a few menial jobs."[25]

During this period of political flux, the Republican administration in Louisville began to hire African Americans in clerical and white-collar positions throughout city government. This shift in policy and political power was also evident in the initial hiring of black policemen, as well as in the construction of a new fire station at Thirteenth and Broadway manned entirely by African Americans. But blacks wanted more than patronage. They demanded to speak for themselves, believing they could best represent their own communities. In short, blacks wanted self-determination. As the *Defender* put it, "Whenever there is a necessity for true interpretation of the Negro's needs, his thinking, his feeling; a Negro can best do the job."[26]

In response to these demands, a small number of blacks from both parties were nominated and elected to public office.[27] In 1935 Charles W. Anderson and C. Ewbank Tucker were the Republican and Democratic candidates, respectively, for state representative in the Fifty-eighth District. Anderson received 2,337 votes to Tucker's 956, becoming the first African American elected to the state legislature. He served six consecutive terms from 1935 to 1947, running unopposed in 1945. Ironically, Tucker, one of a handful of black Democrats in Louisville, ran against the Republican Party because of its refusal to nominate an African American candidate in 1931.[28] In 1948 Republican Eugene Clayton defeated the Democratic candidate, William Beckett, to become the first African American seated in the city council.[29] Although Clayton was a native Louisvillian, the next three African Americans to serve as aldermen—William Beckett, Louise Reynolds, and W. J. Hodge—were all migrants. Between 1954 and 1960 Felix S. Anderson, the migrant originally from Wilmington, North Carolina, served as the first African American elected to the state legislature as a Democrat.[30] Similarly, Earl Dearing, a native of Virginia, was the first black elected Police Court prosecutor in 1965, after being appointed deputy clerk of the Police Court in Jefferson County and a Municipal Court judge in Louisville.[31] Despite differences in party affiliation, the majority of African Americans nominated or elected in Louisville shared a commitment to equality.

Often they were also relatively recent arrivals to the city: Anderson originally from Frankfort, Tucker most recently from West Virginia, and Beckett from Baltimore.[32] Nor were these elected officials alone; many of the city's leading black activists were also migrants. Although by no means the only political activists, migrants represented a disproportionate number of the civil rights advocates in Louisville. Migrants not only increased the political power of blacks by their sheer volume, but they also led the effort to make Louisville more livable for African Americans. There was no hint of the "plantation mentality" in the River City.[33] Quite simply, through migration blacks demonstrated a profound unwillingness to accept the status quo.

African American migrants energized the city's civil rights movement. Prior to their arrival in the 1930s, there was not nearly as much militancy in Louisville as one might expect, given the changing political climate and the amount of activism elsewhere in the Upper South. While cities such as Durham, North Carolina, Charlestown, West Virginia, and Norfolk, Virginia, were deeply involved in the NAACP campaign to equalize the salaries of black teachers, the Louisville branch had yet to join the fight.[34] Throughout much of the decade the local branch of the NAACP was chronically in debt and often characterized by inactivity.[35]

African American teachers in the River City were paid 15 percent less than white teachers. According to the Louisville Board of Education, the pay differential was not a matter of racism; rather, the division of public schools into two classes, A and B, was based on the educational background and experience of the faculty. Teachers in Class A schools were supposedly more qualified than teachers in Class B schools and so received a higher salary. That Class A and B schools fell along racial lines was merely a "coincidence."[36] However, a report conducted by the Louisville Association of Colored Teachers demonstrated little difference in the quality or amount of training between black and white teachers in Kentucky.[37]

The national NAACP repeatedly, albeit unsuccessfully, encouraged the Louisville branch to engage in the struggle to equalize teachers' salaries and higher education throughout the 1930s. The effort to equalize teachers' salaries in the Upper South was the beginning of a campaign that would ultimately reach the U.S. Supreme Court in *Brown v. Board of Education* (1954). Yet both the Louisville branch and black teachers themselves seemed reluctant to address the disparity in pay. Charles Anderson, former president of the Louisville NAACP, characterized African American teachers as "unorganized and afraid."[38] Yolanda Barnett, a member of the future Education Equalization Committee (EEC), told Thurgood Marshall that most of the teachers were "a little skeptical of Anderson's sincerity." Many believed he was little more than a "self-seeker." At the same time, black teachers appeared unwilling to risk their jobs for a cause that the local NAACP did not fully support and that seemed likely to fail.[39]

The national NAACP urged the Louisville branch to "do more," "to get involved," to hold more meetings that were not solely membership drives. Time and time again, the NAACP sent inquiries and field secretaries to Louisville to stimulate interest in participating in the teacher salary equalization campaign. In 1937 NAACP field secretary, William Pickens, suggested: "Our campaign for educational equality would be a great subject to discuss in Louisville, Kentucky. I know of no place where it might be more appropriate or where it might bear more fruit."[40] While the association's efforts in other cities had achieved some success, the Louisville branch had yet to seriously consider the issue. NAACP field secretaries reported back that the climate in Louisville was chilly at best.

Throughout 1937, NAACP field secretary Daisy Lampkin gave a number of speeches in Louisville on the 15 percent differential in teachers' salaries in an effort to spur black teachers into action. In an appeal to the Louisville Association of Colored Teachers, she argued: "It is unfair for you who teach in Louisville to receive a difference in salaries. When you have had the same instruction, teach the same subjects and hold the same certificates. It just doesn't make sense for [such] a condition to exist. To say the least, it is not according to American justice."[41] Her speech failed to achieve the desired result. To the contrary, it raised the "ire" of a number of teachers, including W. H. Perry, president of the Louisville Association, who assured the superintendent of schools that while some teachers agreed with Lampkin, "the majority do not."[42] In a November 1937 letter to prominent NAACP litigator Charles Hamilton Houston, Daisy Lampkin blamed the lack of "progress" in Louisville on "spineless," "Uncle Tom Leadership in Public Schools."[43] Nor was the appraisal of NAACP field secretary Leon A. Ransom much better. While he recognized that the majority was "in line," there were still a few individuals "more concerned with their own jobs than they are with progress."[44] Lampkin acknowledged that there were exceptions, including Dr. P. O. Sweeny, a dentist and recently elected president of the Louisville NAACP, Charles W. Anderson, and a number of teachers such as Lyman T. Johnson.

Although Sweeny was a native Louisvillian, many of the others like Johnson and Anderson were relatively new to the city. While the lack of action in Louisville frustrated the national NAACP, migrants Johnson and Anderson represented a group committed to equalizing teachers' salaries. Sweeny may have spoken for the group as a whole when he wrote the NAACP, "This is one battle I mean to win if I must lose some friends."[45] With the full support of Thurgood Marshall and the national NAACP, Anderson, Sweeny, and Johnson urged the city's black teachers to immediately file suit against the Louisville Board of Education. As a sign of its commitment to the cause, the national NAACP offered to help formulate a viable civil rights strategy and provided free legal counsel. Despite that offer and the promised cohort of local activists, the Louisville Association of Colored Teachers in January 1938 voted to postpone any action until they had discussed the salary differential with the superintendent and the Board of Education.[46]

In 1938, at just about the same time Nashville's African American teachers equalized their salaries, Louisville's newly formed Education Equalization Committee (EEC), a twelve-person task force composed of teachers and citizens, began talking and meeting with the Board of Education. After nearly two years of fruitless discussions, it was clear that the white board members were doing everything in their power to delay any action on the matter. Unexpectedly, Mayor Joseph D. Scholtz voiced approval of the teachers' campaign, calling the salary disparity "unfair." In a rather unusual step given Louisville's racial climate, Scholtz pledged support for black teachers should the request for the necessary appropriation come up, saying the

Board of Education had given them the "run around." Despite the mayor's endorsement, blacks found the school board unrelenting on the 15 percent pay differential. Frustrated by inaction, the EEC declared the "indefinite" promises of the board "so vague as to remove, almost, the possibility of ever bringing about the desired adjustment."[47]

Finally, in December 1939 the EEC ended its negotiations with the school board. Although black teachers still received 15 percent less than white teachers, they remained reluctant to file suit against the Board of Education. For Anderson, the major problem was not the board's racism, but the lack of teacher commitment to the movement. While many "talked" about supporting the campaign, only a few teachers were truly involved. "Out of 300 teachers, only 76 contributed to a fund for a purpose which was for their benefit," he informed the national NAACP. "Likewise, we had lots of promises relative to different ones offering to allow their names as 'plaintiff,' but when the final hour arrived each one who had been a 'parlor' or 'living room' talker, couldn't be found on this side of Finland."[48]

As Louisville's black teachers continued their efforts to secure equal pay, the Board of Education released a statement in October 1940 advocating a gradual adjustment to the pay differential. The statement failed to set a specific date when this adjustment might begin, though the board made it plain that, given "budgetary obligations," it would not be anytime soon. The board dismissed Mayor Scholtz's standing offer to increase the city's appropriation for public schools to cover the cost, claiming that "contractual obligations" legally and morally prevented them from "equalizing the salaries in the immediate future."[49] After nearly two years of unfulfilled promises and the same old cut-rate pay, Louisville's black teachers finally agreed on the necessity of legal action.

The reluctance of many teachers to publicly support the campaign to equalize their salaries made it difficult to find a teacher whose name could be used in a court action. While the NAACP may have viewed them as "spineless," many were simply unwilling to risk losing their jobs during the economic crisis of the Great Depression. Then, as her peers shied away from becoming involved with the NAACP, Valla Dudley Abbington, a teacher at Jackson Junior High School, *volunteered* for the job despite the fact that she could be fired. Better educated than the majority of Louisville teachers, black or white, Abbington had earned a B.S. from Michigan State Normal College, attended graduate school at the University of Michigan, and held a certificate of public health from the Delmar Institute of Columbia Teachers College in New York.[50] Her credentials alone suggest that the Class B pay schedule was in reality based on racism rather than qualifications and experience.

Abbington had lived in Louisville less than ten years when, on November 7, 1940, she petitioned the school board to increase her annual salary from $1,490 to $1,750.[51] She requested a salary schedule free of "all racial discrimination" not only for herself, "but also on behalf of all the Negro teachers and principals in the Public Schools of Louisville."[52] By December 3, the day the Board of Education met to consider her petition, a sense of anticipation ran throughout black Louisville. Before the meeting Thurgood Marshall arrived and participated in the "Negro Hour" radio program, where he spoke on behalf of Louisville's black teachers. In the end, neither Marshall nor the teachers themselves swayed the school board. With little deliberation, the board concluded that "no monies would be added to the 1941 education budget in order to equalize salaries during 1941."[53] Two days later, arguing that the 15 percent differential "violates the Constitution and the laws of the Commonwealth of Kentucky and is a denial of the equal protection of the laws guaranteed by the Fourteenth Amendment to the Constitution of the United States," Valla Abbington filed suit in the U.S. District Court.[54] The trial date was set for March 10, 1941, some three months away.

Although the school board was unwilling to seriously consider equalizing black teachers' salaries, a small number of vocal whites in Louisville's mainstream press supported the increase. In the days following the school board's decision, Mark Ethridge, a white southern liberal and editor of the *Louisville Courier-Journal*, penned a series of editorials advocating the black teachers' demands. He asked white Louisvillians, "Do We Want to Be Truly Democratic?" arguing that inequality "shows that the goal of democracy has not been reached." Ethridge continued: "It is a recognized fact that a Negro in competition with a white man must, in order to succeed, have a great deal more ability than the white man. That is not just. It is not democratic and not in keeping with the Constitution, which guarantees all men equal rights. There is no place in the American system for discrimination against any man because of color, race or religion." In another editorial he urged "Let's Throw Off Prejudice," pointing out that "Negro teachers in the public school system of Louisville must have recourse to the courts in order to secure justice is to be everlastingly deplored." For Ethridge, the lack of progress in this arena signaled that there was still "too much of the old feeling left."[55]

Throughout the winter, the school board members remained committed to its discriminatory policy; however, in the weeks before the trial date they approached the NAACP with an offer. Although they had previously claimed that equalization was a fiscal impossibility, the members now agreed to equalize the black teachers' salaries in the fall if the NAACP would drop its suit. Faced with doubts of the school board's sincerity, NAACP attorney Prentice Thomas turned for advice to Thurgood Marshall, chief counsel of the national NAACP. For Marshall, the word of the school board was a less-than-certain guarantee; he strongly advised the Louisville NAACP to secure a court decree, arguing:

> The mere statement by them that they are working this out is not sufficient to protect the Negro teachers. Nothing will protect the Negro teachers short of a court decree and that is what the School Board is trying to dodge. . . . I do not trust any School Board, and this is the result of past experience, unless and until I have a court decree filed in the case. In addition, we have the additional factor that the Louisville School Board is even worse than any I have gone up against so far. We have nothing to gain by allowing the case to be pushed off and this would be in the School Board's favor and our loss.[56]

Marshall's advice proved sound, for the Board of Education flatly refused the NAACP request for a court decree. Instead, it asked that the case be post-poned until May 27 and used the time to negotiate a settlement. On April 1, the board formally abolished its unequal pay scale. While many black teach-ers proclaimed victory, the national NAACP insisted that they secure a declar-atory judgment and an injunction restraining the board from reinstalling a discriminatory pay schedule in the future. In October 1941, the court decree was granted, closing nearly three years of struggle. The impact of this victory extended far beyond a few more dollars in the hands of Louisville's black teachers. For the national NAACP, the win was viewed as groundwork in the larger fight to desegregate education.[57] In Kentucky, black teachers followed the example of black Louisville and initiated their own successful campaigns to equalize teachers' salaries. More importantly, the fight to equalize salaries marked the beginning of a protracted struggle against inequality. Through-out that struggle, African American migrants would continue to be at the forefront of the fight to make Louisville a safer place for blacks to live.

Although the Education Equalization Committee concentrated on equal-izing teachers' salaries, its activities also encompassed challenging the Day Law in higher education. Enacted in 1904, the Day Law banned integrated education, subjecting institutions, instructors, and students to stiff penalties for violating the statute. As early as 1936, migrant Charles Anderson had ap-proached Governor Albert Benjamin "Happy" Chandler about opening the

University of Kentucky to black graduate students. Chandler's caustic reply to Anderson's repeated appeal was "Such will not happen in your time nor mine."[58]

Despite the governor's cryptic warning, the Louisville NAACP, led by Charles Anderson, initiated its first attempt to desegregate higher education in Kentucky. In January 1939 Alfred M. Carroll, a black native of Louisville, applied for admission to the University of Kentucky Law School. Carroll, a graduate of Wilberforce College, attended Howard University Law School but wanted to return home to finish his legal education. His application led Chandler to allocate $1,600 from his emergency fund to send black students to schools outside the state, a measure he previously refused to consider. At the same time, Chandler spurred Rufus Atwood, the African American president of Kentucky State College, to action.

In the eyes of the Louisville NAACP, Atwood turned out to be little more than a "pawn of white politicians." According to Kentucky historian George Wright, in order to secure additional funding for Kentucky State College, Atwood claimed that Kentucky met the needs of African Americans and that blacks had no reason to seek admission to white universities. Indeed, he falsely stated that Carroll was more than satisfied by Chandler's $1,600 appropriation. Although Louisville's black press condemned Atwood as a "spineless coward" and "traitor," the black educator continued to support Chandler's segregationist stance.[59]

By late 1939, African Americans' agitation around the issue resulted in the appointment of a Governor's Advisory Committee to counsel Chandler on Carroll's application. Despite the presence of African Americans such as Charles Anderson and activists and school principals Albert E. Meyzeek and William H. Fouse on the committee, it did little to support Carroll's position. While the committee pointed out numerous disparities in both the access and the quality of African American education, it remained unchanged on the issue of segregation. On a motion forwarded by Rufus Atwood and seconded by the president of the University of Kentucky, the committee refused to even consider a remedy for the lack of black professional or graduate education in the state. Instead, it suggested that blacks look to the relatively deficient and recently accredited Louisville Municipal College for Negroes or Kentucky State College, located in Frankfort, and that the state find a way of "making farm life more attractive for the Negro population."[60] In response to these mild recommendations, Chandler declared: "If you [African Americans] insist on going to the University of Kentucky now, you are making a mistake because there were barriers which we did not make, for which we are not responsible to prevent you from going to the University." As if to remove any shadow of a doubt as to his position, he concluded: "I see no immediate prospects for completely equalizing opportunities."[61]

Governor Chandler was not the only opponent of fully integrated education in Kentucky. Throughout the NAACP's attempts to integrate the university, its presidents, Frank L. McVey and then Herman L. Donovan, unequivocally opposed integration. Paradoxically, McVey's book, *The Gates Open Slowly*, pointed out the shortcomings of education in Kentucky and the lack of adequate support for blacks in higher education. Apparently, he was untroubled by the contradiction between his liberal ideology and his commitment to segregation.[62]

Ultimately, the University of Kentucky Law School denied Alfred Carroll admission. Its dean, Alvin Evans, explained that, first, the Day Law prohibited integrated education, and second, Carroll had not graduated from an accredited college. Concerned that a defeat in court would hinder the national NAACP effort to desegregate higher education, Thurgood Marshall advised Anderson not to pursue the case. If African Americans were to be admitted to the University of Kentucky, another candidate would be needed.

Despite the defeat in the Carroll case, the NAACP remained committed to desegregating higher education in Kentucky. The national NAACP looked to the Louisville branch to build on its recent success with *Murray v. Maryland* (1936) and *Gaines v. Canada* (1938). In those cases the Supreme Court found that Maryland and Missouri, respectively, could not send black students out of state instead of providing truly equal in-state facilities to educate them, nor could they ask African Americans to wait while equal institutions were created. In 1940, desegregation of higher education in Kentucky was integral to the NAACP's national strategy to overthrow segregation.

In January 1940, Charles Hamilton Houston wrote to Prentice Thomas, Anderson's law partner, suggesting that in light of the *Gaines* victory, Berea College in rural Kentucky might present "an excellent chance to overthrow the Day Law."[63] Houston provided Thomas and the Louisville NAACP with a detailed, ten-point plan for attacking segregation in Kentucky's colleges and universities based on the national NAACP's cases in Maryland and Missouri. For Houston and the national NAACP, desegregation in Kentucky would offer a "tremendous contribution to American Democracy."[64] More importantly, as the premier civil rights organization in Kentucky, the national NAACP looked to its Louisville branch to lead the fight for civil rights throughout the state. As Thurgood Marshall bluntly stated, "The National office wants the Louisville branch in the middle of this fight. . . . We have been in the middle of this fight to open up state universities to Negro students and certainly our leading branch in Kentucky ought to be at the forefront of this particular fight."[65]

The Louisville branch did not disappoint the national office. By October 1941, the local NAACP found a candidate with "moral and scholastic qualifications" to challenge the Day Law. Seventeen years old and a recent graduate of the city's all-black Central High School, Charles Eubanks was quiet, brown-skinned, and more than willing to bring a case against the University of Kentucky. He was the son of a hard-working laundress, Mrs. Bodie Henderson, and wanted desperately to pursue a career in civil engineering. In the fall of 1941 Eubanks applied to the civil engineering program at the University of Kentucky, an academic program unavailable to African Americans in the state. In doing so, he and the NAACP embarked on a campaign to gain access to the university that would not be resolved until 1949.

From the beginning, the local NAACP faced a number of problems, including a lack of funding, support from the "leaders" of Louisville's black community that was tepid at best, and a deep commitment by the University of Kentucky and state government to white supremacy. Dean Leo Chamberlain responded to Eubanks's application simply by stating that the University of Kentucky was "prohibited by constitution and law from admitting to the institution a member of your race."[66] Despite Prentice Thomas's assertion that the "Supreme Court has ruled that equal educational opportunities must be furnished within the borders of the state," Kentucky's assistant attorney general, Jessie K. Lewis, remained unmoved.[67] Rather, Lewis countered in the *Courier-Journal* that Eubanks's suit was not brought "in good faith," since it was little more than "part of an organized effort to stir up class feeling." Urging Eubanks and the NAACP to drop the suit, Lewis concluded: "The colored people and the white people have been getting along fine in Kentucky and we don't like the idea of stirring people up."[68]

Few whites liked the idea of challenging even the "progressive" race relations so many whites believed existed. The NAACP initiative on higher education exposed the limits of white southern liberals' commitment to equality. Like McVey, Mark Ethridge proved unwilling or unable to support a campaign to desegregate higher education. He seemed constrained by a more gradual view of racial progress. Ethridge's 1937 address, entitled "America's Obligation to Its Negro Citizens," to the Southwide Conference on Education and Race Relations captured his and other southern white liberals' thinking on equality. Indeed, "America's Obligation" was so popular that its first printing of ten thousand copies quickly sold out and thousands more were printed at two dollars per hundred by the Commission on Interracial Cooperation (CIC). In that speech Ethridge attempted to dispel the "fog of misunderstanding, distrust, suspicion and ignorance." Speaking out against lynching and for improved health care and sanitation, he admitted that "we of the white race have been neither fair nor democratic."[69]

Though he acknowledged that African Americans simply wanted equality, Ethridge also suggested that they should think in "terms of generations, rather than of years," pointing out that even if given full citizenship rights "there is legitimate doubt as to whether the majority would use them wisely."[70] The newsman advocated "adequate" public accommodations but not integration. Claiming that blacks themselves did not want the "abolition of segregation" or "so-called social equality," he baldly stated: "Nor is it certain that segregation is altogether bad for the Negro." In closing, he said: "Even if these were his aspirations, I should consider him foolhardy if he pressed them, as friendly as I am, I would consider them against his own best interests and against general welfare and peace."[71] Given the context of black life in the South, one wonders how much "peace" African Americans attained and whether it was worth the price of equality.

When in 1941 Walter White, executive secretary of the NAACP, asked him to champion desegregation at the University of Kentucky with the same vigor he lent to the equalization of teachers' salaries, Ethridge absolutely refused. Rather, he advised White against filing any suit, arguing that it would "retard rather than advance the cause of Negro education." He cautioned White that Carroll had "stirred up resentment your activity would crystallize." Less than a year later, Ethridge opened the southern hearings of the Fair Employment Practices Commission (FEPC) in Birmingham by chastising black leaders for challenging segregation. In doing so, he spoke not only for himself, but also for white southern liberals as a whole, who believed in racial progress so long as it was not too much or too fast. In fact, for whites like Ethridge there was no contradiction between being "fair and democratic" and maintaining white supremacy. His refusal to endorse the NAACP exposed the gulf between what blacks wanted for themselves and what whites wanted them to have. In essence, it laid bare the divergence in how blacks and whites defined equality and democracy in the River City and in Kentucky generally.

In 1941 the actions of many whites in the state suggest that their vision of equality did not entail integration, much less African Americans' access to the University of Kentucky. Not only were the majority of southern whites unwilling to support the NAACP's suit against the university, but also Governor Keen Johnson and President Herman Donovan actively prevented the admission of black students. With the help of Rufus Atwood, they created an "engineering school" at Kentucky State College that existed in name only. Neither Donovan nor Johnson attempted to hide the fact that they established the school to circumvent desegregation by providing separate-but-equal facilities. Although the facilities were clearly separate, they were hardly equal. According to George Wright, the school was barren of equipment, its one teacher held a B.S. degree in industrial education, and the core curriculum was an industrial course that provided instruction in welding.[72]

At the same time, the local NAACP's suit exposed fissures between Louisville's small black middle class and the larger working-class black community. In March 1943, the NAACP held a mass meeting to raise funds for the Eubanks case—in part, because much of Louisville's black middle-class "leadership" refused to fund the suit. In a confidential letter to Stephen A. Burnley, president of the Louisville NAACP, Prentice Thomas revealed that many of the "first families of Louisville" were not interested in or were openly "antagonistic" toward Eubanks.[73] The lack of support, financial or otherwise, Charles Eubanks received from Louisville's black middle-class "leadership" reflected their views of his working-class background more than their desire for equal access at the University of Kentucky. As the son of a laundry worker and an unemployed absentee father, Eubanks apparently presented Louisville's black middle class with a difficult figure to rally behind. Despite the lack of support, according to Thomas, Eubanks demonstrated more "social stamina" than many of Louisville's so-called black leaders.[74] Eubanks withstood offers to attend Kentucky State College and schools in Ohio, as well as money to simply leave the state.

In the end, his case failed not because of the lack of funding or black middle-class support, but because the state deployed an array of tactics to delay the trial. In January 1945, more than three years after the case began, the state dismissed it "due to a lack of prosecution." In the *Louisville Defender*, Charles Anderson blamed Rufus Atwood for the defeat. While Atwood had some responsibility, it was the university and the state that obstructed the case long enough to take advantage of Kentucky law that permitted the dismissal of any suit if no action had occurred within a two-year period. In fact, as early as April 15, 1942, Prentice Thomas informed Thurgood Marshall there were rumors in Lexington that the state would attempt to delay the case.[75] Nonetheless, for Thurgood Marshall the defeat was an "awful licking." Meanwhile, Charles Hamilton Houston advised Marshall that the case had "fizzled" and should not be revived until the NAACP found "a student who is absolutely determined on his own initiative."[76]

George Wright believed that the NAACP's defeat in the Eubanks case only strengthened the resolve of blacks in Louisville to desegregate Kentucky's lily-white universities. Three years later the Louisville NAACP renewed the struggle against segregation when Lyman Johnson applied for admission to the graduate program in history at the University of Kentucky. On receipt of Johnson's application, the university signaled its commitment to segregation in a brief statement: "Our policy has been pretty well defined. We are prohibited by State law and the State Constitution from accepting the registration of a Negro." Johnson responded to the university's Board of Trustees saying: "I do understand that both State law and the State Constitution prohibit Negroes from being admitted to the university. But both of these seem to be in conflict with the basic law of the land, the United States Constitution."[77] In Lyman Johnson the NAACP found a person "who would not quit for any reason." As he publicly stated in the *Louisville Times*, "I have no apology to make for being a Negro. I stand on my rights as an American citizen."[78]

As before, the University of Kentucky collaborated with the state to launch a strategy to circumvent desegregation. Within three months of Johnson's application, the governor allocated $25,000 from his emergency fund to create "equal" graduate and undergraduate courses at Kentucky State College. More than thirty black teachers followed Johnson's example and applied for admission to the University of Kentucky in the summer of 1948. Rather than admit them, the university funneled these students to the newly created programs at Kentucky State. It also sent books, bibliographies, and white professors to Kentucky State to teach black students. Although Johnson enrolled in Kentucky State's "graduate program," the NAACP continued its campaign to desegregate the University of Kentucky.

The NAACP suit argued that Johnson was denied admission to the University of Kentucky on the basis of race alone. During the pretrial conference, the NAACP urged that the case be determined by the answers to three questions: Had graduate education been provided for African Americans at Kentucky State College? Did the makeshift plan for African Americans developed by the University of Kentucky fulfill the requirements of the Fourteenth Amendment? And lastly, could any educational institution founded on the basis of racial segregation satisfy the requirements of the Fourteenth Amendment? On the other hand, the University of Kentucky contended that the graduate programs it established at Kentucky State College, along with its willingness to supply books for Kentucky State's library and to send white professors to Frankfort, demonstrated that equal education was a reality for blacks statewide.[79] Foreshadowing future debates in higher education, M. B.

Holifield, Kentucky's assistant attorney general, later claimed that it was Kentucky's white students who were actually discriminated against since the state paid black students' out-of-state tuition, whereas white students had to pay their own way.[80]

Unlike the NAACP's prior suit against the University of Kentucky, the local branch shouldered the burden of the Johnson case with little support from the national association. With the failures in the Carroll and Eubanks cases in mind, the national NAACP wanted the Louisville branch to "hold up the [Johnson] case" while it focused its energies on what would become the Supreme Court cases *Sweatt v. Painter*, *McLaurin v. Oklahoma State Board of Regents*, and *Sipuel v. Oklahoma State Board of Regents*—all dealing with similar issues.[81] On behalf of the Louisville NAACP, Lyman Johnson and James Crumlin repeatedly asked the national NAACP to provide more than verbal support. In December 1948, for example, Crumlin requested that the national office "give proper attention to the preparation for trial in the Johnson case," apparently with little success.[82] In 1949, Johnson wrote Thurgood Marshall, asking for the funding and legal aid necessary to properly prepare and present the case. The frustration of the Louisville NAACP was evident in Johnson's dispatch: "Frankly, we have not been able to cash in on the many nice expressions of encouragement to stay in the matter and see the suit through to successful completion."[83] The national NAACP quietly determined that there was no reason to pay "a huge sum of money when other cases address the issue." More importantly, it feared that another defeat in Kentucky would "gravely damage the prestige" of the association.[84]

The Louisville branch relied heavily on fund-raising and membership drives among black Louisvillians to pay the suit's expenses. Although roundly supported within the local black community, Johnson's case also suffered from internal discord within the Louisville NAACP. A series of suits brought by Dr. P. O. Sweeny, NAACP attorney James Crumlin, and Alfred Carroll against the city to desegregate the public golf courses generated a rash of hostilities. Though Johnson's suit was part of a larger strategy to challenge segregation in municipal parks, its timing effectively strained the Louisville branch's limited financial resources.

There was opposition not only from local whites (Democratic mayor Leland Taylor, for example, was "convinced" that integrated parks "would touch off a race riot") but also from the black community—albeit for different reasons. Many African Americans, including some members of the NAACP, believed that Crumlin, as attorney in the suit, was lining his own pockets with NAACP money. Moreover, Sweeny's case raised the ire of many working-class blacks. According to the *Louisville Leader*, although most blacks supported the desegregation of higher education, the desegregation of public golf courses seemed to benefit only the elite. In an article entitled, "Masses Fail to Grasp Principle," journalist William Ealy claimed that as many as twenty of thirty working-class blacks believed that the case was more about the desire of elite blacks to play golf than it was about civil rights. One editorial suggested that Louisville's "street corner philosophers . . . pooh-poohed" Sweeny's militancy, convinced that his suit risked nothing. Perhaps with a pun intended, the editor responded: "I must publicly advise these men that any time a Negro steps to the fore on anything involving race in the South he is taking a chance with his worldly goods and his life as well."[85] Eventually, Sweeny quieted such complaints by agreeing to pay for the suit. Although Louisville's parks would not be completely open to blacks until 1955, Sweeny's persistence resulted in the desegregation of its public golf courses in 1952.[86]

Despite the internal dissension within the NAACP and Louisville's African American community, as well as the lack of full support from the national NAACP, the Louisville branch approached the March 30 trial date of Lyman T. Johnson's suit with a strong case. The Louisville NAACP secured experts from a variety of disciplines to argue that the facilities at Kentucky State were inadequate. The NAACP also arranged for Charles Parrish, a black sociologist at Louisville Municipal College, and John Hope Franklin, the leading black historian of the day, to present testimony on the poor quality of education Johnson would receive at Kentucky State. Although Franklin traveled to Lexington, it was unnecessary for him to testify.[87]

In the U.S. District Court, Judge H. Church Ford reached a quick decision on behalf of Johnson and the NAACP. The NAACP suit challenged the validity of the arrangement at Kentucky State, "contending that it did not offer training equal to that available to white students on the campus of the University."[88] According to Judge Ford, the only issue was the equality of facilities. While higher education in Kentucky was separate, it was by no means equal. He asked, "How can anyone listen to this evidence without seeing that it is a makeshift plan?"[89] Since the state failed to provide equal graduate and professional schools for blacks, the University of Kentucky was now obligated to admit qualified African American students. On March 31, after more than nine years of struggle, an NAACP press release proclaimed: "NAACP Win Suit to Ban Jim Crow at Kentucky University."[90]

With the encouragement of the NAACP, Johnson and thirty other African Americans enrolled at the University of Kentucky. Two weeks into the summer semester, Johnson reported to the national NAACP that everything had proceeded "smoothly":

> The only open segregation is in the cafeteria. There we have been asked to sit at three tables with the signs on them: reserved. At first they said, "reserved for negroes." I asked the lady in charge, the hostess, if that was necessary. She replied that she had been told to put up the signs. Thereupon she returned to the office and clipped off the bottom line and came back to my table with "reserved" on the cards. In the class-rooms and libraries we experience no noticeable segregation. Professors and students are cordial. Two Deans have called me in for conference. They want the thing to work. But they are afraid of the Federal Judge and the Kentucky law. I have told both that we would not "put ourselves on the white students" in return if they will not resort to the objectionable signs, "For Negroes," "For Colored," etc. so far the "Reserved" is the only indication of open segregation I know about here.[91]

While the transition may have gone "smoothly" for Johnson, the sentiments that initially created segregation did not fade away with Judge Ford's decision. The University of Kentucky Board of Trustees debated whether to appeal the ruling. Assistant Attorney General M. B. Holifield suggested that the university circumvent the spirit of the law by simply maintaining segregation within the university. He issued a statement on behalf of the state claiming that "Judge Ford's ruling did not change the application of the Day Law. . . . Negroes must be taught at different times and in different places from whites."[92] Dean H. L. Donovan revealed in his memoirs that he believed successful integration could only be achieved if black students "segregated" themselves on campus. He personally told them to "sit together in the classroom rather than scatter over the room, that when they entered the cafeteria, they sit at a table with their fellow Negro students instead of each occupying a separate table." During the summer that Johnson desegregated the university, the *Louisville Leader* reported that more than seventeen Ku Klux Klan crosses were burned on or near campus.[93]

Despite the hopes of the NAACP, the Johnson case did not immediately open higher education statewide. Barely a month after the judge's decision, the Kentucky Negro Education Association (KNEA), at a meeting in Louisville, pointed out the inequities that remained in education across the state. Stressing the need for "Equal Educational Opportunity for Every Kentucky Child," the KNEA summed up the "sad yet truthful story": "After some eighty-five years of a 'separate-but-equal' school system we still have separation but not equality."[94] In an oblique reference to the Johnson suit, the KNEA stated that it was "convinced by recent events and the present climate of public opinion that segregated graduate and professional work in the South is unnecessary, and constitutes a backward step in the educational progress of the South." Refuting the notion of separate but equal, its members rejected the old cliché "half a loaf is better than no bread" and dismissed the segregated graduate and professional programs available to blacks in Kentucky as "grossly inferior."[95]

Although the Day Law had been amended in 1948 with the passage of Charles Anderson's act allowing black nurses and doctors to receive postgraduate and in-service training at white hospitals, the statute remained an obstacle to the admission of African Americans to all Kentucky colleges. The University of Louisville flatly refused to integrate, arguing that it was a private rather than a public institution because only part of it received federal funding. With the amendment of the Day Law in 1950, which allowed colleges and universities to desegregate at their own choosing, and with the threat of more NAACP suits, the University of Louisville and colleges throughout the state finally opened their doors to African Americans. However, integration had an ironic and unintended consequence for Louisville Municipal College. After nearly twenty years the University of Louisville closed the college permanently, retaining only sociologist Charles Parrish for its own faculty.[96]

Although in the mid-to-late thirties and forties the NAACP focused on desegregating higher education, it also pursued a broad range of civil rights measures using increasingly more militant strategies. In doing so it mirrored the actions of African Americans nationwide who "struggled on several fronts to break down barriers."[97] For instance, in 1935 Murray Walls left Indianapolis to conduct a housing survey in Louisville for the federal government. By 1938 she was involved with the NAACP, raising funds for the equalization of teachers' salaries. While in Louisville, Walls served on the Tenant Selection Committee for the Municipal Housing Commission and increasingly became active in a variety of civil rights projects. She worked with the NAACP to desegregate the public libraries, open public accommodations, and secure open housing; she worked with the Urban League to obtain employment for African Americans in downtown department stores; and she worked in a number of interracial organizations such as the Girl Scouts and the Human Relations Commission (HRC) on a range of civil rights concerns. On April 7, 1941, Walls wrote to Rabbi Joseph Rauch, president of the Louisville Free Public Library Board, asking that it live up to its name and desegregate.

Frustrated that, as an African American, she was forced to use Louisville's two substandard "colored" branches when there were three libraries for whites within a few blocks of her house, Walls began an eleven-year fight to gain equal access to all of the city's libraries. In her initial letter to Rauch, she argued:

> I, like many other Negroes in Louisville, find it almost unbearable not to be able to visit the Main Library or any convenient Branch. . . . Is there a law forbidding me entrance to certain libraries or is it just one of these unwritten prejudices which we have thoughtlessly allowed to exist? Dr. Rausch [sic], it must be men like you, who are Christian and honest in your declarations of the things that are right for all citizens alike, who should and must make this democracy a real thing if democracy is to stand; otherwise, as sure as there is God, it will not. . . . May I, in the name of all that is fair for all citizens alike, ask that your Library Board take the lead in making possible our participation in the libraries of this city.[98]

Rabbi Rauch himself declined to respond to Walls's letter. Instead, she received a reply from librarian Harold F. Brigham merely reiterating the Free Public Library's policy on the exclusion of African Americans. He concluded his letter by stating: "We realize that this plan is fraught with some inconveniences and delays and some embarrassment to our colored patrons, but we have also felt the necessity of recognizing the limitations imposed by local considerations so well known to us all."[99] Over the next weeks, months, and years, Walls sent a flurry of letters and participated in a number of meetings along with a delegation of ministers and NAACP members that netted no results. At a May 13, 1941, library board meeting, Walls and members of a delegation including Reverend W. P. Offutt Jr. and migrants George Wilson and Floyd Crawford of Louisville Municipal College forcefully made the case for desegregating the Free Public Library. During this and every other meeting to follow, the board members sat, listened, and adjourned without any response. As Walls recalled, "They wouldn't say a word, ask a question, comment, anything. We'd walk out of there feeling like a bunch of monkeys."[100]

Despite continued meetings with the library board, and the sympathy of Mayor Wilson W. Wyatt, the Public Library did not change its policy. Like A. Phillip Randolph's call for a March on Washington protesting segregation in the same year, the failure of negotiation led Walls's delegation to use direct action to dramatize the issue. When President Roosevelt declared December 15, 1941, Bill of Rights Day, all white Louisvillians were invited to the city's public libraries to hear his radio address. Although the invitation excluded African Americans, an NAACP delegation presented itself at the main library to hear the program in which the president "urged against discrimination because of race." Apparently Louisville's library officials did not share FDR's expansive notion of democracy, as they informed the group that "the library was for whites." After trying to keep them out, the library decided to allow them access rather than create a disturbance. According to the *Louisville Leader*, "All in attendance at the public library joined in the singing of the National Anthem without anybody getting hurt."[101]

Meetings and protests continued throughout 1942, including one of the first sit-ins of Louisville's modern civil rights movement by sixteen members of the NAACP in the library board's conference room. Nevertheless, the library policy remained unchanged. During World War II agitation on this issue lessened, only to revive afterward. By 1948, Murray Walls and the NAACP secured a partial victory when the library board voted 5–4 to open the main branch to African Americans. Blacks would not gain access to all library branches until 1952. As NAACP historian Patrick McElhone noted, "Complete desegregation occurred, but hardly for the right reason."[102] The newly desegregated University of Louisville and the Free Public Library initiated an interlibrary loan program, making desegregation necessary since the facilities of each library were open to patrons of the other.

While the NAACP was indispensable to African Americans in their struggles for equality in the city, it was not the only tool migrants used to address their concerns. Indeed, even though black Louisvillians were united in their commitment to achieve equality, their efforts encompassed a broad spectrum of activism: from Republican to Democrat and from strategies of negotiation to direct action—all advocating an immediate end to Jim Crow. At times they worked through the NAACP and other black organizations; in other instances they relied on interracialism and the support of liberal whites. Throughout the World War II era, the rise of what Beth Bates terms "protest politics" provided African Americans with new strategies for taking control of their own destiny on their own terms.[103] Moreover, as they challenged accepted norms in the city, even limited success justified their increasing militancy and assertiveness. While some black migrants acted alone, many others utilized multiple organizations to achieve their goals. While their choice of strategy, organization, and action reflected profound intraracial class differences, in the end African Americans were the greatest advocates of equality.

In Louisville, African Methodist Episcopal (AME) Zion minister Ewbank Tucker was at the forefront of such advocacy. Though born in Baltimore,

Tucker was raised in Jamaica and had lived in Washington, D.C., Philadelphia, and West Virginia by the time he arrived in Louisville. No sooner had he stepped foot in the city than he gained a reputation as a "militant race lawyer," becoming one of the black community's most outspoken and controversial leaders. In 1931, while defending two African Americans, he was attacked by a white mob and narrowly escaped being lynched outside the courthouse in Elizabethtown, Kentucky. He immediately became active in Louisville politics, running as a Democrat against Charles Anderson in 1935. A onetime member of the NAACP, Tucker became one of its most consistent critics, claiming with some accuracy that the association did not represent the "man in the street."[104]

More often than not, Tucker worked independently or in organizations in which he held leadership positions. He served as president of the Kentucky Bureau of Negro Affairs, established in 1944 by Governor Simon Willis. Tucker constantly clashed with the Louisville Police Department over the issue of police brutality throughout the 1940s. He swore out warrants against three police officers for mistreating African Americans; he represented blacks such as Mrs. Grace Miller and her fourteen-year-old daughter after they were arrested for disorderly conduct by Marvin Almon, a police officer especially known for brutality throughout black Louisville.[105] In defending an African American arrested for using the white waiting room at the Greyhound Bus Station, he successfully challenged the authority of city police to enforce segregation in private businesses since there were no state or city laws requiring separation. In 1953 Tucker initiated a successful one-man sit-in to desegregate the Greyhound Bus Lines depot.[106] Despite his contentious relationship with the NAACP, he was no less committed to African American equality.

Like Ewbank Tucker, most activists worked in a variety of organizations, though few were as hostile toward the NAACP. Originally from Tallulah, a small town seventeen miles west of Vicksburg, Louisiana, Dr. Jessie Bell moved to Louisville from Frankfort, Kentucky, in 1935. He served as vice chair of the Urban League and in 1941 joined the staff at Red Cross Hospital. Although Red Cross was a facility founded "by blacks for blacks," it relied on the support of grants and white patrons since most blacks could not afford the high cost of medical care. Bell served as medical director from 1941 to 1946, working to get the hospital accredited because medical facilities in Louisville were "extremely separated." As Bell recalled, "There was no where else for blacks to go."[107]

Throughout the 1940s and 1950s black doctors like Jessie Bell, Maurice Rabb, and Ralph Morris—who arrived in Louisville in 1955—were central in the fight to secure funding for Louisville's black hospital and advocated access for black patients and doctors at Louisville's white hospitals. In 1941 they established a short-lived Nurses Training Program that used nurses from Jewish Hospital as its trainers. Since the Kentucky State Medical Association did not admit blacks, African American doctors in 1947 formed the Falls City Medical Society to address the specific concerns of African Americans. Rabb was the first physician in the state to take advantage of the 1948 amendment of the Day Law allowing black doctors and nurses to receive professional training at white institutions. For Rabb and Bell, it was not only an issue of access but also one of insufficient resources. Given the influx of migrants during this period, their efforts were vital to a community already facing a shortage of hospital beds. As one Red Cross pamphlet noted, between 1944 and 1960 there was almost a 150 percent increase in the patient load.[108]

Significantly, black migrants did not limit their activism to a single organization or strategy. Women such as Lois Morris and Goldie Winstead-Beckett worked to create a "good public image" for Red Cross by doing everything from planting flowers to fund-raising with the Medical Auxiliary and the Hospital Auxiliary. At the same time Morris, a native of Okolona, Mississippi, founded or participated in any number of organizations whose mission was to uplift black women. She was a member of the Urban League Women's Committee and the League of Women Voters; she served on the first Kentucky Human Relations Commission. As a member of the National Housewives League, she advocated the civil rights of African Americans and women. Morris was founder and president of the National Black Women for Political Action and the Louisville branch of the National Council of Negro Women.[109] Like that of Murray Walls, Morris's political participation demonstrates that, more often than not, African Americans in Louisville pursued civil rights through a variety of organizations.

Whites were a small and silent minority in the local NAACP, and few, if any, served on its Executive Board. There were a number of coalitions in Louisville composed of African Americans and well-intentioned whites; the Urban League, the Kentucky Bureau of Negro Affairs, and the Militant Church Movement, an alliance of ministers formed in 1951, were black-led interracial organizations. The Kentucky Council on Interracial Cooperation, the Southern Regional Council, and Americans for Democratic Action comprised of liberal whites all had branches in the River City.

Louisville's interracial movement drew upon a small, though vocal group of labor unions centered at the International Harvester tractor plant. Sharing a militant perspective and a rare commitment to racial equality were the popularly known "Seventh Street Unions," Local 236 of the United Farm Equipment Workers (FE) and its three smaller allies: the Transport Workers' local, covering city bus drivers; the United Public Workers local of garbage collectors; and the United Furniture Workers. At International Harvester, African Americans attained semiskilled jobs denied to them by most unions. Men like James Wright and Sterling Neal even held leadership positions in the FE. Indeed, it was through her association with white journalist Carl Braden and the FE that Anne Braden became politicized after returning to her native Louisville from Alabama.

According to Toni Gilpin, Local 236 of the FE at International Harvester was an important site for interracial political activism. Black member James Wright said that the union included "some of the worse white guys, some of those hard-headed guys who came out of the woods, that had never seen a black guy, and their private name was to call you a nigger."[110] Still, the FE operated on the belief that racial solidarity was a crucial component of labor's power, challenging racial inequality both inside and outside the work space.

While it is not clear whether the actions of FE workers were officially sanctioned by the local, they acted in definitive ways to confront segregation in public parks and hotels. On three different occasions in 1951, black and white members of the FE gathered in Cherokee Park to defy the city's policy of exclusion. Though Louisville did not have any segregation laws, the actions of city police indicate that the government enforced segregation as if it were legal. Each time the police forcibly ejected the group from the park, their willingness to endure being beaten, knocked about the head, and dragged from the area spoke volumes about their commitment to equality. Attempts to desegregate the Earl and Brown hotels downtown were also unwelcome. At the Earl, although the interracial group was repeatedly removed, in the end the protesters were allowed to sit quietly in the lobby. At the more upscale Brown Hotel, Wright remembered that "every time we came in there, they [the Louisville police] stood there and beat us, just drug us out."[111] (The Brown would not be desegregated until the late 1950s.) Regardless of their success, a small number of blacks and whites forged interracial coalitions to fight for equality in the city.

Louisville's interracial coalitions were active in efforts of the 1950s to desegregate Kentucky's hospitals and to ensure fair hiring practices at General Electric (GE). African Americans like Charles Anderson, Dr. Maurice Rabb, and Dr. Jessie Bell had campaigned to integrate Louisville's hospitals since the 1940s. The interracial coalitions became involved in 1950, when three blacks injured in a car wreck nearly died on the floor of a Breckinridge County emergency room while they awaited an ambulance to transport them to a Louisville hospital seventy miles away. The FE "launched" a protest and gathered more than ten thousand signatures on a petition asking the governor to desegregate Kentucky's hospitals. The movement quickly grew beyond the FE into the Interracial Hospital Movement (IHM), a collective of ministers, students, civil rights groups like the NAACP, and organized labor. Confronted by 150 members of the IHM, representing more than 30 organizations across the state, Governor Lawrence Weatherby opened all state-operated hospitals to African Americans over the next few weeks. In 1952 the IHM won a state law requiring all hospitals to treat anyone during an *emergency* situation in order to receive their license.[112]

In 1951, the same year the African American radio station WLOU began to broadcast music and news at 1350 kilohertz (kHz), GE announced its intention to construct a plant making jet engines for the federal government and to hire 15,000 employees according to FEPC guidelines. However, the Urban League discovered that in reality the plant would be segregated, and that labor unions had already negotiated with GE to keep blacks out of skilled positions. The Militant Church Movement immediately organized a campaign to publicly pressure GE into changing its policy. While the labor committee of the NAACP and the Urban League investigated the situation, workers of the United Electrical Workers penned front-page editorials in the *Louisville Defender* highlighting the issue. Eventually, an interracial group of ministers and union representatives formed the Citizens Committee on Fair Employment to address the controversy.

Between 1951 and 1954, GE refused to admit that its hiring policies were discriminatory. In 1954, however, the International Union of Electrical Workers forced the company to accept its nondiscrimination clause when it won the National Labor Relations Board election. Although the Urban League reported in 1957 that, despite a few unpleasant experiences with white workers, the problem was being dealt with, the vast majority of black employees at GE remained in unskilled positions as late as 1967. In its 14,374-person workforce, only 35 skilled workers were African American.[113] As GE employees Wilbur Haskin and William G. Marks, from Winchester and Lexington, Kentucky, respectively, put it, in the 1960s most blacks remained "on the broom."[114]

According to Tracy E. K'Meyer, the gains made in lessening the impact of segregation in public libraries, city auditoriums and offices, hospitals, recreational facilities, and higher education were "accomplished by a coalition of black and interracial organizations working concurrently and in cooperation through persuasion, petition, legislation, and legal challenges toward the goal of full citizenship." In the context of World War II and Cold War propaganda, the use of democratic rhetoric provided African Americans a principle weapon in their fight for equality. This rhetoric combined with the desire of liberal whites to maintain the city's reputation as "a leader in race relations."[115] Blacks and whites joined together in a variety of sacred and secular interracial organizations to challenge segregation, including the YMCA and YWCA, the Louisville Council of Churches, the Farm Equipment Workers, the Congress of Industrial Organizations, the Kentucky Council on Interracial Cooperation, and the Interracial Hospital Movement.[116] For instance, at its inception in 1951, the Militant Church Movement was organized on the principle that "no church or person is a Christian that does not believe in the principles laid down by Jesus Christ, the founder of the church, namely the Fatherhood of God, the Brotherhood of man, and the Golden Rule."[117]

Similarly, K'Meyer points to the importance of a number of white liberal businessmen such as Dan Byck, Arthur Kling, Harry Schacter, Barry Bingham, and *Courier-Journal* editor Mark Ethridge, all of whom worked behind the scenes to foster change or shape "public opinion in favor of better race relations." She notes that "although they did not always agree with black activists about the pace or the extent of desegregation, these white liberal leaders often came down on the side of ending particular cases of discrimination and thus smoothed the way for community acceptance of change."[118] Yet few of these white liberals shared "full citizenship" or equality as their ultimate goal; many simply wanted to slowly improve the lives of African Americans in the context of a segregated society. For many African Americans, such gradualism suggested that white's belief in democracy was not real.

In "My America," his contribution to the African American classic *What the Negro Wants*, Langston Hughes offered an incredibly insightful critique of the limits of white liberalism. In doing so, he indirectly linked the concerns of black activists in Louisville to the growing impatience with liberals' advocacy of gradualism that many blacks expressed across the nation. Hughes wrote:

> Liberals and persons of good will, North and South, including no doubt, our President himself, are puzzled as to what on earth to do about the South—the poll-tax South, the Jim Crow South—that so shamelessly gives the lie to Democracy. With the brazen frankness of Hilter's *Mein Kampf*, Dixie speaks through Talmadge, Rankin, Dixon, Arnall and Mark Ethridge. In a public speech in Birmingham, Mr. Ethridge says: "All the armies of the world, both the United States

and the Axis, could not force upon the South an abandonment of racial segregation."[119]

Thus, for Hughes, even liberal whites like Mark Ethridge existed on a continuum of white supremacy with Adolph Hitler. More importantly, despite their rhetoric, the mistreatment of blacks revealed that whites did not truly believe in democracy.

When blacks and whites in Louisville evoked the "name of democracy," they spoke to a set of values that both surely shared; however, those values held entirely different meanings for African Americans. Throughout World War II blacks in Louisville, as elsewhere in the nation, relied on the icons of democracy as a means of revealing the stark disparities between rhetoric and reality in America. In his challenge to the Day Law, Charles Anderson pointedly argued: "If we are to speak of democracy to the world, then let us have democracy at home."[120] Similarly, Lyman Johnson's claim that he stood on "his rights as an American citizen" and Murray Walls's choice to appear at the public library as Roosevelt read the Bill of Rights, were not just signs of their belief in democracy and citizenship. Rather, Walls and Johnson were tapping into a long tradition—epitomized by Frederick Douglass's 1852 speech, "What to the Slave Is the Fourth of July?"—that called America's claims of liberty and equality little more than a "hollow mockery."[121] The language of democracy provided African Americans with a discourse akin to what Jeremi Suri has called a "language of dissent," which placed whites in the precarious position of either admitting through their deeds or words that they did not truly believe in democracy or acting to end their own unjust or unequal practices.[122]

A migrant from Tennessee, Amelia B. Ray, participated in efforts to remove the onerous word "Negro" from Louisville Municipal College's name and served as the first black woman on the Louisville Police Department at the age of forty-four. At the same time she produced a constant flow of articles in the *Courier-Journal* and *Louisville Times* during World War II challenging America, the South, and Louisville to live up to their democratic ideals. In 1943, echoing African Americans' "Double V Campaign"— victory over fascism abroad and over white supremacy at home—Ray asked, "Can [democracy] survive a double standard of citizenship[?] . . . Segregation and racial discrimination prevent the working of democracy in the United States." In 1948 she wrote, "Communist Russia has been able to breakdown artificial barriers which are conducive to race prejudice, segregation and discrimination, while in so-called Christian, democratic America ways are still being sought to keep vast segments of its citizens submerged."[123] Conversely, during the Eubanks case the University of Kentucky had asked the NAACP to drop the suit for the sake of democracy and national "unity."

Not only did African Americans use the icons of democracy differently from whites, but also whites tended to join more conservative civil rights organizations. For instance, Rabbi Rauch was a leading member of the Kentucky Council on Interracial Cooperation even as he refused to desegregate Louisville's Free Public Library. According to George Wright, only a "handful of whites" participated in Louisville's civil rights movements during the 1940s and 1950s. While many organizations advocated African American equality, they often had a narrow and gradualist view of that equality. Organizations like the Kentucky Council on Interracial Cooperation and the Kentucky Commission on Negro Affairs "pointed out the obvious wrongs that blacks faced in segregated Kentucky" but did little to ameliorate those conditions.[124] Black activist and owner of the *Louisville Defender*, Frank Stanley, quit the Interracial Committee for Kentucky when its chairman, Harry Schacter, refused to support the desegregation of public accommodations. Schacter argued that it was better to go slowly rather than risk the future opportunity for greater change.[125] Though she herself was an exception to this general view, activist Anne Braden observed that, for most whites, segregation "was an accepted part of their lives—unchanged, unchallenged and unquestioned."[126]

Unlike the NAACP, few of Kentucky's "better class of whites" demanded any massive changes to end segregation. Instead, they worked to elevate the status of blacks within the framework of Jim Crow. Because of this, blacks in Louisville hesitated to completely trust even "liberal" whites.[127] As early as 1937, Mark Ethridge insisted that barriers to intermarriage and "social equality" must remain, even as he advocated legal equality.[128] This should not be dismissed as mere hypocrisy or a capitulation to racism, though it was both; white southern liberals genuinely believed that equality was possible within the framework of segregation. Yet, as bell hooks has pointed out in her critique of white liberal feminism specifically and liberalism generally, "The positive impact of liberal reforms . . . should not lead to the assumption that they eradicate systems of domination." Moreover, those reforms seen as "not threatening" by mainstream (white) society are those most likely to be instituted.[129] Thus Ethridge was more than willing to campaign for equal teacher salaries, while supporting desegregation of higher education was inconceivable. Most white southern liberals wanted to ameliorate Jim Crow, not abolish it.

Not only were white southern liberals more apt to advocate reform, but also, according to William A. Link, most white liberals "endorsed some variety of white supremacy."[130] Indeed, few challenged the popular conception of African American inferiority. Ethridge concurred with the opinion of W. T. Couch in his 1944 introduction to *What the Negro Wants*, that—whether by nature or circumstance—African Americans were inferior to whites.[131] As political scientist Michael Dawson has argued, because few liberal whites saw African Americans as equal, they often believed they knew better than blacks themselves what was in blacks' best interests. In 1942 *Southern Frontier*, the voice of the Commission on Interracial Cooperation, argued that African Americans were "fortunate" to have someone like Ethridge to speak on their behalf at the FECP.[132] In doing so, they dismissed black demands for justice and equality as well as their more expansive view of democracy. As editor of the *Courier-Journal*, Ethridge spoke not only for himself but also for white southern liberals, as a whole, who believed in racial progress so long as it was not too much or too fast. In essence, African American activism highlighted the divergence in how blacks and whites defined equality and democracy in the River City and in Kentucky generally. Moreover, the very existence of these white southern liberals suggests that African Americans were increasingly successful in making segregation an issue that could no longer remain hidden behind Louisville's progressive veneer.

In the mid-fifties, two events commanded the attention of Louisvillians, whether white or black, in highlighting these very issues. The first was the Wade-Braden case, which foreshadowed the struggle for open housing in the late 1960s. The second was the peaceful "desegregation" of Louisville's public schools in 1956. Both the Wade-Braden case and the desegregation of public schools emphasized the limits of white liberalism in the River City. While the first event threatened to explode the progressive facade whites had carefully erected in Louisville, the second thrust the city into the national limelight as the model for peaceful integration. Almost overnight Louisville became known as a model southern city where race relations were resolved without incident.

Exacerbated by the influx of migrants in the 1950s and the presence of "unspoken restrictive covenants," the inaccessibility of quality housing was and remained a problem for African Americans in Louisville. Andrew Wade IV, a twenty-year-old electrician and the son of a Nashville migrant, had a two-year-old son and another child on the way; he also had $1,400 in cash to buy a home, but no one would sell him one. Wade attempted to purchase several homes on the outskirts of the city before he eventually turned to a white couple, Carl and Anne Braden. According to a Wade Defense Committee "fact sheet," Wade ran into the unwritten law "that no Negro may buy in a neighborhood that has been set up as 'all-white.'" Although this law, or the racial boundaries mentally mapped across the urban landscape that it represented, did not have any legal standing, it was enforced by real estate agents, money lenders, and insurance agents as well as potential white neighbors.[133] The Bradens were well-known activists in the city, and for some their ties to the left carried the hint of communism. In fact, Andrew Wade was familiar with the Bradens from their shared support of Henry Wallace and the Progressive Party in 1948. Since Wade's color alone made it impossible for him to buy a new home in Louisville, the Bradens purchased one for him on Rone Court in the suburb of Shively. When the Wades refused to submit to local whites' demands to move from their new home, they began to receive threats followed by a burned cross and rifle shots. Finally, on June 27, 1954, the house itself was bombed. The police failed to apprehend the bomber; instead, the Bradens and five others were indicted for "criminal syndicalism and sedition"; Carl was convicted and served less than a year in prison.[134] Unlike many southern white liberals, the Bradens were apparently more than willing to risk their *own lives* by directly challenging segregation itself.

As threats became a daily part of the Bradens' and the Wades' lives, Anne attempted to rally support from Louisville's progressive whites. Religious organizations, whether Catholic or Protestant, proved unwilling to help them. In fact, even the FE, which was known for its radical interracial unionism, refused to become formally involved in the issue. As one worker explained to Carl Braden, "We can talk about equality on the job . . . [but] this gets into social equality and they don't believe in that." Indeed, the actions of the Bradens pointed to the gulf between reform-minded liberals and those who took a more radical path by challenging segregation directly. The *Courier-Journal* was no more willing to support this issue than it had the desegregation of higher education. On May 18, the newspaper claimed that the Bradens set civil rights back "for a generation," by their "artificial forcing"—as opposed to a "careful, steady," and above all gradual community effort.[135] Anne Braden recalled that when confronted by the demands of African Americans in the Wade case, Louisville's "white Christians and liberals simply looked the other way."[136]

Louisville's blacks were only slightly more responsive. Although C. Ewbank Tucker served as the primary lawyer for the Wade Defense Committee, the reaction of the local NAACP was more typical. The association supported Andrew Wade but took a number of steps to dissociate itself from the Bradens. At the time they agreed to purchase a house for the Wade family, Anne was one of a few whites participating in a current NAACP membership drive. As elsewhere in the nation, the effort to distance the struggle for equality and the NAACP from the hint of communism led its local president, James Crumlin, to ask Anne Braden to step down from the NAACP.[137] Yet, as much as the NAACP sought to distance itself from the taint of communism, it is also clear that, given the limits of white liberalism, they hesitated to fully trust whites. Not even Anne Braden was above reproach; as Crumlin, a longtime friend, recalled, "She was not quite as liberal as she thought she was."[138] Nonetheless, Crumlin's comment dismisses her lifelong commitment to equality unmatched by many—black or white. In Louisville, or anywhere else, few people were as willing to risk the threat of violence, daily harassment, or ostracism for decades to help African Americans gain equality.

Whereas the Wade-Braden case threatened to destroy the city's "progressive" image, two years later the desegregation of its public schools propelled Louisville into the national spotlight as *the* model for progressive race relations. Outside of the formation of a chapter of the White Citizens Council to boycott local schools, the burning of three crosses at three schools (including one in front of Parkland Junior High School), and a picket at Male High School by a white man claiming to be president of the National Association for the Advancement of White People, desegregation was for the most part peaceful.[139] The national media, television networks, and print journalists—from the White House to *Newsweek*—focused on "The Louisville Plan." As Omer Carmichael, superintendent of Louisville schools, observed: "Implicit in most such 'outside' views of Louisville is its identification as a southern city, no matter how near the Midwest or true Yankeeland." African Americans represented 27 percent of Louisville's student body, the highest of any city initiating desegregation in 1956. Carmichael's widely acclaimed desegregation plan became the model nationwide.

Yet Carmichael's "Louisville Plan" resulted in very little desegregation. The plan rested on "freedom of choice," or "permissiveness" for students, and white community support. Louisville waited for over a year before it even began to implement it. While the NAACP accused the school board of "stalling," white liberals like Mark Ethridge cautioned them against "trying to hurry too fast." For desegregation to succeed, Superintendent Carmichael believed that he first had to create a "climate opinion favorable to the smooth desegregation of our schools." Thus "permissiveness" was at the heart of desegregation in Louisville—the school system would face neither compulsory integration nor desegregation. Instead, students would have the "freedom of choice" as to whether or not they would attend integrated schools.[140] Not surprisingly, most whites opted to remain in all-white schools.

The desegregation of public schools in Louisville was both a radical departure from and a continuation of the pattern found in many southern cities—or, for that matter, in northern ones like Boston or Harlem.[141] Louisville differed from Prince Edward County, Virginia, where whites chose to abolish public schools rather than integrate. It also differed from larger cities like Atlanta, New Orleans, or Little Rock, where widespread violence or obstruction ran rampant during the late 1950s and 1960s. In New Orleans, whites rioted in the streets, attacked one of the four first-grade children integrating two elementary schools, and withdrew their children from public schools in large numbers. In Little Rock, African Americans integrated public schools only after federal intervention. In Atlanta, desegregation witnessed massive protests, the bombing of English Avenue Elementary School, and what came to be called, "The Second Battle of Atlanta."[142] Concurrent efforts of black and Puerto Rican mothers to desegregate schools in New York City, as well as ex-educator Jonathan Kozol's *Death at an Early Age*, exposed opposition to desegregation in Harlem and Boston. By comparison, Louisville was by far the most peaceful of any sizable southern city. On the other hand, desegregation in Louisville, like desegregation in each of these cities, entailed very little real integration. It is often overlooked that in Little Rock, only nine students attended a "white" school of more than two thousand, leaving the majority of black students mired in substandard education.

In Louisville, desegregation meant that a few blacks enrolled in white schools; no white students transferred to all-black Central High School, and no blacks were allowed to teach in white schools. According to the Human Relations Commission, fifty-one of Louisville's schools had levels of "extreme racial isolation"; only seven of sixty-seven schools did not have racial isolation.[143] By 1971, the commission's observation that racial isolation in the city reached a ten-year high led it to conclude that "Louisville is running a segregated school system and it's getting worse, faster."[144] Moreover, the "extreme racial isolation" in the schools also resulted in "other serious, but often more subtle, aspects of segregation and discrimination," including segregated activities, facilities, and programs within schools; unequal discipline based on race; and demotions and/or dismissals of minority faculty and school administrators.[145] Until school busing almost twenty years later, only a small number of students were involved in desegregation. Grace Lewis, who had moved to Louisville from Brownsville, Tennessee, as a young girl, was among the first blacks to attend integrated schools in the city. She recalled that white faculty and students gave her a "rough time"; students would often "call us out of our names" by hurling the epithet "nigger."[146] At the same time, she felt pressure to earn "straight As" and, on behalf of all black people, "to be the best, represent the best."[147]

Nor were the schools in Jefferson County any better. According to the 1960 Commonwealth of Kentucky's "Report on Integration-Desegregation," few black students were enrolled in formerly white schools. At Medora Elementary School, the ratio of black to white students was 6 to 834; at St. Matthews Elementary School, 3 to 510; at Schaffner Elementary School, 7 to 505; and at Zachary Taylor Elementary School, 11 to 1,010. The high schools showed the same pattern: at Valley High School, the ratio was 11 to 2,415; at Fairdale High School, 5 to 894; at Waggner High School, 3 to 2,433; and at Durrett High School, 1 to 2,103. There were 1,100 teachers employed at a combined twenty-seven elementary and high schools in Jefferson County, but none of them were black.[148] In 1972, the HRC declared that the Louisville school system "failed—either by design or by lack of effort—to deliver the promise of full student and faculty desegregation."[149] The limited impact of Omer Carmichael's plan was demonstrated by the virulent and often violent resistance to genuine integration that accompanied Louisville's busing program in 1975. Nonetheless, in 1957 the "smooth" desegregation of public schools allowed whites to remain secure in their belief that Louisville was progressive and a leader on race relations in the South.

In doing so, whites dismissed the hardships many African Americans endured on a daily basis. Not only did they face segregation and an overabundance of poor housing, but they also struggled to find decent jobs. As Louisville's industrial base expanded after World War II, the prosperity experienced by the city as a whole was not shared by African Americans. Throughout the 1950s they continued to labor in the same service and unskilled occupations. Until the late 1950s, the NAACP primarily concerned itself with political and civil rights, while the Urban League concentrated on equal employment. As African Americans constantly sought out more and better jobs, the slight improvements they achieved amounted to little more than tokenism.

In 1928, for instance, the Louisville Police Department hired its first African Americans, decades before southern cities like Atlanta or Memphis. But it was not until 1945 that three black policemen were promoted to the rank of sergeant. A year before, the Urban League had suggested that Harry Schacter, president of Kaufman Straus Department Store, contact Murray Walls to serve as its personnel director for blacks. Kaufman's move to hire African Americans was by no means altruistic; rather, as Schacter explained to the Urban League, "Louisville is a War boom town, and there were many more jobs than there were people to fill them." Kaufman's turned to Walls to find "desirable" black women with the proper attitude, "deportment and behavior" to work as domestics and elevator girls. So, even though blacks at Kaufman's could take you to the second floor, they still were prohibited from trying on clothes or eating in its segregated cafeteria.[150] The few jobs blacks received at businesses like Kaufman Straus did little to change the overarching pattern of African American employment as a whole.

Throughout the 1950s economic equality increasingly became a civil rights concern for African Americans in Louisville. In 1953 the *Louisville Defender* called for a "penny protest" against the Southern Bell Telephone Company after failing to convince the company to hire African Americans. Although many blacks, supported by the NAACP, paid their phone bills with pennies, Southern Bell refused to hire African Americans until 1956. Between 1951 and 1954, the NAACP successfully campaigned to have racial designations removed in advertisements for civil service jobs. After "white" and "colored" no longer appeared in the ads, it is unclear whether this tactic increased the number of African Americans hired.[151]

In 1957, the local NAACP launched a series of campaigns to offer Louisville blacks wider employment opportunities. In the process, it revived its Labor and Industry Committee, dormant since its efforts in 1941 to gain African Americans jobs in defense industries. The committee was led by Maurice Rabb, Rufus Stout, and John Walls. The NAACP's strategy targeted businesses with a large black clientele—the telephone company, grocery stores, and the bus company—and attempted to persuade them to hire African Americans on an equal basis.[152]

With varying degrees of success the NAACP challenged Kroger, A&P, and Winn-Dixie grocery stores to hire and upgrade African American employees. The NAACP campaign began when it learned that a new Kroger store would open at Twenty-second and Jefferson, a neighborhood more than two-thirds black. A NAACP investigation revealed that Kroger intended to hire blacks only as janitors. Citywide, many of Kroger's black employees worked the same jobs, at the same pay, as when they were first hired ten to fifteen years earlier. The NAACP, backed by a number of African American ministers, insisted that qualified blacks be placed in visible positions such as checkers. Surprisingly, Jack Nichols, regional vice president, offered little resistance to upgrading blacks in all Kroger stores. The NAACP met with similar success with A&P. In fact, the association was astonished to find that the southern regional vice president was a member of the NAACP; within two weeks A&P

became an equal opportunity employer. Flush with its victories, the NAACP turned its attention to Winn-Dixie. When the grocery store refused to change its employment policy, the NAACP led a series of small, ineffective boycotts. Since African Americans accounted for only a minimal amount of the grocery chain's business, Winn-Dixie saw little reason to integrate its workforce.[153]

Rather than waste its resources on an ineffective campaign, the NAACP now directed its energies to the Louisville Transit Company, which refused to hire blacks as anything other than menial labor. As early as 1953, there were concerted efforts to compel the company to hire blacks as bus drivers. However, when the Labor and Industry Committee met with representatives of the Transit Company, it demanded that the company not only hire blacks to drive their buses, but also employ and upgrade African Americans in all departments. Louisville Transit did agree to hire black drivers, but it claimed that the upgrading in other departments must be a gradual process to avoid the resentment of white workers. In fact, the process was so gradual that, other than bus drivers, no blacks were hired or upgraded until the passage of a more expansive employment law in the 1960s.[154]

Although the material success of these economic campaigns was limited, like the larger civil rights movement they served as a powerful critique of progressivism in Louisville. Many whites, liberal or otherwise, could sit back confident in their belief that their city possessed the ideal southern race relations. Nonetheless, African Americans' civil rights between 1930 and 1959 painted a completely different portrait of the River City. The actions of whites revealed that, despite its progressive reputation, Louisville offered neither educational opportunities, economic equality, fair housing, nor genuine political representation for African Americans. Louisville and the South as a whole existed as place where democracy and equality for blacks was more a fiction than a reality.

More importantly, the activism of the period demonstrated that if African Americans did not act to secure equality themselves, then no one would. Increasingly, activism in Louisville would shift from negotiation to direct action. Black migrants were not just involved in the struggle for equality; they were often leaders within those movements. They were at the forefront of campaigns to desegregate libraries and municipal parks, universities and public schools, public accommodations, and private businesses throughout the city. Almost from the moment they arrived, migrants leaped into the work desegregation demanded. Charles Anderson, who moved to Louisville in 1932, was president of the local NAACP by 1934 and Kentucky's first black state representative by 1936. After making a home in the River City in 1931,

Lyman Johnson plunged into the civil rights struggle. He campaigned to equalize teachers' salaries, then initiated a successful attempt to gain access for African Americans to higher education at the University of Kentucky, and, finally, played a seminal role in desegregating public accommodations in Louisville—all while serving six terms as president of the local NAACP.[155]

The struggle to desegregate public accommodations and secure open housing in the 1960s sprouted from ground carefully cultivated in the period before. For blacks in Louisville, as throughout the nation, civil rights did not suddenly flower in 1954. Instead, it emerged as a continuous, evolving battle against inequality. Developing an array of new protest politics, African American activists anticipated and shaped the nature of later civil rights movements in the city. As Murray Walls put it, civil rights were achieved not all at once but "step by step."

BEHOLD THE LAND

TO STAY AND FIGHT AT HOME AND
STRUGGLE FOR CIVIL RIGHTS

"The future of Negroes is in the South" were the first words of W. E. B. Du Bois's 1946 speech, "Behold the Land." The speech was delivered in Columbia, South Carolina, to an interracial group at the Southern Youth Legislature hosted by the Southern Negro Youth Congress. Speaking more directly to African Americans, Du Bois urged young blacks to remain in the South, saying, "Young people, instead of running away from the battle here in Carolina, Georgia, Alabama, Louisiana, and Mississippi, instead of seeking freedom and opportunity in Chicago and New York—which do spell opportunity— nevertheless grit your teeth and make up your minds to fight it out right here if it takes everyday of your lives and the lives of your children's children."[1]

Du Bois captured a sentiment shared by many African Americans in the South. Their activism was an outgrowth of self-identification as southerners and of the South as Home. Here it is important to recall the words of political activist and Louisville migrant Lyman T. Johnson:, "I'm glad I didn't tuck tail and run like most of my kinpeople. To them I say: 'You ran away from the problem.'"[2] He continued: "When I see the opportunities blacks have now in Kentucky and throughout the South, I feel so pleased that I stayed and helped remove some of the barriers. . . . You ran to Detroit, Chicago, New York and Philadelphia. But when you arrived you opened up your suit case, the first thing that jumped out was the problem you thought you left behind."[3]

Whether in the Carolinas, Georgia, Alabama, Mississippi, or Kentucky, a number of African Americans proved more than willing to stay and battle for freedom. At a time when roughly half the black population left the South seeking greater opportunity and freedom in the North and West, that same desire was often a catalyst for some blacks to remain in the South. For many African Americans, in and of itself the South was not a bad place; it was and remained Home. Their commitment to making the South a safe space for African Americans points to an intersection of migration, civil rights, and southern identity that has been largely overlooked.[4]

While studies of the era, such as Glenda Gilmore's *Defying Dixie*, stress that some of the "brightest minds and most bountiful spirits" left the South, many others chose to stay.[5] The activism of black migrants in Louisville mirrored that of other African Americans during the civil rights era who consciously chose to remain in the South and battle for equality. Like blacks in Louisville, civil rights activist Medgar Evers directly connected his decision *not* to migrate north to the fight for freedom within the South that ultimately cost him his life. By situating the actions of black migrants in Louisville in a broader context of African American history, the significance of their actions becomes clearer. Blacks in Louisville continued a tradition of activism that linked the struggle for equality in the River City to the black southern political mandate that African Americans *must* stay and fight for freedom in the South.[6]

While few migrants expected to find a racial paradise in Louisville, it does seem that many newcomers were highly politicized and that their civil rights activism was intimately linked to their decision to remain in the South. Prior to their arrival, migrants like Charles W. Anderson and Willie Bell were active in civil rights organizations. Dr. Maurice Rabb, a native of Mississippi, fought residential segregation in Shelbyville, Kentucky, before moving to Louisville in 1946.[7] A lifelong commitment to civil rights and fair housing brought Murray Walls from Indiana to the city in 1935 to conduct a survey on housing for the Works Progress Administration. In Louisville, she immediately became active in the NAACP and initiated the campaign to desegregate the Free Public Library. Jessie Irvin's work with the Non-Partisan Registration League was a continuation of her father's efforts in Hopkinsville, Kentucky, as a precinct captain.[8] In fact, the majority of the African Americans nominated or elected to local government posts during the 1930s were relatively recent arrivals to Louisville. Charles W. Anderson (from Frankfort) and C. Ewbank Tucker and William Beckett (from Baltimore) were all migrants to the River City.[9] Later, Felix Anderson, originally from Wilmington, North Carolina, was the first African American elected to the state legislature as a Democrat.[10]

Further, from 1930 to 1960 the majority of the local NAACP's presidents were migrants. Charles Anderson, Lyman Johnson, James Crumlin, Earl

Dearing, and Reverend W. J. Hodge all assumed leadership of the preeminent civil rights organization soon after settling in Louisville. Other migrants were no less involved. Jewel Rabb coordinated student sit-ins with the Youth Council, while her husband Maurice, vice president of the council, secured funding for its work. Willie Bell's outlook mirrored that of many migrants, whether they sat on the Executive Board or merely held a one-dollar membership. Arriving in Louisville from La Grange, Georgia, in July 1944, Bell immediately asked for directions to the local NAACP, saying, "I want to stay in touch with you all because I will always be a member of the NAACP."[11]

Whether they remained in their native states, returned to the South from the North, or chose to migrate within the South, many migrants in Louisville were united in their desire to "battle" for freedom within the South. Moreover, many of them emphasized the importance of not "running away" from the lack of opportunity and freedom endemic throughout the South. Like others in the region, black migrants in Louisville were well aware of the greater opportunity and freedom that existed in the North and West, but they seemingly felt compelled to make the South a better place, a safe space, if not for themselves then for future black generations. NAACP president Earl Dearing publicly claimed that he was motivated to challenge discrimination in public accommodations after facing the anguish of informing his seven-year-old son that blacks were not allowed at a theater showing *Bambi*.[12] Many, like Dearing, were politicized and committed to the struggle for equality before coming to Louisville, but the decision to relocate to the River City itself was fueled by the view of the South as Home, one that many migrants shared. African Americans who remained in the South often viewed it contextually as Home, a site of oppression, resistance, agency, and identity.

African Americans stayed in the South for a variety of reasons, including family ties, the lack of resources, or, as Mississippi native Mildred Flemming put it after a six-year stint in Chicago, "The city is not for everybody and I was one of those people it wasn't for."[13] But for many African Americans, their commitment to equality and their view of the South as Home proved decisive. Unita Blackwell, of Lula, Mississippi, recalled that as more and more of her family and friends moved to Chicago, she felt if other African Americans "got away then maybe one of these days then you were going to go." But, she said, "I decided to stay and in come a group of people in nineteen-hundred and sixty-four. And Civil Rights. And I had found in life what I wanted to do and that was to fight for freedom. And I'm here and I've been here every since."[14] Blackwell's words struck a deep cord with many blacks in Louisville, as well as throughout the South.

A participant in the Student Nonviolent Coordinating Committee (SNCC) voter registration campaigns in Greenwood, Mississippi, Hollis Watkins expressed much the same outlook. In a 1964 speech, he urged local blacks to join the effort to register at the Greenwood courthouse. For Watkins, the desire for "first-class citizenship" was linked to his decision not to join the mass exodus to the North and West. He concluded his speech saying, "There are many in Greenwood jail fighting for you and me in Mississippi, you see I'm from Mississippi too, that's why I'm here fighting. People have tried to get me to go up North, but I plan to stay here and make Mississippi a better place to live. [Applause] And as long as we continue to go up North and run away from the situation, we will never make it any better."[15] Similarly, Constance Curry's *Silver Rights* recounts the narrative of Mae Bertha Carter and her children's struggle to desegregate public schools in Drew, Mississippi. Her first five children left the state immediately after graduating from high school; the oldest, Edna, candidly stated, "We ran . . . we just left." Despite the "problems," however, the next youngest child, Carl, chose to stay: "You just got to stick in there in Mississippi and if you see something wrong you got to let people know about it and straighten it out. Mississippi is home for me and I want to stay."[16]

Perhaps this commitment to remain in the South was best captured by Medgar Evers in a 1958 interview published in *Ebony*. After serving in World War II, Evers returned home to Decatur, Mississippi, determined to secure "Victory at Home." In short order, he led five friends in an attempt to register to vote, organized a NAACP branch in Cleveland, Mississippi, and tried to enter the law school at Ole Miss.[17] Despite death threats, he adamantly refused to leave the South. As he explained, "Mississippi is part of the United States. And whether whites like it or not, I don't plan to live here as a parasite. The things that I don't like I will try to change."[18] He continued to say, "It may sound funny, but I love the South."[19] His love for the South combined with his desire to make it a better place—if not in his lifetime, then perhaps in his children's—ultimately cost Medgar Evers his life. Yet, as he put it most powerfully, "This is home."[20]

Like many Louisvillians and Mississippians, a number of activists—ranging from Martin Luther King Jr. to Pauli Murray to Ella Baker—emphasized the linkage between their involvement in civil rights struggles and their decision to remain or relocate in the South.[21] For Baker, the connection to "her people" and her home was the central source of her "political and personal leanings." As she put it in 1947, "The Negro must quit looking for a savior, and work to save himself." This same belief led her to return to the South time and time again as field secretary for the NAACP, as field organizer for the Southern Christian Leadership Conference (SCLC), and as an adviser and mentor to the grassroots organization SNCC.[22] This sentiment was best captured by NAACP chief counsel Thurgood Marshall, who said before an enthusiastic crowd at the third annual meeting of the Regional Council of Negro Leadership: "This is an unbelievable crowd! You couldn't get such a crowd in New York to meet and talk on integration. Only in the South is this possible, because here is where the fight is. The weak ones have moved on to Detroit and Chicago while the real ones have remained to fight."[23]

Rather than "goin' to Chicago," many African Americans from states like Tennessee, Alabama, Georgia, Louisiana, and Mississippi found Kentucky's peculiar position in the Upper South compelling. While millions moved North and West, those that stayed in the South demonstrated a commitment to freedom that combined a desire to make the South a safer place and the recognition that they could not "run away" from the problems of the South. By claiming the South as Home, African American migrants acted on the belief that equality could only be achieved in the South.

Beginning in the mid-1950s, black activism in Louisville set out upon a new trajectory. Unlike the civil rights movements of the Deep South, there was no Freedom Summer, no children were attacked with fire hoses and police dogs; there was no Birmingham or Bloody Sunday. Instead, as in other southern cities like Atlanta and Memphis, African Africans in Louisville were confronted by white moderates immersed in the belief that their city was a leader in race relations in the urban South.[24] Nevertheless, even in such cities with liberal white leaders and a sizable black voting bloc, equality remained difficult to achieve. Over time, the strategies of civil rights organizations in Louisville became increasingly militant; this newfound militancy emerged from the struggles of prior decades. With the successful desegregation of higher education and the city's parks and libraries, African Americans embarked on a civil rights agenda to challenge discrimination in public accommodations, employment, and housing. According to George Wright, black leaders "firmly believed it would be easier to desegregate downtown facilities than housing and employment, and that a successful movement in that area would be a lever to other racial advances."[25] Many accurately believed that securing equality in housing would prove to be a far more difficult and volatile struggle.

By 1956, in response to national NAACP pressure to use and support the work of its Youth Division, the local branch created the Youth Council to coordinate the activities of students working to desegregate public accommodations. At the same time, the success of Ewbank Tucker in Louisville and the inroads made by the Congress of Racial Equality (CORE) and the SCLC across the South prompted the Louisville NAACP to grudgingly accept a more aggressive approach. The Youth Council was headed by three of the NAACP's more militant members, Jewel Rabb, J. Andrew Bishop, and Lyman Johnson—all teachers at Central High School. Both Rabb and Johnson were migrants and veterans of Louisville's civil rights struggles during the 1940s. The NAACP initiated a three-stage plan to desegregate establishments in the Fourth Street business district, starting with dime store lunch counters, then the lunch counters at Walgreen's and Taylor Drugstore, and finally the restaurants and tearooms of the major department stores. The NAACP hoped that eventually its campaign would radiate out from Fourth Street to encompass all of the downtown.[26]

Predating the student movements of the early 1960s, the Youth Council throughout 1956–57 conducted a number of unpublicized sit-ins against five-and-dimes that refused to serve African Americans at their lunch counters despite profiting from black patronage. The national civil rights narrative often points to Greensboro, North Carolina, as the starting point of a student movement that spread across the South; however, the earlier campaign in Louisville was more a result of indigenous agitation. More often than not, blacks in the River City received little or no support from national civil rights organizations, the federal government, or organized labor in their struggle to desegregate public accommodations.

Before the sit-ins in Greensboro and Nashville, groups of 250 or more young people picketed segregated restaurants, clothing stores, and theaters along Fourth Street. Students carried signs reading "segregation is immoral, undemocratic and anti-american," "race hate is a crime against humanity," jim crow must go!" and "don't patronize stores where we are segregated."[27] More than six months later, a small number of Louisville's dime stores began to serve African Americans at their lunch counters. By the middle of 1957, the Youth Council moved to desegregate Louisville's drugstores.

At the same time Earl Dearing, president of the Kentucky State Conference of the NAACP, drafted a city ordinance prohibiting discrimination in privately owned restaurants, theaters, and amusement parks, as well as in employment at public utilities such as the Louisville-Transit Company, Southern Bell Telephone and Telegraph Company, and Louisville Gas and Electric. In an unsuccessful effort to enable Louisville to pass a desegregation ordinance, state representative Felix Anderson introduced three similar antisegregation bills in the Kentucky legislature.[28] At a Frontiers of American Negroes

African Americans demonstrated throughout 1956–61 to desegregate downtown businesses along Fourth Street. © *Louisville Courier-Journal*.

luncheon, the Democratic candidate for mayor, Bruce Hoblitzell, rejected the possibility of passing any local legislation prohibiting private businesses from racial discrimination. Speaking to a crowd that included members of the NAACP, Hoblitzell argued: "This is a most inopportune time to start forcing people to do things. . . . Everything is going so well in race relations that I think it would be terrible to stir-up things at this time. . . . I appeal to you not to push this thing now and muddy the waters." Increasingly, blacks in Louisville would echo Maurice Rabb's response to Hoblitzell's position: "If we're going to listen to people who tell us how nice things are, nothing will happen. The things that have happened here [happened] because we did something, because we did muddy the waters."²⁹

After a year the Youth Council's pickets had not duplicated even the limited success of the dime store crusade. On November 29, 1958, however, the NAACP received an unexpected boost from what one historian termed "an international incident of minor proportions."³⁰ Iris King, mayor of Kingston, Jamaica, was refused service at Walgreen's and loudly protested her mistreatment. The public embarrassment created by the episode apparently induced the drugstore to abandon its racial restrictions. Although the Youth Council attempted to build upon this success at Taylor's Drugstore, the chain never officially abandoned its segregation policy until a more inclusive civil rights ordinance was passed in 1963.³¹

A wintry day in late December 1959 saw a new era in Louisville's civil rights movement. The actions of a small group of students who tried and failed to buy tickets for a Christmas season production of *Porgy and Bess* at the Brown Theater signaled the beginning of an all-out assault against segregation in downtown theaters, hotels, cafeterias, and restaurants. Led by members of the Youth Council, the NAACP established a picket line to underscore the irony and inconsistency of excluding blacks from seeing the all-black play. For more than two months students carried placards stating "This Theater Does Not Admit Negroes," outside the Brown Theater. Long after the play had gone, black students still gathered outside the Brown demanding an end to segregation.³²

Although the NAACP called off the protest at the end of the Christmas season, black civil rights activists served notice that "the 1960's would witness changes in downtown accommodations."³³ The protest and picketing surrounding *Porgy and Bess* represented a departure in terms of pace, scale, and strategy from prior forms of black activism in the city. It was also the first volley in a new series of campaigns challenging segregation in public accommodations, employment, and housing citywide. As before, African American

Despite their differences, CORE and the NAACP joined together to desegregate public accommodations. Here, African Americans picket Kaufman's Department Store and theaters along Fourth Street in 1961. © *Louisville Courier-Journal*.

migrants remained at the forefront of the struggle against inequality. Although the NAACP preferred "the conference [room] and the courtroom" to confrontation, throughout the decade the civil rights activists increasingly came to rely on direct action—pickets, protests, and economic boycotts—as their primary tools.[34]

But over the short term, the protest at the Brown Theater was called off to begin negotiations with Bruce Hoblitzell—now mayor of Louisville. On January 4, 1960, black activists gathered at City Hall to ask Hoblitzell to introduce a city ordinance banning discrimination in public accommodations.[35] The mayor's response was unfortunate, though not unexpected: "He would not promote legislation to force a business to accept anyone." Although he believed integration was "morally right," he also claimed that "to pass a law of non-selectivity was ridiculous."[36] In essence, Hoblitzell outlined a position from which he and the aldermen would not budge: Desegregation should be voluntary, and a public accommodation ordinance would be unjust.

When the mayor refused to endorse a public accommodations ordinance, local black leaders asked William Beckett, the city's only black alderman, to introduce a desegregation bill. Although Beckett was something of an activist in his own right, his relationship with civil rights organizations such as the NAACP was tenuous at best. In 1958 the association had cited his unwillingness "to take a forceful stand in support of our civil rights ordinance."[37] Beckett declined to introduce any civil rights legislation. He believed that the eleven other aldermen would oppose a public accommodations ordinance, as well as any other measures he might propose. But the city's black leaders wanted to use the accommodations bill to compel the board of aldermen to publicly acknowledge that they would not support desegregation. Consequently, a black committee threatened to lead a boycott of Beckett's Funeral Home unless he introduced the measure.

On February 9, 1960, eight days after the Greensboro Woolworth sit-in, Beckett presented a "Public Accommodations" ordinance making it unlawful to deny patronage to any person because of race or religion. Excluding bars or taverns, Ordinance 79 called for the complete desegregation of downtown restaurants, hotels, and theaters. Any business refusing to comply would be subject to a penalty of twenty-five to one hundred dollars. As expected, the white aldermen voted against Beckett's bill 11 to 1. The chairman of the Rules and Grievances Committee, Clifford J. Haury, explained: "After giving the ordinance the full consideration as printed, it is the opinion of the majority of this committee that the Board of Aldermen has no jurisdiction in this matter as the power invested in the Board does not give it authority to pass laws in this regard and we concur in the opinion of our law department."[38] In doing so, Beckett declared, the Board of Aldermen "stymie[d] the progress of this community of 600,000, which has a minority of 70,000 who are not treated equally."[39]

After Beckett obtained a ruling from the state attorney general, John Breckinridge, that Louisville could constitutionally pass an antisegregation ordinance, he introduced a slightly revised version of the bill. It was also defeated by the same 11–1 vote. The Board of Aldermen then denied Beckett's request for a public hearing on the matter. Instead, in a move that took local black leaders by surprise, the board passed the following resolution: "Be it resolved that the Board of Aldermen of the City of Louisville, are opposed to any ordinance, which takes the right away, the right of an owner of a private business, to select his or its customers or clientele."[40] Mayor Hoblitzell voiced his support of the resolution by reiterating his position on a desegregation ordinance: "I don't think this is the time to tell people who and what they should do with their private businesses, I can't be an angel."[41]

Dissatisfied that their resolution did not go far enough, the white aldermen went on the offensive by introducing an antitrespassing ordinance. With an eye toward the waves of sit-ins washing across the South, the board passed an ordinance making it illegal to picket or demonstrate in downtown Louisville; offenders would be arrested. The aldermen also defeated a bill sponsored by Beckett to create a city Human Relations Committee that would have encouraged better race relations through education, persuasion, and conciliation. Although the committee would have had no enforcement powers, the board vetoed even this mild proposal by the usual 11–1 vote.[42] The board made it clear that it would vote against any antisegregation legislation and actively oppose "forced integration."

Given the board's unwavering opposition to desegregation, black civil rights activists made plans to resume the initiative in the public accommodations struggle. C. Ewbank Tucker, Reverend M. M. D. Purdue, and Reverend Daniel J. Hughlett—all members of the Southern Conference Educational Fund, Incorporated, an interracial organization working for racial justice—called a protest meeting. Local activists Carl and Anne Braden arranged for Len Holt, a field secretary for CORE, to be the primary speaker. As a result of the meeting, a branch of CORE was organized in Louisville; its twenty-five members represented a motley band of black adults, white liberals and pacifists like the Bradens, and a small interracial group of high school students.[43] The diminutive size of CORE was more than compensated for by its enthusiasm; its first act was to take seven students to the Char-Mont Room of the Kaufman-Straus department store, where they were denied service at the tearoom. Despite its size, August Meier and Elliot Rudwick contended, this small chapter of CORE provided a "vital stimulus" for Louisville's black protest movement.[44]

In a series of strategy sessions attended by prominent local civil rights activists, Lyman Johnson, Reverend C. Ewbank Tucker, Reverend W. J. Hodge, and Frank Stanley Jr. emerged as leaders of the effort to desegregate public accommodations. Hodge had relocated to Louisville from Virginia, and in

1959 he was president of the local NAACP and pastor of Fifth Street Baptist Church, the most prestigious black church in Kentucky. Stanley, son of the publisher of the *Louisville Defender* and the group's youngest member, became its primary spokesperson. Together, along with Reverend D. E. King, they formed the Integration Steering Committee, which coordinated demonstrations throughout the public accommodations struggle. Johnson relied on his prior experience in Louisville's civil rights movement, as well as his position as a teacher at Central High School, to mobilize students. Unlike the southern sit-in movement, which relied primarily on college students, in Louisville high school students were central to this campaign since there were so few black college students in the city. In light of the school superintendent's threat to fire Johnson for using students in civil disobedience demonstrations, the majority of the protests were carried out after school hours or on weekends. Johnson recalled:

> I told my students: "Well, young folks, the superintendent says he'll fire me. The judge says he'll hold me in contempt of court if he found me using school children. So I'm not going to ask a single one of you—I'm not even going to invite you—to help with the demonstration this afternoon at Walgreen's at a half past three. School will be out at three o'clock, which will give you plenty of time to go home and tell your mothers that Mr. Johnson will not invite you to participate in the demonstration that he'll be leading at half past three at Walgreen's on Fourth Street."[45]

As one of the student leaders in the demonstrations, Frank Stanley argued that the Youth Council could succeed only if all the civil rights groups in the black community supported the effort. According to Stanley, the Interdenominational Ministers Council, comprised of black clergy, had the means to mobilize masses of people. The NAACP had the financial and legal resources to deal with any arrests resulting from the demonstrations. More importantly, the central role that the association played in Louisville's prior civil rights movements would lend the demonstrations immediate credibility. Even typically more conservative organizations, such as the Urban League, could use their personal contacts with the city's white leadership to help negotiate desegregation. Stanley also pointed out that CORE, one of the new organizations on Louisville's political landscape, was skilled in training large numbers of students in nonviolent demonstration techniques. In his view, even white civic leaders could lend their support to African Americans attempting to desegregate downtown Louisville. Yet, with the exception of the few whites affiliated with CORE such as long-term local activist Anne Braden, none came forward.[46]

Stanley's dream of a cohesive, unified protest movement never materialized. From the start, CORE and the NAACP disagreed on how desegregation could be achieved. Tucker and his organization were convinced that nonviolent direct action, rather than negotiation, was essential. On the other hand, the NAACP called for a series of meetings with white business leaders. While the NAACP assured the white merchants that there would be no demonstrations during their negotiations, CORE and the Civil Rights Commission of the Kentucky Conference of the African Methodist Episcopal (AME) Zion Church, led by Tucker, renewed sit-ins at the very businesses with which the NAACP was negotiating. Even though the NAACP and CORE sporadically assisted each other during the remainder of the public accommodations campaign, the relationship between them turned decidedly chilly.

Although CORE and the NAACP worked well together in other cities, such as St. Louis, Missouri, and Lexington, Kentucky, the Louisville chapter of CORE suffered from a number of difficulties. First, Tucker clashed with nearly every other black leader in the River City. As early as 1931, members of the local NAACP characterized Ewbank Tucker as "shabby and unkempt," an "opportunist" with "a reputation for dishonesty."[47] Nearly thirty years later, Tucker printed thousands of fliers labeling members of the black fraternity Alpha Phi Alpha "Tea sippers and pseudo aristocrats." He claimed they "never made any contribution to the integration fight in Louisville" and looked "down with derision upon the masses of people."[48] It was no coincidence that Lyman Johnson and Maurice Rabb were prominent members of both Alpha Phi Alpha and the NAACP. Second, CORE and the Bradens carried the taint of communism. A number of NAACP members questioned the sincerity of CORE; they viewed the organization as little more than a "band of white radicals" and affluent blacks. In 1958, following the path of the national office laid out by executive director Roy Wilkins, the local NAACP described the Highlander Folk School as a "questionable institution" and decided against sending NAACP representatives.[49] Nor was the NAACP the only group to hold this view. CORE's national leadership cautioned field secretaries not to accept food or lodging from the Bradens. Ultimately, the Bradens would dissolve any "formal association with the chapter." Given the Cold War climate, the NAACP in Louisville was no more immune to the "threat" of communism than the nation as a whole.[50]

While the disagreements within Louisville's civil rights community appeared personal, the negative views of CORE were more indicative of differences in civil rights strategies. The tension between the NAACP and CORE was compounded by the presence of a number of other civil rights groups advocating their own solution to segregation. For instance, the Independent Improvement Club, organized by Alberta O. Jones, perhaps Kentucky's first female black barrister, argued that the solution to desegregation lay in political power. The only group both the NAACP and CORE commonly worked with was the Non-Partisan Registration Committee (NPRC), organized in 1960 by Frank Stanley Jr.; Neville Tucker, a black attorney; and Woodford Porter Sr., a leader in the creation of the Lincoln Independent Party during the 1920s. Unlike blacks in the Deep South, there was no need of a Freedom Summer, since African Americans in Louisville already possessed the right to vote. Rather, the NPRC was engaged in expanding the number of black registered voters. The *Louisville Courier-Journal* described the situation as one of "too many cooks" who have "succeeded only in getting in each other's way."[51] In reality, the paper failed to recognize the complexity and diversity of strategies of the local and national civil rights movements.

No matter what created the tension between CORE and the NAACP, their bickering and the recalcitrance of white segregationists effectively hamstrung the black protest movement. In 1960, little desegregation occurred. Though it rarely had more than seven or eight participants, and often as few as three, CORE continued to engage in scattered protests and pickets for the rest of the year. In June, its demonstrations targeted Taylor's Drugstore. On August 15, CORE staged a sit-in at Ben Snyder's Department Store, where white employees informed them: "You, understand, we have orders not to serve you." The next day, Tucker's Civil Rights Commission of the Kentucky Conference of the AME Zion Church focused on discrimination in the Louisville Police Department. A week later, African Americans demonstrated at Algonquin Bowling Center, after the new 72-lane bowling alley refused to admit thirty blacks, announcing that its company policy was to segregate. On September 10, the pickets were attacked by a violent group of white youths wielding iron poles.[52] By the end of the year, CORE lapsed into inactivity. Meanwhile, the NAACP persisted in holding a series of ineffective meetings with the city's leaders.

In January 1961, African American high school students, tired of "patience and meaningless promises," resumed the sit-ins and pickets without the leadership or approval of the adult organizations.[53] As W. J. Hodge remembered, these youths "took the initiative, seized the headlines, and bypassed the older organization." The sit-in of seven students, and their subsequent arrest at Stewart's Department Store, reignited the protest movement in Louisville.

As the frequency and size of the demonstrations increased, CORE and the NAACP scrambled to keep pace. The newfound reliance on public demonstrations and the city's black youth was not so easily accepted by many civil rights veterans. Murray Walls organized older blacks to "meet behind closed doors" and marched with students throughout 1961, though it was something she found difficult to do. As Walls later explained, "I didn't want to do it. . . . Mainly because I grew up in an age when my people had led me to believe it was degrading to sing and march in public. . . . It was just embarrassing for me to get in the streets and yell, as simple as that."[54]

In part, the increasingly aggressive nature of the civil rights movement in Louisville was simply a realization by African Americans that despite the city's "liberal" image, equality would only become a reality if blacks forced the issue. E. Deedom Alston, migrant and minister of the Church of Our Merciful Saviour, described himself as more of a negotiator than an activist, yet he realized the importance of joining the Youth Council's protest marches. He spoke for many blacks when he characterized Louisville's progressive reputation as a "velvet glove" that can "sort of *sooth* your victim, make them think you're doing a lot, when you're not doing nothing."[55] Although many older activists may have initially hesitated to join the sit-ins movement, most recognized their necessity. As Murray Walls put it, "People don't give up power easily, sometimes it has to be taken."[56]

In February 1961, Louisville's black protest movement enjoyed a surge of new vitality. More than one hundred members of the NAACP Youth Council and CORE were arrested in demonstrations that month. At the same time, Frank Stanley Jr. called for a massive campaign of "economic withdrawal" from the downtown business district. His strategy gained widespread support from the black community, as well as from national civil rights leaders such as Martin Luther King Jr. In fact, as a close confidant of Stanley, King telegraphed his approval saying, "If 50,000 blacks in a month can walk in dignity for a year surely 75,000 Negroes in Louisville can stop buying in protest for a month."[57] The "Nothing New for Easter" boycott was slated to begin on February 28 to take advantage of the $18 million that blacks spent in the downtown each year. The campaign was so successful that it extended beyond Easter, April 3, to last the entire month.

According to George Wright, more than 98 percent of Louisville's black population supported the boycott, "as only a handful of blacks ventured into department and dime stores to make purchases." The *Louisville Defender* reported that the sales of white businesses in the downtown declined as much as 25 to 50 percent. At least one store dependent on black patronage was forced to close during the boycott. The majority of white business establishments refused not just to serve blacks but to hire them as well. The Urban League maintained that in 1961 more than 39.8 percent of African American workers were out of a job, compared to 8.3 percent of Louisville's whites.[58] Clara Wims, a native of Tennessee, was among those few blacks employed at segregated restaurants such as the Blue Boar Cafeteria; at age sixty-one she worked as a "silver girl."[59] As Reverend W. J. Hodge explained, the boycott was intended not only to open all public accommodations but also to gain black jobs.[60] For blacks in Louisville, economic opportunity was closely linked to the effort to desegregate public accommodations.

In the attempt to integrate Louisville's 118 segregated restaurants and 6 downtown theaters, the pace and size of the black protest demonstrations began to increase at an alarming rate for white Louisvillians. After the arrest of fifteen students during a series of demonstrations against Stewart's and Kaufman's department stores, Mayor Hoblitzell established an emergency committee to deal with the public accommodations crisis. He had been urged to do so in meetings with Governor Bert Combs, who led the Kentucky General Assembly to institute a merit system to ensure that state agencies used fair employment practices and to create a Commission on Human Rights. Hoblitzell's emergency committee was comprised of white business leaders and African American civil rights advocates, including white entrepreneurs Dillman Rash, president of the Louisville Tile Company; Thomas Ballantine, vice president of Glenmore Distilleries; William Henderson, head of Taylor's Drugstore; George Norton, president of *WAVE* Broadcasting Incorporated; and Barry Bingham, publisher of the *Louisville Courier-Journal* and the *Louisville Times*. African Americans appointed to the new Commission on Human Rights were Frank Stanley Jr., chief spokesman for the demonstrators, and W. J. Hodge and Earl Dearing of the NAACP. The emergency committee was primarily concerned with the negative image black protests created for Louisville. With the rapidly approaching Kentucky Derby in mind, and the national media the event annually drew, the committee urged business owners to voluntarily desegregate by May 1, 1961.[61]

Despite the presence of the mayor's emergency committee, white businesses were no more willing than before to desegregate. As black journalist Mervin Aubespin noted, even "White Castle, the cheapest of them all, had a window in the back, you couldn't even go in the White Castle to get a White Castle."[62] Yet blacks were no less active. If anything, they became increasingly more aggressive in their demands for open access. Over 750 students participated in the almost daily marches and stand-ins at downtown theaters, restaurants, tearooms, and department stores refusing to serve African Americans on an equal basis. On March 14, 1961, the city witnessed one of the largest demonstrations of the public accommodations struggle at the intersection of Fourth and Broadway, called the "magic corner" due to its centrality in the economic life of the city. A four-block-long group of marchers passed through the center of the downtown business district from Fourth Street to Broadway. The march directed particular attention to Kaufman's, Stewart's, and two of the Blue Boar restaurants. L. Eugene Johnson, owner of the Blue Boar, explicitly stated that no African Americans would ever be served in the Blue Boar.[63]

The following day the NAACP Youth Council and CORE coordinated a rally to protest the arrest of 177 high school and college students participating in a march "against segregation . . . and for expansion of job opportunities." W. J. Hodge, Frank Stanley Jr., Bishop Tucker, president of the local NAACP Youth Council Arthur Smith, and CORE member Beverley Neal led a group 500 strong from Quinn Chapel AME Church, the starting point of many demonstrations to City Hall. Throughout March, African Americans held marches, rallies, Sunday meetings at businesses and City Hall, and met with the Board of Aldermen. In late March, 350 black youths staged a protest march through downtown, ending at the office of the mayor. On Easter Sunday, a prayer meeting drew nearly 3,500 participants to City Hall. By March 25, 272 arrests had been made in connection with the public accommodations protest and the "Nothing New for Easter" boycott.[64] Well over 300 students were determined to march, sing, and picket until their goals were met; they were arrested in the final week of the month. In terms of the pace and scale of the protests, March both came in and went out like a lion.

The "vanloads" of young blacks "hauled" to jail by the police often turned to the NAACP to secure their freedom. Throughout the public accommodations fight, the NAACP conducted numerous rallies to raise bail money for students. By all accounts Dr. Rabb's work as an NAACP fund-raiser was unparalleled; in essence, he begged and borrowed to raise bail money. He helped coordinate rallies, sold numerous "Life-Time" memberships in the NAACP, and solicited donations from a variety of sources.[65] At one public meeting, the NAACP drew 2,800 African Americans who contributed $2,100 to the public accommodations campaign.[66] Every penny proved necessary, as the Louisville police ultimately arrested more than 600 students. On at least one occasion, established civil rights leaders Tucker, Hodge, and Stanley were among those under lock and key. The *Louisville Defender* observed: "The police obtained a dubious record . . . in the arrest of juveniles and adults conducting 'stand ins' and 'squat ins' protesting segregation in public accommodations by bringing the total number to 685—the highest in the nation—since the demonstrations intensified on February 20."[67]

Linking Louisville's civil rights campaign to the national movement, local activists received a psychological boost from the "triumphal entry" of Martin Luther King Jr. on April 19, 1961. Recognizing the importance of Louisville to the civil rights movement throughout the South, King challenged 1,500 students at the Southern Baptist Theological Seminary to propel the Christian Church away from "the old order of exploitation and humiliation and segregation to the new order of human dignity and freedom."[68] He called on the churches themselves to desegregate and cultivate among their congregants a "world perspective that rises above the shackles of race prejudice." He spoke to the Integration Steering Committee and the mayor's emergency committee, urging the latter to "move right along on integrating facilities such as restaurants, theaters and hotels." At Quinn Chapel AME Church, King spoke to an overflowing crowd of black students and adults, cautioning Louisville's protesters against the use of violence. At the same, he asserted: "Any law by which the majority imposes on the minority a code which it does not impose on itself is unjust."[69]

As the Kentucky Derby approached, the mayor's emergency committee urged black leaders to end their demonstrations. The mayor released a statement requesting "no later than Monday, May 1, that the operations of all downtown eating facilities quietly, without publicity, desegregate." He asked that groups of three to four blacks under the supervision of the Integration Steering Committee confirm the status of all downtown facilities. In the meantime, he demanded "that there be no further demonstrations during this period, and in no event prior to May 3rd."[70]

The Integration Steering Committee found that thirty-two of the fifty-seven restaurants surveyed still refused to serve blacks. While the emergency committee sent telegrams pleading with the thirty-two holdouts to desegregate, the Louisville Hotel and Restaurant Association objected to the idea that they should even attempt to meet the mayor's May 1 deadline. Association president Fred Latham declared, "As far as Monday is concerned, I feel the mayor is moving a little too fast to expect a great deal of cooperation." Despite this refusal, the mayor's committee argued that blacks should be encouraged by the fact that since February 1961, eighty-eight restaurants had desegregated, a figure representing more than 80 percent of Louisville's downtown eateries. The committee informed African Americans that "under these circumstances, we would strongly urge that there be no more mass demonstrations as we feel that this very probably would hurt rather than help the cause of integration by creating resentment and by tending to alienate some of those who to date have been strong supporters of the local integration movement."[71]

After considerable debate, Louisville's civil rights leaders decided to end the public accommodations demonstrations and the "Nothing New for Easter" boycott, even though thirty-two restaurants and virtually all of the city's theaters and hotels remained segregated. It did not take the black protest movement long to realize it had made a tactical mistake. Although the emergency committee advocated integration, it did so strictly on a voluntary basis. Any doubts African Americans might have had about the sincerity of the mayor's intentions were quickly removed. At the very moment black activists encouraged the committee to use its influence to pass a public accommodations ordinance, arguing that partial desegregation was no real victory, Mayor Hoblitzell and the emergency committee formally refused to press the Board of Aldermen to enact legislation outlawing segregation. Adding insult to injury, the committee dissolved itself, proclaiming that "most of the city is desegregated."[72] In hindsight, it appears that the mayor's committee was more committed to ending the demonstrations before Derby Day than it was to achieving African American equality.

Much to the dismay of CORE and the NAACP, the mayor and Board of Aldermen would not move from their initial segregationist stance. In the wake of the emergency committee's decision to disband, the Board of Aldermen endorsed yet another resolution reaffirming their opposition to integration. In that resolution, passed by an 11–1 vote, the aldermen stated they "opposed any ordinance that would impose enforced segregation."[73] At the same time they maintained their resistance to the creation of a city human relations committee. As George Wright described the situation, "Despite mass demonstrations, mass arrests, an economic boycott, and persuasion from the governor, Louisville's Democratic board of aldermen—led by William S. Milburn—had not budged in their view of desegregation of public accommodations."[74]

On June 1, 1961, the Integration Steering Committee surveyed the status of integration in downtown Louisville from First to Ninth Street and from Oak Street to Main Street. The committee "tested" and "re-tested" the restaurants by sending groups of blacks to eat at the various establishments. Among the 142 restaurants tested, 100 were integrated, 26 were segregated, and 12 were listed as "indefinite." But as Urban League member Arthur Walters, a migrant from Magnolia, Kentucky, remembered, the test team was "stoned out [of] sixty-five percent of accommodations we tried to get served at."[75] The survey demonstrated both the success of Louisville's public accommodations demonstrations as well as the need for their continuance. For instance, the committee's report revealed that out of the fifty-one restaurants at which blacks held demonstrations, only seven remained segregated. Even Eugene Johnson's Blue Boar Cafeteria had submitted under the constant pressure of student demonstrations.[76]

On the other hand, the Dizzy Whizz, Music Man, Whizz Hamburger, Williams Food Shop on West Market and West Chestnut, W & F Coffee, Saratoga Restaurant, and aptly named White Swan resisted all efforts to integrate. The inability of student protesters to open these particular restaurants demonstrates that white Louisvillians would concede as little as possible to integration. While the Dizzy Whizz and two Williams Food shops refused to desegregate, other locations of the same restaurant had already agreed to admit black patrons. Although the Dizzy Whizz at 216 West Broadway opened to black customers, the 217 West Catherine Street shop unequivocally refused to serve them. The mayor's appeal for voluntary desegregation obscured the fact that whites had denied equal service to blacks in the first place. The "indefinite" status of twelve restaurants suggests that on any given day whites could still turn blacks away. It was only pressure that made them serve African Americans on an equal basis. While the survey noted the progress made in desegregating restaurants, the majority of theaters, hotels, and amusement parks remained closed to African Americans. In short, in the weeks after the Kentucky Derby, it became increasingly clear that public accommodations would only be desegregated if blacks themselves took the initiative.

In the summer of 1961, the NAACP and CORE renewed the protest demonstrations but only drew a small number of people. Historian George Wright believed that "discontinuing the demonstrations in early May sapped the momentum that had been built up since February."[77] Moreover, they were poorly coordinated as the long-standing conflict between the NAACP and CORE resurfaced. The two organizations held marches independent of one another. CORE along with Frank Stanley Jr. initiated a campaign to desegregate Fountain Ferry Amusement Park during the summer, which resulted in the first arrests since May 6. The NAACP refused to lend the protest its support. At the same time, CORE launched a highly successful boycott against Sealtest and Coca-Cola, but ten weeks later the campaign had stalled. According to CORE historians Rudwick and Meyer, the boycott was "undermined by Bishop Tucker's enemies in the Urban League and NAACP."[78] As the demonstrations staggered on toward the end of the year, businesses that had previously integrated began to discriminate once again.

As the protest movement continued to falter under the weight of internal dissension and white resistance, the work of the Non-Partisan Registration Committee gained greater significance for black leaders. Like the Non-Partisan Voters' League in Memphis, blacks in Louisville used the vote to secure political representation and to effect social change.[79] The NPRC worked under the banner, "Fifty-one thousand Registered Voters Can Totally Desegregate Louisville."[80] When it was organized in 1960, there were an estimated 18,000 to 19,000 African American registered voters in a voting population that exceeded 51,000. With the support of more than 800 workers, the NPRC added thousands of black voters to the rolls. Through its efforts more than 15,000 new voters were registered by November 1960.[81]

Jessie Irvin was one of the eight hundred workers involved in the NPRC initiative to increase the pool of black registered voters. In 1951 Irvin moved to Louisville from Hopkinsville, Kentucky; by 1960 she had spent more than seven years working at the precinct level in the Eighth Ward as a Democrat. However, as a member of the NPRC, she "didn't care how they voted as long as they voted. Naturally, I wanted them to vote Democrat, but it didn't matter."[82] As they went "door to door," Irvin said, initially blacks were not overly receptive to their efforts. She encountered migrants from places like Mississippi, for example, who "didn't even know they could vote or weren't listening when they were told."[83] But after more than three years, the hard work of Irvin and the NPRC paid off. In Irvin's precinct, the number of registered black voters swelled from 328 to well over 1,000. By November 1961, the work of the NPRC resulted in more than 40,000 registered black voters, effectively giving African Americans the political balance of power.

Although blacks had amassed sufficient political power to sway the upcoming election by a "one-shot" vote, they faced the difficult question of who deserved their ballot. The *Louisville Defender* described both mayoral candidates as "cut from the same cloth." Democrat William Milburn was president of the Board of Aldermen and the leading opponent of desegregating public accommodations. The Republican candidate, William Cowger, promised to establish a Human Relations Commission HRC) if elected, but like Hoblitzell favored "voluntary" integration. But the majority of blacks in Louisville balked at the idea of voting for Milburn. Even Lyman Johnson's NAACP and Bishop Tucker's CORE, which were so often at odds, could agree on that. As Reverend Hodge put it, Milburn was "an outright, first-class, super segregationist."[84] For the first time, the *Defender* refused to support either candidate, declaring: "Both have failed to display sufficient positive leadership required to advance the cause of human dignity so sorely needed in our community."[85]

Despite their reservations, African American voters gave the Republican Party a startling victory. On November 7, 1961, Cowger defeated Milburn by a vote of 61,651 to 50,219.[86] For the first time in twenty-eight years Louisville elected a Republican mayor. Along with Cowger's election, the Republican Party carried every seat on the Board of Aldermen for the first time in fourteen years. Although the sole black alderman, William Beckett, openly campaigned on the issue of public accommodations, promising that he would present an accommodations ordinance if elected, he was swept out of office along with the other Democrats.[87] Among the new aldermen were African Americans Russell Lee and Louise Reynolds. Reynolds was the first black woman elected to the Board of Aldermen. A migrant from Lewisburg, Tennessee, she had worked in Republican campaigns as a committeewoman since 1950.[88] In addition, Amelia Tucker, originally from Alabama and the wife of activist C. Ewbank Tucker, became the first African American woman to win a seat in the Kentucky legislature.[89] The NPRC immediately and loudly proclaimed that black voters had achieved the Republican victory. The *Louisville Defender* called attention to the fact that 60 to 70 percent of blacks voted Republican, compared to 54 percent in 1957.[90]

If African Americans believed the demonstration of their collective political muscle in the election of William Cowger ensured the passage of a public accommodations ordinance, then they were surely disappointed. In January 1962, Cowger met with a delegation of black leaders to urge them not to resume public accommodations demonstrations. Instead, he asked that they give him time to establish a Human Relations Commission to negotiate with white businesses. In March, Louise Reynolds sponsored the bill that created the HRC, though no members were appointed until June. In an apparent stalling tactic, the commission spent the balance of 1962 organizing subcommittees to investigate discrimination in Louisville. As black leaders began to insist that the mayor and Board of Aldermen pass a desegregation ordinance, CORE presented the mayor with an ultimatum: the organization would march on City Hall in thirty days if an ordinance was not passed prohibiting racial discrimination in public accommodations.

The *Louisville Defender*'s advocacy of black equality merged with a growing chorus of civil rights groups such as the NAACP, CORE, and the HRC, clamoring for the passage of a public accommodations ordinance in 1963. With the hundredth anniversary of the Emancipation Proclamation in mind, the black press argued: "Emancipation is not yet achieved."[91] On April 10, 1963, the HRC submitted a draft ordinance to the Board of Aldermen. Meanwhile, CORE and the NAACP threatened to renew demonstrations if the ordinance was vetoed. The threats of Louisville's black protest movement combined with the political support of the African American community achieved their desired effect. Faced with increasing pressure from civil rights organizations, Cowger reversed his initial position on "voluntary" integration and began to speak out in favor of an ordinance. On May 14, 1963, after more than three years of struggle, the Board of Aldermen enacted the first public accommodations ordinance in Kentucky. The ordinance made it unlawful for any public place providing food, shelter, entertainment, or amusement to refuse service to anyone on the basis of race, color, or religious belief. The statute called for fines of up to one hundred dollars for each violation; after three violations, the city would seek an injunction against the violator. Failure to comply with the injunction would lead to a jail sentence.[92]

On the heels of the victory in Louisville, the black protest movement shifted its attention to securing a statewide antidiscrimination law. Rather than introducing state civil rights legislation, Governor Combs issued an executive order prohibiting racial discrimination in all establishments and by all professions licensed by the state. While segregationists accused Combs of infringing on whites' privacy and property rights, African American activists labeled the executive order a "hoax."[93] The efforts to obtain a state civil rights law culminated in a march led by the Allied Organization for Civil Rights to the steps of the capitol in Frankfort.[94] In March 1964, an interracial coalition of 10,000 demonstrators, including Carl and Anne Braden as well as a host of national figures such as Martin Luther King Jr., Reverend Ralph Abernathy, Jackie Robinson, Mahalia Jackson, and comedian Dick Gregory, joined in the protest. Mattie Jones was one of the many blacks in Frankfort on that cold, snowy day. Recalling her decision to march, Jones said: "I was doing what I had to do. . . . The only thing I could see was that I didn't want my children to suffer."[95] After two years of intense pressure, including a 32-person hunger strike at the General Assembly, Kentucky became the first southern state to pass a civil rights law. The statute—one of the strongest in the nation—prohibited discrimination in public accommodations and employment.

Though elated by its passage, civil rights leaders said the battle was far from over. While the Civil Rights Act and the public accommodations ordinance may have erased the "last visages of racial discrimination from public accommodations" in the River City, few blacks viewed it as a complete success. The struggle for public accommodations was not only to secure equal

March on Frankfort, 1964. Nearly ten thousand people gathered at the state capitol to demand a state desegregation law. © *Louisville Courier-Journal.*

access but part of a larger fight to obtain better jobs and housing as well. The progress that blacks made in the arena of public accommodations did not end racial discrimination in Louisville, as the specter of segregation continued to linger in the lives of African Americans. The victory was important, but it did little to ameliorate the inequities in employment and housing. Frank Stanley, editor of the *Louisville Defender*, pointed to this fact in a commentary entitled, "The Negro in Kentucky: Is His Apparent Progress More Apparent Than Real?" Despite the progress in opening public accommodations, he wrote, "Negroes generally—the masses—have not benefited greatly from local, state and federal civil rights laws. The barometer is the widening of the economic gap between Negroes and whites both on a per capita and a per family average."[96] Now, with public accommodations assured, employment and fair housing would become the primary terrain on which the battle for racial equality—for black migrants to remake the South, to make Home a safe place—would be fought.

UPON THIS ROCK

AFRICAN AMERICAN MIGRATION AND THE

TRANSFORMATION OF THE POSTWAR URBAN LANDSCAPE

By 1960, African Americans created a strong, vibrant, and completely segregated community in Louisville. At the center of this community stood the Old Walnut Street business district spanning from Sixth to Thirteenth streets and overflowing onto the side streets along Walnut. As early as 1860, when Martha A. Cozzens, a free woman of color, operated a rooming house in the nine hundred block, Walnut Street became the center of black business in the city.[1] Although Walnut Street's heyday peaked between 1930 and 1950, blacks had owned a substantial number of the businesses along the street since the turn of the twentieth century. Decades later African Americans still remembered Walnut Street as more than a business district; for many, it was "the heart and soul of the black community." In "Footing It Down the Block," poets George Ann Berry and Estella Conwill Alexander memorialized Walnut Street as a place "where energy rich and dark pulsated real through the block / and life forces transfuses and folk fused together."[2]

In 1984 James Syndor, a black photographer, described Walnut as "a street of great smells. The aroma of home-cooked food poured out of the Wilson Restaurant, Buckhart's, Givens Goodies, Teeken's Bakery, out of Betty's and the Little Palace Café." Within the seven blocks of Walnut Street, there was the only black-owned filling station in the city, located at Eighth Street; white-owned department stores, such as Byck's and Waterman's, that allowed black shoppers to try on clothes; businesses like the Lucky Morris Pawn Shop, rumored to be "run by Negroes but not owned by Negroes"; and the Mammoth Life Insurance Company. At theaters like the Lyric and the Grand, African American actors always received the top billing, and in *Imitation of*

Life, Miss Louise Beavers was the headliner. Although created by the realities of residential and social segregation, it was a street of "laughter and music," of stylish nightspots such as the Top Hat, the Joe Louis Club, the Little Doggie, and Charlie Moore's Café, where on any given night Duke Ellington, Lionel Hampton, Count Basie, Dinah Washington, or Sarah Vaughan performed. For blacks with more limited resources, there was the Fifth Avenue Pool Hall, the Moonglow Café, or the Orchid Bar. As Syndor observed, Walnut Street was "a stage on which all social classes performed."[3]

While blacks were not allowed to enter the Orange Bar or the Fountain Ferry Amusement Park, or to consistently try on clothes in downtown department stores, within the Walnut Street corridor there existed what Christopher Silver and John Moeser have termed a "separate city." In cities such as Memphis, Atlanta, and Louisville the black community existed as a "city within a city," served almost entirely by black business people and professionals. In spite of a narrow economic base, African Americans "served their own community in matters such as financing, insurance, jobs, personal services and patronage, as well as offering a social life that rivaled that of the white world in its depth and diversity."[4] Indeed, for many blacks the culture and community centered on Walnut Street was unrivaled in the River City.

During its heyday, the majority of black businesses, or those catering to blacks, were located along Walnut Street, including flower shops, grocery stores, doctors, lawyers, real estate agents, and at least one private detective, Lewis C. Olive. Blacks could walk along the street and get their hair done at any one of a number of shops—among them, Ella's Beauty Salon, the John Miller Barber Shop, and the Red Star Barber Shop, which advertised itself as the place to go "for a good haircut and shave." At Tenth and Chestnut streets stood the Pythian Temple, which was the headquarters of the Universal Negro Improvement Association in the 1920s. Just outside of the Walnut Street business district they might choose to visit Mrs. Fannie Jordan, the "wonderful hair grower," who claimed to be the person to see "if you want your scalp cleaned and your hair to grow." Back on Walnut, blacks might stop at Your Shop or F. L. Stith to have clothes pressed, altered, or cleaned. If they hungered for chili on a cold day, it could be found at Helen's Chili Parlor or John's Mexican Chili Parlor, which reminded its customers: "Do not forget to see us when you are hungry." If chili was not appealing, there were other black-owned eateries to choose from such as Davis Eat Shop, operated by Willa Davis Cross, "proprietress." The Domestic Life Building, located at 601 Walnut Street, alone housed the offices of dentist P. O. Sweeny; T. Lomax Nichols, M.D.; the Ray and Hawes Agency, realtors; and the Service Drug

Company. The comings and goings of black Louisville were reported in the *Louisville Defender*, the *Louisville News*, and the *Louisville Leader*, which advertised itself saying, "It Champions your cause . . . it prints your news . . . [and] it employs your people."[5] As James Syndor put it, "You could find *everything* you wanted on that street. You could make some fast money and you could go broke. You could get entertained, get embalmed and get fed."[6]

In Harlem, there was 125th Street; in Memphis, there was Beale Street. In Louisville, Walnut Street was no less vital in the lives of African Americans. According to migrant George D. Wilson, there was a saying in Louisville "that if one would just stand 'by the corner' long enough, any person he or she wished to see would pass by."[7] Although whites would often come downtown to "see the sights," as Goldie Winstead-Beckett, a migrant from Hopkins County, Kentucky, recalled, Walnut Street was a "haven," a safe place, where blacks could "go and be free after work." After their arrival in Louisville, the Becketts purchased A. B. Ridley Funeral Home, located in the heart of the black community at Eleventh and Walnut. Although clearly tinged by nostalgia, Goldie Beckett spoke for many blacks when she noted that times spent in the "Old Walnut Street district . . . were the happiest days of my life."[8]

In less than ten years, the Church of Our Merciful Saviour and the Mammoth Life Insurance Company would be the only buildings left standing within the Walnut Street district. By 1968, there were 150 fewer black-owned businesses in Louisville than in 1942, although the black population had nearly doubled.[9] Monte Edwards and Tommie Burns, both migrants from Mississippi, were two of the few black entrepreneurs left in the city. The destruction of the Walnut Street business district was the result of a combination of factors: the integration of public accommodations, suburbanization, and urban renewal. Integration had the unintended consequence of undermining black business. Before integration, Red Cross Hospital was sustained by the fact that, except for the emergency room at General Hospital, African Americans had no access to white hospitals. They patronized Louisville's small black clinics and Red Cross not just because they wanted to, but because they had no other choice. Red Cross consistently drew black patients from the surrounding counties as well. Between 1951 and 1953, 457 out-of-town patients used the facilities at Red Cross; many of them, like Elizabeth Roberts, were from small towns, such as Bardstown, Kentucky, without black doctors. As Dr. C. Milton Young, a migrant from Nashville and a member of the hospital staff, recalled, "When white hospitals opened to blacks . . . it [Red Cross Hospital] just faded away."[10]

It is important, however, not to overstate the significance of integration in the demise of black business in Louisville. First, blacks had always patronized white establishments to some extent. There were no black-owned grocery stores comparable to Kroger, A & P, or even Winn-Dixie. In fact, the 1961 "Nothing New for Easter" campaign revealed that despite their preference not to shop at businesses that "Jim Crowed" them, many did just that. And second, while Louisville's newly integrated hospitals were clearly an improvement over Red Cross in terms of medical equipment and financial resources, white funeral homes, restaurants, bars, and taverns were not necessarily perceived as better.

In Louisville, the struggle for open housing was intimately linked to urban renewal, the demise of Walnut Street, and the creation of a "ghetto." This was not what Arnold R. Hirsch termed the "making of the second ghetto," but the creation of one where it had not existed before.[11] While blacks in Louisville clearly confronted residential segregation before, they had not experienced the degree of spatial isolation, the lack of community and social resources, or the grinding poverty ushered in by urban renewal and white flight. Walnut Street's importance to African Americans should not be viewed as a nostalgic look backward toward a "golden age" of the ghetto; rather, it is simply a recognition that urban renewal created conditions that were fundamentally different in kind and scale from what they had confronted previously. As the black population grew, city planners slated entire communities for renewal. As housing conditions worsened, open housing became of paramount importance as a civil rights issue linking the issues of freedom and equality, urban renewal and ghettoization, and migration in the minds of many African Americans.

The process that would culminate in urban renewal, or "Negro Removal," began before World War II ended. In 1943 Mayor Wilson W. Wyatt established the Louisville Area Development Association (LADA) to manage the city's and Jefferson County's postwar economic development. Led by the mayor and comprised of local businessmen, labor leaders, and city and county government officials, LADA sought to preserve wartime economic advances, avoid postwar unemployment, and rebuild deteriorating public facilities. During its eight-year life, LADA essentially plotted the future of Louisville by developing extensive plans for population trends, economic growth, education, the fine arts, pubic health, housing, parks and recreation, streets and highways, and public transportation. In the 1950s LADA laid the groundwork for every major urban renewal project of the 1960s, including the construction of expressways, the building of a medical center, and a series of housing projects. Although LADA planned these projects, local leaders believed a new organization was necessary to implement them. In 1950 the LADA merged with the Louisville Board of Trade, the Retail Merchants Association, and the Louisville Convention and Publicity Association to form the Louisville Chamber of Commerce, which in turn funneled its plans through the Louisville and Jefferson County Planning and Zoning Commission.[12] On one hand, the elite members of LADA and the Louisville Chamber of Commerce could be viewed as visionaries who had the foresight to plan in the best interests of the city; on the other, they could be seen as subverting the democratic process by planning the future of the city and its inhabitants without their consent.

Yet the LADA and urban renewal were made possible by the National Housing Acts of 1933 and 1934 and the Housing Act of 1937, which created the Federal Housing Administration (FHA) and the low-rent public housing program directed by the Public Housing Administration. The 1937 act also made possible the establishment of the Louisville Housing Commission. Nationally, urban renewal began in 1949 with the passage of the Federal Housing Act, authorizing federal assistance for slum clearance. By 1950, when Kentucky passed the state law enabling cities to undertake urban renewal projects, LADA already had eight years of planning civic projects. A series of amendments in 1954, 1956, 1957, 1959, and 1961 authorized slum clearance and relocation payments, sought to prevent the spread of slums through rehabilitation and conservation, and increased federal funding, which permitted local government to pool its resources for urban renewal projects.[13] In short, urban renewal was a federally funded means for city planners to redevelop abandoned, vacant, or "blighted" property.

In the pamphlet, "Urban Renewal?" the Urban Renewal and Community Agency proclaimed its mission was to "improve Louisville" and to "stop" blight and decay. For the Urban Renewal Commission, as neighborhoods deteriorated to the "point of no return," renewal became a necessity fueled by "the natural increase in population," the in-migration of a "formerly rural population," and the growth of urbanization.[14] During the ten years between 1950 and 1960, Louisville's black population grew three times as fast as the white population.[15] Between 1957 and 1962, the city approved four different urban renewal projects. The first began in 1957, when voters accepted a $5 million bond that paved the way for the start of various renewal projects. Two years later the Urban Renewal Commission described the first project as an "effort to revitalize our city areas which are decaying, and prevent good areas from starting to decay. . . . The objectives of urban renewal are simple:

Architects John H. Bickel and A. B. McCulloch receive an award for their design of the Village West, West Downtown redevelopment project, 1965. Typically, residents in redevelopment areas were excluded from the planning process. © *Louisville Courier-Journal.*

to clear or rehabilitate slum and blighted areas; to rehouse those displaced into standard accommodations; and to rebuild the cleared areas for productive and desirable uses."[16]

The first renewal project was characterized by wholesale demolition, where newly cleared sites remained vacant for extended periods of time. The effort to redevelop "blighted" areas led to the construction of streets, sewers, and running water in some of Louisville's black communities for the first time. The Southwick Redevelopment Project, approved in 1960, concentrated on a primarily African American community bounded by Dumesnil Street, Shawnee Park, Thirty-fourth Street, and Bohn Avenue. Within this 49-acre zone, houses, churches, and businesses were slated for demolition and replacement by the Cotter Homes housing project, parks, and schools. In 1965 it was followed by Southwick II, a 38-acre site whose borders were Young Avenue to the Louisville and Nashville Railroad tracks, Thirty-second Street, and Thirty-fourth Street. The East Downtown Renewal Area and the West Downtown Renewal Area were both approved in 1962 and intended to work in tandem as "buffer zones on the east and west sides of the downtown business core."[17] Second Street, Broadway Street, Jackson Street, and Jefferson Street bound the East project. Officially known as the Medical Center, the 215-acre site paved the way for the construction of the University of Louisville medical campus, hospitals, motels, and office buildings. Meanwhile, the West project, commonly known as the Civic Center Project, became the site for city, state, county, and federal office buildings, including the courthouse and county jail. The site extended from Second Street to Fifteenth Street and from Broadway to Market Street, encompassing the Walnut Street business district. For the Urban Renewal Commission, these projects represented an attempt to save downtown "by breaking the strangling noose of blight and slum that has surrounded the core of the city."[18]

Black business owner Joseph Hammond spoke for black Louisville as a whole when he said, "The clearing of Walnut vandalized the social fabric of the black community."[19] The city's efforts to "quarantine blight" amounted to little more than a systematic process by which African Americans were pushed out of downtown. Black businesses suffered the brunt of urban renewal, since few blacks could afford to relocate and those who did confronted the difficulties of finding a new home in a segregated housing market. Goldie Beckett recalled that during the height of urban renewal, her business—Beckett Funeral Home—stood on a razed block surrounded by rubble. Like many black entrepreneurs unable to relocate, she was forced to sell the funeral home and auction off its equipment. When her spacious

Urban renewal devastated black businesses in the Walnut Street business district, including the Calas cleaners, which was forced to close in 1974. © *Louisville Courier-Journal.*

four-bedroom home at 1024–26 West Walnut Street was consumed by urban renewal, she packed her belongings and moved to Philadelphia, after living in Louisville for nearly thirty years.[20]

As Goldie Beckett's personal history suggests, urban renewal affected not only black businesses but also the black community as a whole. Urban renewal intensified the housing shortage in Louisville. Although the Urban Renewal Commission recognized that limited housing was a "severe problem for negroes," the few public housing units it created to alleviate this problem were little more than a stopgap measure. Nor did African Americans have a legitimate voice in the process of urban renewal. When public hearings were held, they were most often to inform blacks of what would happen to their homes and businesses, rather than to solicit their input to the process. Because blacks overwhelmingly lived in Louisville's poorest neighborhoods, displacement mainly impacted those with the least social and economic resources to challenge urban renewal or to shape it to suit their own interests. In the Southwick Redevelopment area, for instance, the project displaced 333 African American families, but only 1 white family.[21] Although blacks represented more than 85 percent of the people dislocated by "slum" clearance, the city relocated less than 30 percent of the families so displaced.[22]

While it is easy enough to note that 333 families were displaced, it is much harder to fathom what that meant for African Americans in those communities. In the Southwick Redevelopment area, nearly every building was razed. New Ark Baptist Church and Pleasant View Baptist Church were among the ten congregations whose place of worship were destroyed.[23] Businesses, such as the filling station at the corner of Thirty-fourth Street and Southwick Avenue, were gutted and torn down along with hundreds of homes in the area. After decades in the city, migrants like William Carter, Louise Cobb, and Paul Floyd were all forced to leave the homes they owned along Kirby Avenue. Carter, from Tennessee, had been a resident for twenty-five years when his home at 3618 Kirby Avenue was destroyed; Louise and Harris Cobb were thirty years removed from their prior home in Alabama, while Floyd had relocated to Louisville from Georgia twenty years earlier. Others, such as Tennessee migrant Corine Baskett, faced the difficulty of finding a new place to rent as a single mother of two on her income as a domestic worker.[24]

The influx of African American migrants into the city exacerbated the housing pressures. As more and more blacks crowded into the River City, they found less housing available; the housing that was available was often more segregated. As African Americans struggled to cope with overcrowding, entire black neighborhoods were torn down to "make way" for the Med-

According to the Integration Steering Committee, the Saratoga Restaurant was one of a few remaining segregated establishments on June 1, 1964. © *Louisville Courier-Journal.*

ical Center, the Civic Center, new businesses, and parking lots.[25] In what University of Louisville sociologists Scott Cummings and Michael Price called "classic patterns of 'invasion' and 'succession,'" African Americans turned toward the adjacent, less densely populated white neighborhoods in the West End to meet their housing needs.

In a speech she delivered to the Louisville section of the National Council of Jewish Women, Murray Walls—on behalf of the Human Relations Committee and the NAACP—described the nature of housing for blacks in the city. Walls pointed out that racial discrimination created a separate housing market for African Americans. For those with the desire and resources to buy a new home, there were only two alternatives: either stay in an already crowded area or try to expand into the areas not currently open to them. It became apparent that "no money was available to Negroes wanting to build houses east of 18th Street."[26] Instead, the greatest expansion of African American home ownership was in the neighborhoods directly south and west of Broadway. In a similar speech, Human Relations Committee member Frederick William Woolsey argued that African Americans "found that the only freedom of choice that existed for them was between one home in the West End and another in the West End."[27] However, as Murray Walls discovered, "When the Negro began to expand, if one family entered a block [occupied by whites], for sale signs would go up all along the street. There was panic selling at its worst."[28] Whites often responded to their new black neighbors by "fleeing" to the suburbs in Jefferson County. Although restrictive residential covenants were deemed unconstitutional, many blacks, like Andrew Wade, detected the presence of an "unspoken restrictive covenant"—meaning that few blacks could expect to find housing in Louisville's suburbs.[29]

For African Americans in Louisville, as elsewhere in the nation, urban renewal became synonymous with "Negro Removal." Historians have demonstrated that through the complex interplay of African American migration, federally financed programs of urban renewal and interstate highway construction, the Home Owners Loan Corporation (HOLC) and the FHA, real estate practices, and white flight to suburbia, blacks were trapped in increasingly deteriorating inner cities. In cities such as Atlanta, Richmond, Miami, Cincinnati, and Chicago, suburbanization and urban renewal combined to create what many historians have termed the "second ghetto."[30] Increasingly, poor whites and people of color were spatially isolated in inner cities surrounded by a suburban ring existing as a residential haven for a more affluent and mostly white population.

Middle-class black homes along "Teachers' Row" bore the brunt of urban renewal along Chestnut Street. © *Louisville Courier-Journal.*

While in other cities urban renewal and white flight combined to make the "second ghetto," this was not the case in Louisville. Instead, for many blacks white flight and urban renewal created a ghetto where one did not exist before. Residential segregation in the River City was enforced by custom rather than by law. Whereas Atlanta and other cities used zoning laws to spatially contain its black population, no such laws were enacted in Louisville.[31] Although African Americans were clearly segregated and forced to accept the city's worst housing stock, until the 1960s they lived in a number of enclaves throughout the downtown area. In Louisville residential discrimination was more of a "checker board" or a "layer cake" than the continuous ghetto that existed for blacks in Chicago and Cincinnati, for example. Since middle-class African Americans were no more immune to the realities of residential segregation than those in poverty, many black neighborhoods were more economically diverse than they would become over time. Blacks in Louisville commonly lived in close proximity to whites, albeit on racial homogenous blocks or streets. For instance, in the more prosperous Highlands, located in the East End, a few small pockets of blacks lived in the overwhelmingly white section. Although a number of them resided along Yale Drive, they were unable to buy homes on the adjoining Douglas Boulevard. On Hite Avenue, there was a cluster of "modest new homes" next to an older black neighborhood; however, realtors and white homeowners refused to sell African Americans homes on Brownsboro Road, which was connected to it.[32]

African American expansion into the West End was fueled by demands for better housing and the practices of a number of Louisville realtors. As Murray Walls explained in her speech to the National Council of Jewish Women, real estate agents took advantage of the segregated housing market to "make hay while the sun shines," despite a "Code of Ethics" that prohibited them from changing the racial character of a neighborhood. In a practice known as "blockbusting," realtors opened segregated housing to African Americans. Blockbusting played upon whites' fear of a black residential "takeover" by selling a single African American a home on a white block with the understanding that whites would leave in response. Newly vacated homes would then be sold to African Americans at a price much higher than realtors initially paid for them. Often entire blocks would undergo the transition from white to black in a matter of months. At the same time that blacks expanded into the West End housing market block by block, a larger sectoral pattern of residential segregation emerged.[33]

Despite the presence of a few East End settlements along Yale Drive and Hite Avenue, African Americans increasingly found the only housing available to them was west of Eighteenth Street. When urban renewal kicked into high gear, they were forced from the central city as businesses, apartments, and houses, including the prestigious Teachers' Row, were deemed blighted and removed. In a brief history of segregation in Louisville, Vernon Robertson argued that blacks "were carefully contained by what seems to be an overall plan to limit Negro housing to an extension of the central areas going toward the west end."[34] The process of ghettoization ensnared all African Americans, including many with the resources to buy quality housing. When Ruth Bryant and her family arrived in Louisville from Tulsa, Oklahoma, the only available housing was in the Du Valle section of Southwick,

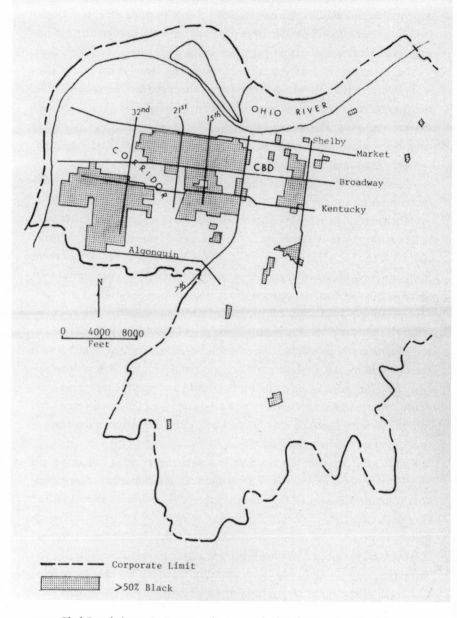

MAP 2 Black Population, 1960. By 1960, urban renewal, white flight, and residential segregation began to create a "ghetto" where one did not previously exist. Courtesy of John L. Anderson and the University of Louisville Archives and Records Center.

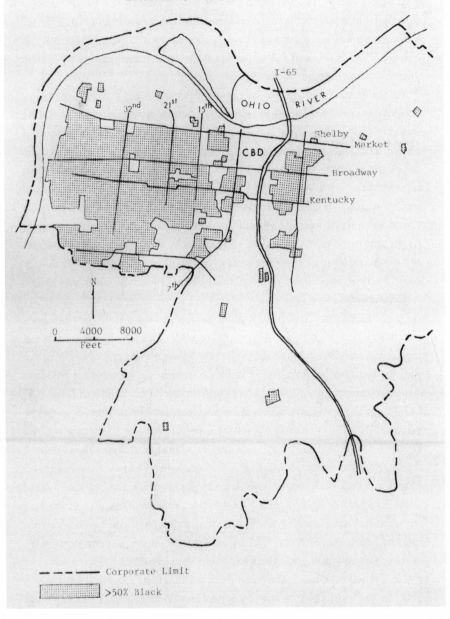

MAP 3 Black Population, 1970. Comparing the distribution of the black population in 1950–60 to that in 1970 shows clearly increasing residential segregation. Courtesy of John L. Anderson and the University of Louisville Archives and Records Center.

an area where pigs ran freely and outdoor toilets were the norm. There was "nowhere to move" until they were able to purchase a two-story house on 27th Street and West Jefferson from two white women in a neighborhood tipping from white to black.[35] For African Americans searching for a better home, there was "no chance of buying a single house outside the established pattern."[36] As black journalist William Ealy put it some years later, "These ghettos are nothing but Indian Reservations."[37]

As residential segregation increased, open housing became a pressing civil rights concern. The fight against residential segregation in Louisville was about more than the ability to buy a nice home in the neighborhood of choice. The goal of African Americans was not to get closer to white people, but to get closer to equality. Blacks saw open housing as an opportunity to transform the urban landscape by challenging the boundaries of margin and inclusion. Here, blacks demonstrated a "collective imagination" that produced a vision of what the city could be, one that was radically different from its present or its past. Blacks had the hope, the dream of equality, that necessitated the struggle for open housing and against ghettoization. In Louisville, as across the nation, they acted on the belief that they could "make their world anew."[38]

While many historians have applied Jacquelyn Dowd Hall's powerful notion of the "long civil rights movement" to understand the linkages between the activism of the 1950s and 1960s to the "civil rights unionism" of the 1930s, the emphasis on "civil rights" struggles obscures the even longer freedom struggles initiated by African Americans themselves.[39] Blacks in Louisville fought against residential segregation and for the hope of transforming the urban landscape to suit their interests throughout the twentieth century. The Louisville branch of the NAACP was organized in 1914 to oppose a residential segregation ordinance prohibiting blacks and whites from buying homes on blocks in which their race was not already the majority, and that opposition culminated in the 1917 Supreme Court case *Warley v. Buchanan*. In the late 1930s African Americans such as E. E. Pruitt, manager of the Beecher Terrace housing project, and Murray Walls, then a tenant selection supervisor, simultaneously fought alongside the NAACP and the Urban League to ensure that blacks gained equal consideration during the construction of Louisville's first housing projects.[40] In the 1950s, Andrew Wade and P. O. Sweeny were among a handful of blacks who risked their lives in an attempt to buy a home outside the "established pattern."

The open housing campaign of the later 1960s was a direct descendant of earlier struggles initiated by blacks in the city; however, in the context of urban renewal open housing took on even greater importance. In seeking equal access to housing, blacks also sought to fundamentally alter the boundaries of race and class throughout the city. Open housing served as a way to gain access to better schools and employment opportunities. It also represented the African American vision of a radically different urban landscape from the one pictured by either municipal government or local whites. Blacks did not fight for integration just for the privilege of sitting next to whites in darkened theaters, or of buying a home next door to whites. As Amelia B. Ray aptly put it: "What we don't want is laws saying what I can't do. Don't fence me in."[41] Not only did black migrants protest being "fenced in" both literally and figuratively, but as Frank Stanley Jr., a leader in the open housing campaign, argued: "Louisville's racial practices represented paradoxical inconsistencies," and African Americans were "tired of patience and meaningless promises."[42] Dr. Maurice Rabb, an NAACP member who fought restrictive covenants in Shelbyville, Kentucky, prior to his arrival in Louisville, explained that many blacks believed open housing was the solution to "all our problems."[43] His vision of a different future was echoed by Murray Walls, who maintained: "So long as people live in isolation as we do . . . our schools will remain segregated, our churches will remain segregated, our young people will grow up the one with a belief in his superiority, the other with a badge of inferiority."[44]

In 1957, the local NAACP sued the Louisville Municipal Housing Commission on behalf of twelve plaintiffs who were challenging the doctrine of "separate but equal." Even though blacks received a fair share of public housing, Louisville's projects were segregated. The NAACP forced the commission to adopt a plan of "gradual integration," but four years later less than 1 percent of public housing was integrated. Clearly, the city placed its emphasis on *gradual* rather than on integration. The Municipal Housing Commission refused to "compel a White applicant against his wishes to occupy a unit in a project which is occupied predominantly by Negro tenants."[45] Once again, blacks found that reliance on white Louisvillians' willingness to "voluntarily" desegregate provided no remedy. As members of Mayor Hoblitzell's public accommodations emergency committee, Murray Walls and Maurice Rabb urged the mayor to confront the African American housing crisis in Louisville, asserting that "we must not condone discrimination . . . and confine Negroes to a ghetto."[46]

The struggle against residential segregation from 1962 to 1967 was markedly different from prior attempts to obtain open housing. First, like the fight for the public accommodations ordinance, the battle for open housing during 1962–67 was characterized by increasing militancy among African Americans. Second, it focused on the private housing market rather than on public housing. Lastly, for the first time the protest movement involved more than a handful of whites. Ultimately, the effort to end residential segregation was led by the Human Relations Commission (HRC) and the Committee on Open Housing (COH), an African American organization created in 1966 to obtain an open housing ordinance.

Created in June 1962, the HRC was a moderate civil rights agency composed of a majority of liberal whites, including the chairman, Monsignor Alfred, president of Bellarmine College; Rose Tarbis, a member of the Urban League and the Council of Jewish Women; Ray Bixler, head of the Psychology Department at the University of Louisville; Dorcas Ruthenburg, a playwright and writer for the *Louisville Courier-Journal*; and Mansir Tydings, the executive director. Increasing numbers of white Louisvillians began to speak out in favor of opening housing and through the HRC assumed an important role in the effort to secure an open housing ordinance as negotiators with the mayor's office and the Board of Aldermen. According to one estimate of white activists' support of open housing, nearly 20 percent of the protest marchers were white. However, few of these white supporters were active members of the COH. Although white participation was not solicited, the presence of white marchers (Anne Braden, Eric Tachau, Charles Tachau, an insurance agent and Episcopal minister from St. George's Church, and Henry Wallace, a member of the Kentucky Civil Liberties Union) was important because the COH believed it was imperative that the open housing movement not be viewed as a "black rebellion," but a concern of whites as well.[47] Given the context of urban unrest such as the Watts Uprising in 1964 and the growth of Black Power politics in organizations ranging from the Student Nonviolent Coordinating Committee to the Black Panthers, as well as the racial violence of the Birmingham church bombing and Bloody Sunday in Selma, Alabama, white participation dispelled fears of a black rebellion in Louisville. At the same time it allowed many whites in the city to maintain the decades-old illusion that Louisville was a leader in race relations despite its rapidly eroding progressive veneer.

Liberal whites in the HRC were joined by a small number of African Americans, including Frank Stanley Sr., editor of the *Louisville Defender*; Lois Morris, a migrant from Mississippi who served on the Urban League Women's Committee, the League of Women Voters, and the first Kentucky Commission on Human Relations; Murray Walls, a veteran of the efforts to desegregate Louisville's public libraries; and Maurice Rabb, an NAACP member who was active in numerous desegregation campaigns. As its long-term goal, the HRC sought improved interracial; relations that would ultimately end discrimination in Louisville. HRC members viewed their mission as promoting and securing mutual understanding and respect among the city's various religious, racial, and ethnic groups. Unlike the COH, the HRC, as a government agency, had neither the option nor the desire to conduct protests or demonstrations to achieve its goal; rather, it would act as a negotiator in interracial controversies.[48]

Although the HRC had already begun to discuss the open housing issue, in 1964 the West End Community Council (WECC) urged the HRC to actively endorse an open housing ordinance. The WECC was organized in May 1963 by native Louisvillian Anne Braden as a group of white and blacks citizens working to "keep the West End a balanced community, neither all Negro nor all white." In an effort to stabilize desegregating communities, the WECC sponsored art, theater, and musical programs to unite the West End community. It directly challenged white flight through an "I'm Not Moving" campaign in which members like Ruth Bryant went door-to-door educating West End residents on integrated housing. In distributing placards labeled "House Not for Sale" and "Well, I'm Not Moving," they attempted to create a markedly different vision of Louisville's urban landscape from their white neighbors who had fled to the suburbs of Jefferson County.[49] Although the organizer of the WECC, Braden acknowledged that her communist reputation could potentially harm the council and so assumed a background role in its work. Instead, African Americans such as Hulbert James, Gladdis Carter, head of the West End YWCA, and Ruth Bryant became the primary spokespersons for the group.

Bryant's activism in Louisville was closely linked to her experiences elsewhere in the South. As a junior at Fisk University in Nashville, she had participated in a housing survey of the local black community. Bryant remembered that it was the "first time I saw rock bottom housing. I didn't know people lived like that: no furniture, eating out of tin cans—dirtsville. It began to depress me and it changed my mind about social work. There was always a guilt complex 'cause I knew what was there and hadn't done anything." For Bryant, her activities for the WECC and the COH linked the lives of blacks in Louisville with those in Nashville.

On June 25, 1964, the HRC endorsed a fair housing plan. The proposal was drafted by Harry S. McAlpin, a black barrister and former migrant, and approved by the HRC before submission to the Board of Aldermen. The proposed ordinance outlawed the refusal to sell, rent, or lease housing on the basis of race, religion, or national origin; the false representation of homes or apartments as unavailable when they, in fact, were available; and racial discrimination in the terms, conditions, or privileges of any property deal. It also provided fines of up to one hundred dollars for noncompliance. The HRC soon discovered, however, that such an ordinance would receive little support from City Hall. Not only was the document unpopular among many white Louisvillians, but also Mayor Cowger refused to comment on the proposal, the Louisville Area Board of Realtors openly condemned it, and the members of the Board of Aldermen indicated they would vote against it.

As the aldermen considered the proposed ordinance, the HRC conducted a number of surveys on housing, including "What Happens to Property Values in Integrated Urban Housing" and "Facts for Action." Collectively, these studies examined the population trends in the West End and contradicted popular discourse suggesting property values fell as blacks moved into formerly white neighborhoods. At the same time, studies conducted by Ray Bixler demonstrated that, due to segregated housing, African Americans were increasingly concentrated in a narrow corridor extending throughout the West End along Walnut and Jefferson streets. The HRC hoped that, by publicizing the results of their surveys, public opinion might be swayed in favor of an open housing ordinance.[50] But their findings only further inflamed a white community already incensed over the issue. According to one historian, the fact that the HRC actually thought the studies would sway public opinion only "illustrates the Commission's naïve belief that education and discussion of the issue would gain acceptance of an ordinance among the [white] population."[51]

Since they expected the Board of Alderman to reject the proposed ordinance, the HRC decided to focus its energies on a voluntary approach to open housing, with the understanding that it could work for an enforceable fair housing ordinance in the future. In September 1964, the HRC drafted the "Declaration of the Principles of the Freedom of Residence." Under its terms, the Louisville Area Board of Realtors, financial institutions, and other real estate organizations would agree to sell, lease, or rent property without regard to race, creed, color, or national origin. The HRC combined the declaration with a proposed ordinance creating a seven-member panel to process racial discrimination complaints through negotiation and arbitration. The panel would consist of representatives from the Board of Realtors, the Home Builders Association, the Louisville League of Loan Associations, the Louisville Real Estate Brokers, and the HRC. The mayor, the Board of Aldermen, and the Board of Realtors all supported the proposal. Maurice Rabb cast the only vote against it, calling the plan "toothless."

On August 25, 1965, the Board of Aldermen passed the ordinance. However, it was not long before the HRC realized the accuracy of Rabb's critique. In a report submitted to Republican mayor Kenneth Schmied, elected in March 1965, the commission concluded: "A SERIOUS PROBLEM EXISTS NOW AND THERE IS NO EVIDENCE WHATSOEVER TO SUPPORT THE BELIEF THAT THE DECLARATION OF PRINCIPLES HAS HAD ANY SIGNIFICANT EFFECT UPON THE PRACTICE OF REAL ESTATE AGENTS, INCLUDING REALTORS, OR UPON THE PRACTICE OF INDIVIDUAL OWNERS."[52] In early August, the HRC expressed its "deep frustration" with the ordinance in the *Louisville Courier-Journal*:

> The commission can handle complaints about racial discrimination in housing through negotiations only. If the accused person refuses to negotiate, there is nothing the commission can do about it. The commission has no subpoena powers and there are no enforcement provisions in the ordinance. It contains a declaration of principles aimed at freedom of housing, which has been endorsed by real-estate, home-loan, and other organizations in the housing industry.[53]

Mrs. William Flarshiem, chairman of a commission panel empowered to hear complaints, lamented: "It's a lost sound of fury signifying nothing."[54]

The HRC came to realize the necessity of a "law with some teeth in it." When Mayor Schmied refused to seek a stronger ordinance, African Americans founded the COH in March 1966 to organize a protest movement seeking an open housing statute. Although a few whites, including Ray Bixler, served on the committee, the COH was primarily a black organization. Its leaders were Reverend A. D. King, a recent arrival in the River City, who was pastor of the Zion Baptist Church and the brother of Martin Luther King Jr.; Reverend W. J. Hodge of the NAACP; Hulbert James, executive director of the WECC; and Reverend Leo Lesser, president of the Greater Louisville Area AME Ministerial Alliance. The COH served as a lobbyist group for fair housing as the HRC began to draft a new, enforceable, open housing ordinance.

Concurrently, the COH drafted an open housing ordinance of its own. On September 13, 1966, representatives of the Kentucky Christian Leadership Conference, the WECC, and the NAACP presented the Board of Aldermen with a proposal for an enforceable ordinance, calling for fines of up to five hundred dollars and jail sentences. The aldermen promised to give the plan "due consideration." Since it would only have jurisdiction within the city of

Louisville, leaving the surrounding suburbs open to residential segregation, the COH submitted the same proposal to the Jefferson County Fiscal Court on October 3. But county attorney E. P. Sawyer claimed that the court was not empowered by the state to enact such legislation. Four days, later the HRC approved an open housing ordinance that was essentially the same as the COH draft. The COH abandoned its own document and concentrated on the passage of the HRC proposal.[55]

Despite its pledge to do so, the Board of Aldermen had yet to consider the open housing proposal in December 1966. In an effort to spur City Hall into action, the COH sent a telegram to the U.S. Department of Housing and Urban Development (HUD) on December 12 stating that it would oppose Louisville's attempt to obtain federal aid as a Model City until the city enacted enforceable open housing legislation. The Model Cities Program was created by President Lyndon B. Johnson to fund the removal of urban blight. After attending Fisk University's Race Relations Institute in 1963, Ruth Bryant encountered activists who were using federal dollars for Model Cities as a lever in the fight for open housing. Her hope was that Louisville would pass an open housing ordinance rather than lose federal funding. As Bryant recalled, "Louisville was a model city looking to get another year of funding. Lots of money and careers were riding on this."[56] On behalf of COH, Reverend Hodge enlisted the support of the national NAACP in an attempt to sway Dr. Robert Weaver, secretary of HUD, to "hold allocations to Louisville's model cities application until fair housing is passed."[57] While it is unclear whether COH's request ever reached the desk of Robert Weaver, barely two weeks later, on December 27, the proposed bill received its first reading by the Board of Aldermen.

At that same meeting, J. W. "Boots" Young, president of the Board of Aldermen, proposed that several hearings on open housing be held throughout the city to "get a pulse of the people on it."[58] On January 17, 1967, Young announced that the board had settled on six hearings. In what was a clear recipe for failure, the first hearing was scheduled for February 2 at Southern Junior High, "in the heart of the area most opposed to open housing."[59] The hearing degenerated into a debacle. The Board of Aldermen insisted on conducting the hearings without discussion of any potential changes to the bill. Opponents of open housing jeered and booed the ten people who spoke in favor of the ordinance. Meanwhile, the Louisville Board of Realtors publicly denounced what it termed "forced housing," claiming that it would "take away the right from the owner to sell to whom he pleased."[60] The hearing at Southern Junior High proved to be the first and the last.

On February 14, the HRC presented the Board of Aldermen with a revised ordinance in response to the "concerns" Mayor Schmied raised about the "broad powers" of enforcement given to the HRC. The HRC revisions eliminated jail sentences and fines for noncompliance; they also exempted from the ordinance property sold by individuals (as opposed to realtors). Under the new proposal, a committee appointed by the mayor and the circuit court judge would handle discrimination complaints. Not surprisingly, the HRC revisions drew criticism from both sides of the issue. The mayor let it be known that no action would be taken on the plan while there were demonstrations or even the threat of demonstrations. The Board of Realtors protested that the noncoverage of homes sold by individuals would discourage people from using real estate agents. Neville Tucker, an African American lawyer and a member of COH, denounced the revised bill as "totally ineffective." In reality, it was no better than the earlier declaration advocated by the HRC.

As a moderate civil rights agency, the HRC found itself wedged between the opponents of open housing and an increasingly militant group of open housing supporters. Even though more radical members of the HRC, such as Murray Walls and Maurice Rabb, increasingly urged the commission to adopt a more activist strategy, as a whole the HRC refused, arguing that its governmental mandate did not extend beyond the conference room. Although neither the mayor nor the Board of Aldermen demonstrated any support for a fair housing ordinance, Chairman Alfred Horrigan remained convinced that its passage would come through arbitration and discussion rather than direct action. The HRC seemed unable or unwilling to acknowledge that an appeal to the conscience of white Louisvillians would not result in equal treatment, much less an open housing law.[61]

From this point on there was a decided split between the HRC and the COH. The rift stemmed not only from a disagreement in strategy, but also from a fundamental difference in their reading of race and racism in the River City. The HRC refused to acknowledge the depth of white Louisvillians' commitment to white supremacy. Here, the state in the form of municipal government and white "hecklers" through their "defensive localism" were wedded in their resistance to open housing. The COH totally rejected the HRC's revisions and warned, if the open housing ordinance was not passed, they would initiate a campaign of nonviolent direct action to pressure city officials to act. At the request of the COH, five field representatives of the Southern Christian Leadership Conference (SCLC) arrived in Louisville directly from "Operation Breadbasket," the Chicago open housing campaign, to help organize and prepare activists for demonstrations. Although historians have not devoted the same attention to southern cities like Louisville, concurrent open housing campaigns in Cicero, Illinois, and New York, were all equally important to the SCLC. Martin Luther King's presence in the city, along with the SCLC field representatives, forged an important link between Louisville's local movement and the national civil rights movement.

The arrival of the five SCLC representatives prompted the HRC to speak out against the plan to demonstrate, as well as against the SCLC associates and the COH itself. Led by Harry S. McAlpin of the HRC, eighteen African Americans released a statement denouncing the COH and its SCLC representatives. The statement included the signatures of Felix Anderson, pastor and former state representative, and Frank Stanley Sr., editor of the *Louisville Defender*, which provided only limited coverage to the open housing demonstrations. In part, the statement read:

> The threat by imported "Civil Rights Leaders," with the approval of a handful of Louisville residents, some of very recent origin, to loose chickens in the streets, dump garbage in front of City Hall, parade in tense areas, and demonstrate for open housing or open hell has aroused the better-thinking, more responsible elements of our community, both white and black, to publicly express our disagreement and detachment from any such procedure. This may sound like division among civil rights and interested groups and persons. And it is! But despite the disadvantages that may accompany an open split, we believe it to be harmful to our community for us to remain quiet and give the appearance of unity behind such irresponsible proposals. . . . We deplore demonstrations for the sake of demonstrating. We deplore demonstrations designed to make work for itinerant rabble-rousers who disrupt a community, accomplish nothing, and move on. . . . We anticipate because we are now expressing disagreement and detachment from irresponsible demonstration proposals, we will be called Uncle Toms. As erroneous as such a connotation is, we would prefer that to being Tom Fools.[62]

The next day the *Courier-Journal* showed a photograph of Commissioner Bishop Tucker pointing a finger at Reverend A. D. King labeling him an "outsider."[63] The statement eerily echoed the mayor, who claimed that the open housing activists were little more than a bunch of "uppity negroes" led by "outside agitators." Ironically, Felix Anderson and Tucker were migrants themselves, albeit not of "recent origin." However, the issue might have signaled differences in strategy as much as the consternation an older generation of activists might have felt as a new group of activists stepped to the forefront of the black protest movement.

Regardless of the motivation, Reverend Hodge stated that many COH members found the statement "unnecessary, offensive, insulting and directed at the wrong persons."[64] On February 28, the committee released a biting rebuke, asserting:

> The committee on open housing is pleased that the board of aldermen is moving forward on an open housing bill. . . . The ordinance is little more than the existing resolution calling for voluntary compliance. . . . We are pleased to have heard from the so-called better thinking Negroes of the community, stating their willingness to accept this token ordinance. We are, however, disillusioned that they would knowingly betray the Negro. Their statement that there are those of us who wish to demonstrate for the sake of demonstrations is of course a flat lie. We have stated repeatedly that demonstrations would be our last resort. We have maintained our patience and restraint since August of last year. . . . We will continue to press forward for true equality and we will not be deterred by those of lesser strength.[65]

For some open housing advocates, the distinction between negotiation and direct action was less stark than either COH or its African American opponents would suggest. Although he had participated in the public accommodations marches, E. Deedom Alston viewed himself as more of a negotiator during the open housing fight. He chose not to demonstrate because "I am a quick reactor: If you hit me, I'm going to hit you back, so I did not want to expose myself to this type of activism." For Alston, activism and negotiation were two sides of the same coin. Activism was a tool used to facilitate negotiation. With an apt analogy, he explained: "Were it not for activism negotiation could never have been accomplished. If you see me point the gun [at you] and though I leave it back at the car, though you know it's pointed at you, I don't have to say anything about the gun, you see it pointed at you."[66] African Americans like Alston believed that black protest demonstrations were the "gun" that would make the task of negotiating with the Board of Aldermen and the mayor that much easier.

The COH advocated a series of amendments to the HRC proposal that it believed would ensure that African Americans secured an enforceable ordinance. These amendments included extending coverage to all housing and conferring enforcement powers on the HRC that would enable it to freeze a property transaction while an investigation was pending. At the same time the COH initiated a series of demonstrations protesting residential segregation. Throughout the remainder of March the COH launched over eleven marches and protests. On March 12, more than 650 delegates of the NAACP attending a regional convention of association branches marched on City Hall in support of open housing. The following day, the COH conducted the first of three marches outside the homes of white aldermen and that of Joseph Krieger, a South End insurance agent and founder of the Concerned Citizens Committee, which opposed open housing legislation. After a dramatic sit-in at City Hall during an aldermanic meeting where the police bodily dragged twenty demonstrators from the chambers, Mayor Schmied reiterated his position that no further action would be taken on the open housing ordinance until "outsiders" ceased their protests. Concurrently, the mayor introduced seven amendments to the proposed ordinance, the cumulative effect of which was to exempt more rental housing from the ordinance. On March 30, Dr. Martin Luther King Jr. arrived in Louisville to lead 370 demonstrators to Memorial Auditorium, where the Concerned Citizens Committee was holding a meeting against fair housing.[67]

Fueled by the historic "Don't Buy Where You Can't Work" boycotts of the 1930s, as well as by the more recent example of the Montgomery bus boycott in 1955, the NAACP initiated a "Don't Buy Downtown" campaign in support of open housing and threatened to boycott the Kentucky Derby scheduled for May 6. At the same time COH moved the focus of its demonstrations from downtown to the all-white neighborhoods of the South End. On April 1, the COH conducted the first of more than twenty demonstrations in the South End. The marches became almost nightly affairs, involving several hundred demonstrators and attracting crowds of white "hecklers" numbering between 900 and 2,000 on any given night. More than 160 demonstrators marched through the South End, followed by growing numbers of white hecklers waving Confederate flags and hurtling rocks, eggs, and obscenities at the open housing advocates. Though few white hecklers were ever arrested, by the end of April more than 600 demonstrators had been taken into custody.[68]

The actions of these white agitators were reminiscent of the "defensive localism" used by whites in Detroit to "protect" their property from perceived threats from blacks—that is, to defend whites' "rights" at the expense of equality.[69] The frustrations shared by many whites were captured in a letter by businessman Ray Fuhs. Writing to the Urban Renewal Commission, Fuhs complained that the government was "tearing up the whole city and building back nothing"; that "[the] little man don't have a chance in this country,

Described as "hecklers" in the *Courier-Journal*, mobs of young whites threw bottles and rocks, and jeered at open housing demonstrators in the South End in 1967. © *Louisville Courier-Journal*.

ought to found a country that is run by the people"; that [the] "country can't even whip a small country like Vietnam. Everything the Government does is backwards." In closing, he declared: "I'll move to another country. Give this country to the negros [*sic*], they about have it now. Dumb and stupid men in Washington can't tell the difference in black and white." In his lament, Fuhs linked the war in Vietnam, urban renewal, and open housing to a general sense of loss experienced by many whites.[70]

On April 11, 1967, the Board of Aldermen met to consider the open housing proposal. The bill was defeated by a count of 9 to 3, with Louise Reynolds, Eugene Ford Sr., and attorney Oscar G. Stoll voting in favor of the ordinance. For one historian of the fair housing movement, April 11 was "Black Tuesday—the day on which racism's burning fires of hate and fury were brought out in full-dress revue before an awed and vacillating citizenry; it had professed to see the housing dilemma settled in favor of equal justice and freedom for all but now did not lift a finger in favor of an open housing bill."[71] After the board's decision, the majority of aldermen issued a statement declaring that they would not surrender to pressure from "either side." The statement characterized the protest demonstrations as "mob rule of the worst sort and a tragedy on the orderly process of government."[72] It ended by asserting that no further action would be taken on open housing "until our community regains its composure and the outsiders have gone home."[73]

In the wake of the aldermen's decision, the HRC released its own statement asserting that its recommendations had been dealt with in a manner that "raises a serious question about the future functions of the Commission."[74] In fact, the majority statement of the Board of Aldermen made no mention of the HRC or the possibility of further negotiations on an open housing ordinance. The HRC urged the board to stop focusing on "outside agitators" and address the central "issue of human freedom and dignity and the right of all Americans to one class of citizenship unqualified by prejudice and discrimination." The commission concluded that the aldermen's reasoning in discarding the ordinance "bordered on the frivolous."[75]

While the HRC debated its future, the Jefferson Circuit Court—on April 13, at the behest of Mayor Schmied—issued an injunction banning night marches. The following day the mayor demanded that the HRC stop criticizing him and the Board of Aldermen. In a somewhat veiled threat, Schmied stated that he had no plans to abolish the commission but reminded its members that they were "appointed for the specific purpose of improving race relations, not as a lobbying group for civil rights legislation."[76] Their mandate, he pointed out, was to represent all of the people in the community, not just African Americans. In doing so, he revealed the primary tension within the HRC as well as between it and the COH. The HRC had overstepped its bounds. As a government agency its role was to negotiate, not to lobby for an open housing ordinance.

Despite the court injunction and subsequent arrests, the protests continued. Jessie Irvin was one of the many African Americans who turned out for open housing; along with the other demonstrators led by Reverend A. D. King and Reverend Leo Lesser, she marched down Chestnut and Jefferson streets to the downtown area and to Central Avenue in the South End. Irvin recalled: "The thing that stood out in my mind was when we marched on Central they threw rocks and bottles[; they] threatened us and physically abused us, they had knives and guns. I was scared but not scared enough not to march. I was pregnant at the time. I marched not because it was something I thought I'd see the fruit of but because my children would. I marched for that and because I was tired of staying in substandard housing."[77]

Open housing "hecklers" in 1967. Each night six hundred to seven hundred whites gathered to protest open housing demonstrators, who often numbered less than one hundred. © *Louisville Courier-Journal.*

Open housing advocates like Jessie Irvin marched almost daily in the hope of reforming the urban landscape to benefit her children, if not herself. Not only did blacks envision a radically different city, they actively attempted to make their aspirations a reality. Rather than seeing themselves at the onset of an urban crisis, they saw themselves at a moment of possibility, a moment where a future could be forged to end the current realities of substandard housing, threats of violence, and racism. Many African Americans wielded their hopes and dreams as sword and shield in the struggle for open housing. Like Irvin, blacks in Louisville demonstrated their commitment by marching night after night, despite the ordinance's defeat and the impasse between the HRC and City Hall. Throughout late April the level of nightly violence increased, as fair housing advocates continued to march. By April 18 and 19 the police used tear gas for the first time to quell the hundreds of rock-throwing whites. On the twentieth, thirty protesters were arrested as soon as they stepped out of two trucks to march.

According to the *New York Times*, "White hecklers, unable to reach the marchers, battled the police with bottles and chunks of concrete and bricks. An unoccupied police cruiser was overturned in the melee." In at least one instance the police found a carload of Molotov cocktails that whites intended to use against the protesters.[78] Yet, according to demonstrators such as Eric Tachau, few white "hecklers" were ever arrested.[79] On the evening of May 6, 125 protesters were seized attempting to march in the South End and in the parking lot of Churchill Downs. During an open housing meeting at Bishop David High School, Hulbert James declared that inaction on open housing would guarantee "open hell" for the upcoming Kentucky Derby. James's words signaled an acceleration of the COH initiative to disrupt the ninety-third running of the Derby. Under the slogan, "No Housing Bill, No Derby," the committee's marchers demanded action from the mayor and Board of Aldermen.[80]

Led by Reverend A. D. King and the Kentucky Christian Leadership Conference, blacks began nightly marches from Wyandotte Park to Churchill Downs in the South End. A. D. King termed the marches "home shopping," saying "You can't buy anything til you've looked at it." As on previous occasions, large crowds of "hecklers" threw bottles, rocks, and bricks at the white and black demonstrators.[81] Unsure whether the COH would act on this threat, the Kentucky Derby Festival Committee decided to cancel the twelfth annual Pegasus Parade as well as the Free Country and Western Music Show. Prior to 1967, the parade attracted the largest crowds of any event associated with the Derby; its cancellation cost the city an estimated $550,000. The only parade that year was held by black and white open housing advocates marching through downtown Louisville.

The threat of disrupting the Kentucky Derby was not the only source of national attention. Louisville was but a few years removed from the infamous return of Cassius Clay (now Muhammad Ali) from the 1960 Olympics. Although the city hosted a parade in his honor, Clay was denied service at a segregated diner while wearing his gold medal. By his own account, he went to a bridge and threw his Olympic medal into the Ohio River, saying: "I went all the way to Italy to represent my country, won a gold medal, and now I come back to America and can't even get served at a five-and-dime store. . . . That gold medal didn't mean a thing to me if my black brothers and sisters were treated wrong in a country I was supposed to represent."[82] While there is some debate about whether Clay actually tossed his gold medal into the Ohio River, no one disputes that the Olympic champion was denied service. More importantly, his vocal denunciation of racial segregation in Louisville directed public attention to the realities blacks faced in his hometown and across the nation.

In 1967, as part of his refusal to be inducted into the military, Muhammad Ali again directed attention to the racial situation in Louisville: "Why should they ask me to put on a uniform and go ten thousand miles from home and drop bombs and bullets on brown people in Vietnam while so-called Negroes in Louisville are treated like dogs?"[83] Stokely Carmichael, of the Student Nonviolent Coordinating Committee, addressed students at Howard University in similar terms: "Mr. Muhammad Ali is from Louisville, Kentucky. Did you know that? He was born in Louisville, Kentucky. Do you know what's happening in Louisville, Kentucky today? They're marching for open housing. They're marching for open occupancy. Now, here's a black man who can't live where he wants to live in Kentucky and the honkies are going to send him to Vietnam to fight for freedom."[84]

Though white Louisvillians were increasingly panicked by the national attention accorded open housing as well as by the prospects of a disturbance at the Derby, Mayor Schmied refused to meet with open housing advocates. In an effort to circumvent any violence on Derby Day, the city law director, Eugene H. Alvey, announced that three laws already existed whose combined effect would provide enforcement powers against racial bias in the sale and rental of property. Not surprisingly, Alvey's legal discovery consisted of the Declaration of Principles on Freedom of Residence, the ordinance creating the HRC and the Kentucky Civil Rights Act.

As the HRC and the COH debated whether the three laws would actually solve the open housing crisis, the demonstrations continued within twenty-four hours of the Derby. On May 5, Reverend A. D. King returned to the city to address an evening rally of several hundred open housing advocates at a West End church. According to the *New York Times*, King stated: "We are aiming at bringing the issues out into the open and exposing injustice." Somewhat disingenuously, he claimed to be unaware of any dissension among open housing advocates and refused to participate in strategy sessions regarding the Kentucky Derby. But King warned, "We are not playing about it."[85] Following the rally, over two hundred demonstrators marched in the downtown business district in support of the NAACP's "Don't Buy Downtown" boycott. After meeting with local leaders of the open housing movement, however, King announced that the plan to protest at the Derby had been terminated. He said he had advised the COH not to demonstrate as a "gesture of good faith to refute the claim that we are interested only in disruption for disruption's sake."[86]

The decision brokered by King to call off the demonstration at the Kentucky Derby turned out to be a mistake. By failing to protest or to at least retain the threat of a protest, local black leaders allowed King to give away one of their most important points of leverage without gaining anything in return. Furthermore, without the threat of disruption COH lost its spotlight in the national media, which made the mayor at least more willing to consider negotiation.

Yet in the weeks following the Kentucky Derby, the demonstrations escalated. By May 10, Reverend A. D. King returned to Louisville and led seventy demonstrators in a march in the South End. During an attempt to reason with a group of young white hecklers, a rock was thrown out of the crowd, ricocheting off King's car and through the window. He later said that the rock "shaved my neck and the bottom part of my face, and it caused me to start thinking about the purpose of that rock." As his car attempted to speed away, white teenagers swarmed the vehicle screaming "vicious epithets." During an address to several hundred people at the Greater St. James AME Church in the West End, King approached the pulpit carrying a large rock symbolic of his earlier confrontation. In what John Benjamin Horton called a "prophetic speech," King proclaimed the intent of the local open housing struggle: "We shall tell the young men and young ladies in the South End that upon this rock.... Upon this rock, we are going to build an open city, and the gates of injustice will not prevail again."[87]

The idea of open housing as the rock, the foundation of a new city was at once biblical and indicative of a radical vision of the urban landscape and American society. For Peter, the "rock" was the foundation of the church in the New Testament; for African Americans like A. D. King, open housing would be the rock, the foundation of a new society. Taken further, open housing, the "stone the builder refused," would become the "headstone for the corner." For blacks, open housing was the foundation not only for a radically transformed city but also for society itself. In the radical black imagination, this was not so much the origin of an urban crisis as it was an opportunity to remake the urban landscape. As Martin Luther King Jr. argued in *Strength to Love* (1963), "We Negroes have long dreamed of freedom, but still we are confined in an oppressive prison of segregation and discrimination.... We need the vision to see in this generation's ordeals the opportunity to transfigure both ourselves and American society."[88]

The demonstrations in the South End continued until the end of May, whereupon the COH began to focus its attention on the Highlands in the East End of Louisville. The protests in the more economically affluent Highlands were no more peaceful than those in the South End. During one demonstration, two men dressed in full Ku Klux Klan regalia confronted fair housing marchers. At a sit-in in the middle of Bardstown Road, some fifteen to twenty white opponents of open housing were enlisted by Police Chief William Bindner to load housing demonstrators into waiting paddy wagons. Yet there were increasingly fewer and fewer demonstrators at each march, and by mid-June the COH discontinued the demonstrations altogether. Some protesters, like Charles Tachau, quit marching after they were arrested and spent a night in jail. Others were reluctant to face the increasingly hostile white crowds drawn by the protests.

But the primary reason for discontinuing the marches was a shift in strategy with the approach of the November elections. Perhaps with the earlier struggle to desegregate public accommodations in mind, the black protest movement turned to voter registration as a way to secure an open housing ordinance. Although none of the Democratic nominees openly advocated a fair housing ordinance, according to Richard R. Bernier, "Many marchers believed that a secret deal was made between civil rights leaders and the candidates."[89] The *Louisville Courier-Journal* reported that "some leaders in the Negro community said that they privately received campaign commitments that the Democrats would do something about a strong housing law."[90] As Lyman Johnson put it, "We helped kick the Republicans out and put the Democrats back in. We told the Democrats: 'Remember two terms ago you wouldn't pass a public accommodations ordinance, and you paid for it. In a sixty-five percent Democratic community, you had to put up with two terms of Republicans.' The message got across."[91]

On November 7, 1967, Democrats replaced eleven of the twelve Republican aldermen. Louise Reynolds, who supported open housing, was the only alderman reelected. On December 13, the new aldermen passed an enforceable housing ordinance by a 9–3 vote. Through the efforts of three African Americans—state senator and former migrant Georgia Davis Powers and representatives May Street Kidd and Hughes McGill—this victory was followed in March by the passage of a state law banning housing discrimination. This was one of the first open housing laws enacted in the South. By April 1968 Congress passed the Civil Rights Act (Fair Housing Act), which contained housing provisions. However, this bill was too watered down to prevent housing discrimination.

Blacks in Louisville did not view their open housing victory as the ultimate answer to discrimination, but rather as a necessary tool in the fight against residential segregation. It is difficult to measure the success of the struggle

Open housing advocates gathered at City Hall in 1967 to appeal to the Board of Aldermen. Eventually, an open housing ordinance was achieved when blacks voted as a bloc to remove Mayor Schmied and the majority of the Board of Aldermen. © *Louisville Courier-Journal*.

for open housing, since the passage of the open housing ordinance did little to halt white flight. While the ordinance was important, it was foremost a tool to build the dream of equality. Blacks envisioned a very different future from that created by urban renewal, one where the "haven" that existed on Walnut Street could be wed to the freedom to live in quality housing. Hope, a radical imagination, and the will to act fueled the open housing struggle. Yet, in the end, the hope of securing a nice home—for themselves and their children—where they did not have to pay more for housing of lesser quality, or live in the shadow of segregation, eluded many blacks. In "A Dream that Failed: An Analysis of the Life and Death of the West End Community Council," Anne Braden wrote that the WECC was "built on a dream with no more validity in the minds of people—integration."[92] Although the WECC slowed white flight, ultimately it was unable to stop it.

Within four years, 1960–64, nearly 15,600 whites left the West End in favor of the East End, the South End, or the suburbs of Jefferson County.[93] During the 1960s alone, the white population in the West End decreased by roughly 50 percent. As Louisville's population declined, that of Jefferson County increased by nearly 80 percent by 1986. At the same time that blacks were left isolated in Louisville's West End, African Americans comprised 28 percent of the population in Louisville but only 7 percent of the population in Jefferson County. The few whites who remained in the West End primarily lived in Portland, a working-class neighborhood of Irish Catholic heritage. As in cities like Atlanta, what Kevin Kruse calls the "politics of suburban secession" was no less evident in Louisville.[94] Despite the success of the open housing campaign in achieving an ordinance barring discrimination, blacks entered the 1970s more segregated than ever. In 1940 Louisville's segregation index stood at 70.0; by 1970 it had risen to 89.2.[95]

Not only did housing conditions worsen, but so too did economic opportunities for blacks in the River City. Throughout the period, African Americans made only slight economic gains and remained at the bottom of Louisville's socioeconomic ladder. But due to the destruction of many black businesses and the onset of deindustrialization, that ladder now had a few more rungs on it. In 1968 a U.S. Department of Labor study revealed that blacks comprised only 5 percent of the local building trades; while a study of black employment across the state showed that 98.3 percent of skilled and white-collar positions in industry were held by whites.[96] During the 1970s the number of black families below the poverty line rose by 22 percent, and African Americans continued to work in the same menial jobs, at the same menial pay, as before. The majority of them—67 percent—were employed as domestics or increasingly in service industries as unskilled labor.[97] For entrepreneurs, integration and urban renewal decimated black business. By 1968 there were only 490 black-owned businesses in Louisville representing 0.6 percent of those employed in Jefferson County.[98]

The results of the open housing campaign were somewhat paradoxical. On one hand, the struggle itself represented a significant challenge to white supremacy and the progressive veneer of equality in Louisville. Sparked by worsening housing conditions, urban renewal, and the ongoing fight for equality, the open housing campaign drew much-needed attention to the way residential segregation brutally truncated black lives. Not only did blacks in Louisville gain national attention, but they also served notice that they would take action to achieve equality. While their militancy clearly surprised many whites in the city, it was an important step toward freedom and self-determination. Moreover, their campaign to obtain legal recognition of equal housing succeeded. But legal success was undermined by white flight and the bleak economic realities blacks faced in the city. Ultimately, their dream of the urban landscape was not of integration, but of equality. Like the blues in earlier times, here the sentiments of many blacks in Louisville were echoed by Nina Simone's "Mississippi Goddamn," where she sang, "You don't have to live next to me, just give me my equality." Thus, it seems more accurate to view the "Dream That Failed" as equality itself.

At the moment of blacks' greatest civil rights triumph, they faced escalating spatial isolation as African Americans nationwide were increasingly marooned in "ghettos" such as the one created in the West End of Louisville. The construction of a ghetto combined with limited economic opportunity, increased residential segregation, and unending police brutality created conditions that led many African Americans to question whether freedom could in fact be legislated. In black Louisville, much of the economic and communal infrastructure was razed along with buildings deemed as blighted. Increasingly, African Americans questioned the U.S. commitment to equality and found the nation lacking. In Louisville, like many cities across America during the 1960s, blacks began to answer Langston Hughes's decades-old query, "What happens to a dream deferred?"

CONCLUSION

A TALE OF TWO CITIES

What white Americans have never fully understood—but what the Negro can never forget—is that white society is deeply implicated in the ghetto. White institutions created it, white institutions maintain it, and white society condones it.

—*The Kerner Report on National Disorders* (1968)

On April 4, 1968, Martin Luther King Jr. was murdered in Memphis, Tennessee. Across the nation, from Washington, D.C., to Chicago to Los Angeles, some African Americans responded with violent protests. In more than 168 cities blacks expressed their sorrow and frustration with ongoing inequality as much as with King's death by burning, looting, and destroying property in the neighborhoods around them. Other African Americans reacted with shock, disbelief, and dismay. Nina Simone captured the sentiments of many blacks when she asked in the song "Why," "What will happen now that the King of love is Dead?" But in Louisville, all remained quiet, all remained calm.

Indeed, King's death seemed to pull blacks and whites closer together. Dozens of white and black Louisvillians attended the funeral in Atlanta, traveling on buses provided by Mayor Kenneth Schmied, as well as government officials representing the city. The following Saturday thousands gathered at a memorial service on the steps of the courthouse in Louisville. Later, the mayor led a march through the downtown in King's honor. Thus, many white residents remained secure in their decades-old belief that the city was a leader in race relations throughout the South. Overlooking the years of black protest, the bombing of Andrew Wade's home, and the violent encounters during the open housing campaign in the South End, whites doggedly clung to the progressive veneer that whitewashed racial conflict in the River City. They proudly pointed to the fact that Louisville was among the first—and largest—southern cities to desegregate public schools in 1956 without violence, that it was the first city south of the Mason-Dixon Line to pass a public accommodations law, and that it was one of eleven cities to receive an All American City Award presented by *Look* magazine and the National Municipal League.[1] For many whites, the lack of violence in the city after King's murder confirmed the belief that "race relations in the community were harmonious and everybody was happy."[2]

This illusion was shattered less than two months later, on May 27, when a political rally protesting police brutality erupted in anger, frustration, and violence that lasted nearly a week. This disturbance in the West End would leave the neighborhood surrounding Twenty-eighth Street and Greenwood Avenue devastated and force the city at large to confront the reality of racism. For blacks, it signaled a new direction in the struggle for equality. For many whites, it killed their belief that Louisville was immune to the racial tensions present in the rest of the South and in the nation as a whole. The riot was significant not only in and of itself, but also because it exposed the gulf between black and white Louisvillians. Many whites were "shocked" by the protest, yet this gulf had long existed beneath the "progressive" veneer of the city's race relations.

Though the riot—or rebellion, depending on one's point of view—began around 8:30 on the evening of the twenty-seventh, it stemmed from a series of events following the arrest of Charles Thomas, a thirty-one-year-old elementary schoolteacher, on May 8. Two patrolmen, James Minton and Edward Wegenast, stopped him in the West End under the suspicion that his car was used in a burglary earlier in the day. Maintaining his innocence, Thomas allowed the police to search his vehicle before a growing crowd of African Americans. As more than two hundred blacks looked on, Officers Michael Clifford and Ralph Zehnder arrived as backup. The situation escalated when Manfred Reid, a black real estate dealer, stopped to ask why his friend Thomas was being arrested. A scuffle broke out when Officer Clifford tried to force Reid and other blacks off the street and onto the sidewalk. During the altercation, Clifford's hat was knocked off and his uniform torn. The patrolman reacted by hitting Reid multiple times after first "thumping" him in the chest. Reid was charged with breach of peace and assault and battery; Thomas was initially arrested on grand larceny (the charge was later dismissed). The four officers were suspended, and Clifford was ultimately fired for using excessive force after black leaders protested his actions. Days later, however, Clifford was reinstated by the Civil Service Board under pressure by the Louisville Lodge Six of the Fraternal Order of Police, which voted to support him.[3]

In May 1968, the intersection of Twenty-eighth and Greenwood became the center of the uprising in the West End. © *Louisville Courier-Journal*.

After a series of fruitless meetings with the mayor, Samuel Hawkins and Robert Kuyu Sims, leaders of the Black Unity League of Kentucky (BULK), called for a protest rally on May 27. BULK had been formed earlier in 1968 as a branch of the West End Community Council to give younger, more militant blacks an organization of their own. As part of the rally, BULK sent one hundred dollars to the Student Nonviolent Coordinating Committee in Washington, D.C., to bring Stokely Carmichael to speak at the rally; instead, they got James Cortez, who claimed to be Carmichael's "right-hand-man." In reality, Carmichael was never contacted about attending the rally. Nonetheless, on May 27 between 350 and 400 blacks gathered at Zion Baptist Church on the corner of Twenty-eighth and Greenwood to protest the police treatment of Charles Thomas and Manfred Reid; to advocate for black political and economic power, and black pride; and to protest the city government's failure to responds to blacks' needs or concerns. In other words, they put forward a Black Power platform or, as Cortez asserted, "Black Power is Black Unity."[4] Sims concluded the rally by saying: "The reason we're up here is that the honky policemen have been brutalizing our black brothers. We going to tell the mayor that next time this happens, he's going to see smoke signals coming up from the West." As the crowd began to disperse, someone threw a brick and some light bulbs off the roof of Moon Cleaners overlooking the intersection. The brick hit a policeman in the face and, as reported in the *Courier-Journal*, "All hell broke loose."[5]

Spiraling outward from the intersection of Twenty-eighth and Greenwood, the disturbance resulted in 2 deaths, 472 arrests, and the deployment of 2,187 National Guardsmen to restore order, with more than $200,000 in property damage.[6] The fatalities were two black youths, James Grove, age fourteen, and Mathias Washington, age nineteen; both were killed under suspicion of looting, though bystanders maintained that neither were looters. A policeman shot Grove as he fled from Rose Grocery Store a few minutes before midnight. Washington was shot and killed by the owner of the Vermont Liquor Store for supposedly stealing liquor through a broken window, but the only thing found in his hand was a fish sandwich he had just purchased from Jean's Grill across the street. On the night after the disturbance began, a pharmacy, a community center, and Zion Baptist Church were all bombed in the same neighborhood. Zion Baptist Church was a hub of Black Power militancy in the city and the site of a voter registration drive.[7] Despite the presence of the National Guard and an eleven p.m. to five a.m. curfew (later amended to eight p.m. to five a.m.), "heavy rioting" would last for almost three days. Ironically, the area around Twenty-eighth and Greenwood was one of the few places where black businesses survived urban renewal, only to be destroyed during the disturbance and never rebuilt.[8] Ultimately, order was restored by A. D. King, Samuel Hawkins, Robert Sims, James Cortez, and other black leaders, who implored blacks in the West End to "cool it," and by the National Guardsmen who patrolled the streets with fixed bayonets.

Though many whites in Louisville were surprised by the protest in the West End, the *Courier-Journal* located the source of the riot in the numerous inequities confronting African Americans in the city, such as "restricted and inadequate housing, unemployment and underemployment, unsatisfactory schools, exclusion from community decision-making, discriminatory consumer and credit practices, poor police relations, inadequate welfare and other public services, disrespectful white attitudes, and the withdrawal of whites from the inner city to the nearly all-white suburbs, magnifying the division between races and making communication more difficult."[9] In light of these concerns/injustices, many blacks viewed the violence in the West End as problematic but understandable. In the opinion of one onlooker, Doris Kirby, the riot was a valid means to voice their concerns, given their

More than two thousand National Guardsmen were called into Louisville in May 1968 to reestablish order by imposing a curfew. © *Louisville Courier-Journal.*

long-standing battle for equality in Louisville. "I don't approve of destroying property," she remarked, "but it seems like that is the only way to open people's eyes."[10]

In a series of interviews conducted by the local press in the immediate aftermath of the riot, African Americans expressed their ongoing frustrations with their continuing unequal treatment in the city, as well as the limitations of nonviolent protest. Like many blacks nationwide, particularly in the context of the Vietnam War and urban renewal, nonviolence seemed to be less and less a viable strategy to attain equality. One middle-aged black woman, Kathleen Washington, believed the riot was simply another means of protest. She declared: "I don't approve of the looting, window breaking, and vandalism, but I approve of their standing up for their rights. I believe in standing up so you can be heard." In a similar vein, an unidentified man said that the riot "might get us recognition. It might make people realize that we are being pushed around. The non-violent movement is just about over with. If we couldn't get it non-violently, we'll do it with violence. You know they say, 'It's going to be a long hot summer,' but in Louisville, we've had all this and it isn't even summer yet."[11]

BULK's leaflet, "City Shifts Blame for Civil Disorders; Frames Black Leaders," explained the growth of Black Power militancy among many African Americans when it stated: "White Louisville must face the fact that this set of circumstances says one thing very clearly—that when white property appears to be threatened we do something about it, but when black lives are taken, we do not."[12] Nor was BULK alone in its assessment of white Louisville. The Southern Conference Education Fund's report, "Lessons from Louisville," argued: "You stop a police state by defending and freeing its first victims."[13] And the White Emergency Support Team (WEST), an ad hoc organization supporting the black community, stated: "For 300 years, America has demanded that black people be nonviolent in the face of white people. Now the debt must be repaid. Today the white community must be nonviolent— even in the face of black violence. This is a rich country, we can replace any property lost in the uprising. But the lives of black people shot by police and merchants cannot be returned."[14]

In the aftermath of the protest in the West End, Manfred Reid, James Cortez, Samuel Hawkins, and Robert Sims were arrested on a range of charges. Reid was accused of passing a bad check for $113.44, as well as assault and battery stemming from his earlier encounter when he claimed Officer Clifford hit *him*. Cortez was said to have been a "common nuisance" and to have passed worthless money orders in the amounts of $35.00 and $85.00; a later charge of second-degree burglary was added from the court system in Washington, D.C. Cortez joined Sims and Hawkins in the allegation that they had conspired to dynamite oil refineries and destroyed five other properties during the riot—among them, the Moon Cleaners, the Louisville Taxi Cab and Transfer Company, and a pawn shop. Nearly three months later, charges were also brought against Walter "Pete" Crosby, who was with Reid during the initial incident, and Ruth Bryant, a leader of the WECC and an outspoken critic of race relations in the city. Collectively, Reid, Crosby, Sims, Hawkins, Cortez, and Bryant became known as the "Black Six" during the two years their cases wound their way through the courts. The trial was eventually moved to Munfordville, Kentucky, where Southern Conference Educational Fund activists Mike Honey and Martha Allen were arrested for urging citizens to protest the trial. In the end, after two years of protests and demonstrations, all conspiracy charges were dropped.[15]

The false accusations against the Black Six were but one response to the violent protest in the West End. Another was the report on race relations conducted by Roper Research Associates and published in the *Louisville Courier-Journal* and the *Louisville Times*. The local press commissioned this 1969 study with an eye toward understanding the disturbances of 1968. Its purpose was "to explore community relations among whites and Negroes in the Louisville area," with special attention to living conditions and perceptions of race and racism in the city. The study sought to divine public opinion on issues ranging from housing, crime, and the cost of living to "attitudes" toward integration, the effects of urban renewal, the causes of the May 1968 riot, and later disturbances in 1969.[16]

According to the Roper report, the survey could appropriately be called *A Tale of Two Cities* "due to the stark differences in the conditions blacks and whites faced in the city." It revealed that "the real 'racial problem' in Louisville is the gulf between the two races—both in terms of the conditions in which they live and in terms of the attitudes toward the struggle for equality for Negroes in society."[17] Moreover, the study found blacks remarkable for their restraint, stating that, given the deplorable conditions they faced in the city, their behavior showed surprising moderation.[18] The African Americans surveyed listed the cost of living, a lack of decent housing, and juvenile delinquency among their biggest concerns; whites, on the other hand, cited crime (though only 7 percent said crime was a serious problem in their own neighborhood) and the "racial problem" as their foremost concerns. Whereas whites listed street lighting as their number one neighborhood issue, blacks indicated the lack of quality housing. African American anxiety about crime centered around housebreaking, drunkenness, gambling, drug use among young people, prostitution, and knifings and shootings, whereas whites said that only housebreaking in their own neighborhood was a significant problem. Given the concerns blacks voiced about crime, the Roper report ironically concluded: "Negroes are the ones who *most* want 'law and order.'"[19]

In short, the Roper study found that blacks and whites lived in "two different worlds" and that "the conditions of Negroes in Louisville relative to whites, are dismal." Whereas blacks felt alienated from the local government and the society in which they lived, whites did not. Whites claimed that job discrimination on the whole did not exist, or, if so, only in a few job categories. Not surprisingly given the conflict over open housing, nearly 83 percent of the whites surveyed wanted to live in white only or majority-white neighborhoods.[20] Yet, in spite of these findings, the majority of whites believed that African Americans in Louisville were better off than elsewhere and that the pace of racial progress was fine. The Roper report concluded that whites demonstrated a "frightening . . . unawareness and unconcern" for the hardships confronting African Americans in the city.[21] As it pointed out, "Negroes clearly want more and faster progress than whites want or see a need for."[22] Despite the success of the civil rights movements of the 1960s, blacks in Louisville entered the new decade with the dream, rather than the reality, of equality.

By 1970 the flow of migrants streaming into the River City had dwindled to a trickle. For many African Americans, Louisville now appeared to be a less-than-desirable destination. As the right to vote and access to higher education became more widespread in the South, the city was less of a lure.[23] Despite the passage of civil rights legislation and the constant efforts of activists, discrimination remained a constant in the daily lives of blacks. Although it was a central goal of the struggle for equality throughout the period, blacks only made slight economic gains. African Americans remained at the bottom of Louisville's socioeconomic ladder. Sociologists Scott Cummings and Michael Prince demonstrate that black poverty rates "remained relatively unchanged between 1969, 1979 and 1989."[24] In each era, roughly 30 percent of all blacks lived in poverty compared to 9 percent of whites. More than 16 percent of Louisville's manufacturing jobs were lost as many of the city's largest employers—International Harvester, Seagrams, and Brown and Williamson—relocated to other cities. During the 1970s, the number of black families below the poverty line rose by 22 percent and African Americans continued to work many of the same menial jobs, at the same menial pay, as before. The majority of African Americans, or 67 percent, were employed as domestics or increasingly as unskilled labor in service industries.[25] Even grocery stores such as A&P and Kroger, which had been the target of NAACP employment campaigns, witnessed a loss of black employees.[26] For entrepreneurs, integration and urban renewal emaciated black business in the River City.

Just as the economic picture in Louisville was bleak at best, so too was its standing in race relations. By its opposition to public accommodations, fair housing, and civil rights generally throughout the 1960s, Louisville proved its progressive reputation was little more than a veneer. Despite the accolades of Omer Carmichael's "Louisville Plan," the majority of students attended same-race schools. Moreover, a 1972 study by the Kentucky Commission on Human Rights revealed not only the lack of integration in the city, but also the fact that resegregation had occurred. Yet, one wonders when *desegregation* itself actually took place since the commission's report states:

As late as 1968, only 55.7 percent of the city's students were in schools with extreme segregation but the level had increased to 73.5 percent in 1971. Meanwhile, the national level dropped from 64.3 per cent in 1968 to 43.3 percent in 1970 and the level in Southern states dropped from 77.8 percent in 1968 to 33.4 percent in 1970. . . . The Louisville school system has failed—either by design or by lack of effort—to deliver on the promise of full students and faculty desegregation. The myth of "neighborhood schools" has been put forward to conceal this basic failure.[27]

In response to the absence of racial progress in the realm of education, a group of organizations, including the West End and Mid-City Citizens for Desegregation, Kentucky Civil Liberties Union, Kentucky Commission on Human Rights, NAACP, and Louisville Legal Aid Society, filed lawsuits against the city in 1971 and 1972.[28] In 1975, after a series of appeals, the Sixth Circuit Court of Appeals ordered the merger of the Louisville and Jefferson County school systems "to the end that all the remaining vestiges of the state imposed segregation shall be removed from the said school district."[29]

To achieve the racial balance required by the court decision in each school, Louisville and Jefferson County schools embarked on a busing program in which 22,600 of the school system's 130,000 students (half black and half white) would be bused to different schools. In response, local whites initiated widespread, violent demonstrations against busing, mobilizing a host of protest organizations such as the Ku Klux Klan, Save Our Community Schools, Concerned Citizens, Inc., Citizens against Busing, Union Labor against Busing, and Restore Our Alienated Rights. In an interview by *Time* magazine, Susan Connor, head of Concerned Citizens, one of the largest groups with a membership of 16,000, described the antibusing movement as a "war."[30] The effort to desegregate schools in Louisville resulted in a series of often violent protests, demonstrations, and boycotts.

On the first day of school in September 1975, half of the white students in the school system stayed home. At the Ford Motor Company, the plant was shut down when 38 percent of its workforce walked out in opposition to busing, while at the General Electric plant, union members threatened to close the factory by walking out in protest. At city and county schools, a Ku Klux Klan cross was burned and school buses were firebombed; at least one protest devolved into a riot when more than ten thousand whites at Valley High School threw rocks and bottles at police, attacked police cars, and started a bonfire. At Southern High School, whites broke windows, slashed the tires of forty school buses, firebombed two other buses, lit a number of bonfires, and chanted "We don't want niggers in our schools."[31] At Fairdale High School, nearly 81 percent of the white students stayed away. When 300 black students arrived at the school, city and county police were joined by 350 state troopers, and ultimately 1,000 National Guardsmen who used tear gas to quell white protesters. The ambivalence of many blacks attending schools under these conditions was captured by Leslie Lacy, a seventeen-year-old at Fairdale, who quipped: "I think I'll paint myself white and go back to Shawnee [High School]."[32] Nor were schools the only site of protest. Susan Connor and Concerned Citizens led a march of more than 8,000 whites downtown to protest busing; ironically, this march was larger than any held in the city in support of civil rights or black equality.[33]

Five years later, the *Louisville Courier-Journal* noted that the issue of school busing had ignited a "powder keg of emotions" that exploded "with a ferocity that shook the town."[34] For many whites, the antibusing movement was not a racist undertaking; rather, it was a protest for quality education and against the interference of the government in their lives. Public opinion polls conducted at the time revealed that, although busing was in fact spurred by racism, many antibusing protesters expressed the "belief that discrimination no longer exists, that blacks are making unfair demands and illegitimate gains and that powerful persons and institutions in the nation are giving blacks undue recognition and respect."[35] In the end, the ferocity of the antibusing movement in Louisville dealt a death blow to the decades-old "progressive" veneer that the city was a leader in race relations and drew national attention.[36] While busing evoked white protests in many U.S. cities, the controversy in Louisville was rivaled only in Boston, where a photograph of an African American being speared with an American flag by white protesters and the violence in South Boston was broadcast across the nation. Like Boston, Louisville's antibusing protests were detailed nationally in the *New York Times* and in *Time* magazine, as well as on NBC and ABC news.

Despite widespread protests, busing continued, as did segregation in Louisville's public schools. While whites could not stop busing, they could remove their children and send them to private schools. Between the fall of 1973 and the fall of 1976, white enrollment in the public schools fell by 23,000 students, or 21 percent. The trend continued into the 1980s, as each year between 1974 and 1982 the enrollment of white students declined by 5.9 percent.[37] At the same time, white students' enrollment in private schools increased by 22 percent.[38] By 1983, the Kentucky Commission on Human Rights noted: "Since 1980, there has been a steady erosion of the desegregation gains made after 1975–76. . . . The school administration has allowed the school system to slide back toward the levels of segregation which existed before 1975–76."[39] More recently, the U.S. Supreme Court heard the same concerns about busing and Louisville's ongoing attempts to achieve desegregation in the public schools. Crystal Meredith sued to keep her white son, Joshua McDonald, from being bused ninety minutes to Bloom Elementary School to help achieve a racial balance in the school. In a 2007 ruling that is widely understood to counteract the impact of the 1954 *Brown v. Board of Education* decision, the Supreme Court determined that race could no longer be used as a factor in student school assignments.[40]

Similarly, except for the Irish Catholics residing in the Portland neighborhood and a few whites like Anne Braden who refused to move, the West End was transformed into a black neighborhood, housing 62,000 of the 80,000 blacks in the city by 1970.[41] Indeed, by that year Louisville was one of the most segregated cities in the South.[42] By 1975, the Kentucky Commission on Human Rights reported: "The evidence is that most of our cities are as segregated or more segregated than they were ten years ago."[43] In part, the rising segregation in Louisville reflected a mass exodus by whites; between 1960 and 1990, the city's population declined by 32 percent, while Jefferson County's increased by 8 percent. And while blacks comprised 30 percent of Louisville's population, they were 9 percent of Jefferson County's.[44] Yet segregation was caused not just by white flight but also by the city itself; between 1984 and 1988, Louisville's Housing Authority of Jefferson County was the most segregated in the state.[45] With seemingly prophetic insight, in 1970 the Kerner Report revisited noted: "The city as seen by the two groups [blacks and whites] is in the main not the same city, and the problems faced by the two groups—particularly at the neighborhood level—are so different that the gulf between white and Negro citizens appears wide indeed."[46]

The Roper report concluded that "the challenge faced in Louisville, it seems to us, is really the challenge faced by the nation."[47] Louisville, like many cities across America, stood at the center of what was less the "origin" of any crisis than it was a continuation of the inequalities African Americans always confronted. The problem became an "urban crisis" when blacks moved to cities across America and found an adherence to white supremacy no less powerful than in their former southern homes. Indeed, if there was an "urban crisis" it was rooted in white supremacy, in the unwillingness of whites to share a radical egalitarian vision of the urban landscape, of the nation as a whole. As Louisville entered the 1970s, the "modern conservatism" of many whites held tightly to old ideologies: white supremacy, gradualism, and the notion that they knew what was best for African Americans. Yet the lesson of Louisville is not to discount the power of the aspirations that motivated black migrants to relocate there in order to create a better future for themselves and their children, as well as for Louisville, the South, and the nation.

Despite the gulf the existed between blacks and whites in the River City, the efforts of African American migrants such as Lyman Johnson, Charles Anderson, Murray Walls, and Jessie Irvin did make Louisville a "better" city. Though aware of the harsh reality of racism, they envisioned a city and a society that was radically different. As important as their dreams were the actions they took to make their world anew. Throughout the 1970s black migrants would remain an integral part of ongoing attempts to eradicate racial discrimination from Louisville's landscape. W. J. Hodge, Lois Morris, and others would continue the tradition of African American migrants holding office. Arthur Walters, an activist and migrant from Magnolia, Kentucky, would go on to become the executive director of the Louisville Urban League. As African Americans shifted strategies toward Black Nationalism, migrants like Ruth Bryant remained at the forefront of the civil rights movement in Louisville. Bryant was among the founding members of the Black Unity League of Kentucky and the local branch of Junta Militant Organizations, which sought a more nationalistic brand of black equality.

Not only did migrants come to Louisville with expectations that racial discrimination would be less, that housing and jobs would be more plentiful and of better quality. More often than not they worked hard to make such aspirations a reality. By 1970 the majority of black migrants had been in the city nearly twenty years; nevertheless, they remained as tied to their former homes through visiting and kinship as to Louisville. While they continued to see themselves as migrants, many viewed themselves as Louisvillians as well. In the process of fighting to make the city and the South a safe place, Louisville became Home to many African Americans. Their efforts did not make Louisville completely safe, but in many ways complete success was impossible; racism would not, and could not, be erased overnight. Yet the actions of black migrants in Louisville, whether political, social, or economic, illustrate the ways in which they claimed the South and Louisville as their own.

APPENDIX

MIGRATION, POPULATION, AND EMPLOYMENT DATA

TABLE 1. Total and Black Population, 1920–1980

Year	Total Population	Black Population	% Black
1900	204,731	39,139	19.1
1910	223,928	40,522	18.0
1920	234,891	40,087	17.0
1930	307,745	47,354	15.3
1940	319,077	47,158	14.8
1950	369,129	57,657	15.6
1960	390,639	70,075	17.9
1970	361,472	86,040	23.8
1980	298,451	84,080	28.2
1990	269,555	79,783	29.5
2000	256,231	84,586	33.0

Sources: J. Blaine Hudson, "African Americans," in Encyclopedia of Louisville, ed. John E. Kleber (Lexington: University of Kentucky Press, 2001), 18; Twenty-second U.S. Census (Census 2000) (Washington, D.C.: U.S. Government Printing Office, 2000).

TABLE 2. Total Migration, Selected Southern Cities, 1935–1940

City	Out-Migration	In-Migration	Urban In-Migration
Atlanta	58,563	39,904	24,211
Birmingham	38,008	31,223	15,925
Charlotte	16,520	17,329	12,219
Louisville	33,828	28,179	14,946
Memphis	37,789	40,396	19,277
New Orleans	37,716	27,503	19,362

Source: Leon Truesdell, Population, Internal Migration, 1935 to 1940, Sixteenth Census of the United States (Washington, D.C.: U.S. Government Printing Office, 1943).

TABLE 3. Total African American Migration, Selected Cities, 1935–1940

City	Out-Migration	In-Migration	Net Migration
Atlanta	8,779	5,526	−3,253
Birmingham	8,112	8,140	+28
Charlotte NA	2,685	NA	
Louisville	2,738	2,801	+63
Memphis	11,057	9,774	−1,283
New Orleans	6,159	3,580	−2,579

Source: Leon Truesdell, *Population, Internal Migration, 1935 to 1940, Sixteenth Census of the United States* (Washington, D.C.: U.S. Government Printing Office, 1943).

TABLE 4. Number and Percentage of African American Male
Urban In-Migrants, Selected Cities, 1935–1940

City	In-Migration	Urban >100,000	Urban <100,000	% Urban
Atlanta	2,489	355	768	45.1
Birmingham	3,699	210	1,146	36.6
Charlotte	1,242	119	550	53.8
Louisville	1,316	338	463	60.8
Memphis	5,184	346	975	25.5
New Orleans	1,652	273	644	55.5

Source: Leon Truesdell, *Population, Internal Migration, 1935 to 1940, Sixteenth Census of the United States* (Washington, D.C.: U.S. Government Printing Office, 1943).

TABLE 5. Number and Percentage of African American Female
Urban In-Migrants, Selected Cities, 1935–1940

City	In-Migration	Urban >100,000	Urban <100,000	% Urban
Atlanta	3,037	400	1,041	47.0
Birmingham	4,441	276	1,484	39.6
Charlotte	1,443	110	690	55.4
Louisville	1,485	352	532	59.5
Memphis	5,873	336	1,223	26.5
New Orleans	1,928	227	800	53.2

Source: Leon Truesdell, *Population, Internal Migration, 1935 to 1940, Sixteenth Census of the United States* (Washington, D.C.: U.S. Government Printing Office, 1943).

TABLE 6. Racial Composition of CIO Unions, 1948

Industry	Total Members	African American Members	% Black
Clothing Industries	3,000	30	10
Enro Shirt Company	600	60	10
Auto Workers	3,500	35	10
Breweries	800	70	8.7
Gas, Coke, and Chemical Workers	150	141	94
Furniture Workers	50	3	6
Office and Professional Workers	130	2	1.5
Papers Workers	400	5	1.3
Public Workers	400	100	25
Garbage Collectors	70	63	90
Shipyard Workers	300	24	8
Textile Workers	1,200	12	1
Transport Workers	1,000	25	2.5
Steel Workers	1,500	60	4
Paper Box Industries	400	40	10
Total	13,370	670	5

Source: Harvey Kerns, *A Survey of the Economic and Cultural Conditions of the Negro Population of Louisville, Kentucky, and A Review of the Program and Activities of the Louisville Urban League* (Louisville: Louisville Urban League, 1948).

TABLE 7. Black Employment in Louisville, Selected Industries, 1968

		AFRICAN AMERICANS		
Employer	*Total Employees*	*Skilled*	*Unskilled*	*Total*
General Mills	82	0	4	4
P. S. Royster Guano Company	20	0	0	0
Globe Battery Division	100	0	0	0
Griffin & Company	92	0	0	0
Kentucky Trust Company	166	0	0	0
Killion Motor Express	188	0	2	2
Glenmoer Distilleries	690	2	28	30
Thomas Industries	2,520	9	71	80
Anaconda Aluminum	3,294	31	103	134
Kingsford Company	247	0	0	0
Wood Mosaic Company	564	5	42	47
Boone Box Company	186	0	2	2
Bank of Louisville-Royal	405	7	12	19
Kentucky Security Police	108	0	0	0
Kentucky Farm Bureau	158	0	0	0
Kentucky Store Company	195	2	13	15
Kister Lumber Company	110	0	2	2
United Furniture Company	127	0	5	5
Terminal Transport Company	46	0	1	1
A & H Truck Lines	54	0	1	1
Girder Corporation	343	5	0	5
Citizen's Fidelity Bank	740	6	24	30
W. M. Cissell Manufacturing Company	400	0	3	3
George J. Meyer Manufacturing Company	73	0	2	2
Mother's Cookie Company	160	1	22	23
Mopco Chemical Company	27	0	0	0
Ohio River Sand Company	50	0	3	3
Oscar Ewing Incorporated	100	0	2	2
Cosmodyne Corporation	121	1	3	4
W. E. Caldwell	171	0	2	2
Martin A. Cedar Incorporated	79	0	0	0
Campbell Tobacco Company	209	1	191	192
Creasey Company of Kentucky	168	0	4	4
N & N Construction Company	54	0	1	1
Columbia Manufacturing Company	123	0	8	8
Alton Box Board Company	174	0	3	3
Famco Incorporated	452	1	6	7

American Air Filter	1,161	7	32	39
Stitzel Weller Distillery	223	0	10	10
United Parcel Service	237	2	4	6
K. M. White Company	200	4	6	10
Winn-Dixie Stores	542	1	6	7
K & I Railroad	732	1	22	23
L & N Railroad	2,027	2	38	40
Reliance Universal Incorporated	256	2	13	15
Mason & Dixon Line	225	1	5	6
Marley Company	315	0	25	25
Paramount Foods	279	1	10	11
Porcelain Metals	219	0	5	5
H. J. Scheirich Company	472	1	8	9
Schenly Distilleries	634	0	34	34
James E. Smith & Sons	274	0	4	4
Smith's Transfer Corporation	355	0	4	4
Liberty National Bank	472	3	26	29
Levy Brothers	235	10	21	31
Louisville Bedding Company	256	0	1	1
Kentucky Manufacturing Company	475	0	13	13
Kentucky Transport Company	218	1	5	6
Kroehler Manufacturing Company	892	16	39	55
Gamble Brother Incorporated	397	1	3	4
First National Lincoln Bank	623	3	25	28
Adams & Mulberry Corporation	144	1	4	5
Belknap Hardware & Manufacturing Company	1,157	0	63	63
Meadow Gold Dairy	100	0	4	4
Shedd-Barrush Foods	130	1	3	4
Blue Cross Blue Shield	288	3	4	7
General Electric	14,374	35	784	819
Ford Motor Company	4,792	28	230	258
Brown-Forman Distilleries	1,316	11	111	122
Dover Corporation (Peerless Manufacturing Division)	233	11	26	37
Dover Corporation (C. Lee Cook Division)	96	11	47	58
Courier-Journal Lithographing Company	245	0	7	7
	47,690	228	2,202	2,430

Source: "Black Business in Louisville," Kentucky Commission on Human Rights, October 1968, Charles Parrish Papers, box 14, University Archives and Records Center, University of Louisville.

NOTES

ABBREVIATIONS

EL-UARC   Ekstrom Library, University Archives and Records Center,
             University of Louisville
KHS   Kentucky Historical Society, Frankfort
LC   Library of Congress, Manuscript Division, Washington, D.C.
LMA   Louisville Metro Archives (formerly City of Louisville Archives)
NAACP   National Association for the Advancement of Colored People
NYCC   Negro Youth at the Crossways Collection,
             Charles Henry Parrish Jr. Papers, EL-UARC
UARC   University Archives and Records Center, University of Louisville

INTRODUCTION

1   Interview with Goldie Winstead-Beckett, September 12, 1978, Black Oral History Collection, UARC.
2   "One Decade of Desegregation," 1966, box 1, folder 1, Woolsey Papers, EL-UARC. The first black alderman was Eugene S. Clayton, elected in 1945.
3   Urban Renewal Papers, R-10 Project Relocation Files and Inactive Families, LMA.
4   Interview with Goldie Winstead-Beckett.
5   Ibid.
6   Ibid.
7   By "fellowship" I mean the African American practice of holding church services with members of one's own church or other churches, which serves to create and maintain community.
8   Interview with Rev. William G. Marks, November 29, 1997, by author.
9   "Employment by Race in Selected Plants in Louisville, Kentucky, January 1967," Woolsey Papers, box 1, folder 4, EL-UARC.
10 Interview with Rev. William G. Marks, November 29, 1997, by author.
11 Woodson, *Century of Negro Migration*; Scott, *Negro Migration during the War*; Woofter, *Negro Migration*; Charles Johnson, *Negro in Chicago*; Kennedy, *Negro Peasant Turns Cityward*; Edward E. Lewis, *Mobility of the Negro*; Kiser, *Sea Island to City*; Florant, "Negro Internal Migration"; Tuttle, *Race Riot*; Pleck, *Black Migration and Poverty*; Borchert, *Alley Life in Washington*; Henri, *Black Migration*; Trotter, "Black Migration in Historical Perspective," 4–5; Du Bois, *Philadelphia Negro*, 73, 81–82. W. E. B. Du Bois was one

of the first scholars attentive to black migration in his classic study, *The Philadelphia Negro*. He viewed the relocation of southern blacks as central to black community development and population growth in Philadelphia. In asking, "Whence came these people?" Du Bois pointed to the role of migration in the conditions blacks faced in northern cities.

12 For overviews of the scholarship on the national migration that began in the 1910s, see Trotter, *Great Migration in Historical Perspective*, and Alferdteen Harrison, *Black Exodus*. On specific case studies, see Gottlieb, *Making Their Own Way*; Trotter, *Black Milwaukee*; Grossman, *Land of Hope*; Earl Lewis, *In Their Own Interests*; Taylor, *Forging of a Black Community*; Clark-Lewis, *Living In, Living Out*; Griffin, *"Who Set You Flowin'?"*; Phillips, *Alabama North*; and Hicks, "'In Danger of Becoming Morally Depraved.'" On migration in the West, see Lemke-Santangelo, *Abiding Courage*; Taylor, *In Search of the Racial Frontier*; Wilson-Moore, *To Place Our Deeds*; Sides, *L.A. City Limits*; and Gregory, *Southern Diaspora*. On the connections between black religion and the process of migration, see Gregg, *Sparks from the Anvil of Oppression*; Sernett, *Bound for the Promised Land*; and Best, *Passionately Human, No Less Divine*.

13 Painter, *Exodusters*.

14 Hine, "Rape and the Inner Lives of Black Women."

15 See Earl Lewis, *In Their Own Interests*, and Grossman, *Land of Hope*.

16 Grossman, *Land of Hope*; Earl Lewis, *In Their Own Interests*; Wilson-Moore, *To Place Our Deeds*; Lemke-Santangelo, *Abiding Courage*; Phillips, *Alabama North*.

17 Gregory, *Southern Diaspora*; Gilmore, *Defying Dixie*.

18 Gilmore, *Defying Dixie*, 4.

19 Laurie Green, *Battling the Plantation Mentality*, 3.

20 Ibid., 3–4, 285, 291.

21 Ibid., 5.

22 Charles Johnson, *Shadow of the Plantation*, 6. Johnson also notes: "The Negro of the plantation—though the two are closely related and the history of the one goes far to explain the history of the existence of the other—is not to be identified with the mobile and migratory Negro laborers who crowd the slums of southern cities," xxi. Green does not cite Johnson.

23 Ibid., 16. Johnson asks: "How in the world did those poor, downtrodden, compliant people in Alabama's Black Belt ever mount and support a civil rights revolution? The answer is that those people were neither totally downtrodden nor altogether compliant. This book shows they resented the cruel exploitation, callous contempt, and withholding of personal respect that was their almost universal experience with whites," xii.

24 Truesdell, *Population, Internal Migration*.

25 Laurie Green, *Battling the Plantation Mentality*, 291. Similarly, Green argues that "the process of claiming freedom was about simultaneously uprooting white racist thought and liberating black minds," 4.

26 Throughout the period, African Americans commonly referred to less militant blacks, or even figures prone to negotiation (including Martin Luther King Jr.), as "Uncle Tom's." Similarly, in his "Message to the Grassroots," Malcolm X refers to his audience as "handkerchief headed Uncle Toms"; much to their amusement, it was more a chal-

lenge to join activism than a description of reality. At the same time, whites called African American activists "uppity," "inferior," "communists," and "outside agitators," yet few would say those terms were accurate. Rather, the historians' task is to understand what they meant, not simply accept them at face value.

27 On blacks in Louisville, see Horton, *Not without Struggle*; George C. Wright, *Life Behind a Veil*, *History of Blacks in Kentucky*, "Desegregation of Public Accommodations," and "Civil Rights Movement in Kentucky"; Wade Hall, *Rest of the Dream*; K'Meyer, *Civil Rights*, "To Bring People Together," "Building Interracial Democracy," and "'Gateway to the South'"; Trotter, *River Jordan*; Braden, *The Wall Between*; Fosl, *Subversive Southerner*; Luther J. Adams, "African American Migration to Louisville," "It Was North of Tennessee," "Headed to Louisville," and "Way Up North in Louisville"; Ernest Collins, "Political Behavior of the Negroes"; McElhone, "Civil Rights Activities"; Bernier, "White Activists and Support"; Shirley Mae Harmon, "Black and White Women War Workers"; and Gilpin, "Left by Themselves."

28 See Hirsch, *Making the Second Ghetto* and "With or without Jim Crow"; Jackson, *Crabgrass Frontier*; Carolyn T. Adams et al., *Philadelphia*; Casey-Leininger, "Making the Second Ghetto in Cincinnati"; Sugrue, *Origins of the Urban Crisis*; Mohl, "Making the Second Ghetto in Metropolitan Miami"; Bayor, *Race and the Shaping of Twentieth-Century Atlanta*; Self, *American Babylon*; and Rhonda Y. Williams, *Politics of Public Housing*. On real estate practices, see Oser, *Blockbusting in Baltimore*. On the "Underclass Debate," or what I would call the "urban crisis" literature, see William Julius Wilson, *Truly Disadvantaged*; Jencks, *The Urban Underclass*; Massey and Denton, *American Apartheid*; Katz, *"Underclass" Debate* and *Improving Poor People*; Gans, *War against the Poor*; Marris, *How to Save the Underclass*; and Reed, *Stirrings in the Jug*.

29 Sugrue, "Revisiting the Second Ghetto," 283; Thompson, "Making a Second Urban History," 284; Hirsch, "Second Thoughts on the Second Ghetto." These papers appear in a series of articles by urban scholars that consider the impact of Hirsch's *Making the Second Ghetto*. In his essay, Hirsch notes that "making the second ghetto" was "race relations and urban history, not black history."

30 Hirsch, "Second Thoughts on the Second Ghetto," 300, 308, 308n4. Hirsch poses a series of questions on the role of "black agency," including "How 'free' were the choices of black Chicagoans to move due south and west, as opposed to southwest? What role did white ethnicity, political dominance, or economic competence play in such decisions? If emphasis is placed on black 'agency' (autonomy?) without regard to the issue of power, where does responsibility lie? Does the decision not to move carry the same weight as an affirmative act?" Yet it does not seem that an analysis of black agency would necessitate eliding power; in fact, understanding black agency would seemingly result in a more complex understanding of the nature of power in postwar urban America.

31 Ibid.

32 Even a cursory examination of the titles of these works suggests the extent to which these historians focused on the creation of ghettos as well as on how far back the roots of black migration lay; see Osofsky, *Harlem*; Spear, *Black Chicago*; and Kusmer, *A Ghetto Takes Shape*. Driven by the desire to explain the ills of urban America, Lemann's *The Promised Land* led both scholarly and popular audiences to focus more on the connec-

tion between the Second Great Migration and urbanization, though he substituted the culture of poverty thesis for historical analysis.

33 Biondi, *To Stand and Fight*; Wiese, *Places of Their Own*; Rhomberg, *No There There*; Rhonda Y. Williams, *Politics of Public Housing*; Countryman, *Civil Rights and Black Power*; Adam Green, *Selling the Race*.

34 The literature on civil rights is voluminous. A selected bibliography includes Chafe, *Civilities and Civil Rights*; Carson, *In Struggle*; McNeil, *Groundwork*; Doug McAdam, *Freedom Summer*; Garrow, *We Shall Overcome*; Weisbrot, *Freedom Bound*; Hill, *Race in America*; Sitkoff, *Struggle for Black Equality*; Dittmer, *Local People*; Payne, *I've Got the Light of Freedom*; Branch, *Pillar of Fire*; Lee, *For Freedom's Sake*; Tyson, *Radio Free Dixie*; Collier-Thomas and Franklin, *Sisters in the Struggle*; Ransby, *Ella Baker*; Hill, *Deacons for Defense*; Ogbar, *Black Power*; Crosby, *Little Taste of Freedom*; Lovett, *Civil Rights Movement in Tennessee*; Theoharis and Woodard, *Groundwork*; Strain, *Pure Fire*; Greene, *Our Separate Ways*; Branch, *At Canaan's Edge*; and Joseph, *Black Power Movement*.

35 Davis, *Blues Legacies and Black Feminism*, 81.

36 My articulation of "Home" draws from Dorinne Kondo's "The Narrative Production of 'Home.'" Of Home, Kondo says: "It stands for a safe place, where there is no need to explain oneself to outsiders; it stands for community; more problematically it can elicit a nostalgia for a past golden age that never was, a nostalgia that elides exclusion, power relations, and difference" (p. 97). She speaks of the production of Home from the resonance of the "sensory memory" in which foods, sounds, and smells serve as "symbolic vehicles of ethnic identity" (p. 106).

37 Osofsky, *Harlem*; Kusmer, *A Ghetto Takes Shape*; Katzman, *Before the Ghetto*; Lemann, *Promised Land*. For many historians, southern migrants became the loud-talking, ignorant, uncouth, and unclean "Negroes" whom northern blacks made them out to be. Taken as a whole, these studies posit black migrants from the South as unable to cope with life in the urban landscapes to which they relocated. See also Griffin, *"Who Set You Flowin'?"* In a different light, Griffin describes southern migrants' "initial confrontation" with the urban landscape as characterized by fear and confusion, in part because of the subtlety of power relations in the North.

38 Kondo, "Narrative Production of 'Home,'" 97.

CHAPTER 1

1 Gilpin, "Left by Themselves," 417.

2 Ibid., 417–19.

3 Harmon, "Black and White Women War Workers," 22. See also Karen Tucker Anderson, "Last Hired, First Fired."

4 Kerns, *Economic and Cultural Conditions*, 40; Harmon, "Black and White Women War Workers," 34, 36, 54.

5 "Employment by Race in Selected Plants in Louisville, Kentucky, January 1967," Woolsey Papers, box 1, folder 4, EL-UARC. According to the survey, of the forty African Americans employed, only two were skilled workers.

6 Harmon, "Black and White Women War Workers," 30, 35, 66.

7 Interview with Dr. Maurice Rabb, August 15, 1977, Black Oral History Collection, UARC.

8 Miller, *Net Intercensal Migration*, 89, 161, 220. On the decade 1950–60, see Bowles, *Net Migration*, 649; on 1935–40, see Truesdell, *Population, Internal Migration*; on 1960–70, see Marcus E. Jones, *Black Migration*, 71. For an overview of Louisville and Kentucky, see Yater, *Two Hundred Years*; Lucas, *History of Blacks in Kentucky*, and George C. Wright, *History of Blacks in Kentucky*, which provides background on African Americans in the state. Wright's *Life Behind a Veil* focuses on the city before the Depression. On black migration in Kentucky, see Luther J. Adams, "It Was North of Tennessee" and "African American Migration to Louisville." Trotter's *River Jordan* compares the formation of black communities in Louisville, Cincinnati, Pittsburgh, and Evansville, Ind.

9 Kyriakoudes, *Social Origins of the Urban South*.

10 Grossman, *Land of Hope*, 95, 111–12; Gottlieb, *Making Their Own Way*, 44–45; Jacqueline Jones, "Southern Diaspora," 40.

11 Grossman, *Land of Hope*, 111.

12 On specific case studies of the national migration that began in the 1910s, see Osofsky, *Harlem*; Spear, *Black Chicago*; Tuttle, *Race Riot*; Pleck, *Black Migration and Poverty*; Henri, *Black Migration*; Borchert, *Alley Life in Washington*; Trotter, *Black Milwaukee*; Earl Lewis, *In Their Own Interests*; Taylor, *Forging of a Black Community* and *In Search of the Racial Frontier*; Clark-Lewis *Living In, Living Out*; Griffin, *"Who Set You Flowin'?"*; and Gregory, *Southern Diaspora*.

13 Daniel, "New Deal, Southern Agriculture," 57.

14 Kirby, *Rural Worlds Lost*, 167.

15 Brinkley, "New Deal and Southern Politics"; Mitchell, *Depression Decade*, 99–101; Daniel, "New Deal, Southern Agriculture," 48–49, and "Going among Strangers," 886–87; Sitkoff, *New Deal for Blacks*, 48, and "Impact of the New Deal," 121; Whayne, *A New Plantation South*, 162–65; Wolters, *Negroes and the Great Depression*, 12–13. According to the AAA contracts established in 1933, landowners and cash tenants would receive the entire "parity payment." While tenants and sharecroppers would get between three-quarters to one-half the payment depending on their status and interest in the crop, farmer laborers working for wages would not collect any of the payment.

16 Daniel, "New Deal, Southern Agriculture," 56; Wolters, *Negroes and the Great Depression*, 60.

17 Kirby, *Rural Worlds Lost*, 72.

18 Daniel, "New Deal, Southern Agriculture," 55.

19 Mitchell, *Depression Decade*, 220–21.

20 Daniel, "New Deal, Southern Agriculture," 59; Kirby, *Rural Worlds Lost*, 319.

21 Brinkley, "New Deal and Southern Politics," 113.

22 Wolters, *Negroes and the Great Depression*, 93.

23 Ibid.; Sitkoff, *New Deal for Blacks*, 55.

24 Wolters, *Negroes and the Great Depression*, 109.

25 Sitkoff, *New Deal for Blacks*, 55; Wolters, *Negroes and the Great Depression*, 13.

26 Chad Berry, *Southern Migrants, Northern Exiles*, 31–32, 60.

27 Webb and Brown, *Migrant Families*, 4. See also Lively, *Rural Migration in the United States*, and Dennis, *African-American Exodus and White Migration*. For out-migration in eastern Kentucky during 1950–60, see Schwarzweller's *Mountain Families in Transition*, "Sociocultural Origins of Migration Patterns," "Career Placement and Economic Life Chances," and "Family Ties, Migration, and Transitional Adjustment."

28 Truesdell, *Population, Internal Migration*.

29 Unemployment Committee of the National Federation of Settlements, *Case Studies*, 112–13. None of the case studies reveal their subjects full names, hence Mr. Leighton.

30 Silver and Moeser, *Separate City*, 6. According to these authors, segregation led to the development of "separate cities" where African Americans lived in communities balanced between the denial of access and a full range of opportunities and a self-reliance that fostered the establishment of independent black-owned businesses.

31 Associates of Louisville Municipal College et al., *Study of Business and Employment among Negroes*, 37, 42–43.

32 Ibid., 28.

33 Ibid., 62–63, 68.

34 Brandon, "American Negro Migration," 153.

35 Earl Lewis, "Expectations, Economic Opportunities," 23.

36 Clippings from "Methods of Pro-integration Groups Differ," *Louisville Courier-Journal*, September 14, 1960, NAACP Branch Files, Louisville, 1956–65, pt. 2, C-50, NAACP Papers, LC.

37 "Brief Sketch," NAACP Branch Files, Louisville, pt. 1, G-76, NAACP Papers, LC. Although Anderson is widely believed to have been a Louisville native, a handwritten note he wrote to Thurgood Marshall indicates that he was, in fact, from Frankfort, Ky. According to the 1900 census, his parents, Tabitha Murphy and Charles Anderson, lived in Louisville. Charles Jr. was not born until 1907; by 1910 the four-year-old child was living in the home of Charles and Tabitha in Frankfort. Similarly, he is also listed as a member of their Frankfort household in 1920 at age fourteen. Afterward he attended Kentucky State University and graduated in 1925; he left the state to continue his education at Wilberforce University in Ohio (1927), then at Howard University in Washington, D.C. (1930). Thus, it seems more accurate to view Anderson as a migrant from Frankfort. See U.S. Bureau of the Census, *Twelfth Census, Thirteenth Census*, and *Fourteenth Census*.

38 Wade Hall, *Rest of the Dream*, 10, 7.

39 Associates of Louisville Municipal College et al., *Study of Business and Employment among Negroes*, 73–74.

40 Wilson Papers, EL-UARC; George D. Wilson, *Footprints in the Sand*, 82, 89.

41 Beers and Heflin, *Negro Population*, 5, 14, 21.

42 Ibid., 24–27; interview with Goldie Winstead-Beckett, September 12, 1978, Black Oral History Collection, UARC.

43 Interview with Lyman T. Johnson, Black Oral History Collection, UARC.

44 Urban Renewal Papers, Relocation Files, LMA.

45 Ibid., Inactive Families, boxes 20, A–Bolin; 22, E–F; 23, Ha–I; and 24, LMA.

46 Interview with W. L. Holmes, August 15, 1978, Black Oral History Collection, UARC.

47 Ibid.

48 Harmon, "Black and White Women War Workers," 21.

49 Interview with Amelia B. Ray, August 25, 1978, Black Oral History Collection, UARC.

50 Interview with Goldie Winstead-Beckett, September 12, 1978, Black Oral History Collection, UARC; Municipal Reference Collection, Louisville, Planning Urban Renewal, LMA.

51 Charles Hall, *Negroes in the United States*, 48. Ironically, this stands in stark contrast

with northern blacks, two-thirds of whom lived in cities whose population exceeded 100,000.

52 On Kentucky's black population, see Beers and Heflin, *Negro Population*, 24. See also Coleman, Pryor, and Christiansen, *Negro Population of Kentucky at Mid-Century*; De Jong and Hillery, *Kentucky's Negro Population in 1960*; and "Let's Pull Together Kentuckians!: A Digest Report of the Kentucky Commission on Negro Affairs," Kentucky Commission on Negro Affairs, 1946, Wade Hall Collection, KHS.

53 Interview with Rev. A. J. Elmore, August 21, 1996, by author.

54 Urban Renewal Papers, R-10 Project Relocation Files, boxes 22, 29, LMA.

55 Miller, *Net Intercensal Migration*, 220.

56 Weaver, *Negro Labor*, 135; Kerns, *Economic and Cultural Conditions*, 22.

57 Brandon, "American Negro Migration," 31–32.

58 Reid, "Special Problems of Negro Migration," 287–88.

59 Daniel, "Going among Strangers," 901.

60 Kerns, *Economic and Cultural Conditions*, 11.

61 U.S. Senate, Committee on National Defense Migration, *Hearings*, 6770; Yater, *Two Hundred Years*, 206.

62 Yater, *Two Hundred Years*, 208.

63 Ibid., 206; U.S. Senate, Committee on National Defense Migration, *Hearings*, 6770.

64 Interview with Mattie Jones, February 5, 1999, Kentucky Civil Rights Oral History Project, KHS.

65 Ibid., 207–9.

66 Ibid., 209.

67 Ibid., 209–10.

68 U.S. Senate, Committee on National Defense Migration, *Hearings*, 6771.

69 Yater, *Two Hundred Years*, 209.

70 Ibid., 208, 210.

71 Ibid., 208.

72 Ibid.

73 Trotter, *River Jordan*, 146–47; George C. Wright, *History of Blacks in Kentucky*, 16.

74 Trotter, *River Jordan*, 146–47.

75 Kerns, *Economic and Cultural Conditions*, 22. It is important to note that the president's Executive Order 8802 establishing the FEPC led not only to the employment of blacks in the defense industries as a whole, but also in all branches of the U.S. government. For the first time African Americans gained access to a host of jobs such as supervisors, foremen, chemists, clerical, and postal workers throughout the various federal agencies.

76 Harmon, "Black and White Women War Workers," 20–21.

77 Urban Renewal Papers, R-10 Project Relocation Files, boxes 20, 29, LMA.

78 Interview with James Glass, Black Oral History Collection, LMA.

79 Ibid.

80 Ibid.; Kerns, *Economic and Cultural Conditions*, 34–35.

81 Walls Papers, box 2, folder 17, EL-UARC.

82 Interview with Lillian Hudson, February 19, 1999, Kentucky Civil Rights Oral History Project, KHS.

83 U.S. Senate, Committee on National Defense Migration, *Hearings*, 6772.

84 Ibid.

85 Ibid., 6772, 6776, 6780.

86 Ibid., 6773.

87 Interview with James Glass, February 29 [no year listed], Black Oral History Collection, UARC.

88 Kerns, *Economic and Cultural Conditions*, 2.

89 *Report of the Kentucky Commission on Negro Affairs*, 28; Kerns, *Economic and Cultural Conditions*, 18.

90 Kerns, *Economic and Cultural Conditions*, 18, 20.

91 Ibid., 22.

92 Ibid., 18–19.

93 Fosl and K'Meyer, *Freedom on the Border*, 156.

94 Du Bois, *Black Reconstruction*, 700.

95 Ibid.

96 Ibid., 701.

97 Roediger, *Wages of Whiteness*, 13. The literature on whiteness is extensive. See Guterl, *Color of Race*; Lipsitz, *Possessive Investment in Whiteness*; Hale, *Making Whiteness*; Ignatiev, *How the Irish Became White*; Roediger, *Towards the Abolition of Whiteness*; and, predating all of these, Du Bois, *Dusk of Dawn*. For criticism, see Kolchin, "Whiteness Studies." See also Kelley, *Race Rebels*, 30–31. Alluding to Du Bois and Roediger's studies, Robin D. G. Kelley argues that much of black labor was stigmatized as "nigger work," which gave white workers "a sense of superiority and security" from being white and not holding the same jobs as African Americans. Given the relegation of black workers to domestic and manual labor in Louisville, it does not seem to be a great leap to suggest that whiteness played a similar role in the city.

98 *Report of the Kentucky Commission on Negro Affairs*, 28.

99 Kerns, *Economic and Cultural Conditions*, 22–23.

100 Ibid.

101 Ibid., 31.

102 Ibid., 34.

103 Ibid., 31; Urban Renewal Papers, Relocation Files, Inactive Families, box 27, LMA.

104 Cited in Kerns, *Economic and Cultural Conditions*, 31.

105 Ibid., 37.

106 Urban Renewal Papers, Relocation Files, Inactive Families, box 27, LMA.

107 Karen Tucker Anderson, "Last Hired, First Fired," 82, 84.

108 Kerns, *Economic and Cultural Conditions*, 22. See also Harmon, "Black and White Women War Workers." On the lack of employment prospects for black Louisvillians after the war, see George C. Wright, *History of Blacks in Kentucky*, 16, and Kerns, *Economic and Cultural Conditions*, 22–25, 40.

109 Ibid., 97.

110 Kerns, *Economic and Cultural Conditions*, 11.

111 Miller, *Net Intercensal Migration*, 161. Of that number, 3,909 were women and 3,286 were men.

112 See, e.g., Woodson, *Century of Negro Migration*; Scott, *Negro Migration during the War*; Woofter, *Negro Migration*; Charles Johnson, *The Negro in Chicago*; Osofsky, *Harlem*; Spear, *Black Chicago*; and Kusmer, *A Ghetto Takes Shape*.

113 Wade Hall, *Mae Street Kidd*; interview with Rev. A. J. Elmore, September 23, 1996, by author.

114 Beers and Heflin, *Negro Population*, 2–3, 20.

CHAPTER 2

1 Clara Smith, "L & N Blues."

2 Marcus E. Jones, *Black Migration*, 71; Miller, *Net Intercensal Migration*, 99, 161, 220; Luther J. Adams, "Headed to Louisville" and "African American Migration to Louisville."

3 Ayers, *Southern Crossing*, 63.

4 Interviews with codes 011, 119, 048, box 10, NYCC, EL-UARC.

5 Ernest Collins, "Political Behavior of the Negroes," 29.

6 Ibid. Collins asserts that whites in Paris and Danville excluded African Americans from local politics by reconfiguring town boundaries so black areas were no longer within the town limits.

7 Carmichael and Johnson, *Louisville Story*, 12–13.

8 George C. Wright, "Civil Rights Movement in Kentucky," 47.

9 Ayers, *Southern Crossing*, 107.

10 George C. Wright, *Racial Violence in Kentucky*, 5, and *History of Blacks in Kentucky*, 2:79–83. At least one of these lynchings appeared on a widely disseminated postcard. See Allen, *Without Sanctuary*.

11 George C. Wright, *History of Blacks in Kentucky*, 41.

12 Wade Hall, *Rest of the Dream*, 59.

13 Ibid.

14 *Race Relations in Louisville*, 4–5.

15 Kerns, *Economic and Cultural Conditions*, 80, 111, 159, 33. See also George C. Wright, *History of Blacks in Kentucky*, 54.

16 George C. Wright, *Life Behind a Veil*, 4.

17 Ibid., 5.

18 Ibid., 53–55. In brief, the case began when three African Americans—Horace Pearce and brothers Robert and Samuel Fox—boarded a streetcar on the Market Street line after church one Sunday in 1871. Their actions led to a disturbance and ultimately to their arrest. The black community united behind them and, at a meeting the next night at Quinn Chapel Church, decided to settle the matter in court. Pearce and the Fox brothers won their suit, but that did not end the problem. Blacks were often attacked for exercising their right to ride streetcars, as the city continually tried to pass Jim Crow laws on streetcars well into the next century.

19 Hudson, "History of Louisville Municipal College," 28, and "Establishment of Louisville Municipal College," 111–23.

20 Hudson, "History of Louisville Municipal College."

21 Kerns, *Economic and Cultural Conditions*, 175.

22 Ibid., 48.

23 Lohman, *Principles of Police Work*, 18–19; John L. Anderson, "Changing Patterns of Louisville's Black Residential Areas," presented at the Conference of the Southeast Division of the Association of American Geographers, November 14, 1976, in "Blacks" Vertical Reference File, EL-UARC.

24 Woolsey Papers, box 4, folder 2, EL-UARC.

25 *Louisville Defender*, February 17, 1940; Pruitt Papers, box 1, EL-UARC.

26 *Louisville Leader*, June 25, 1949; Lohman, *Principles of Police Work*, 16, 24.

27 Lohman, *Principles of Police Work*, 19, 22, 24; Kerns, *Economic and Cultural Conditions*, 49.

28 Lohman, *Principles of Police Work*, 28–29.

29 Kerns, *Economic and Cultural Conditions*, 52.

30 Ibid., 50, 53.

31 Powers, *I Shared the Dream*, 14, 74.

32 Kerns, *Economic and Cultural Conditions*, 58.

33 Lohman, *Principles of Police Work*, 21, 28; Kerns, *Economic and Cultural Conditions*, 49. Dr. Lohman cites a local study demonstrating that although only 12 percent of African Americans in the neighborhoods surrounding Central High School paid fifteen dollars or more for rent, 74 percent said they would and could pay more.

34 Kerns, *Economic and Cultural Conditions*, 53, 60.

35 Ibid., 60.

36 WPA, *The Real Property and Sanitary Survey of Louisville, Kentucky, 1939–1940*, Official Project No. 665-43-3-320, WPA No. 5544–56, in Pruitt Papers, box 1, EL-UARC.

37 Kerns, *Economic and Cultural Conditions*, 70–71.

38 Ibid., 172–75.

39 Ibid., 87.

40 Ibid., 87–82.

41 Ibid., 61.

42 Ibid., 52.

43 Ibid., 51; Pruitt Papers and Beecher Terrace Scrapbook, EL-UARC; *Louisville Defender*, June 8, 1940.

44 Kerns, *Economic and Cultural Conditions*, 58.

45 Lohman, *Principles of Police Work*, 20.

46 "Ghettoization in Kentucky Cities," Housing, Louisville, 1967, in NAACP Papers, pt. 4, LC. See also Cummings and Price, "Race Relations and Public Policy." According to Scott Cummings and Michael Price, the segregation index stood at 83.6 percent.

47 George C. Wright, "Civil Rights Movement in Kentucky," 59.

48 George C. Wright, *History of Blacks in Kentucky*, 62.

49 George C. Wright, *Life Behind a Veil*, 5. Similarly, the 1948 Urban League report notes that many black leaders in Louisville attributed the advancements in the African Americans' status to whites' "progressivism." The report claims: "These achievements, they state, would not have been possible without a liberal attitude on the part of whites, even though it was necessary for Negroes to initiate many of the proposals through protest" (pp. 174–75).

50 Interview with code 011, box 10, NYCC, EL-UARC.

51 Interview with code 003, ibid.

52 Interview with code 011, ibid.

53 Ibid.

54 Interview with code 003, ibid.

55 Interview with code 119, ibid.

56 Ibid.; interview with Rev. William G. Marks, November 29, 1997, by author; Wade Hall, *Rest of the Dream*, 38–39, 58.

57 Wade Hall, *Rest of the Dream*, 58.

58 Interview with code 048, box 10, NYCC, EL-UARC.

59 Ibid.

60 Interview with Dr. Maurice Rabb, August 15, 1977, Black Oral History Collection, UARC.

61 "Law Sought to Prohibit Racial Bias," Clippings, Louisville, 1956–59, pt. 3, C-50, NAACP Papers, LC.

62 Interview with Rev. William G. Marks, November 29, 1997, by author.

63 Wade Hall, *Rest of the Dream*, 60.

64 Le Roi Jones, *Blues People*, x. The literature on blues is extensive. Key texts are Oliver, *Blues Fell This Morning*; Keil, *Urban Blues*; Albert Murray, *Stomping the Blues*; Daphne Duval Harrison, *Black Pearls*; Barlow, *"Looking Up at Down"*; *Wild Women Don't Have the Blues*; Carby, "It Jus' Be's Dat Way Sometime"; Thomas, "A Sense of Community"; Lomax, *Land of Where Blues Began*; and Floyd, *Power of Black Music*.

65 Oliver, *Blues Fell This Morning*, 12.

66 Litwack, *Trouble in Mind*, xvi–xvii.

67 Wilson-Moore, *To Place Our Deeds*, 130, 133.

68 Barlow, *"Looking Up at Down,"* xii, 117.

69 Thomas, "A Sense of Community," 79–82.

70 Ibid.

71 Hughes, *Vintage Hughes*, 177.

72 Oliver, *Meaning of the Blues*, 67.

73 Oliver, *Story of the Blues*, 82–83.

74 Guy, "Stone Crazy."

75 Cited in Oliver, *Meaning of the Blues*, 63–64.

76 Hine, "Black Migration to the Urban Midwest," 138.

77 Cited in Oliver, *Meaning of the Blues*, 72. See also Peetie Wheatstraw's "C & A Blues," ibid., 85.

78 Beaman, "Goin' Away Blues."

79 Urban Renewal Papers, R-10 Project Relocation Files, box 30, LMA.

80 Interview with Ruth Bryant, July 24 [no year listed], Black Oral History Collection, UARC.

81 Wade Hall, *Rest of the Dream*, 10, 7.

82 George C. Wright, "Civil Rights Movement in Kentucky," 51.

83 Wade Hall, *Rest of the Dream*, 60.

84 Interview with Rev. William G. Marks, November 29, 1997, by author.

85 Interview with code 036.

86 Interview with W. L. Holmes, August 15, 1978, Black Oral History Collection, UARC.

87 Ibid.

88 Interview with Dr. Jessie Bell, July 28, 1979, Black Oral History Collection, UARC.

89 Interview with Amelia B. Ray, August 25, 1978, Black Oral History Collection, UARC.

90 Interview with Rev. William G. Marks, November 29, 1997, by author. In fact, members of the Marks family have lived in Kentucky since at least the 1830s, when James Herndon transported them as slaves from Virginia to Mountain Island in Owen County.

91 Powers, *I Shared the Dream*, 75. Jim Crow Town, also known as "Jimtown," is located just outside Lexington.

92 Interview with E. Deedom Alston, August 15, 1979, Black Oral History Collection, UARC.

93 Kondo, "Narrative Production of 'Home,'" 106. On Home, see also Martin and Mohanty, "Feminist Politics."

94 Barbara Smith, *Home Girls*, xxii–xxiii, li. See also Wald, *Crossing the Line*, 19, 50–51.

95 Kondo, "Narrative Production of 'Home,'" 97–98.

96 Ibid.

97 Davis, *Blues Legacies and Black Feminism*, 81.

98 Wade Hall, *Rest of the Dream*, 183.

99 Martin and Martin, *Black Extended Family*, 7–8.

100 Interview with Rev. William G. Marks, November 29, 1997, by author.

CHAPTER 3

1 Wade Hall, *Passing for Black*, 37–38.

2 Ibid.

3 Ibid., 32. After the death of her first husband, Horace Street, Mae married James Meredith Kidd. The Lincoln Institute was a school established for rural blacks in Kentucky from towns or counties that did not support adequate education.

4 Ibid., 34.

5 Ibid., 38, 41.

6 Ibid., 39.

7 Interview with Amelia B. Ray, August 25, 1978, Black Oral History Collection, UARC.

8 Interview with Goldie Winstead-Beckett, September 12, 1978, Black Oral History Collection, UARC; Municipal Reference Collection, Louisville, Planning Urban Renewal, LMA.

9 Interview with Rev. A. J. Elmore, August 21, 1996, by author.

10 Interview with Dr. Maurice Rabb, August 15, 1977, Black Oral History Collection, UARC.

11 Wilson Papers, EL-UARC; George D. Wilson, *Footprints in the Sand*, 82, 89.

12 Wade Hall, *Passing for Black*, 41; Interview with Dr. John and Murray Walls, July 31, 1973, Black Oral History Collection, UARC; Wade Hall, *Rest of the Dream*, 128; George C. Wright, *History of Blacks in Kentucky*, 60–61.

13 Wade Hall, *Passing for Black*, 38; Urban Renewal R-10 Project Relocation Files (Southwick I to West Downtown), 1960–67, LMA.

14 Wilson Papers, EL-UARC; George D. Wilson, *Footprints in the Sand*, 100.

15 Interview with code 025, box 10, NYCC, EL-UARC.

16 Kerns, *Economic and Cultural Conditions*, 253, 193. The Urban League's failure to provide migrants with direct aid during this period stands in stark contrast to the earlier migration when the league was "concerned primarily with helping to adjust the problems of Negro families who came to Louisville in large numbers from rural areas of Kentucky and near by states after the close of WWI."

17 Interview with Rev. A. J. Elmore, August 21, 1996, by author.

18 Anniversary Brochure of the Fifteenth Street Memorial AME Church, Pruitt Papers, box 2, EL-UARC. The Paducah Club was organized in 1943, and all of its members were former residents of Paducah, Ky.

19 Interview with Rev. William G. Marks, November 30, 1997, by author; interview with
    W. L. Holmes, August 154, 1978, Black Oral History Collection, UARC; "Blacks" Verti-
    cal Reference File, EL-UARC.
20 Hale, *Making Whiteness*, 136.
21 Ibid.
22 Barkley Brown and Kimball, "Mapping the Terrain of Black Richmond," 83.
23 Ibid., 41.
24 Ibid. Kidd's father was white and her mother was of mixed heritage, which accounted
    for her light skin.
25 Trotter, *River Jordan*, 107.
26 *Louisville Leader*, May 7, 1939.
27 George C. Wright, *Life Behind a Veil*, 72–73.
28 Ibid., 117.
29 Ibid., 257.
30 *Louisville Leader*, May 18, 1935.
31 George C. Wright, *Life Behind a Veil*, 257.
32 *Louisville Leader*, June 25, 1949.
33 *Louisville Leader*, June 3, 1939.
34 *Louisville Leader*, June 25, 1949.
35 *Louisville Leader*, June 3, 1939.
36 Ibid.
37 *Louisville Leader*, April 20, 1935.
38 *Louisville Leader*, June 3, 1939.
39 Elizabeth Miller to Bessie Etherly, October 10, 1932, sent from *Chicago Defender*, and
    Harris to Louisville NAACP, NAACP Branch Files, Louisville, 1914–39, pt. 1, G-76,
    NAACP Papers, LC.
40 Ibid.
41 Wolcott, *Remaking Respectability*, 8. See also Higginbotham, *Righteous Discontent*, and
    Shaw, *What a Women Ought to Be and to Do*.
42 Parrish Papers, EL-UARC.
43 *Louisville Leader*, September 20, 1947.
44 *Louisville Leader*, October 20, 1945.
45 George C. Wright, *Life Behind a Veil*, 254–56.
46 Ibid., 254.
47 *Louisville Courier-Journal*, September 12, October 5, 23, 29, 1927.
48 NAACP press release, "18th Victim of Louisville Police Rouses NAACP to Stop Shoot-
    ings," 1932, NAACP Branch Files, Louisville, 1914–39, pt. 1, G-76, NAACP Papers, LC.
49 George C. Wright, *Life Behind a Veil*, 255–56. Wright's work contains a detailed discus-
    sion of police corruption and police brutality in Louisville between the late 1890s and
    1930.
50 *Louisville Leader*, April 16, 1938.
51 *Louisville Leader*, June 3, 1939.
52 Ibid.
53 Ibid.
54 *Louisville Leader*, September 20, 1947.
55 *Louisville Leader*, June 3, 1939.

56 Lohman, *Principles of Police Work*, 14–15. Lohman's report attempts to walk a tightrope in acknowledging police brutality as a reality without labeling the individual actions of a specific officer, or the Louisville Police Department as a whole, as unjust or racist. In doing so, he views the problems African Americans faced in the city as ones of "maladjustment" on their part, resulting in unequal treatment by the police generally.

57 *Louisville Leader*, June 25, 1949; Lohman, *Principles of Police Work*, 16, 24.

58 Woolsey Papers, folder 1, EL-UARC; Vernon Robertson, "A Buried History of Segregation in Louisville," 1961.

59 Lohman, *Principles of Police Work*, 65.

60 *Louisville Leader*, May 1, 1948.

61 Wade Hall, *Passing for Black*, 36.

62 Ibid., 36–38.

63 Ibid., 62.

64 Higginbotham, *Righteous Discontent*, 190–92, 196–97.

65 Abrams, "Negotiating Respect," 65.

66 Higginbotham, *Righteous Discontent*, 194.

67 Interview with Eleanor Jordan, February 3, 1999, Kentucky Civil Rights Oral History Project, KHS.

68 *Louisville Leader*, April 20, 1935.

69 *Louisville Leader*, April 13, 1935.

70 *Louisville Leader*, December 15, 1945.

71 Ibid.

72 Interview with Dr. Maurice Rabb, August 15, 1977, Black Oral History Collection, UARC.

73 Interview with Dr. John and Murray Walls, July 31, 1973, Black Oral History Collection, UARC.

74 My thinking on race has been most influenced by Fields, "Ideology and Race in American History"; Anzaldua, *Borderlands/La Frontera*; Du Bois, *Dusk of Dawn*; Prakash, "Subaltern Studies as Postcolonial Criticism" and "Writing Post-Orientalists Histories of the Third World"; and Chakrabarty, "Postcoloniality and the Artifice of History."

75 Hine, "Rape and the Inner Lives of Black Women," 292, 294–95.

76 See James Baldwin, "Stranger in the Village," 135–49; Blassingame, *Slave Community*, 313–14; Roberts, *From Trickster to Badman*; Richard Wright, *Black Boy*, 149, 182–86, 227–29; and Malcolm X, *Autobiography*, xi. Each author suggests that dissemblance (whether in the form of trickster or not) has a long history among African Americans as a whole. Malcolm X and Baldwin emphasize its place for men specifically, whereas Hine rightly directs our attention to how the "same" strategy may have offered protection for women from a variety of oppressors.

77 Wade Hall, *Rest of the Dream*, 115.

78 Ibid.

79 Interview with Rev. A. J. Elmore, August 21, 1996, by author.

80 Wade Hall, *Rest of the Dream*, 118. See also Richard Wright, *Black Boy*, 149, 182–85, 196, 200.

81 Hine, "Rape and the Inner Lives of Black Women," 295.

82 Wade Hall, *Rest of the Dream*, 9, 119.

83 Ibid., 119.

84 Wald, *Crossing the Color Line*, 5. See also Nielson, *Reading Race*, who argues that "race serves simultaneously as the means by which hegemonic discourse organizes its policing functions, erecting boundaries that define and oppress an other" (p. 3). On passing, see Ginsberg, *Passing and the Fictions of Identity*; Piper, "Passing for White, Passing for Black"; Browder, *Slippery Characters*; and Carole Anne Tyler, "Passing."

85 Ginsberg, *Passing and the Fictions of Identity*, 16.

86 Wade Hall, *Passing for Black*, 174, 177–78.

87 Ibid., 74.

88 Ibid., 17.

89 Ibid., 178. See also Piper, "Passing for White, Passing for Black."

90 Ernest Collins, "Political Behavior of the Negroes," 70.

91 Ibid.; interview with Lyman T. Johnson, Black Oral History Collection, UARC.

92 Ginsberg, *Passing and the Fictions of Identity*, 8.

93 Ibid.

94 Carole Anne Tyler, "Passing," 213.

95 Interview with Amelia B. Ray, August 25, 1978, Black Oral History Collection, UARC.

96 Wald, *Crossing the Line*, 134.

97 Interview with Amelia B. Ray, August 25, 1978, Black Oral History Collection, UARC.

98 Ibid.

99 Interview with code 048, box 10, NYCC, EL-UARC.

100 Interview with Amelia B. Ray, August 25, 1978, Black Oral History Collection, UARC.

101 *Louisville Leader*, January 10, 1942.

102 Interview with Amelia B. Ray, August 25, 1978, Black Oral History Collection, UARC.

103 Interview with Dr. John and Murray Walls, July 31, 1973, Black Oral History Collection, UARC.

104 Wade Hall, *Rest of the Dream*, 128. Johnson described *Gone with the Wind* as a "shameful glorification of the fantasy known as the Old South and the myth that such a fine civilization was shamelessly destroyed by a damnable bunch of nigger-loving Yankees!"

105 *Louisville Leader*, February 11, 1939.

106 *Louisville Leader*, April 13, 1935.

107 *Louisville Leader*, June 8, 1946. The large number of African Americans involved in the "Sugar Chile" incident suggests that they could have not all been migrants. My point here is not that this strategy was unique, but rather that migrants brought it with them to the city.

CHAPTER 4

1 *Louisville Leader*, April 20, 1935. In the same article Cole shifted to a discussion of how African Americans "should at all times" shop in stores that did not segregate. In doing so, he intimately linked political action with the fight against segregation. Significantly, Cole had relocated in Louisville during the era of the Great Migration.

2 Ernest Collins, "Political Behavior of the Negroes," 75; Kerns, *Economic and Cultural Conditions*, 11. On black political participation in Louisville, see also Kesselman, "Negro Voting," and George C. Wright, "Black Political Insurgency."

3 George C. Wright, *Life Behind a Veil*, 247.

4 Ernest Collins, "Political Behavior of the Negroes," 79.

5 Ibid., 73–75.

6 George C. Wright, *Life Behind a Veil*, 239–40.

7 Ernest Collins, "Political Behavior of the Negroes," 74.

8 *Louisville Leader*, September 24, 1921.

9 Ernest Collins, "Political Behavior of the Negroes," 76.

10 Ibid., 77.

11 Ibid.; George C. Wright, *Life Behind a Veil*, 251.

12 George C. Wright, *Life Behind a Veil*, 247–49.

13 Ernest Collins, "Political Behavior of the Negroes," 79.

14 Ibid., 81.

15 *Louisville Leader*, October 29, 1932.

16 Weiss, *Farewell to the Party of Lincoln*. See also Berry and Blassingame, *Long Memory*, 176–80, and Sitkoff, *New Deal for Blacks*, 40–42, 84, 93–97.

17 *Louisville Defender*, November 30, 1935.

18 *Louisville Defender*, November 16, 1940, cited in Ernest Collins, "Political Behavior of the Negroes," 89.

19 Ernest Collins, "Political Behavior of the Negroes," 90.

20 Cited in ibid., 97.

21 *Louisville Defender*, October 30, 1948.

22 Ernest Collins, "Political Behavior of the Negroes," 96.

23 Cited in ibid., 104–5.

24 Miller, *Net Intercensal Migration*, 89, 161, 220.

25 Cited in Ernest Collins, "Political Behavior of the Negroes," 190–91.

26 *Louisville Defender*, October 21, 1944.

27 George C. Wright, *Life Behind a Veil*, 252–57.

28 Ernest Collins, "Political Behavior of the Negroes," 146; George C. Wright, "Desegregation of Public Accommodations," 192.

29 Ernest Collins, "Political Behavior of the Negroes," 146.

30 Interview with Felix S. Anderson, n.d., Black Oral History Collection, UARC.

31 "Earl Dearing," in Kleber, *Encyclopedia of Louisville*, 240.

32 *Louisville Courier-Journal*, September 14, 1960; interview with Goldie Winstead-Beckett, September 12, 1978, Black Oral History Collection, UARC.

33 Laurie Green, *Battling the Plantation Mentality*.

34 Subject File: Discrimination; Teachers Salaries, February–September 1933, and Letters, NAACP Branch Files, Louisville, pt. 1, C-281, NAACP Papers, LC: Charles Hamilton Houston to Rev. J. A. Johnson, 1936; Thurgood Marshall to Louisville Branch President, August 30, 1937; and William Pickens to Bessie S. Etherly, October 20, 1937.

35 Letters, May 23, 1925; December 28, 1929; February 27, 1930; April 30, 1930; and May 21, 1930—all in NAACP Branch Files, Louisville, pt. 1, G-76, NAACP Papers, LC.

36 McElhone, "Civil Rights Activities," 81.

37 George C. Wright, *History of Blacks in Kentucky*, 163.

38 Charles W. Anderson to Charles Hamilton Houston, March 6, 1936, NAACP Branch Files, Louisville, pt. 1, G-76, NAACP Papers, LC.

39 Yolanda Barnett to Thurgood Marshall, September 16, 1940, in Teachers Salaries, Cor-

respondence 1940–42, NAACP Branch Files, Louisville, pt. 2, B-127, NAACP Papers, LC; George C. Wright, *History of Blacks in Kentucky*, 165.

40 William Pickens to B. S. Etherly, Secretary, Louisville NAACP, October 20, 1937, NAACP Branch Files, Louisville, pt. 1, G-76, NAACP Papers, LC.

41 Daisy Lampkin to Charles Hamilton Houston, November 4, 1937, NAACP Branch Files, Louisville, pt. 1, G-76, NAACP Papers, LC.

42 William Perry to P. O. Sweeny, n.d., ibid.

43 Daisy Lampkin to Charles Hamilton Houston, November 4, 1937, NAACP Branch Files, Louisville, pt. 1, G-77, NAACP Papers, LC. Houston was vice dean of the Howard Law School (1929–35) and litigation director of the NAACP.

44 L. A. Ransom to William Pickens, November 19, 1937, NAACP Branch Files, Louisville, pt. 1, G-76, NAACP Papers, LC.

45 P. O. Sweeny to William Perry, n.d., NAACP Branch Files, ibid.

46 George C. Wright, *History of Blacks in Kentucky*, 163.

47 "Negroes," box 5-2, Louisville Free Public Library; *Louisville Times*, March 5, 1939.

48 Cited in George C. Wright, *History of Blacks in Kentucky*, 163.

49 Cited in ibid., 165–66.

50 Handwritten note in Teachers Salaries, Correspondence 1940–42, NAACP Branch Files, Louisville, pt. 2, B-177, NAACP Papers, LC.

51 Ibid.

52 NAACP press release, ibid.

53 George C. Wright, *History of Blacks in Kentucky*, 166.

54 NAACP press release in Teachers Salaries, Correspondence 1940–42, NAACP Branch Files, Louisville, pt. 2, B-177, NAACP Papers, LC.

55 *Louisville Courier-Journal*, December 9, 1941; George C. Wright, *History of Blacks in Kentucky*, 166–67.

56 Cited in George C. Wright, *History of Blacks in Kentucky*, 167–68.

57 McNeil, *Groundwork*. Although McNeil emphasizes the larger groundwork Charles Hamilton Houston and the NAACP participated in before *Brown*, she devotes little attention to Louisville or Kentucky's role in that process.

58 Cited in George C. Wright, "Civil Rights Movement in Kentucky," 49.

59 George C. Wright, *History of Blacks in Kentucky*, 167–68.

60 B. S. Etherly to Dr. Frank L. McVey, 1940, NAACP Branch Files, Louisville, pt. 1, C-200, NAACP Papers, LC.

61 *Louisville Courier-Journal*, November 26, 1939.

62 George C. Wright, *History of Blacks in Kentucky*, 175.

63 Charles Hamilton Houston to Prentice Thomas, January 22, 1940, NAACP Branch Files, Louisville, pt. 1, C-200, NAACP Papers, LC.

64 Ibid.

65 Acting Secretary to Lyman T. Johnson, February 29, 1944, ibid.

66 Leo Chamberlain to Charles Eubanks, September 6, 1941, University of Kentucky, *Eubanks v. University of Kentucky*, Correspondence 1940–41, NAACP Branch Files, Louisville, pt. 2, B-200, NAACP Papers, LC.

67 *Louisville Courier-Journal*, October 14, 1941.

68 Ibid.

69 Ethridge, "America's Obligation to Its Negro Citizens," 11.

70 Ibid., 2, 6.

71 Ibid., 7, 11.

72 George C. Wright, "Civil Rights Movement in Kentucky," 51.

73 Prentice Thomas to Stephen A. Burnley, March 24, 1943, University of Kentucky, *Eubanks v. University of Kentucky*, Correspondence 1940–41, NAACP Branch Files, Louisville, pt. 2, B-200, NAACP Papers, LC.

74 Prentice Thomas to Stephen A. Burnley, April 14, 1943, ibid.

75 Prentice Thomas to Thurgood Marshall, April 15, 1942, ibid.

76 Charles Hamilton Houston to Thurgood Marshall, February 1943, ibid.

77 Lyman T. Johnson to University of Kentucky Board of Trustees, March 27, 1948, Lyman T. Johnson Correspondence 1948–49, ibid.

78 *Louisville Times*, March 24, 1948.

79 George C. Wright, "Civil Rights Movement in Kentucky," 52–53.

80 *Louisville Defender*, October 16, 1948.

81 Robert Carter to Thurgood Marshall, February 18–20, 1949 (memo), Lyman T. Johnson, Correspondence 1948–49, NAACP Branch Files, Louisville, pt. 2, B-200, NAACP Papers, LC.

82 James Crumlin to Franklin K. Williams, Assistant Special Counsel, December 21, 1948, ibid.

83 Lyman T. Johnson to Thurgood Marshall, January 15, 1949, ibid. Johnson sent a similar letter to the Kentucky State Conference of the NAACP (in ibid.).

84 Robert Carter to Thurgood Marshall, February 18–20, 1949 (memo), and note dated January 7, 1949, Lyman T. Johnson, Correspondence 1948–49, NAACP Branch Files, Louisville, pt. 2, B-200, NAACP Papers, LC.

85 *Louisville Leader*, July 12, August 30, 1947.

86 For more on the desegregation of Louisville's parks, see McElhone, "Civil Rights Activities," 53–70.

87 George C. Wright, "Civil Rights Movement in Kentucky," 53.

88 NAACP press release, March 31, 1949, in Lyman T. Johnson Correspondence 1948–49, NAACP Branch Files, Louisville, pt. 2, B-200, NAACP Papers, LC.

89 George C. Wright, *History of Blacks in Kentucky*, 80, and "Civil Rights Movement in Kentucky," 53.

90 NAACP press release, March 31, 1949, in Lyman T. Johnson Correspondence 1948–49, NAACP Branch Files, Louisville, pt. 2, B-200, NAACP Papers, LC.

91 Lyman T. Johnson to R. Carter, June 29, 1949, Lyman T. Johnson Correspondence 1948–49, ibid.

92 *Louisville Leader*, May 21, 1949.

93 McElhone, "Civil Rights Activities," 107.

94 "Equal Education for Every Kentucky Child: Resolutions of the Kentucky Negro Education Association," Kentucky Negro Education Association, April 20–23, 1949, 5, box 13, folder 13, Wade Hall Collection, KHS.

95 Ibid., 8.

96 Wilson Papers, EL-UARC.

97 Bates, *Pullman Porters*, 150.

98 Murray Walls to Rabbi Rauch, April 7, 1941, Walls Papers, EL-UARC.

99 Harold F. Brigham to Murray Walls, 1941, Walls Papers, EL-UARC.

100 Interview with Dr. John and Murray Walls, July 31, 1973, Black Oral History Collection, UARC; McElhone, "Civil Rights Activities," 112.

101 *Louisville Leader*, January 3, 1942.

102 McElhone, "Civil Rights Activities," 114.

103 Bates, *Pullman Porters*, 187, 183.

104 *Louisville Courier-Journal*, January 25, 1953.

105 *Louisville Leader*, September 20, 1947.

106 McElhone, "Civil Rights Activities," 151; Horton, *Not without Struggle*, 58.

107 Interview with Dr. Jessie Bell, July 28, 1979, Black Oral History Collection, UARC.

108 Ibid.; interview with Dr. Maurice Rabb, August 15, 1977, Black Oral History Collection, UARC; "With Charity for All" (Red Cross pamphlet), box 13, Morris Papers, and box 3, General Correspondence, Red Cross Papers, EL-UARC.

109 Morris Papers, boxes 7, 13, EL-UARC.

110 Gilpin, "Left by Themselves," 500.

111 Ibid., 522–26.

112 K'Meyer, "Building Interracial Democracy"; Braden, "Civil Rights," in Kleber, *Encyclopedia of Louisville*, 192.

113 "Employment by Race in Selected Plants in Louisville, Kentucky[,] January 1967," Woolsey Papers, box 1, folder 4, EL-UARC. According to this report, GE employed 784 blacks in unskilled positions. Similarly, the Ford Motor Company employed 28 skilled blacks and 230 unskilled blacks in its 4,792-person workforce.

114 Interviews with Wilbur Haskin, Lexington, Ky., July 5, 1997, and Rev. William G. Marks, November 29, 1997, by author.

115 K'Meyer, "Building Interracial Democracy," 417.

116 Ibid., 419–20.

117 Ibid.

118 Ibid., 422.

119 Hughes, "My America," 303.

120 Cited in K'Meyer, *Civil Rights*, 33.

121 See ⟨http://douglassarchives.org/doug_a10.html⟩ (January 12, 2007). The extended quotation offers a sense that African Americans in Louisville, like many before and after them, utilized the icons of democracy not only rhetorically but also literally to point out the gulf between ideology and reality. Frederick Douglass ultimately answers his question, saying, "What, to the American slave, is your 4th of July? I answer: a day that reveals to him, more than all other days in the year, the gross injustice and cruelty to which he is the constant victim. To him, your celebration is a sham; your boasted liberty, an unholy license; your national greatness, swelling vanity; your sounds of rejoicing are empty and heartless; your denunciations of tyrants, brass fronted impudence; your shouts of liberty and equality, hollow mockery; your prayers and hymns, your sermons and thanksgivings, with all your religious parade, and solemnity, are, to him, mere bombast, fraud, deception, impiety, and hypocrisy—a thin veil to cover up crimes which would disgrace a nation of savages. There is not a nation on the earth guilty of practices, more shocking and bloody, than are the people of these United States, at this very hour."

122 Suri, *Protest and Politics*, 88. Suri examines the "words of prominent iconoclasts . . . that allowed men and women to express their anger as they had not before."

123 Clippings by Amelia B. Ray from *Louisville Times*, February 19, 1943, June 3, 1949, and *Louisville Courier-Journal*, June 23, 1946, January 30, 1948, September 24, 1950, in Louisville Municipal College Scrapbook, AL-UARC.

124 George C. Wright, *History of Blacks in Kentucky*, 191–92.

125 Cited in K'Meyer, "Building Interracial Democracy," 428.

126 Braden, *The Wall Between*, 51. According to Anne Braden, white liberals in Louisville were "generally gradualist in their approach and their methods," 43.

127 George C. Wright, *History of Blacks in Kentucky*, 191–92.

128 Kneebone, *Southern Liberal Journalists*, 90–91.

129 hooks, *Feminist Theory*, 20–21. See also Link, *Paradox of Southern Progressivism*. He points out that many southern white liberals explicitly stated they sought solutions that were "not radical"; their efforts were "directed largely toward the eradication of the various causes of irritation and friction" (p. 260).

130 Link, *Paradox of Southern Progressivism*, 257.

131 Janken, Introduction to *What the Negro Wants*, xxv.

132 Dawson, *Black Visions*, 244–45; *Southern Frontier* 3, no. 7 (July 1942). Ironically, the editorial, published with a copy of Ethridge's FEPC speech, was placed directly under an article by Virginius Dabney entitled, "Paternalism in Race Relations Is Outmoded."

133 Wade Defense Committee, "They Broke the Unwritten Law." On the Wade-Braden case, see interview with Anne Braden, March 5–18, 1981, Black Oral History Collection, UARC, and interview with Anne Braden, March 23, 2003, "Living the Story" Collection, KHS.

134 Others were arrested along with the Bradens: Vernon Bown, who volunteered to help protect the Wades and was charged with bombing the house; Larue Spiker, an unemployed grain millworker who offered the Wades her support; Lousie Gilbert, a social worker who sent letters to Shively residents asking for goodwill toward the Wades; and I. O. Ford, who lived with Vernon Bown. At their trial for sedition, Ewbank Tucker led the Wade Defense Committee.

135 *Louisville Courier-Journal*, May 18, 1956, cited in Carmichael and Johnson, *Louisville Story*, 79–81.

136 Braden, *The Wall Between*, 118. According to Anne Braden, any activities that supported racial equality were called communist even before the era of the Cold War. See interview with Anne Braden, March 23, 2003, "Living the Story" Collection, KHS.

137 Von Eschen, *Race against Empire*; Dudziak, *Cold War and Civil Rights*; Carole Anderson, *Eyes Off the Prize*; Biondi, *To Stand and Fight*. On the relationship between anticommunism and white supremacy, see Honey, *Southern Labor and Black Civil Rights*.

138 Fosl, "'Once Comes the Moment to Decide,'" 167.

139 McElhone, "Civil Rights Activities," 141. McElhone notes that desegregation was marked by a few "minor" incidents: an interracial fight at Eastern Junior High and a cross burning at Parkland Junior High. See also K'Meyer, "Building Interracial Democracy," 427.

140 George C. Wright, "Civil Rights Movement in Kentucky," 56.

141 Kozol, *Death at an Early Age*; Inger, "New Orleans Schools Crisis of 1960"; Back, "Exposing the Whole Segregation Myth"; Kruse, *White Flight*.

142 Kruse, *White Flight*, 146–47.

143 Kentucky Commission on Human Rights, "Louisville School System Retreats to

Segregation," "Highlights" and 11. The commission reported: "Twenty-seven of the schools have a white majority of at least 90 percent this year [1971], compared to just twenty-two in 1968. Twenty-four schools have a black majority of at least 90 percent this year, compared to just 17 in 1968." Extreme racial isolation was defined as a black or white majority of 90–100 percent.

144 Ibid., 2, 8. According to the commission, 81.4 percent of black students attended schools with at least 80 percent minority enrollment.

145 Kentucky Commission on Human Rights, "Louisville School System Retreats to Segregation," and "Southern Cities—Except Louisville—Desegregate Schools," 2.

146 Interview with Grace Lewis, February 4, 1999, Kentucky Civil Rights Oral History Project, KHS.

147 Ibid.

148 Commonwealth of Kentucky, "Report on Integration-Desegregation [for the] School Year[s] 1950–60," Department of Education, October 1960, in Wilson Papers, box 5, EL-UARC. The report actually covered the years 1956–60 for selected counties in the state. Ironically, it considered figures that were typical of all schools included in the survey of Jefferson County a sign of successful integration. The ratio of black and white students for other schools listed were (Elementary) Auburndale, 7/368; Bates, 6/642; Chenoweth, 2/600; Eastwood, 4/157; Hikes, 10/687; Indian Trail, 84/740; Kennedy, 12/451; Kenwood, 2/633; Middletown, 54/527; South Park, 7/505; Stonestreet, 2/685; Wilder, 35/737; and Wilson, 13/748. Also (High Schools) Butler, 12/2471; Eastern, 166/1452; Fern Creek, 29/1411; Seneca, 196/1810; and Southern, 45/1532. Schools within the city were not listed.

149 George C. Wright, *History of Blacks in Kentucky*, 210.

150 Harry Schacter to Miss Ann Tanneyhill, Secretary, National Urban League, October 17, 1944, in Walls Papers, EL-UARC; interview with Murray Walls, July 27, 1977, Black Oral History Collection, UARC.

151 McElhone, "Civil Rights Activities," 127.

152 Ewbank Tucker (as well as some NAACP documents), suggests that the revival of the Labor and Industry Committee was in part a response to the declining membership in the NAACP and to the claim that the NAACP did not represent the interests of working-class blacks; see McElhone, "Civil Rights Activities," 132. On the conflict between Tucker and the NAACP, see also Meier and Rudwick, *CORE*, 120–21, 191.

153 McElhone, "Civil Rights Activities," 127–29.

154 Ibid., 130.

155 NAACP Branch Files, Louisville, 1940–55, pt. 2, C-66, NAACP Branch Files, 1940–55.

CHAPTER 5

1 Du Bois, "Behold the Land," 233.

2 Wade Hall, *Rest of the Dream*, 183.

3 Ibid.

4 Patricia Hill Collins, *Black Feminist Thought*, 95; Griffin, *"Who Set You Flowin'?,"* 8–10, 134–35. Griffin (pp. 134–35) offers an especially insightful discussion of how the "streets" served as a "safe space" for Malcolm X. Collins defines a "safe space" as a place where domination is not present as a hegemonic ideology and where black women

can "speak freely." "Safe spaces" and the relatively safe discourse they offer were necessary conditions for black women's resistance to objectification as "other." While Griffin adopted Collins's notion of "safe spaces," she complicated it by extending the idea to encompass both men and women, by pointing out that hegemonic ideology exists even within sites of resistance, and by suggesting "safe spaces" were more often sites of sustenance and preservation than sites of resistance. However, it seems that there *are* times when preservation alone is an act of resistance.

5 Gilmore, *Defying Dixie*, 4.

6 Frederick Douglass's speech, "We Have Decided to Stay," was delivered on May 9, 1848, at the American Anti-Slavery Society in New York. Speaking with Governor John B. Pinney of Liberia in the audience, Frederick Douglass remarked to the American Colonization Society that African Americans had as much right to this country as anyone else. Nearly three decades later Douglass's position had not changed. In the context of the post–Reconstruction exodus of more than 20,000 blacks from the South to Kansas, he espoused his commitment to attaining equality in the South. In his speeches against the exodus, he argued: "That they who would solve the problem of freedom and free institutions by emigration rather than protection, by flight rather than by right, by going into a strange land rather than by staying in our own, by a change of soil rather than by a change of heart; instead of an egg, would give us a stone, instead of a fish, a serpent, instead of substance, a shadow; and would leave the whole question of equal rights upon the soil of our birth still an open question, with the moral influence of Exodus against us as a confession of the impracticability of equal rights upon the soil of the South."

7 Interview with Dr. Maurice Rabb, August 15, 1977, Black Oral History Collection, UARC.

8 Interview with Jessie Irvin, June 28, 1978, ibid.

9 *Louisville Courier-Journal*, September 14, 1960; interview with Goldie Winstead-Beckett, September 12, 1978, Black Oral History Collection, UARC. On civil rights in Louisville, see George C. Wright, "Civil Rights Movement in Kentucky," *History of Blacks in Kentucky*, and "Desegregation of Public Accommodations"; McElhone, "Civil Rights Activities"; Horton, *Not without Struggle*; Bernier, "White Activists and Support"; Fosl, "'Once Comes the Moment to Decide'"; Luther J. Adams, "Way Up North in Louisville"; and K'Meyer, *Civil Rights*.

10 Interview with Felix S. Anderson, n.d., Black Oral History Collection, UARC.

11 Willie Bell to National NAACP, July 7, 1944, 1940–55, NAACP Branch Files, Louisville, 1940–55, pt. 2, C-66, NAACP Papers, LC.

12 "Law Sought to Prohibit Racial Bias," clippings, NAACP Branch Files, Louisville, 1956–59, pt. 3, C-50, ibid.

13 *Goin' to Chicago*.

14 Ibid.

15 "Mass Meeting and Prayer," in *Sing for Freedom*.

16 Curry, *Silver Rights*, 188, 193.

17 "Why I Live in Mississippi," *Ebony*, November 1958, 67.

18 Ibid., 65.

19 Ibid., 69.

20 Ibid., 65.

21 Fairclough, *Martin Luther King, Jr.*, 16; Curry, *Silver Rights*; Pauli Murray, *States' Laws on Race and Color*, x–xi; Ransby, *Ella Baker*, 6.

22 Ransby, *Ella Baker*, 171.

23 Laurie Green, *Battling the Plantation Mentality*, 192.

24 Ibid., 22; Kruse, *White Flight*, 35–36, 40. Perhaps most famously, Mayor William Harts-field proclaimed Atlanta the "city too busy to hate," while Green notes that under Mayor E. H. Crump's leadership contemporaries viewed Memphis as a model of "racial harmony" in the South.

25 George C. Wright, "Desegregation of Public Accommodations," 195.

26 Ibid., 196; McElhone, "Civil Rights Activities," 153.

27 *Louisville Courier-Journal*, March 11, 1967; Negroes: Demonstrations, Louisville, folder 1, Photographic Archives, *Louisville Courier-Journal*.

28 Clippings, March 4, 1958, NAACP Branch Files, Louisville, pt. 3, C-50, NAACP Papers, LC.

29 Clippings, 1957, Louisville, 1957–61, ibid. Hoblitzell's position was no different from that of Republican candidate Robert B. Diehl.

30 McElhone, "Civil Rights Activities," 154.

31 George C. Wright, "Desegregation of Public Accommodations," 196; McElhone, "Civil Rights Activities," 154.

32 George C. Wright, "Desegregation of Public Accommodations," 197; McElhone, "Civil Rights Activities," 155–56; Horton, *Not without Struggle*, 55–57.

33 George C. Wright, "Desegregation of Public Accommodations," 197.

34 McElhone, "Civil Rights Activities," 152.

35 Woolsey Papers, box 1, folder 4, EL-UARC; George C. Wright, "Desegregation of Public Accommodations," 198.

36 Woolsey Papers, box 1, folder 4, EL-UARC; George C. Wright, "Desegregation of Public Accommodations," 198.

37 Clippings, January 28, 1958, NAACP Branch Files, Louisville, 1957–61, pt. 3, C-50, NAACP Papers, LC.

38 Woolsey Papers, box 1, folder 4, EL-UARC.

39 *Louisville Times*, February 24, 1960. Beckett commented that he wished he could "put you in my shoes and walk with you into some places so you could understand and appreciate what I mean."

40 Woolsey Papers, box 1, folder 4, EL-UARC.

41 Ibid.

42 Horton, *Not without Struggle*, 57; George C. Wright, "Desegregation of Public Accommodations," 198.

43 Meier and Rudwick, *CORE*, 120; Horton, *Not without Struggle*, 57.

44 Woolsey Papers, box 1, folder 1, EL-UARC; Meier and Rudwick, *CORE*, 120.

45 Wade Hall, *Rest of the Dream*, 134.

46 George C. Wright, "Desegregation of Public Accommodations," 196.

47 Daisy Lampkin to William T. Andrews, June 20, 1931, NAACP Branch Files, Louisville, 1924–39, pt. 1, G-76, NAACP Papers, LC.

48 Woolsey Papers, box 1, folder 1, EL-UARC.

49 Gloster Current to George Cordery, March 4, 1958, NAACP Branch Files, Louisville, 1924–39, pt. 1, G-76, NAACP Papers, LC.

50 Von Eschen, *Race against Empire*; Dudziak, *Cold War and Civil Rights*; Carole Anderson, *Eyes Off the Prize*. The Highlander Folk School was established in 1932 near Monteagle, Tenn., to provide education and training for numerous labor and civil rights activists across the South.

51 *Louisville Courier-Journal*, September 14, 1960.

52 Woolsey Papers, box 1, folder 4, EL-UARC.

53 Frank Stanley Jr., "While the World Waits" (pamphlet), Report to the Mayor's Citizen Committee, March 9, 1961, in Woolsey Papers, box 1, folder 4, EL-UARC.

54 Walls Papers, Professional and Civic, box 2, EL-UARC. Fanny Rosenbaum of the Louisville HRC recalled that Walls was an "extremely dignified lady . . . [who] always had on white gloves." Interview with Rosenbaum, February 11, 1999, Kentucky Civil Rights Oral History Project, KHS.

55 Interview with E. Deedom Alston, August 15, 1979, Black Oral History Collection, UARC.

56 Walls Papers, Professional and Civic, box 2, EL-UARC.

57 George C. Wright, "Desegregation of Public Accommodations," 201. In a report to Mayor Hoblitzell, Stanley remarked of the campaign: "The New Negro recognized his strength. He was aware that there are 19 million Negro Americans, who spend 21 million dollars annually, larger than the Dominion of Canada."

58 Frank Stanley Jr., "While the World Waits."

59 Clara Wims, box 28, Willis-Young, West Downtown, Urban Renewal Papers, Relocation Files, R-10 Project Relocation Files and Inactive Families, LMA. A "silver girl" would set and serve food at dining room tables.

60 George C. Wright, "Desegregation of Public Accommodations," 202.

61 Ibid., 203; NAACP press release, March 2, 1961, NAACP Branch Files, Louisville, 1957–61, pt. 3, C-50, NAACP Papers, LC.

62 Interview with Mervin Aubespin, October 22, 1999, Kentucky Civil Rights Oral History Project, KHS.

63 George C. Wright, "Desegregation of Public Accommodations," 200; NAACP press release, March 16, 1961, NAACP Branch Files, Louisville, 1957–61, pt. 3, C-50, NAACP Papers, LC.

64 "No Buying Drive," March 25, 1961, NAACP press release, NAACP Branch Files, Louisville, 1957–61, pt. 3, C-50, NAACP Papers, LC.

65 Interview with Dr. Maurice Rabb, August 15, 1977, Black Oral History Collection, UARC; NAACP Branch Files, Louisville, pt. 3, C-50, NAACP Papers, LC.

66 George C. Wright, "Desegregation of Public Accommodations," 201.

67 Cited in ibid.

68 Horton, *Not without Struggle*, 65.

69 Cited in ibid.

70 Cited in ibid., 66–67.

71 George C. Wright, "Desegregation of Public Accommodations," 205.

72 Mayors' Papers, cited in ibid., 203n24.

73 George C. Wright, "Desegregation of Public Accommodations," 205.

74 Ibid.

75 Interview with Arthur Walters, June 14, 1977, Black Oral History Collection, UARC.

76 Integration Steering Committee, "Official Results of Sit-Ins, Testing and Re-Testing 142 Downtown Restaurants," June 1, 1961, in Wilson Papers, box 5, EL-UARC.

77 George C. Wright, "Desegregation of Public Accommodations," 205.

78 Meier and Rudwick, *CORE*, 191.

79 Laurie Green, *Battling the Plantation Mentality*, 206, 208–9.

80 George C. Wright, "Desegregation of Public Accommodations," 206.

81 Horton, *Not without Struggle*, 58.

82 Interview with Jessie Irvin, June 28, 1978, Black Oral History Collection, UARC.

83 Ibid.

84 Interview with W. J. Hodge, December 4, 1977, Black Oral History Collection, UARC.

85 Cited in George C. Wright, "Desegregation of Public Accommodations," 206.

86 "William Owen Cowger," in Kleber, *Encyclopedia of Louisville*, 228.

87 Horton, *Not without Struggle*, 82.

88 Interview with Louise Reynolds, [no month listed] 13, 1979, Black Oral History Collection, UARC.

89 "Amelia Tucker," in Kleber, *Encyclopedia of Louisville*, 893. Representing the Forty-second District in Louisville, Tucker worked to secure a public accommodations bill without success.

90 George C. Wright, "Desegregation of Public Accommodations," 207.

91 Ibid., 208.

92 Ibid., 209.

93 George C. Wright, "Civil Rights Movement in Kentucky," 191.

94 Interview with Georgia Davis Powers, January 29, 2003, "Living the Story" Collection, KHS. Powers was a central figure in organizing the march in Frankfort. Bishop Tucker, ever the iconoclast, led a separate march the day before.

95 Interview with Mattie Jones, February 5, 1999, Kentucky Civil Rights Oral History Project, KHS.

96 Cited in George C. Wright, "Civil Rights Movement in Kentucky," 61. Stanley continued: "Frankly, the average Caucasian Kentuckian is mostly unaware of the important goals yet to be achieved, or more specifically, of the amount of non-progress that has been made. Certainly most are totally incapable of realizing the tortures of hellish racial prejudice and what it does to the souls and minds of people who are forced to suffer it. . . . The plain truth is, regardless of how many civil rights laws we pass, Negroes cannot win complete equality or total integration without broad cash programs for full employment, abolition of slums, the reconstruction of our education system and new definitions of work and leisure."

CHAPTER 6

1 Kleber, *Encyclopedia of Louisville*, 919.

2 George Ann Berry and Estella Conwill Alexander, "Footing It Down the Block," n.d., Old Walnut Street, in "Blacks" Vertical Reference File, EL-UARC.

3 Clipping, *Louisville Courier-Journal*, 1984, Old Walnut Business District, in ibid.

4 Silver and Moeser, *Separate City*, 6. According to these historians, segregation led to the development of "separate cities," where African Americans lived in communities

balanced between the denial of access and a full range of opportunities and a self-reliance that fostered independent black-owned businesses.

5 "Souvenir Program," Broadway Temple, AME Zion Church, April 9, 1944, box 13, folder 8, Wade Hall Collection, KHS.

6 Clipping, *Louisville Courier-Journal*, n.d. 1984, Old Walnut Business District, in "Blacks" Vertical Reference File, EL-UARC.

7 Wilson Papers, EL-UARC; George D. Wilson, *Footprints in the Sand*, 91.

8 Interview with Goldie Winstead-Beckett, September 12, 1978, Black Oral History Collection, UARC.

9 "Black Business in Louisville," October 1968, Kentucky Commission on Human Rights, in Parrish Papers, EL-UARC.

10 Interview with Dr. C. Milton Young, October 7, 1978, and Correspondence, box 3, Red Cross Hospital Papers, all in EL-UARC.

11 Hirsch, *Making the Second Ghetto*. See also Casey-Leininger, "Making the Second Ghetto in Cincinnati," and Mohl, "Making the Second Ghetto in Metropolitan Miami."

12 For a short history of the role of the LADA and the Louisville Chamber of Commerce in urban planning, see Kramer, "Louisville Area Development Association," 532, 707. For a bit more depth on planning in Louisville, see also Kramer, "James C. Murphy" and "Two Centuries of Urban Development."

13 "A Study of Urban Renewal and Related Agencies in the Metropolitan Area," League of Women Voters of Louisville, January 1963, in Informational Services, boxes 1–2, Publications, Newsletters, 1964–76, Louisville, Planning Urban Renewal, LMA.

14 Ibid.

15 Woolsey Papers, box 1, folder 4, EL-UARC.

16 "The Facts on Urban Renewal," n.d., in Informational Services, boxes 1–2, Publications, Newsletters, 1964–76, Louisville, Planning Urban Renewal, LMA.

17 "Annual Report, 1959," General Files, boxes 1–2, Louisville, ibid.

18 "Annual Report, Additional Site (8), Indian Trail," ibid.

19 Woolsey Papers, box 1, folder 4, EL-UARC; clipping, *Louisville Courier-Journal*, 1984, Old Walnut Business District, in "Blacks" Vertical Reference File, EL-UARC.

20 Interview with Goldie Winstead-Beckett, September 12, 1978, Black Oral History Collection, UARC.

21 *Louisville Courier-Journal*, February 10, 1960.

22 Woolsey Papers, box 1, folder 1, EL-UARC; "The Facts on Urban Renewal," Urban Renewal and Community Development Agency, n.d., in Informational Services, boxes 1–2, Publications, Newsletters, 1964–76, Louisville, Planning Urban Renewal, LMA.

23 "Southwick Redevelopment Project: Project Proposals: Property Acquisition," June 1, 1959, Department of Building and Housing Inspection, Urban Renewal Papers, LMA.

24 Urban Renewal Papers, R-10 Project Relocation Files, boxes 20, 28–30, LMA.

25 Lohman, *Principles of Police Work*, 20.

26 Walls Papers, Professional and Civic, box 2, EL-UARC. On the role of women activists in housing and civil rights campaigns, see Greene, *Our Separate Ways*; Rhonda Y. Williams, *Politics of Public Housing*; Naples, *Grassroots Warriors*; and Kornbluh, "'To Fulfill Their Rightly Needs,'" 69, 76–113.

27 Woolsey Papers, box 1, folder 1, EL-UARC.

28 Murray Walls, "Housing for Negroes in Louisville," Walls Papers, Professional and Civic, box 2, folder 17, EL-UARC. According to Anne Braden (*The Wall Between*, 39), between World War II and 1954 only three hundred new houses were built for blacks in Louisville. Moreover, she noted, "The United States Census for 1950 showed 84.4 percent of the city's Negroes were living in dwellings rated as poor or very poor, and the Health Department reported that thousands were living in coal sheds and chicken coops."

29 George C. Wright, "Civil Rights Movement in Kentucky," 59.

30 For more recent treatments of these issues, see Rhonda Y. Williams, *Politics of Public Housing*; Wiese, *Places of Their Own*; and Self, *American Babylon*. See also Casey-Leininger, "Making the Second Ghetto in Cincinnati"; Carolyn T. Adams et al., *Philadelphia*; Sugrue, *Origins of the Urban Crisis*; Mohl, "Making the Second Ghetto in Metropolitan Miami"; Jackson, *Crabgrass Frontier*; Hirsch, *Making the Second Ghetto* and "With or without Jim Crow"; and Bayor, *Race and the Shaping of Twentieth-Century Atlanta*. On real estate practices, see Oser, *Blockbusting in Baltimore*. On regional distinctions, see Flowerdew, "Spatial Patterns of Residential Segregation."

31 Bayor, "Roads to Racial Segregation," 15, and *Race and the Shaping of Twentieth-Century Atlanta*. His essay compelled historians to also think about where roads were not built; the lack of access to certain areas in Atlanta was also effective as "racial roadblocks" (pp. 12–14).

32 Walls Papers and Woolsey Papers, box 1, folder 4, EL-UARC.

33 Flowerdew, "Spatial Patterns of Residential Segregation," 97. In her work on residential segregation in Memphis, Robin Flowerdew notes that "black residence in the southern city might be expected to extend from the central edge outwards in one or more directions, perhaps extending as far as the edge of the city."

34 Woolsey Papers, box 1, folder 4, EL-UARC.

35 Interview with Ruth Bryant, July 24 [no year listed], Black Oral History Collection, UARC.

36 "The Need for a Fair Housing Law: A Report Submitted to the Human Relations Commission of the City of Louisville," 1966, in Woolsey Papers, box 1, folder 4B, EL-UARC. This study, conducted on August 10, 1966, documented the refusal of eighty real estate agents and individual owners to sell or rent housing to twenty middle-class African Americans. Even those with an excess of income were given "the run around."

37 Interview with William Ealy, August 22, 1977, Black Oral History Collection, UARC.

38 Kelley, *Freedom Dreams*; Hughes, "To Make Our World Anew."

39 Jacquelyn Dowd Hall, "Long Civil Rights Movement." Hall's remarkable essay urged historians to expand their understanding of the civil rights movement beyond the narrow time frame of 1954–65, to its origins in the "civil rights unionism" of the 1930s as well as after 1965, in order to incorporate issues such as Black Power, the rise of conservatism, residential and school segregation, and the prison industrial complex. While I generally agree with this argument, a broader emphasis on "freedom" and "equality" reveals that prior to the liberal New Deal coalitions of the 1930s African Americans organized around the similar issues of employment, housing, and political and social rights on their own behalf. Moreover, such an approach signals that "civil rights" was one of many strategies African Americans adopted to fight for equality. On "civil rights

unionism," see Korstad, *Civil Rights Unionism*. For a critique of the "Long Civil Rights Movement" perspective, see Chau-Jau, Keita, and Lang, "The 'Long Movement' as Vampire."

40 Pruitt Papers, box 1, EL-UARC.

41 Interview with Amelia B. Ray, August 25, 1978, Black Oral History Collection, UARC.

42 Frank Stanley Jr., "While the World Waits" (pamphlet), Report to the Mayor's Citizen Committee, March 9, 1961, in Woolsey Papers, box 1, folder 4, EL-UARC.

43 Interview with Dr. Maurice Rabb, August 15, 1977, Black Oral History Collection, UARC.

44 Walls Papers and Woolsey Papers, box 1, folder 4, EL-UARC.

45 *Leola Eleby, Etc . . . v. City of Louisville Municipal Housing Commission, Etc . . .*, U.S. District Court for the Western District of Kentucky, Louisville Division, Civil Action #3240, and Municipal Housing Commission press release, May 24, 1957, both in Urban Renewal Papers, Informational Services, box 1, LMA.

46 Report of the Mayor's Committee on Human Rights, December, 1961, p. 4, in Walls, "Housing for Negroes in Louisville," Walls Papers, Professional and Civic, box 2, EL-UARC.

47 Bernier, "White Activists and Support," 88.

48 Ibid., 33–35.

49 Ibid., 20–21; Horton, *Not without Struggle*, 125; Woolsey Papers, box 1, folder 4C, EL-UARC.

50 Bernier, "White Activists and Support," 40–42, 117.

51 Ibid., 42.

52 "The Need for a Fair Housing Law: A Report Submitted to the Human Relations Commission of the City of Louisville," 1966, in Woolsey Papers, box 1, folder 4b, EL-UARC.

53 *Louisville Courier-Journal*, August 6, 1965.

54 "The Need for a Fair Housing Law."

55 Bernier, "White Activists and Support," 49; Horton, *Not without Struggle*, 127.

56 Interview with Ruth Bryant, July 24 [no year listed], Black Oral History Collection, UARC.

57 Gloster Current to Clarence Mitchell, Director, Washington, D.C., May 22, 1967, NAACP Branch Files, Louisville, Housing, 1967, pt. 4, A-35, NAACP Papers, LC. Current "belatedly" forwarded a letter from Hodge requesting that the national NAACP attempt to influence Weaver.

58 Bernier, "White Activists and Support," 50.

59 Ibid., 50–51; Horton, *Not without Struggle*, 128.

60 Bernier, "White Activists and Support," 51.

61 Ibid., 48–49.

62 "Statement," NAACP Branch Files, Louisville, Housing, pt. 4, A-35, NAACP Papers, LC.

63 Bernier, "White Activists and Support," 53.

64 Handwritten note by Rev. W. J. Hodge, NAACP Branch Files, Louisville, Housing, pt. 4, A-35, NAACP Papers, LC.

65 COH, press release, February 28, 1967, ibid.

66 Interview with E. Deedom Alston, August 15, 1979, Black Oral History Collection, UARC.

67 Horton, *Not without Struggle*, 129.

68 Ibid., 149.

69 Sugrue, *Origins of the Urban Crisis*.

70 Ray Fuhs to Urban Renewal Commission, July 25, 1968, Louisville, Planning Urban Renewal, Informational Services, box 1, LMA.

71 Horton, *Not without Struggle*, 133.

72 Bernier, "White Activists and Support," 57.

73 Horton, *Not without Struggle*, 134.

74 Bernier, "White Activists and Support," 57.

75 Ibid.; Horton, *Not without Struggle*, 134.

76 Bernier, "White Activists and Support," 58–59.

77 Interview with Jessie Irvin, June 28, 1978, Black Oral History Collection, UARC.

78 *New York Times*, April 22, 1967.

79 Interview with Eric Tachau, May 1, 22, 2000, Kentucky Civil Rights Oral History Project, KHS.

80 Horton, *Not without Struggle*, 143; *New York Times*, May 6, 1967.

81 *New York Times*, May 5, 1967.

82 "Muhammad Ali," *Contemporary Black Biography*, vol. 16, ⟨http://www.gale.cengage.com/free_resources/bhm/bio/ali_m.html⟩ (October 28, 2008). For the range of debate on the topic, see Marqusee, *Redemption Song*; Remnick, *King of the World*; and Hauser, *Muhammad Ali*.

83 Remnick, *King of the World*, 289.

84 Cited in Blackside, Inc., "Ain't Gonna Shuffle No More (1964–1972)," *Eyes on the Prize*.

85 *New York Times*, May 5, 1967.

86 Horton, *Not without Struggle*, 145.

87 Ibid., 148. See Matthew 7:25, 16:18, and Psalm 118:22.

88 Cited in Kelley, *Freedom Dreams*, x.

89 Bernier, "White Activists and Support," 27.

90 *Louisville Courier-Journal*, November 13, 1967.

91 Cited in Wade Hall, *Rest of the Dream*, 177.

92 Anne Braden, "A Dream That Failed: An Analysis of the Life and Death of the West End Community Council," in Woolsey Papers, box 1, folder 4C, EL-UARC.

93 Bernier, "White Activists and Support," 16–17.

94 Kruse, *White Flight*, 234. Kruse notes that white flight represented a mind-set as well as a physical movement to the suburbs.

95 "Ghettoization in Kentucky Cities," 1967, NAACP Branch Files, Louisville, Housing, pt. 4, NAACP Papers, LC. See also Cummings and Price, "Race Relations and Public Policy," 4–5. According to Cummings and Price, the segregation index stood at 83.6 percent. On suburbanization in the nation as a whole, see Jackson, *Crabgrass Frontier*.

96 K'Meyer, *Civil Rights*, 150–51.

97 *Race Relations in Louisville*, 12.

98 "Black Business in Louisville," Kentucky Commission on Human Rights, October 1968, in Parrish Papers, box 14, EL-UARC.

CONCLUSION

1 Louisville and Jefferson County HRC, "Civil Rights in Louisville, 1961–1972," 4, EL-UARC.

2 Ibid., 7.

3 Tachau, "Why Louisville must Support the Black Six"; Ad Hoc Committee for Justice, "What Louisville Should Know About the 'Black Six' Conspiracy Case." See also Kenneth H. Williams, "Oh Baby . . . It's Really Happening"; Hudson, "African Americans"; Braden, "Civil Rights"; and Bruce Tyler, "The 1968 Black Power Riot," ⟨http://louisville .edu/a-s/history/tyler/kentuckyriots.html⟩ (November 20, 2008).

4 Cited in Kenneth H. Williams, "Oh Baby . . . It's Really Happening," 53. For recent scholarship on Black Power, see Woodard, *A Nation within a Nation*; Tyson, *Radio Free Dixie*; Cleaver and Katsiaficas, *Liberation, Imagination*; Moore, *Carl B. Stokes and the Rise of Black Political Power*; Brown, *Fighting for US*; Ogbar, *Black Power*; Spencer, "Inside the Panther Revolution"; Patrick Jones, "'Not a Color but an Attitude'"; Hasan Kwame Jefferies, "Organizing for More Than the Vote"; Tracye Matthews, "'No One Ever Asks'"; Smethurst, *Black Arts Movement*; Joseph, *Black Power Movement*; and Jefferies, *Bloody Lowndes*.

5 *Louisville Courier-Journal*, May 28, 1978.

6 Cited in Kenneth H. Williams, "Oh Baby . . . It's Really Happening," 59–60.

7 Childress, *Louisville Division of Police*, 70; Cummings and Price, "Race Relations and Public Policy," 636.

8 The area was home to numerous businesses, including Moon Cleaners, the Metro Lounge, the Little Palace Restaurant, Champs Poolroom, a hardware store, an A&P, a Masonic Lodge, and the NAACP headquarters.

9 Cummings and Price, "Race Relations and Public Policy," 49.

10 Ibid., 58.

11 Ibid., 58–59.

12 Southern Conference Educational Fund, "Lessons of Louisville," 8.

13 Ibid.

14 Ibid., 4. At WEST's inception, "It was made clear that it was not to be a negotiating committee, or a go-between, that its purpose was not to 'quiet things down' but to try to bring influence to bear to see that Louisville faced its basic problems." Ibid.

15 Ad Hoc Committee for Justice, "What Louisville Should Know about the 'Black Six' Conspiracy Case"; Kenneth H. Williams, "Oh Baby . . . It's Really Happening," 56–57. "What Louisville Should Know . . ." includes a comprehensive "fact sheet" detailing every event in the Black Six conspiracy case.

16 Roper Research Associates, Inc., "A Community Study among Whites and Negroes in Louisville," July 1969, UARC. The researchers interviewed 508 whites and 506 blacks aged eighteen and older. Of the whites interviewed, 272 lived in the city of Louisville and 236 in the surrounding suburbs. On the other hand, 461 of the blacks in the survey lived in the city, while only 45 lived in the suburbs, which itself reflected white flight and the lack of access to housing that many blacks continued to face. Interestingly, the Roper report does not indicate the distribution of male and female respondents, though it does state that a large number of women were interviewed.

17 Ibid., 5–6.

18 Ibid. Of the whites in the study, 64 percent wanted to live in all-white neighborhoods

and 19 percent wished to reside in majority white neighborhoods. By contrast, nearly 75 percent of the blacks surveyed preferred to live in mixed neighborhoods.

19 Ibid., 7.

20 Ibid., 9, 12, 14.

21 Ibid., 5.

22 Ibid., 105.

23 While many scholars have noted a rise in "return migration" among African Americans beginning in the 1970s, Louisville does not appear to have attracted substantial "return migrants" until the 1990s. See Hudgens, "Coming Home Again," University of Chicago, ⟨http://www.inmotionaame.org-AAME:/⟩ (October 23, 2008); Stack, *Call To Home*; Cromartie and Stack, "Reinterpretation of Black Return"; and Frey, "Black Migration to the South." For a brief discussion of "return migration" in Louisville, see Luther J. Adams, "African American Migration to Louisville," 382.

24 Cummings and Price, "Race Relations and Public Policy," 626. See also *Race Relations in Louisville*, 12–14.

25 *Race Relations in Louisville*, 12.

26 K'Meyer, *Civil Rights*, 232–33. According to K'Meyer, the number of black employees at A&P fell from 8 to 6 percent, and Kroger refused to hire and promote people of color.

27 Kentucky Commission on Human Rights, "Louisville School System Retreats to Segregation," 16; George C. Wright, *History of Blacks in Kentucky*, 210–11. Not only was desegregation an issue for students, but also the Commission on Human Rights noted that Louisville's employment of black teachers lagged behind that of nine other southern cities, including Jackson, Mississippi; Birmingham, Alabama; Little Rock, Arkansas; and Columbia, South Carolina.

28 George C. Wright, *History of Blacks in Kentucky*, 210; "Busing," in Kleber, *Encyclopedia of Louisville*, 148; McConahay, *Racial and Non-Racial Correlates*; Cummings and Price, "Race Relations and Public Policy," 639. On busing controversies, see Formisano, *Boston against Busing*, and Rubin, *Busing and Backlash*. On massive resistance, see Bartley, *Rise of Massive Resistance*; Douglass, *Reading, Writing, and Race*; Hirsch, "Massive Resistance in the Urban North"; Lassiter and Lewis, *Moderates' Dilemma*; Meyer, *As Long as They Don't Move Next Door*; and Durr, *Behind the Backlash*.

29 "Busing," in *Encyclopedia of Louisville*, 148. Appeals to the U.S. Supreme Court to hear the case were denied.

30 "Busing," in *Encyclopedia of Louisville*, 148; "Rehearsal for Busing," *Time*, September 8, 1975, ⟨http://www.time.com/time/magazine/article/0,9171,917781-1,00.html⟩ (December 10, 2008). Connor's full quote was "We have a war going, I think Boston will be small compared to Louisville."

31 "Busing and Strikes: Schools in Turmoil," *Time*, September 15, 1975. In 1975–76, *Time* published a series of articles that focused on busing, the majority highlighting Boston and Louisville as northern and southern representatives of the issue—see "Rehearsal for Busing," September 8, 1975; "The Busing Battle," September 12, 1975; "The Busing Dilemma," September 22, 1975; "White Flight Continued," September 29, 1975; "Defiance on Trial," March 15, 1976; "Busing Battle Revives," May 31, 1976; "Desegregation Grades," September 6, 1976; and "A New Idea on Busing," November 10, 1976.

32 "Busing and Strikes: Schools in Turmoil," *Time*, September 15, 1975.

33 Clotfelter, *After Brown*, 75–76; "Busing," in Kleber, *Encyclopedia of Louisville*, 148; Mc-Conahay, *Racial and Non-Racial Correlates*, 4; "Rehearsal for Busing," *Time*, September 8, 1975, ⟨http://www.time.com/time/magazine/article/0,9171,917781-1,00.html⟩ (December 10, 2008). By the end of September, more than 600 people were arrested, 200 were injured, and students rode to school with armed National Guardsmen on their buses.

34 Cited in Cummings and Price, "Race Relations and Public Policy," 638.

35 McConahay, *Racial and Non-Racial Correlates*, 19, 24. With funds from the Ford Foundation and the Louisville Foundation, McConahay conducted a series of public opinion polls on the issue of busing. Despite white protesters' claims to the contrary, he concluded that "busing is a racial issue." However, he identified a new form of racism evident in the actions of whites, which he termed "symbolic racism." "Old fashioned racism" was defined as the cognitive component of racism from years gone by, the belief in stereotypes that black people are lazy or dumb, and epitomized by public figures like Bull Connor and George Wallace. "Symbolic racism," by contrast, is expressed in abstract, moralistic, and ideological symbols, the racist content of which may not be obvious to its adherents. Nonetheless, both behave in the same way. Mc-Conahay, *Reactions to Busing* and *Is It the Buses or the Blacks?*

36 George C. Wright, *History of Blacks in Kentucky*, 211.

37 Clotfelter, *After Brown*, 76.

38 "Busing," in Kleber, *Encyclopedia of Louisville*, 148.

39 Kentucky Commission on Human Rights, "School and Housing Desegregation Are Working Together," 3.

40 Joe Atkinson, "Busing in the Balance," *Louisville Magazine*, November 2006; Nina Totenberg, "Supreme Court to Weigh Schools' Racial Plans," ⟨http://www.npr.org/templates/story/story.php?storyId=6567985⟩ (December 10, 2008); Chris Kenning, "5–4 Ruling Limits Use of Race by District," *Louisville Courier-Journal*, June 29, 2007, ⟨http://www.Louisville Courier-Journal.com/apps/pbcs.dll/article?AID=/20070629/NEWS0105/706290504⟩ (December 20, 2008). The Louisville case, *Meredith v. Jefferson County Board of Education*, was heard jointly with a case regarding a dormant school assignment policy in Seattle, Washington, *Community Schools v. Seattle School District Number One*. Ironically, in 1971 Bloom was one of two all-white elementary schools in Louisville.

41 Hudson, "African Americans" (p. 17), and Braden, "Civil Rights" (p. 192), in Kleber, *Encyclopedia of Louisville*; interview with Ruth Bryant, July 24 [no year listed], Black Oral History Collection, UARC.

42 *Race Relations in Louisville*, 6. See also Massey and Denton, *American Apartheid*.

43 Cited in George C. Wright, *History of Blacks in Kentucky*, 222.

44 Cummings and Price, "Race Relations and Public Policy," 623; *Race Relations in Louisville*, 8.

45 Cummings and Price, "Race Relations and Public Policy," 622. According to these authors, five of the eight housing projects in Louisville were over 90 percent black.

46 "Pamphlet on Louisville Riot," The Kerner Report, Black Files: Violence in 1960s, UARC.

47 "A Community Study among Whites and Negroes in Louisville," 105, Roper Research Associates, Inc., July 1969.

BIBLIOGRAPHY

MANUSCRIPT COLLECTIONS
Frankfort, Kentucky
  Kentucky Historical Society
    Special Collections
      Wade Hall Collection
Louisville, Kentucky
  Louisville Metro Archives (formerly City of Louisville Archives)
    Municipal Reference Collection
      Planning Urban Renewal
    Police Personnel Files
    Urban Renewal Papers
      Informational Services
      General Files
      Project Proposals—Public Improvements
      Redevelopment Project—Neighborhood Land Use
      Relocation Files, 1960–65
        Inactive Families, 1963–67
        Publications, Newsletters, 1964–76
        R-10 Project Relocation Files (Southwick I to West Downtown), 1960–61
  Ekstrom Library, Archives and Records Center, University of Louisville
    Beecher Terrace Scrapbook
    "Blacks" Vertical Reference File
    Green St. Baptist Church Papers, 1844–1964
    Louisville Municipal College Scrapbook
    Lois Morris Papers
    Municipal College for Negroes Papers
    Charles Henry Parrish Jr. Papers
    E. E. Pruitt Papers
    Red Cross Hospital Papers
    Murray B. Atkins Walls Papers
    George D. Wilson Papers
    Frederick William Woolsey Papers
  Louisville Free Public Library
    "Negroes" Papers

Washington, D.C.
    Library of Congress
        Manuscript Division
            National Association for the Advancement of Colored People Papers

NEWSPAPERS AND MAGAZINES
Louisville Courier-Journal
Louisville Defender
Louisville Leader
Louisville Magazine
Louisville News
Louisville Times
New York Times
Southern Frontier
Time

INTERVIEWS
By author (in author's possession)
    Elmore, A. J., August 21, 1996
    Ferris, Charles (via telephone), November 11, 2000
    Haskin, Wilbur, July 5, 1997
    Marks, Reverend William G., November 29, 1997
Black Oral History Collection, Oral History Center, Archives and Records Center,
        University of Louisville
    Alston, Deedom E. (interview by Kenneth Chumbley), August 15, 1979
    Anderson, Felix S. (interview by Kenneth Chumbley), n.d.
    Beard, D. W. (interview by Olivia M. Frederick, transcribed by Mindy Glenn),
        November 29, 1979
    Bell, Dr. Jessie (interview by Olivia M. Frederick). July 28, 1979
    Braden, Anne (interview by Ruthie Pfisterer), January 5–March 18, 1981
    Bryant, Ruth (interview by Kenneth Chumbley), July 24 [no year listed]
    Ealy, William (interview by Dewayne Cox, transcribed by Natalie Fowler),
        August 5, 22, 1977
    Edwards, Monte (interview by Mary D. Bobo), March 24, 1979
    Glass, James (interview by James Montgomery), February 29 [no year listed]
    Hammond, Joseph (interview by Mary D. Bobo), April 16, 1979
    Hodge, W. J. (interview by Chuck Staiger), December 4, 1977
    Holmes, W. L. (interview by Mary D. Bobo), August 15, 1978
    Irvin, Jessie (interview by Kenneth Chumbley), June 28, 1978
    Johnson, Lyman T. (interview by Regina Monsour), March 15, 25, 1977
    Kidd, Mae Street (interview by Kenneth Chumbley), October 30, December 5, 1978
    Powers, Georgia Davis (interview by Kenneth Chumbley), July 6, 1978
    Rabb, Dr. Maurice (interview by Dwayne Cox), August 15, 1977
    Ray, Amelia B. (interview by Kenneth Chumbley), August 25, 1978
    Reynolds, Louise (interview by Mary D. Bobo), [no month listed] 13, 1979

Stanley, Vivian (interview by Janet Hodgson, transcribed by Shawntriss M. Simms),
     August 5, 1985
Walls, Dr. John, and Murray B. Atkins Walls (interview by Patrick McElhone),
     July 31, 1973
Walls, Murray B. Atkins (interview by Dwayne Cox), July 27, 1977
Walters, Arthur (interview by Kenneth Chumbley), June 14, 1977
Winstead-Beckett, Goldie (interview by Kenneth Chumbley), September 12, 1978
Young, Dr. C. Milton (interview by Kenneth Chumbley), October 7, 1978
Kentucky Civil Rights Oral History Project, Kentucky Oral History Commission,
     Kentucky Historical Society, Frankfort
  Aubespin, Mervin (interview by Betsy Brinson), October 22, 1999
  Childress, Mort (interview by Betsy Brinson), October 28, 1999
  Hudson, Lillian (interview by Betsy Brinson), February 19, 1999
  Hutchins, Walter T. (interview by Betsy Brinson), August 3, 2000
  Jones, Mattie (interview by Betsy Brinson), February 5, 1999
  Jordan, Eleanor (interview by Betsy Brinson), February 2, 1999
  Lewis, Grace (interview by Betsy Brinson), February 4, 1999
  Martin, Galen (interview by Betsy Brinson), November 4, 1999
  Rosenbaum, Fanny (interview by Betsy Brinson), December 11, 1999
  Tachau, Eric (interview by Ethel White, transcribed by Lucinda Spangler),
     May 1, 22, 2000
  Zriny, Mary (interview by Betsy Brinson), February 22, 2001
"Living the Story" Collection, Kentucky Oral History Commission, Kentucky Historical
     Society, Frankfort (interviews by Kentucky Oral History Commission)
  Braden, Anne, March 23, 2003
  Breathitt, Edward T., January 28, 2003
  Davis Powers, Georgia, January 29, 2003
Negro Youth at the Crossways Collection, 1938, in the Charles Henry Parrish Jr. Papers,
     Ekstrom Library, Archives and Records Center, University of Louisville [Because
     the Parrish Papers stipulate that all interviewees are to remain anonymous, codes
     are used throughout this book.]
  Interview with code 003
  Interview with code 011
  Interview with code 048
  Interview with code 119

GOVERNMENT DOCUMENTS, PAMPHLETS, AND REPORTS
Ad Hoc Committee for Justice. "What Louisville Should Know about the 'Black Six'
     Conspiracy Case: And Why It Should Be Known," October 17, 1968. Southern
     Conference Educational Fund, Louisville, 1968.
Associates of Louisville Municipal College, University of Louisville, Louisville Urban
     League, and Central Colored High School, *A Study of Business and Employment among
     Negroes in Louisville*. Louisville, 1942.
Beers, Howard W., and Catherine P. Heflin. *The Negro Population of Kentucky*. Kentucky
     Agricultural Experiment Station, Bulletin 481, January 1946.

Carmichael, Omer, and Weldon Johnson. *The Louisville Story*. New York: Simon and
Schuster, 1957.

Coleman, A. Lee, Albert C. Pryor, and John R. Christiansen. *The Negro Population of
Kentucky at Mid-Century*. Kentucky Agricultural Experiment Station, Bulletin 643,
June 1956.

De Jong, Gordon F., and George A. Hillery Jr. *Kentucky's Negro Population in 1960*.
Kentucky Agricultural Experiment Station, Bulletin 704, November 1965.

Emergency Civil Liberties Committee. "A Would Be Murderer Walks the Streets of
Louisville." New York, N.Y., 1955.

Ethridge, Mark. *America's Obligation to Its Negro Citizens*. Atlanta: Conference of Education
and Race Relations, September 1937.

Human Relations Commission. "The Need for a Fair Housing Law: A Report Submitted
to the Human Relations Commission of the City of Louisville." Human Relations
Commission, Louisville, 1966.

Kentucky Commission on Human Rights. "Black Business in Louisville." Commission on
Human Rights, Louisville, ca. 1969.

———. "Louisville School System Retreats to Segregation: A Report on the Public Schools
in Louisville, Kentucky, 1956–1971." Commission on Human Rights, Louisville, 1972.

———. "School and Housing Desegregation Are Working Together in Louisville and
Jefferson County." Commission on Human Rights, Louisville, May 1983.

———. "Southern Cities—Except Louisville—Desegregate Schools." Louisville, 1972.

Kentucky Commission on Negro Affairs. "Let's Pull Together Kentuckians: A Digest of
the Report of the Commission on Negro Affairs." Southern Regional Council, Atlanta,
1946. Wade Hall Collection, Kentucky Historical Society.

Kentucky Negro Education Association. "Equal Opportunity for Every Kentucky Child."
Resolutions of the Kentucky Negro Education Association. Louisville, April 20–23,
1949. Wade Hall Collection, Kentucky Historical Society.

Kerns, J. Harvey. *A Survey of the Economic and Cultural Conditions of the Negro Population
of Louisville, Kentucky, and A Review of the Program and Activities of the Louisville Urban
League*. Louisville: Louisville Urban League, 1948.

Lively, C. E. *Rural Migration in the United States*. Washington, D.C.: U.S. Government
Printing Office, 1939.

Lohman, Dr. Joseph. *Principles of Police Work with Minority Groups*. Division of Police,
Committee on Police Training, Louisville, 1950.

Louisville and Jefferson County Human Relations Commission. "Civil Rights in Louisville,
1961–1972: Progress, Failures, and What Remains to Be Done." March 1972.

Price, Margaret. "Toward a Solution of the Sit-In Controversy." *Southern Regional Council*
16 (May 31, 1960).

Race Relations in Louisville: Southern Racial Traditions and Northern Class Dynamic. Policy
Paper Series, Urban Research Institute, University of Louisville, June 1990.

The Report of the Kentucky Commission on Negro Affairs, November 1, 1945. Louisville: Lost
Cause Press, 1976.

Roper Research Associates. "A Community Study among Whites and Negroes in
Louisville." Conducted for the *Louisville Courier-Journal* and the *Louisville Times*,
July 1969.

Southern Conference Educational Fund. "Lessons of Louisville: A White Community Response to Black Rebellion." Louisville, 1970.

Stanley, Frank, Jr. "While the World Waits." Pamphlet. Report to the Mayor's Citizen Committee, March 9, 1961.

Tachau, Charles. "Why Louisville must Support the Black Six." Speech Delivered to Ad Hoc Committee for Justice, 1968. In author's possession.

Truesdell, Leon. *Population, Internal Migration, 1935 to 1940, Sixteenth Census of the United States*. Washington, D.C.: U.S. Government Printing Office, 1943.

Unemployment Committee of the National Federation of Settlements. *Case Studies of Unemployment*. Philadelphia: University of Pennsylvania Press, 1931.

U.S. Bureau of the Census. *Twelfth Census of the United States, 1900*. Louisville, Ward 8, Jefferson, Ky. Washington, D.C.: U.S. Government Printing Office, 1900.

———. *Thirteenth Census of the United States 1910*. Frankfort, Ward 1, Franklin, Ky. Washington, D.C.: U.S. Government Printing Office, 1910.

———. *Fourteenth Census of the United States, 1920*. Frankfort, Ward 1, Franklin, Ky. Washington, D.C.: U.S. Government Printing Office, 1920.

———. *U.S. Census of Population and Housing, 1950: Census Tracts*. Final Report. Washington, D.C.: U.S. Government Printing Office, 1951.

———. *U.S. Census of Population and Housing, 1960: Census Tracts*. Final Report. Washington, D.C.: U.S. Government Printing Office, 1961.

———. *U.S. Census of Population and Housing, 1970: Census Tracts*. Final Report. Washington, D.C.: U.S. Government Printing Office, 1971.

U.S. Senate. Committee on National Defense Migration. *Hearings Before the Select Committee Investigating National Defense Migration*. Part 14, Trenton Hearings. Washington, D.C.: U.S. Government Printing Office, 1941.

Wade Defense Committee. "They Broke the Unwritten Law: A Fact Sheet on the Bombing of the Wade Home at Louisville, Ky." n.d.

Weaver, Robert. *Negro Labor: A National Problem*. Port Washington, N.Y.: Kennikat Press, 1946.

Webb, John N., and Malcolm Brown. *Migrant Families*. Washington, D.C.: U.S. Government Printing Office, 1938.

Wilson, Charles, President's Committee on Civil Rights. *Report of the President's Committee on Civil Rights*. New York: Simon and Schuster, 1947.

SECONDARY SOURCES

Abrams, Roger. "Negotiating Respect: Patterns of Representation among Black Women." *Journal of American Folklore* 88 (1975): 58–80.

Adams, Carolyn T., et al. *Philadelphia: Neighborhoods, Divisions, and Conflict in a Postindustrial City*. Philadelphia: Temple University Press, 1991.

Adams, Luther J. "African American Migration to Louisville in the Mid-Twentieth Century." *The Register of the Kentucky Historical Society* 99, no. 4 (Autumn 2001): 363–84.

———. "Headed to Louisville: Rethinking Rural to Urban Migration in the South, 1930–1950." *Journal of Social History* 40, no. 2 (Winter 2006): 407–30.

———. "It Was North of Tennessee: African American Migration and the Meaning of the South." *Ohio Valley History* 33 (Fall 2003): 37–52.

Allen, James. *Without Sanctuary: Lynching Photography in America*. Santa Fe, N.Mex.: Twin Palms, 2000.

Anderson, Carole. *Eyes Off the Prize: The United Nations and the Struggle for Human Rights, 1944–1955*. Cambridge: Cambridge University Press, 2003.

Anderson, Karen Tucker. "Last Hired, First Fired: Black Women Workers during World War II." *Journal of American History* 69, no. 1 (June 1982): 82–97.

Anzaldua, Gloria. *Borderlands/La Frontera: The New Mestiza*. San Francisco: Aunt Lute Books, 1987.

Ayers, Edward L. *Southern Crossing: A History of the American South, 1877–1960*. New York: Oxford University Press, 1995.

Back, Adina. "Exposing the Whole Segregation Myth." In *Freedom North: Black Freedom Struggles Outside the South, 1940–1980*, edited by Jeanne Theoharis and Komozi Woodard, 65–92. New York: Palgrave Macmillan, 2003.

Baldwin, Davarian L. *Chicago's New Negroes: Modernity, the Great Migration, and Black Urban Life*. Chapel Hill: University of North Carolina Press, 2007.

Baldwin, James. "A Stranger in the Village." *Notes of a Native Son*. 9th ed. New York: Bantam Books, 1964.

Barkley Brown, Elsa, and Gregg D. Kimball. "Mapping the Terrain of Black Richmond." In *The New African-American Urban History*, edited by Kenneth W. Goings and Raymond A. Mohl, 66–115. Thousand Oaks, Calif.: Sage Publications, 1996.

Barlow, William. *"Looking Up at Down": The Emergence of Blues Culture*. Philadelphia: Temple University Press, 1989.

Bartley, Numan. *The Rise of Massive Resistance: Race and Politics in the South during the 1950's*. Baton Rouge: Louisiana State University Press, 1969.

Bates, Beth Tompkins. *Pullman Porters and the Rise of Protest Politics in Black America, 1925–1945*. Chapel Hill: University of North Carolina Press, 2001.

Bayor, Ronald H. *Race and the Shaping of Twentieth-Century Atlanta*. Chapel Hill: University of North Carolina Press, 1996.

———. "Roads to Racial Segregation: Atlanta in the Twentieth Century." *Journal of Urban History* 15 (1988): 3–21.

———. "Urban Renewal, Public Housing and the Racial Shaping of Atlanta." *Journal of Policy History* 1, no. 4 (1989): 419–39.

Beaman, Lottie. "Goin' Away Blues." *Goin' Away Blues, 1926–11932*. Yazoo 1018. 1929.

Berry, Chad. *Southern Migrants, Northern Exiles*. Urbana: University of Illinois Press, 2000.

Berry, Mary Frances, and John Blassingame. *Long Memory: The Black Experience in America*. New York: Oxford University Press, 1982.

Best, Wallace D. *Passionately Human, No Less Divine: Religion and Culture in the Chicago, 1915–1952*. Princeton, N.J.: Princeton University Press, 2005.

Biondi, Martha. *To Stand and Fight: The African American Struggle for Civil Rights in Postwar New York City*. Cambridge: Harvard University Press, 2003.

Blassingame, John. *The Slave Community: Plantation Life in the Antebellum South*. New York: Oxford University Press, 1979.

Borchert, James. *Alley Life in Washington: Family, Community, Religion, and Folklife in the City, 1850–1970*. Urbana: University of Illinois Press, 1980.

Bowles, Gladys. *Net Migration of the Population, 1950–1960, by Age, Sex, and Color*. Vol. 1, pt. 4. Washington, D.C.: U.S. Government Printing Office, 1965.

Braden, Anne. "Civil Rights." In *The Encyclopedia of Louisville*, edited by John E. Kleber. Lexington: University of Kentucky Press, 2001.

———. *The Wall Between*. 1958. Reprint, Knoxville: University of Tennessee Press, 1999.

Branch, Taylor. *At Canaan's Edge: America in the King Years, 1965–1968*. New York: Simon and Schuster, 2006.

———. *Pillar of Fire: America in the King Years, 1963–1965*. New York: Simon and Schuster, 1998.

Brinkley, Alan. "The New Deal and Southern Politics." In *The New Deal and the South*, edited by James Cobb, 117–34. Jackson: University Press of Mississippi, 1984.

Browder, Laura. *Slippery Characters: Ethnic Impersonators and American Identities*. Chapel Hill: University of North Carolina Press, 2000.

Brown, Scot. *Fighting for US: Maulana Karenga, the US Organization, and Black Cultural Nationalism*. New York: New York University Press, 2003.

Carby, Hazel V. "It Jus' Be's Dat Way Sometime." In *Unequal Sisters: A Multi-Cultural Reader in U.S. Women's History*, edited by Ellen Carol Du Bois and Vicki L. Ruiz, 238–49. New York: Routledge, 1990.

Carson, Clayborne. *In Struggle: SNCC and the Black Awakening of the 1960s*. Cambridge: Harvard University Press, 1981.

Casey-Leininger, Charles F. "Making the Second Ghetto in Cincinnati: Avondale, 1925–70." In *Race and the City, 1820–1970*, edited by Henry Louis Taylor Jr., 232–57. Urbana: University of Illinois Press, 1993.

Chafe, William. *Civilities and Civil Rights: Greensboro, North Carolina, and the Black Struggle for Freedom*. New York: Oxford University Press, 1980.

Chakrabarty, Dipesh. "Postcoloniality and the Artifice of History: Who Speaks for 'Indian' Pasts?" *Representations* 37 (Winter 1992): 1–26.

Chau-Jua, Sundiata Keita, and Clarence Lang. "The 'Long Movement' as Vampire: Temporal and Spatial Fallacies in Recent Black Freedom Studies." *Journal of African American History* 92, no. 2 (2007): 265–88.

Childress, Morton O. *Louisville Division of Police, 1806–2002*. Louisville: Turner Publishing Co., 2005.

Clark-Lewis, Elizabeth. *Living In, Living Out: African-American Domestics and the Great Migration*. 1994. Reprint, New York: Kodansha International, 1996.

Cleaver, Kathleen, and George Katsiaficas. *Liberation, Imagination, and the Black Panther Party: A New Look at the Panthers and Their Legacy*. New York: Routledge, 2001.

Clotfelter, Charles T. *After Brown: Rise and Retreat of School Desegregation*. Princeton, N.J.: Princeton University Press, 2007.

Cohen, William. *At Freedom's Edge: Black Mobility and the Southern White Quest for Racial Control, 1861–1915*. Baton Rouge: Louisiana State University Press, 1991.

Collier-Thomas, Bettye, and V. P. Franklin, eds. *Sisters in the Struggle: African American Women in the Civil Rights–Black Power Movement*. New York: New York University Press, 2001.

Collins, Patricia Hill. *Black Feminist Thought: Knowledge, Consciousness, and the Politics of Empowerment*. New York: Routledge, 1990.

Countryman, Matthew. *Civil Rights and Black Power in Philadelphia*. Philadelphia: University of Philadelphia Press, 2006.

Cromartie, John B., and Carol B. Stack. "Reinterpretation of Black Return and Nonreturn Migration to the South, 1975–1980." *Geographical Review* 79 (1989): 297–310.

Crosby, Emilye. *A Little Taste of Freedom: The Black Freedom Struggle in Claiborne County, Mississippi*. Chapel Hill: University of North Carolina Press, 2005.

Cummings, Scott, and Michael Price. "Race Relations and Public Policy in Louisville: Historical Development of an Urban Underclass." *Journal of Black Studies* 27, no. 5 (May 1997): 615–49.

Curry, Constance. *Silver Rights: The Story of the Carter Family's Brave Decision to Send Their Children to an All-White School and Claim Their Civil Rights*. New York: Harcourt Brace and Co., 1995.

Daniel, Pete. "Going among Strangers: Southern Reactions to World War II." *Journal of American History* 77, no. 3 (December 1990): 886–901.

———. "The New Deal, Southern Agriculture, and Economic Change." In *The New Deal and the South: Essays*, edited by James Cobb, 37–62. Jackson: University Press of Mississippi, 1984.

Davis, Angela Y. *Blues Legacies and Black Feminism: Gertrude "Ma" Rainey, Bessie Smith and Billie Holiday*. New York: Pantheon Books, 1998.

Dawson, Michael C. *Black Visions: The Roots of Contemporary African American Political Ideologies*. Chicago: University of Chicago Press, 2001.

Dennis, Sam Joseph. *African-American Exodus and White Migration, 1950–1970: A Comparative Analysis of Population Movements and Their Relations to Labor and Race Relations*. New York: Garland Publishing, Inc., 1989.

Dittmer, John. *Local People: The Struggle for Civil Rights in Mississippi*. Urbana: University of Illinois Press, 1994.

Douglass, Davison. *Reading, Writing, and Race: The Desegregation of the Charlotte Schools*. Chapel Hill: University of North Carolina Press, 1995.

Drake, St. Clair, and Horace R. Cayton. *Black Metropolis: A Study of Negro Life in a Northern City*. 1945. Reprint, New York: Harcourt Brace, and World, 1962.

Du Bois, W. E. B. "Behold the Land." In *Black Titians*, edited by John Henrik Clarke et al., 231–37. Boston: Beacon Hill Press, 1970.

———. *Black Reconstruction in America, 1860–1880*. 1935. Reprint, New York: Simon and Schuster, 1995.

———. *Dusk of Dawn: Towards an Autobiography of a Race Concept*. New York: Library of America, 1986.

———. *The Philadelphia Negro: A Social Study*. 1899. Reprint, Philadelphia: University of Pennsylvania Press, 1996.

Dudziak, Mary L. *Cold War and Civil Rights: Race and the Image of American Democracy*. Princeton, N.J.: Princeton University Press, 2000.

Durr, Kenneth D. *Behind the Backlash: White Working-Class Politics in Baltimore, 1940–1980*. Chapel Hill: University of North Carolina Press, 2003.

Eyes on the Prize: America's Civil Rights Movement, 1954–1985. Vol. 6. Alexandria, Va.: PBS Video, 2006.

Fairclouth, Adam. *Martin Luther King, Jr*. Athens: University of Georgia Press, 1995.

Fields, Barbara J. "Ideology and Race in American History." In *Region, Race and Reconstruction: Essays in Honor of C. Vann Woodward*, edited by J. Morgan Kousser and James M. McPherson, 143–77. New York: Oxford University Press, 1982.

Florant, Lyonel C. "Negro Internal Migration." *American Sociological Review* 7 (December 1942): 782–91.

Flowerdew, Robin. "Spatial Patterns of Residential Segregation in a Southern City." *Journal of American Studies* 13, no. 1 (1979): 93–107.

Floyd, Samuel. *The Power of Black Music: Interpreting Its History from Africa to the United States*. New York: Oxford University Press, 1995.

Formisano, Ronald P. *Boston against Busing: Race, Class, and Ethnicity in the 1960s and 1970s*. Chapel Hill: University of North Carolina Press, 1991.

Fosl, Catherine. *Subversive Southerner: Anne Braden and the Struggle for Racial Justice in the Cold War South*. New York: Palgrave, 2002.

Fosl, Catherine, and Tracy K'Meyer. *Freedom on the Border: An Oral History of the Civil Rights Movement in Kentucky*. Lexington: University of Kentucky Press, 2009.

Frazier, E. Franklin. *The Negro Family in the United States*. 1939. Reprint, Chicago: University of Chicago Press, 1966.

Frazier, E. Franklin, and Charles Parrish. *Negro Youth at the Crossways: Their Personality Development in the Middle States*. 1940. Reprint, New York: Schocken Books, 1967.

Frey, William H. "Black Migration to the South Reaches Record Highs in the 1990s." *Population Today* 26, no. 2 (1998): 1–3.

Gans, Herbert. *The War against the Poor: The Underclass and Antipoverty Policy*. New York: Basic Books, 1995.

Garrow, David. *We Shall Overcome: The Civil Rights Movement in the United States in the 1950s and 1960s*. Brooklyn: Carlson Publishing, 1989.

Gilmore, Glenda. *Defying Dixie: The Radical Roots of Civil Rights, 1919–1950*. New York: Norton, 2008.

Ginsberg, Elaine, ed. *Passing and the Fictions of Identity*. Durham: Duke University Press, 1996.

Goings, Kenneth W., and Raymond A. Mohl, eds. *The New African-American Urban History*. Thousand Oaks, Calif.: Sage Publications, 1996.

Goin' to Chicago. San Francisco: California Newsreel, 1994.

Gottlieb, Peter. *Making Their Own Way: Southern Blacks' Migration to Pittsburgh, 1916–30*. Urbana: University of Illinois Press, 1987.

Green, Adam. *Selling the Race: Culture, Community, and Black Chicago, 1940–1955*. Chicago, 2007.

Green, Laurie. *Battling the Plantation Mentality: Memphis and the Black Freedom Struggle*. Chapel Hill: University of North Carolina Press, 2007.

Greene, Christine. *Our Separate Ways: Women and the Black Freedom Movement in Durham, North Carolina*. Chapel Hill: University of North Carolina Press, 2005.

Gregg, Robert. *Sparks from the Anvil of Oppression: Philadelphia's African Methodists and Southern Migrants, 1890–1940*. Philadelphia: Temple University Press, 1993.

Gregory, James N. *The Southern Diaspora: How the Great Migrations of Black and White Southerners Transformed America*. Chapel Hill: University of North Carolina Press, 2005.

Griffin, Farah Jasmine. *"Who Set You Flowin'?": The African-American Migration Narrative*. New York: Oxford University Press, 1995.

Grossman, James R. *Land of Hope: Chicago, Black Southerners, and the Great Migration*. Chicago: University of Chicago Press, 1989.

———. "The White Man's Union." In *The Great Migration in Historical Perspective: New Dimensions of Race, Class and Gender*, edited by Joe William Trotter Jr., 83–105. Bloomington: University of Indiana Press, 1991.

Guterl, Matthew Pratt. *The Color of Race in America, 1900–1940*. Cambridge: Harvard University Press, 2001.

Guy, Buddy. "Stone Crazy," *Greatest Blues Legends*, MCA, Special Productions, MCAD 20768.

Hale, Grace Elizabeth. *Making Whiteness: The Culture of the Segregation in the South, 1890–1940*. New York: Pantheon, 1998.

Hall, Charles. *Negroes in the United States, 1920–1932*. New York: Greenwood Press, 1969.

Hall, Jacquelyn Dowd. "The Long Civil Rights Movement and the Political Uses of the Past." *Journal of American History* 91, no. 4 (March 2005): 1233–63.

Hall, Wade. *Passing for Black: The Life and Careers of Mae Street Kidd*. Lexington: University Press of Kentucky, 1997.

———. *The Rest of the Dream: The Black Odyssey of Lyman Johnson*. Lexington: University of Kentucky Press, 1988.

Harrison, Alferdteen, ed. *Black Exodus: The Great Migration from the American South*. Jackson: University Press of Mississippi, 1991.

Harrison, Daphne Duval. *Black Pearls: Blues Queens of the 1920's*. New Brunswick, N.J.: Rutgers University Press, 1988.

Hauser, Thomas. *Muhammad Ali: His Life and Times*. New York: Simon and Schuster, 1991.

Henri, Florette. *Black Migration: Movement North, 1900–1920*. Garden City, N.Y.: Anchor Press, 1975.

Hicks, Cheryl. "'In Danger of Becoming Morally Depraved': Single Black Women, Working-Class Black Families, and New York State's Wayward Minor Laws, 1917–1928." *University of Pennsylvania Law Review* 151, no. 6 (2003): 2077–91.

Higginbotham, Evelyn. *Righteous Discontent: The Women's Movement in the Black Baptist Church, 1880–1920*. Cambridge: Harvard University Press, 1993.

Hill, Herbert. *Race in America: The Struggle for Equality*. Madison: University of Wisconsin Press, 1993.

Hill, Lance. *The Deacons for Defense: Armed Resistance and the Civil Rights Movement*. Chapel Hill: University of North Carolina Press, 2004.

Hine, Darlene Clark. "Black Migration to the Urban Midwest." In *The Great Migration in Historical Perspective: New Dimensions of Race, Class and Gender*, edited by Joe William Trotter Jr., 127–45. Bloomington: Indiana University Press, 1991.

———. "Rape and the Inner Lives of Black Women in the Middle West: Preliminary Thoughts on the Culture of Dissemblance." In *Unequal Sisters*, edited by Ellen Carol Du Bois and Vicki L. Ruiz, 238–49. 1st ed. New York: Routledge, 1990.

Hirsch, Arnold R. *Making the Second Ghetto: Race and Housing in Chicago, 1940–1960*. New York: Cambridge University Press, 1983.

———. "Massive Resistance in the Urban North: Trumbull Park, Chicago, 1953–1966." *Journal of American History* 82, no. 2 (September 1995): 522–50.

———. "Second Thoughts on the Second Ghetto." *Journal of Urban History* 29 (March 2003): 298–309.

———. "With or Without Jim Crow: Black Residential Segregation in the United States." In *Urban Policy in Twentieth-Century America*, edited by Arnold R. Hirsch and Raymond A. Mohl, 65–99. New Brunswick, N.J.: Rutgers University Press, 1993.

Honey, Michael. *Southern Labor and Black Civil Rights: Organizing Memphis Workers*. Urbana: University of Illinois Press, 1993.

hooks, bell. *Feminist Theory: From Margin to Center*. Boston: South End Press, 1984.

Horton, Colonel John Benjamin. *Not without Struggle*. New York: Vantage Press, 1978.

Hudgens, Molly. "Coming Home Again: African-American Return Migration to the South." University of Chicago, ⟨http://www.inmotionaame.org-AAME:/⟩. October 23, 2008.

Hudson, J. Blaine. "African Americans." In *Encyclopedia of Louisville*, edited by John E. Kleber. Lexington: University of Kentucky Press, 2001.

———. "The Establishment of Louisville Municipal College: A Case Study in Racial Conflict and Compromise." *Journal of Negro Education* 64, no. 2 (Spring 1995): 111–23.

Hughes, Langston. "My America." In *What the Negro Wants*, edited by Rayford W. Logan, 299–307. 1944. Reprint, Notre Dame, Ind.: University of Notre Dame Press, 2001.

———. "To Make Our World Anew." In *The Collected Poems of Langston Hughes*, edited by Langston Hughes and Arnold Rampersad. New York: Vintage Press, 1995.

———. *Vintage Hughes*. New York: Vintage Books, 2004.

Ignatiev, Noel. *How the Irish Became White*. New York: Routledge, 1995.

Inger, Morton. "The New Orleans Schools Crisis of 1960." In *Southern Businessmen and Desegregation*, edited by Elizabeth Jacoway and David R. Colburn, 82–97. Baton Rouge: Louisiana State University Press, 1982.

Jackson, Kenneth T. *Crabgrass Frontier: The Suburbanization of the United States*. New York: Oxford University Press, 1985.

———. "Race, Ethnicity, and Real Estate Appraisal: The Home Owners Loan Corporation and the Federal Housing Administration." *Journal of Urban History* 6, no. 4 (August 1980): 419–52.

James, Elmore. "Call It Stormy Monday." *Greatest Blues Legends*, MCA, Special Productions, 1995, MCAD 20768.

Janken, Kenneth Robert. Introduction to *What the Negro Wants*, edited by Rayford W. Logan, vii–xxx. 1944. Reprint, Notre Dame, Ind.: University of Notre Dame Press, 2001.

Jefferies, Hasan Kwame. *Bloody Lowndes: Civil Rights and Black Power in Alabama's Black Belt*. New York: New York University Press, 2009.

———. "Organizing for More Than the Vote: The Political Radicalization of Local People in Lowndes County Alabama." In *Groundwork: Local Black Freedom Movements in America*, edited by Jeanne Theoharis and Komozi Woodard, 140–64. New York: New York University Press, 2005.

Jencks, Christopher. *The Urban Underclass*. Washington, D.C.: Brookings Institution, 1991.

Johnson, Charles. "How Much Is the Migration a Flight from Persecution?" *Opportunity*, No. 1 (September 1923): 272–75.

———. *The Negro in Chicago: A Study of Race Relations and a Race Riot*. Chicago Commission on Race Relations. 1922. Reprint, New York: Arno Press, 1968.

———. *Shadow of the Plantation*. Chicago: University of Chicago Press, 1934.

Johnson, Robert. "Ramblin' On My Mind." *The Complete Recordings: Disc One*. Columbia 46233. 1928.

Jones, Jacqueline. "Southern Diaspora: Origins of the Northern 'Underclass.'" In *The "Underclass" Debate: Views from History*, edited by Michael Katz, 27–54. Princeton, N.J.: Princeton University Press, 1993.

Jones, Le Roi. *Blues People: The Negro Experience in White American and the Music That Developed from It*. New York: Morrow Quill Paperbacks, 1963.

Jones, Marcus E. *Black Migration in the United States with Emphasis on Selected Central Cities.* Saratoga, Calif.: Century Twenty-One Publishing, 1980.

Jones, Patrick. "'Not a Color but an Attitude': Father James Groppi and Black Power Politics in Milwaukee." In *Groundwork: Local Black Freedom Movements in America*, edited by Jeanne Theoharis and Komozi Woodard, 259–81. New York: New York University Press, 2005.

Joseph, Peniel, ed. *The Black Power Movement: Rethinking the Civil Rights–Black Power Era.* New York: Routledge, 2006.

Katz, Michael B. *Improving Poor People: The Welfare State, the "Underclass," and Urban Schools as History.* Princeton, N.J.: Princeton University Press, 1995.

———, ed. *The "Underclass" Debate: Views from History.* Princeton, N.J.: Princeton University Press, 1993.

Katzman, David. *Before the Ghetto: Black Detroit in the Nineteenth Century.* Urbana: University of Illinois Press, 1973.

Keil, Charles. *Urban Blues.* Chicago: Chicago University Press, 1966.

Kelley, Robin D. G. *Freedom Dreams: The Black Radical Imagination.* Boston: Beacon Press, 2002.

———. *Race Rebels: Culture, Politics, and the Black Working Class.* New York: Free Press, 1996.

Kennedy, Louise V. *The Negro Peasant Turns Cityward: Effects of Recent Migrations to Northern Cities.* New York: Columbia University Press, 1930.

Kesselman, Louis C. "Negro Voting in a Border Community: Louisville, Kentucky." *Journal of Negro Education* 26, no. 3 (Summer 1957): 273–80.

Kirby, Jack Temple. *Rural Worlds Lost: The American South, 1920–1960.* Baton Rouge: Louisiana State University Press, 1987.

Kiser, Clyde V. *Sea Island to City: A Study of St. Helena Islanders in Harlem and Other Urban Centers.* 1932. Reprint, New York: AMS Press, 1967.

Kleber, John E., ed. *The Encyclopedia of Louisville.* Lexington: University of Kentucky Press, 2001.

K'Meyer, Tracy E. "Building Interracial Democracy: The Civil Rights Movement in Louisville, Kentucky, 1945–1960." In *Time Longer Than Rope: A Century of African American Activism, 1850–1950*, edited by Charles M. Payne and Adam Green, 411–39. New York: New York University Press, 2003.

———. *Civil Rights in the Gateway to the South: Louisville, Kentucky, 1945–1980.* Lexington: University of Kentucky Press, forthcoming.

———. "'The Gateway to the South': Regional Identity and the Louisville Civil Rights Movement." *Ohio Valley History* 4, no. 1 (2004): 43–60.

———. "To Bring People Together: The Arts, Interracialism, and Black Power in the Louisville Freedom Struggle." *Journal of American and Comparative Cultures* 24, nos. 3–4 (2001): 117–26.

———. "The West End Community Council: Building Interracial Community in Louisville's West End." *Ohio Valley History* 7, no. 3 (2007): 6–31.

Kneebone, John. *Southern Liberal Journalists and the Issue of Race, 1920–1944.* Chapel Hill: University of North Carolina Press, 1985.

Kolchin, Peter. "Whiteness Studies: The New History of Race in America." *Journal of American History* 89, no. 1 (June 2002): 154–73.

Kondo, Dorinne. "The Narrative Production of 'Home,' Community, and Political Identity in Asian American Theater." In *Displacement, Diaspora, and Geographies of*

Identity, edited by Smadar Lavie and Ted Swedenburg, 97–118. Durham: Duke University Press, 1996.

Kornbluh, Felicia. "'To Fulfill Their Rightly Needs.'" *Radical History Review* 69 (1997): 76–113.

Korstad, Robert. *Civil Rights Unionism: Tobacco Workers and the Struggle for Democracy in the Mid-Twentieth-Century South*. Chapel Hill: University of North Carolina Press, 2003.

Kozol, Jonathan. *Death at an Early Age: The Destruction of the Hearts and Minds of Negro Children in Boston Public Schools*. New York: Bantam Books, 1967.

Kramer, Carl E. "James C. Murphy and the Urban Planning Movement in Louisville." *Filson Club Historical Quarterly* 64 (July 1990): 317–59.

———. "Louisville Area Development Association." In *Encyclopedia of Louisville*, edited by John E. Kleber. Lexington: University of Kentucky Press, 2001.

———. "Two Centuries of Urban Development in Central and Southern Louisville." In *Louisville Survey: Central and South Report*, 198.

Kruse, Kevin. *White Flight: Atlanta and the Making of Modern Conservatism*. Princeton, N.J.: Princeton University Press, 2005.

Kusmer, Kenneth. "African-Americans in the City since World War II: From the Industrial to the Post-Industrial Era." In *The New African-American Urban History*, edited by Kenneth W. Goings and Raymond A. Mohl, 320–68. Thousand Oaks, Calif.: Sage Publications, 1996.

———. *A Ghetto Takes Shape: Black Cleveland, 1870–1930*. Urbana: University of Illinois Press, 1976.

Kyriakoudes, Louis M. *The Social Origins of the Urban South: Race, Gender, and Migration in Nashville and Middle Tennessee, 1980–1930*. Chapel Hill: University of North Carolina Press, 2003.

Lassiter, Matthew D., and Andrew B. Lewis, eds. *The Moderates' Dilemma: Massive Resistance to School Desegregation in Virginia*. Charlottesville: University of Virginia Press, 1998.

Lee, Chana Kai. *For Freedom's Sake: The Life of Fannie Lou Hamer*. Urbana: University of Illinois Press, 1999.

Lemann, Nicholas. *The Promised Land: The Great Black Migration and How It Changed America*. New York: Alfred A. Knopf, 1991.

Lemke-Santangelo, Gretchen. *Abiding Courage: African-American Migrant Women and the East Bay Community*. Chapel Hill: University of North Carolina Press, 1996.

Lewis, Earl. "Expectations, Economic Opportunities and Life in the Industrial Age: Black Migration to Norfolk, Virginia, 1910–1945." In *The Great Migration in Historical Perspective*, edited by Joe William Trotter Jr., 22–45. Bloomington: Indiana University Press, 1991.

———. *In Their Own Interests: Race, Class and Power in Twentieth-Century Norfolk, Virginia*. Berkeley: University of California Press, 1991.

Lewis, Edward E. *The Mobility of the Negro*. 1931. Reprint, New York: AMS Press, 1968.

Link, William A. *The Paradox of Southern Progressivism, 1880–1930*. Chapel Hill: University of North Carolina Press, 1992.

Lipsitz, George. *The Possessive Investment in Whiteness: How White People Benefit from Identity Politics*. Philadelphia: Temple University Press, 1998.

Litwack, Leon. *Trouble in Mind: Black Southerners in the Age of Jim Crow*. New York: Vintage Books, 1998.

Lomax, Alan. *Land of Where Blues Began*. New York: Pantheon Books, 1994.

Lovett, Bobby. *The Civil Rights Movement in Tennessee: A Narrative History*. Knoxville: University of Tennessee Press, 2005.

Lucas, Marion B. *A History of Blacks in Kentucky*. Vol. 1. Frankfort: Kentucky Historical Society, 1992.

Marks, Carole. *Farewell—We're Good and Gone: The Great Black Migration*. Bloomington: Indiana University Press, 1989.

Marqusee, Mike. *Redemption Song: Muhammad Ali and the Spirit of the Sixties*. London: Verso, 1999.

Marris, Robin. *How to Save the Underclass*. New York: St. Martin's Press, 1996.

Martin, Biddy, and Chandra Talpade Mohanty. "Feminist Politics: What's Home Got to Do with It?" In *Feminist Studies/Critical Studies*, edited by Teresa de Lauretis, 191–212. Bloomington: Indiana University Press, 1986.

Martin, Elmer P., and Joanne Mitchell Martin. *The Black Extended Family*. Chicago: University of Chicago Press, 1978.

Massey, Douglas S., and Nancy A. Denton. *American Apartheid: Segregation and the Making of the Underclass*. Cambridge: Harvard University Press, 1996.

Matthews, Tracye. "'No One Ever Asks, What a Man's Place in the Revolution Is': Gender and the Politics of the Black Panther Party, 1966–1961." In *The Black Panther Party Reconsidered*, edited by Charles E. Jones, 267–304. Baltimore: Black Classic Press, 1998.

McAdam, Doug. *Freedom Summer*. New York: Oxford University Press, 1988.

McConahay, John B. *Is It the Buses or the Blacks?: Self-interest versus Symbolic Racism as Predictors of Opposition to Busing in Louisville*. Durham: Center for Policy Analysis, Institute of Policy Sciences and Public Affairs, Duke University Press, 1981.

———. *Racial and Non-Racial Correlates of Anti-Busing Attitudes in Louisville*. Durham: Duke University Press, 1978.

———. *Reactions to Busing in Louisville: Summary of Adult Opinions in 1976 and 1977*. Durham: Center for Policy Analysis, Institute of Policy Sciences and Public Affairs, Duke University Press, 1978.

McMillen, Neil. *Dark Journey: Black Mississippians in the Age of Jim Crow*. Chicago: University of Illinois Press, 1990.

McNeil, Genna Rae. *Groundwork: Charles Hamilton Houston and the Struggle for Civil Rights*. Philadelphia: University of Pennsylvania Press, 1983.

Meier, August, and Elliot Rudwick. *CORE: A Study of the Civil Rights Movement, 1942–1968*. Urbana: University of Illinois Press, 1975.

Meyer, Stephen Grant. *As Long as They Don't Move Next Door: Segregation and Racial Conflict in American Neighborhoods*. Lanham, Md.: Rowman and Littlefield, 2000.

Miller, Ann Ratner. *Net Intercensal Migration to Large Urban Areas of the United States, 1930–1940, 1940–1950, 1950–1960*. Philadelphia: University of Pennsylvania, 1964.

Mitchell, Broadus. *Depression Decade: From New Era through New Deal, 1929–1941*. 1947. Reprint, New York: Holt, Rinehart and Winston, 1961.

Mohl, Raymond A. "Making the Second Ghetto in Metropolitan Miami, 1940–1960." In *The New African-American Urban History*, edited by Kenneth W. Goings and Raymond A. Mohl, 266–98. Thousand Oaks, Calif.: Sage Publications, 1996.

Moore, Leonard N. *Carl B. Stokes and the Rise of Black Political Power*. Urbana: University of Illinois Press, 2002.

Murray, Albert. *Stomping the Blues*. New York: Vintage Books, 1982.

Murray, Pauli, ed. *States' Laws on Race and Color*. Athens: University of Georgia Press, 1997.

Myrdal, Gunnar. *An American Dilemma: The Negro Problem and Modern Democracy*. 1944. Reprint, New York: Pantheon Books, 1962.

Naples, Nancy A. *Grassroots Warriors: Activist Mothering, Community Work, and the War on Poverty*. New York: Routledge, 1998.

Nielson, Aldon Lynn. *Reading Race: The White American Poet and the Racial Discourse in the Twentieth Century*. Athens: University of Georgia Press, 1988.

Ogbar, John. *Black Power: Radical Politics and African American Identity*. Baltimore: Johns Hopkins University Press, 2004.

Oliver, Paul. *Blues Fell This Morning*. London: Cassell, 1960.

———. *The Meaning of the Blues*. New York: Collier Books, 1963.

———. *Story of the Blues*. Philadelphia, Pa.: Chilton Books, 1969.

Oser, W. Edward. *Blockbusting in Baltimore: The Edmondson Village Story*. Lexington: University Press of Kentucky, 1994.

Osofsky, Gilbert. *Harlem: The Making of a Ghetto: Negro New York, 1890–1930*. New York: Harper and Row, 1966.

Painter, Nell. *Exodusters: Black Migration to Kansas after Reconstruction*. New York: Norton, 1976.

Payne, Charles. *I've Got the Light of Freedom: The Organizing Tradition and the Mississippi Freedom Struggle*. Berkeley: University of California Press, 1995.

Phillips, Kimberley L. *Alabama North: African-American Migrants, Community, and Working-Class Activism in Cleveland, 1915–1945*. Urbana: University of Illinois Press, 1999.

Piper, Adrian. "Passing for White, Passing for Black." *Transition* 58 (1992): 4–32.

Pleck, Elizabeth H. *Black Migration and Poverty: Boston, 1865–1900*. New York: Academic Press, 1979.

Portelli, Alessandro. *The Death of Luigi Trastulli and Other Stories: Form and Meaning in Oral History*. Albany: State University of New York Press, 1991.

Powers, Georgia Davis. *I Shared the Dream: The Pride, Passion and Politics of the First Black Woman Senator from Kentucky*. Tar Hills, N.J.: New Horizon Press, 1995.

Prakash, Gyan. "Subaltern Studies as Postcolonial Criticism." *American Historical Review* (December 1994): 1475–90.

———. "Writing Post-Orientalists Histories of the Third World: Perspectives in Indian Historiography." *Comparative Studies in Society and History* 32 (1990): 383–408.

Pruitt, Bernadette. "'For the Advancement of the Race': Agency, Work and the Great Migration in Houston, Texas, 1900–1941." *Journal of Urban History* 31, no. 4 (2005): 435–78.

Ransby, Barbara. *Ella Baker and the Black Freedom Movement: A Radical Democratic Vision*. Chapel Hill: University of North Carolina Press, 2003.

Reed, Adolph L. *Stirrings in the Jug: Black Politics in the Post–Segregationist Era*. Minneapolis: University of Minnesota Press, 1999.

Reid, Ira De. A. "Special Problems of Negro Migration during the War." *Milbank Memorial Fund Quarterly* 25, no. 3 (July 1947): 284–92.

Remnick, David. *King of the World: Muhammad Ali and the Rise of an American Hero*. New York: Vintage, 1999.

Rhomberg, Chris. *No There There: Race, Class and Political Community in Oakland*. Berkeley: University of California Press, 2004.

Roberts, John. *From Trickster to Badman: The Black Folk Hero in Slavery and Freedom*. Philadelphia: University of Pennsylvania Press, 1989.

Roediger, David R. *Towards the Abolition of Whiteness: Essays on Race, Politics, and Working Class History*. London, 1994.

———. *The Wages of Whiteness: Race and the Making of the American Working Class*. New York: Verso, 1991.

Rubin, Lillian B. *Busing and Backlash: White against White in an Urban School*. Berkeley: University of California Press, 1973.

Schwarzweller, Harry K. "Career Placement and Economic Life Chances of Young Men from Eastern Kentucky." University of Kentucky Agricultural Experiment Station, Lexington, January 1964.

———. "Family Ties, Migration, and Transitional Adjustment of Young Men from Eastern Kentucky," University of Kentucky Agricultural Experiment Station, Lexington, May 1964.

———. *Mountain Families in Transition: A Case Study of Appalachian Migration*. University Park: Pennsylvania State University Press, 1971.

———. "Sociocultural Origins of Migration Patterns of Young Men from Eastern Kentucky." University of Kentucky Agricultural Experiment Station, Lexington, December 1963.

Scott, Emment J. *Negro Migration during the War*. 1920. Reprint, New York: Arno Press, 1969.

Self, Robert O. *American Babylon: Race and the Struggle for Postwar Oakland*. Princeton, N.J.: Princeton University Press, 2003.

Sernett, Milton. *Bound for the Promised Land: African-American Religion and the Great Migration*. Durham: Duke University Press, 1997.

Shaw, Stephanie. *What a Woman Ought to Be and to Do: Black Professional Women Workers during the Jim Crow Era*. Chicago: University of Chicago Press, 1996.

Sides, Josh. *L.A. City Limits: African American Los Angeles from the Great Depression to the Present*. Berkeley: University of California Press, 2003.

Silver, Christopher, and John Moeser. *The Separate City: Black Communities in the Urban South, 1940–1968*. Lexington: University of Kentucky Press, 1995.

Sing for Freedom. Washington, D.C.: Smithsonian Folkways Recordings, 1990.

Sitkoff, Harvard. "Impact of the New Deal on Black Southerners." In *The New Deal and the South*, edited by James Cobb, 117–34. Jackson: University Press of Mississippi, 1984.

———. *A New Deal for Blacks: The Emergence of Civil Rights as a National Issue: The Depression Decade*. Oxford: Oxford University Press, 1978.

———. *The Struggle for Black Equality, 1954–1980*. New York: Hill and Wang, 1981.

Smethurst, James Edward. *The Black Arts Movement: Literary Nationalism in the 1960s and 1970s*. Chapel Hill: University of North Carolina Press, 2005.

Smith, Barbara, ed. *Home Girls: A Black Feminist Anthology*. New York: Kitchen Table: Women of Color Press, 1983.

Smith, Clara. "The L & N Blues," Columbia 14073-D, March 1925.

Spear, Allan. *Black Chicago: The Making of a Ghetto, 1890–1920*. Chicago: University of Chicago Press, 1967.

Spencer, Robyn Ceanne. "Inside the Panther Revolution: The Black Freedom Movement and the Black Panther Party in Oakland, California." In *Groundwork: Local Black Freedom Movements in America*, edited by Jeanne Theoharis and Komozi Woodard, 300–318. New York: New York University Press, 2005.

Stack, Carol B. *Call to Home: African-Americans Reclaim the Rural South*. New York: Basic Books, 1996.

Strain, Christopher. *Pure Fire: Self-Defense as Activist in the Civil Rights Era*. Athens: University of Georgia Press, 2005.

Sugrue, Thomas J. "Crabgrass-Roots Politics: Race, Rights, and the Reaction against Liberalism in the Urban North, 1940–1964." *Journal of American History* 82, no. 2 (September 1995): 551–78.

———. *The Origins of the Urban Crisis: Race and Inequality in Postwar Detroit*. Princeton, N.J.: Princeton University Press, 1996.

———. "Revisiting the Second Ghetto." *Journal of Urban History* 29 (March 2003): 281–90.

Suri, Jeremi. *Protest and Politics: Global Revolution and the Rise of Détente*. Cambridge: Harvard University Press, 2003.

Taylor, Quintard. *Forging a Black Community: Seattle's Central District from 1870 through the Civil Rights Era*. Seattle: University of Washington Press, 1994.

———. *In Search of the Racial Frontier: African Americans in the American West, 1528–1990*. New York: Norton, 1998.

Theoharis, Jeanne, and Komozi Woodard, eds. *Groundwork: Local Black Freedom Movements in America*. New York: New York University Press, 2005.

Thomas, Lorenzo. "A Sense of Community: Blues as Primer for Urbanization." *Popular Music and Society* 14, no. 2 (Summer 1990): 77–86.

Thompson, Heather. "Making a Second Urban History." *Journal of Urban History* 29 (March 2003): 291–97.

Trotter, Joe William, Jr. "Black Migration in Historical Perspective: A Review of the Literature." In *The Great Migration in Historical Perspective: New Dimensions of Race, Class and Gender*, edited by Joe William Trotter Jr., 1–21. Bloomington: Indiana University Press, 1991.

———. *Black Milwaukee: The Making of an Industrial Proletariat, 1915–45*. Urbana: University of Illinois Press, 1988.

———. *River Jordan: African American Urban Life in the Ohio Valley*. Lexington: University Press of Kentucky, 1999.

Tuttle, William. *Race Riot: Chicago in the Red Summer of 1919*. 1970. Reprint, New York: Atheneum, 1974.

Tyler, Bruce. "The 1968 Black Power Riot in Louisville, Kentucky," ⟨http://louisville.edu/a-s/history/tyler/kentuckyriots.html⟩. November 20, 2008.

Tyler, Carole Anne. "Passing: Narcissism, Identity and Difference." *Differences: A Journal of Feminist Cultural Studies* 6.2–3 (1994): 212–48.

Tyson, Timothy. *Radio Free Dixie: Robert F. Williams and the Roots of Black Power*. Chapel Hill: University of North Carolina Press, 1999.

Von Eschen, Penny. *Race against Empire: Black Americans and Anticolonialism, 1937–1957*. Ithaca, N.Y.: Cornell University Press, 1997.

Wald, Gayle. *Crossing the Line: Racial Passing in Twentieth-Century U.S. Literature and Culture*. Durham: Duke University Press, 2000.

Weisbrot, Robert. *Freedom Bound: A History of America's Civil Rights Movement*. New York: Norton, 1990

Weiss, Nancy J. *Farewell to the Party of Lincoln: Black Politics in the Age of FDR*. Princeton, N.J.: Princeton University Press, 1983.

Whayne, Jeannie. *A New Plantation South: Land, Labor and Federal Favor in Twentieth Century Arkansas*. Charlottesville: University Press of Virginia, 1996.

Wiese, Andrew. *Places of Their Own: African American Suburbanization in the Twentieth Century*. Chicago: University of Chicago Press, 2003.

Wild Women Don't Have the Blues. Directed by Christine Dall. Videocassette. Calliope Film Resources, 1989.

Williams, Kenneth H. "Oh Baby . . . It's Really Happening: The Louisville Race Riot of 1968." *Kentucky History Journal* 3 (1998): 48–64.

Williams, Rhonda Y. "Black Women and Black Power." *Magazine of History* 22, no. 3 (2008): 22–26.

———. *The Politics of Public Housing: Black Women's Struggles against Urban Inequality*. New York: Oxford University Press, 2004.

Wilson, George D. *Footprints in the Sand*. Decorah, Iowa: Anindsen Publishing Co., 1982.

Wilson-Moore, Shirley Ann. *To Place Our Deeds: The African American Community in Richmond, California, 1910–1963*. Berkeley: University of California Press, 2000.

Wilson, William Julius. *The Truly Disadvantaged: The Inner City, the Underclass, and Public Policy*. Chicago: University of Chicago Press, 1987.

Wolcott, Victoria. *Remaking Respectability: African American Women in Interwar Detroit*. Chapel Hill: University of North Carolina Press, 2001.

Wolters, Raymond. *Negroes and the Great Depression: The Problem of Economic Recovery*. Westport, Conn.: Greenwood Publishing Corp., 1970.

Woodard, Komozi. *A Nation within a Nation: Amiri Baraka and Black Power Politics*. Chapel Hill: University of North Carolina Press, 1999.

Woodson, Carter G. *A Century of Negro Migration*. New York: Russell and Russell, 1918.

Woofter, Thomas J. *Negro Migration: Changes in Rural Organization and Population of the Cotton Belt*. New York: W. D. Gray, 1920.

Wright, George C. "Black Political Insurgency in Louisville, Kentucky: The Lincoln Independent Party of 1921." *Journal of Negro History* 68, no. 1 (Winter 1983): 8–23.

———. "The Civil Rights Movement in Kentucky, 1900–1970." In *Essays on the American Civil Rights Movement*, edited by W. Marvin Dulaney and Kathleen Underwood, 44–65. College Station: Texas A & M Press, 1993.

———. "Desegregation of Public Accommodations in Louisville: A Long and Difficult Struggle in a 'Liberal' Border City." In *Southern Businessmen and Desegregation*, edited by Elizabeth Jacoway and David Colburn, 191–212. Baton Rouge: Louisiana State University Press, 1982.

———. *A History of Blacks in Kentucky*. Vol. 2 of *In Pursuit of Equality, 1890–1980*. Lexington: Kentucky Historical Society, 1992.

———. *Life Behind a Veil: Blacks in Louisville, Kentucky, 1865–1930*. Baton Rouge: Louisiana State University Press, 1985.

———. *Racial Violence in Kentucky, 1865–1940: Lynchings, Mob Rule and "Legal Lynchings."* Baton Rouge: Louisiana State University Press, 1990.

Wright, Richard. *Black Boy*. 1944. Restored ed., New York: First Perennial Classics, 1993.

X, Malcolm. *The Autobiography of Malcolm X.* With the assistance of Alex Haley. 3rd printing. New York: Grove Press, Inc., 1965.

Yater, George H. *Two Hundred Years at the Falls of the Ohio: A History of Louisville and Jefferson County.* Jefferson County: Heritage Corporation of Louisville, 1979.

DISSERTATIONS AND THESES

Adams, Luther J. "Way Up North in Louisville: African American Migration in Louisville, Kentucky, 1930–1970." Ph.D. diss., University of Pennsylvania, 2002.

Bernier, Richard R. "White Activists and Support in the Louisville, Kentucky, Open Housing Movement, 1962–1967." M.A. thesis, University of Louisville, 1998.

Brandon, Donald. American Negro Migration from 1920 to 1947. Ph.D. diss., Teachers College, Columbia University, 1949.

Collins, Ernest. "The Political Behavior of the Negroes in Cincinnati, Ohio and Louisville, Kentucky." Ph.D. diss., University of Kentucky, 1950.

Fosl, Catherine Anne. "'Once Comes the Moment to Decide': Anne Braden and the Civil Rights Movement." Ph.D. diss., Emory University, 2000.

Gilpin, Toni. "Left by Themselves: A History of the United Farm Equipment and Metal Workers Union, 1938–1955." Ph.D. diss., Yale University, 1992.

Harmon, Shirley Mae. "A Comparison Study of Black and White Women War Workers in Louisville, Kentucky, during World War II." M.A. thesis, University of Louisville, 1999.

Hudson, James Blaine, III. "The History of Louisville Municipal College: Events Leading to the Desegregation of the University of Louisville." Ph.D. diss., University of Kentucky, 1981.

McElhone, Patrick S. "The Civil Rights Activities of the Louisville Branch of the National Association for the Advancement of Colored People, 1914–1960." M.A. thesis, University of Louisville, 1976.

McGreevy, John T. "American Catholics and the African-American Migration, 1919–1970." Ph.D. dissertation, Stanford University, 1992.

Moore, Shirley Ann. "Blacks in Richmond, California, 1915–1960." Ph.D. diss., University of California, 1989.

PERMISSIONS FOR THE REPRINTING OF SONG LYRICS

INDEX

white liberals, 222 (n. 126); on whites' view
of segregation, 114
Braden, Carl, 110, 116–17, 133, 135, 145
Bradley, Mildred, 28
Breckinridge, John, 132
Brigham, Harold F., 106
Brinkley, Alan, 17
Brookins, Beatrice and Catherine, 70
Brown, Elsa Barkely, 63
Brown, Lafayette, 28
Brown v. Board of Education, 91, 195
Bryant, Ruth, 55, 161, 164, 167, 170, 190, 196
Buchanan v. Warley, 46
Building and Construction Workers union,
34
Building trades, 183
BULK. *See* Black Unity League of Kentucky
Burnley, Stephen A., 100
Burns, Tommie, 151
Bus company, 120, 121
Businesses: black-owned and -operated
businesses, 3, 4, 19–20, 149–52, 155–56,
183; blacks' patronage of, 74–75, 82–83,
217 (n. 1); blacks' protests against mistreatment by, 83; department stores, 46, 48,
81–83, 105, 119–20, 133, 136–39, 149, 150;
drugstores, 48, 75, 128, 130, 136; economic
boycotts against, 12, 121, 131, 132, 137–39,
141, 152, 174, 179; funeral homes, 3, 4, 20,
132, 151, 155; grocery stores, 20, 83, 150, 152,
192, 233 (n. 26); law firms, 20–21; restaurants, 20, 46, 63–64, 128, 130, 133, 138–42,
149, 150, 158, 178; Walnut Street business
district, 3, 12, 19–20, 149–52, 155; and war
production, 25–27; white business leaders, 138, 140. *See also* Employment *headings;
and specific companies*
Busing. *See* School busing
Bussey, Gladys, 28
Bus station, 3, 24, 82, 108
Byck, Dan, 112

Carmichael, Omer, 39, 117, 119, 192
Carmichael, Stokely, 179, 187
Carroll, Alfred M., 96–97, 99, 102
Carter, Gladdis, 167
Carter, Mae Bertha, 126
Carter, William, 157
Chamberlain, Leo, 98
Chandler, Albert Benjamin "Happy," 95–97
Charleston, S.C., 25

Charlestown, W.Va., 90
Charlotte, N.C., 18–19, 35, 197–99
Chicago, Ill., 9, 48, 51, 62, 123, 125, 127, 159,
161, 171
Churches: African Methodist Episcopal
Church, 62–63, 107, 135, 136, 139, 140,
180; Baptist Church, 4, 62, 134, 157, 169,
187, 188; Colored Methodist Episcopal
Church, 72; Congregational Church, 62;
desegregation of, 140; destruction of, by
urban renewal, 157; "fellowship" practice
of African Americans, 4, 203 (n. 7); and mi-
grants, 62–63, 72; on Walnut Street, 3, 151
CIC. *See* Commission on Interracial
Cooperation
Cicero, Ill., 172
Cincinnati, Ohio, 18, 159, 161
CIO. *See* Congress of Industrial
Organizations
Citizens against Busing, 193
Citizens Committee on Fair Employment,
111
Civic Center Project, 155, 159
Civil Rights Act (Kentucky), 145, 146, 179
Civil Rights Act (U.S.), 181
Civil rights movements: and African
Americans' commitment to remain in
South, 12, 123–27; arrests of protesters in,
137, 138, 139–40, 142, 174, 176, 181; black
migrants' leadership of, generally, 121–22;
and Black Power, 166, 187–88, 190; court
injunction against night marches, 176;
in Deep South, 127, 136; desegregation
of higher education, 95–105, 114, 122;
desegregation of public accommodations, 12, 105, 114, 121, 122, 125, 127–47;
desegregation of public library, 105–7, 113,
124; different strategies for, 107, 135–36,
171–73; and economic boycotts, 12, 121,
131, 132, 137–39, 141, 152, 174, 178, 179; and
economic equality, 120–21; and hunger
strike, 145; and interracialism, 105, 107,
109–13, 133, 145, 166–67; in Kentucky, 227
(n. 96); Kentucky civil rights law, 145, 146;
longer time frame of, 122, 164, 229 (n. 39);
March on Washington (1941), 24, 106; and
murder of King, 185; and older blacks,
137, 172–73; open housing campaign, 5,
12, 105, 127, 152, 164–84; and ordinance
prohibiting demonstrating in downtown
Louisville, 133; photographs of, 129, 131,

Interdenominational Ministers Council, 134

International Harvester, 13, 109–10, 192

International Union of Electrical Workers, 111

Interracial Hospital Movement (IHM), 111, 112

Interracial movement, 105, 107, 109–13, 133, 145, 166–67. *See also* Commission on Interracial Cooperation; Kentucky Council on Interracial Cooperation

Interstate highways, 159

Irvin, Jessie, 124, 143, 176–77, 196

Jackson, Leo, 22

Jackson, Mahalia, 145

James, Hulbert, 167, 169, 178

Jim Crow. *See* Segregation

Jobs. *See* Employment *headings*

Johnson, Charles S., 8, 204 (nn. 22–23)

Johnson, Cornelia, 54

Johnson, Juanita, 72

Johnson, Keen, 99–100

Johnson, L. Eugene, 139, 142

Johnson, Lyman T.: democratic rhetoric by, 113; and desegregation of public accommodations, 122, 133–34, 143; and desegregation of University of Kentucky, 101–5, 122, 220 (n. 83); on dissemblance, 76–78; on educational opportunities for blacks in Louisville, 53, 54; education of, 53; family background of, 21, 53; and improvement of conditions in Louisville generally, 196; on Louisville and Kentucky generally, 39, 47; migration of, to Louisville, 21, 51, 121–22; and movie *Gone with the Wind*, 82, 217 (n. 104); as NAACP president, 122, 124; and NAACP Youth Council, 128; and open housing campaign, 181; on reasons for staying in South, 55–56, 123; as teacher, 128, 134; and teacher salary equalization, 92, 122; and Tucker, 135

Johnson, Lyndon B., 170

Johnson, Weldon, 39

Jones, Alberta O., 136

Jones, Jacqueline, 15

Jones, Le Roi, 48

Jones, Mattie, 145

Jones, Tom and Mattie, 25

Jordan, Eleanor, 74

Jordan, Fannie, 150

Joseph, E., 70

Judges, 90

Junta Militant Organizations, 196

Kelley, Robin D. G., 210 (n. 97)

Kentucky: antisegregation bills in legislature of, 128; black state legislators in, 90, 124, 144, 181; as border state, 37–38; civil rights law in, 145, 146, 179; civil rights movement in, 227 (n. 96); compared with other southern states, 38–39; economy of, 38; executive order prohibiting racial discrimination in, 145; open housing laws passed by legislature of, 181; segregation in, 39; violence against African Americans in, 39; voting rights of African Americans in, 38, 126, 136, 144. *See also* Lexington, Ky.; Louisville, Ky.

Kentucky Bureau of Negro Affairs, 108, 109

Kentucky Christian Leadership Conference, 169, 178

Kentucky Civil Liberties Union, 166, 193

Kentucky Commission on Human Relations, 166

Kentucky Commission on Human Rights, 138, 192, 193, 194–95

Kentucky Commission on Negro Affairs, 32, 114

Kentucky Conference of the AME Zion Church, Civil Rights Commission of, 135, 136

Kentucky Council on Interracial Cooperation, 109, 112, 114

Kentucky Derby, 138, 140, 174, 178–80

Kentucky Negro Education Association (KNEA), 104–5

Kentucky State College, 2–3, 96, 100, 101, 103

Kentucky State Medical Association, 109

Kerner Report, 195

Kidd, Mae Street, 35–36, 59–64, 71–73, 78–79, 84, 181, 214 (n. 3)

Kimball, Gregg D., 63

King, A. D., 169, 172, 176, 178–80, 188

King, D. E., 134

King, Iris, 130

King, Martin Luther, Jr.: brother of, 169; and decision to remain in South, 126; and economic boycott, 137; on goals of civil rights movement, 140, 180; in Louisville, 140, 172, 174; and March on Frankfort (1964), 145, 146; murder of, 185; negotia-

and desegregation of higher education, 96–105, 114; and desegregation of public accommodations, 128–35, 139–44; and desegregation of public library, 105–7, 124; and desegregation of public schools, 117, 193; and economic boycott, 174; and employment discrimination, 111, 120–21, 192; financial problems and inactivity in Louisville chapter of, 90–92; founding of Louisville chapter of, 5; Houston as litigation director of, 219 (n. 43); internal dissension within Louisville chapter of, 102–3; and Interracial Hospital Movement, 111; Labor and Industry Committee of, 111, 120–21, 223 (n. 152); and open housing, 105, 169, 170, 174, 230 (n. 57); and passing as challenge to segregation, 79–80; on police brutality, 68; and political action generally, 85, 119; presidents of Louisville chapter of, 91, 117, 121, 122, 124–25, 133–34; Rabb as fund-raiser for, 139; and residential segregation, 5, 159, 164; teacher salary equalization campaign of, 90–95, 105; tensions between CORE and, 135–36, 142–43; and Wade-Braden case, 116–17; white membership of, 109, 117; and working-class blacks, 102–3, 223 (n. 152); Youth Council of, 125, 127–28, 137, 139. *See also* Civil rights movement; Political action

Nashville, Tenn., 15, 23, 47, 53, 92, 128, 167

National Association for the Advancement of Colored People. *See* NAACP

National Association for the Advancement of White People, 117

National Black Women for Political Action, 109

National Council of Jewish Women, 159, 161, 166

National Council of Negro Women, 109

National Guardsmen, 187–89, 194

National Housewives League, 109

National Housing Acts (1933, 1934), 153

National Municipal League, 186

National Recovery Administration (NRA), 16, 17, 24

National Synthetic Rubber Company, 25–27

Neal, Beverley, 139

Neal, Sterling, 110

New Deal, 15–19, 24, 88, 207 (n. 15), 229 (n. 39)

New Negro, 226 (n. 57)

New Orleans, La., 19, 20, 35, 118, 197–99

Newspapers. *See specific newspapers*

New York City, 118, 123, 151, 172

New York Times, 178, 179, 194

Nichols, Jack, 120

Nichols, T. Lomax, 150

Nielson, Aldon Lynn, 217 (n. 84)

Non-Partisan Registration Committee (NPRC), 136, 143, 144

Non-Partisan Registration League, 124

Non-Partisan Voters' League, 143

Norfolk, Va., 25, 90

North: blacks' return to South from, 54, 62, 125; reactions to southern migrants by blacks in, 47, 206 (n. 37); segregation in, 10; southern African American migration to, 1–2, 24, 54, 123–24, 204 (n. 11); urban black population in, 208–9 (n. 51)

North Carolina. *See* Charlotte, N.C.; Durham, N.C.; Greensboro, N.C.

Norton, George, 138

NPRC. *See* Non-Partisan Registration Committee

NRA. *See* National Recovery Administration

Nurses. *See* Medical professionals

Offutt, W. P., Jr., 106

Oliver, Paul, 48–49, 50

Olympics, 178–79

"One-Way Ticket" (Hughes), 49–50

Open housing campaign, 12, 164–84; arrests of protesters in, 174, 176, 181; in Chicago, 171; city ordinance for voluntary approach to, 168–69; and Committee on Open Housing, 166, 167, 169–74, 176, 178–81; court injunction against night marches during, 176; and economic boycott, 174, 179; goals of, 180, 182–83; and Human Relations Commission, 166–73, 176, 177, 179; legal basis for, 179; and NAACP, 105, 169, 170, 174, 230 (n. 57); and open housing ordinance passed (1967), 181–82; and police, 177, 178; proposed city ordinances on, 167–71, 173–76; protest demonstrations for, 171–82; results of, 181–84; sit-ins during, 174, 181; and Southern Christian Leadership Conference, 171–72; and threat of boycott and protests at Kentucky Derby, 174, 178–80; and urban renewal, 152, 164–65; violence against protesters during, 176–78, 180, 185; and West End Community Council, 167, 169, 182–83; white hecklers against, 174–78, 180–81; and white liberals, 166, 167; whites' opposition to, 174–75. *See also* Housing

Organized labor. *See* Labor unions

Paducah County Club, 63, 214 (n. 18)
Page, Henry and George, 13
Painter, Nell, 6
Parks, 3, 48, 79–80, 102–3, 110. *See also* Amusement parks
Parkway Place, 29, 45
Parrish, Charles, 81, 103, 105
Passing by African Americans, 63–64, 78–81
Pearce, Horace, 211 (n. 18)
Pemberton, W. E., 68
Perry, W. H., 92
The Philadelphia Negro (Du Bois), 204 (n. 11)
Physicians. *See* Medical professionals
Pickens, William, 91
Pinney, John B., 224 (n. 6)
"Plantation mentality," 7–8
Police: benign neglect of vice and crime by, 64–65; black, 40, 89, 113, 119; and civil rights movement, 127, 137, 139, 177, 178; corruption and brutality of, 64, 67–71, 108, 110, 127, 186–88, 215 (n. 48), 216 (n. 56); and Ku Klux Klan, 86; and open housing demonstrations, 177; segregation enforced by, 110
Political action: of African American elected officials, 3, 89–90, 124, 132, 144, 196, 203 (n. 2); by African American women, 109; black migrants' leadership of, generally, 121–22; Cole's call for, 85; and democratic rhetoric and icons, 112–14, 221 (n. 121); and economic equality, 120–21; interracial movement for, 105, 107, 109–13, 133, 145, 166–67; by labor unions, 109–11; and Lincoln Independent Party, 86–87, 136; and NAACP generally, 85; and southern white liberals, 222 (nn. 126, 129). *See also* Civil rights movement; Democratic Party; Integration/desegregation; NAACP; Republican Party
Porgy and Bess, 130
Porter, A. D., 86, 87
Post Office, U.S., 33
Poverty, 183, 192

Poverty, culture of, 8, 206 (n. 32)
Powers, Georgia Davis, 43, 51, 54, 55, 57, 181, 227 (n. 94)
Price, Michael, 231 (n. 95)
Prince, Michael, 192
Progressive Party, 116
Prostitution, 64–65
Protest politics, 107. *See also* Civil rights movement
Pruitt, E. E., 164
Psychological wages, 31–32, 210 (n. 97)
Public accommodations: city ordinance banning discrimination in, 128, 130–32, 141, 144–45; desegregation of, 12, 105, 114, 121, 122, 125, 127–47; discontinuation of demonstrations for desegregation of, in May 1961, 141, 142; Ethridge on adequacy of, for African Americans, 99; Louisville Board of Aldermen's enactment of antisegregation ordinance for, 145, 186; Louisville Board of Aldermen's opposition to antisegregation ordinance for, 132–33, 141; mayor's emergency committee on desegregation of, 138, 140–41, 165; segregation of, generally, 99, 125. *See also* Amusement parks; Hotels; Parks; Restaurants; Theaters
Public housing. *See* Housing
Public Housing Administration, 153
Public library. *See* Louisville Free Public Library
Public transportation, 37–40, 47, 48, 211 (n. 18)
Public utilities, 28, 32, 33, 128
Purdue, M. M. D., 133

Quin, Huston, 87
Quinn Chapel AME, 139–40, 211 (n. 18)

Rabb, Jewel, 48, 75, 125, 128
Rabb, Maurice: activism by, against residential segregation, 124, 165; on civil rights activism, 130; as doctor, 14, 21; and hospitals for African Americans, 108–9, 110; and Human Relations Commission, 166–67, 171; migration of, to Louisville, 14, 36, 61–62, 71; as NAACP fund-raiser, 139; and NAACP Labor and Industry Committee, 120; and NAACP Youth Council, 125; and open housing campaign, 165, 169; racial discrimination against family of, 48; and Tucker, 135

Race, as social construction, 76

Racism and racial discrimination: in criminal justice system, 39; and Democratic Party, 87; in employment, 30–35, 111, 119–21, 128, 192; in Louisville during 1960s–1970s, 185–96; and Louisville riot, 188–90; and "plantation mentality," 7–8; "polite racism" in Louisville, 39–40, 46, 48; Roper report on, 191–92, 195, 232 (n. 16); symbolic, 234 (n. 35); in teacher salaries, 90–95; and urban crisis and white supremacy, 195–96; and whites' assumptions of black inferiority, 76, 83–84, 115, 234 (n. 35); whites' lack of awareness about, 171, 191–92. See also Education; Employment of African Americans; Housing; Ku Klux Klan; Public accommodations; Segregation; White supremacy

Radio station. See WLOU

Railroads: employment of blacks by, 13, 14, 24, 28, 33; segregation of, 37–38, 79

Randolph, A. Phillip, 106

Ransom, Leon A., 92

Rash, Dillman, 138

Rauch, Rabbi Joseph, 105–6, 114

Ray, Amelia B., 23, 53–54, 61, 80–82, 113–14, 165

Regional Council of Negro Leadership, 127

Reid, Ira, 25

Reid, Manfred, 186, 187, 190

Relocation of African Americans within South. See African American migration

Republican Party: and African Americans, 85–90, 144; in elections of 1921, 87; and elections of 1961, 143–44; and elections of 1967, 181; and Lincoln, 86, 88; and Louisville Board of Aldermen, 144, 181

Residential segregation. See Housing; Open housing campaign

Restaurants, 20, 46, 63–64, 128, 130, 133, 138–42, 149, 150, 158, 178

Restore Our Alienated Rights, 193

Reynolds, Louise, 90, 144, 175, 181

Richmond, Va., 20, 63, 159

Roberts, Elizabeth, 151

Robertson, Vernon, 161

Robinson, Jackie, 145

Robinson, "Sugar Chile," 83, 217 (n. 107)

Roediger, David, 32, 210 (n. 97)

Roosevelt, Franklin D., 15, 24, 27, 87–88, 106–7, 113, 209 (n. 75)

Roper report, 191–92, 195, 232 (n. 16)

Rosenbaum, Fanny, 226 (n. 54)

Rubber production, 25–28

Rudwick, Elliot, 133, 142

Rural-to-urban migration. See African American migration; White migration

Russell, Ruth, 65, 71

Ruthenburg, Dorcas, 166

Sacksteder, C., 70

"Safe space," 55, 124, 125, 147, 223–24 (n. 4). See also Home

St. Louis, Mo., 135

Salaries. See Employment of African Americans

Sanders, Juanita, 33

Save Our Community Schools, 193

Sawyer, E. P., 170

Schacter, Harry, 112, 114, 119–20

Schmied, Kenneth, 169, 171, 172, 174, 176, 179, 185

Scholtz, Joseph D., 92–93

School busing, 118, 119, 193–95, 233 (n. 30), 234 (nn. 33, 35)

Schools. See Education

SCLC. See Southern Christian Leadership Conference

"Second ghetto," 9–10, 12, 152, 159, 205 (nn. 29–30)

Second Great Migration. See African American migration

Segregation: and blacks' refusal to be "Jim Crowed," 82–84; of bus station, 3, 24; city ordinance banning, 128, 130–32, 141, 144–45; Day Law (1904) on, 39, 95–105, 109, 113; dissemblance as survival strategy for, 76–78; in employment, 31, 32, 111, 119–21; Ethridge on, 99; of hospitals, 39, 45, 108–11, 151; in Kentucky generally, 39; and labor unions, 32, 34, 111; Louisville index of, 46, 183, 212 (n. 46), 231 (n. 95); maintenance of, based on custom versus law, 40, 41, 46, 75, 110, 160–61; mental map of, 74–75; Muhammad Ali (Cassius Clay) on, 178–79; in northern cities, 10; passing as challenge to, 79–80; of police force, 40; of public library, 39, 105–7; of public transportation, 37–38, 47, 211 (n. 18); and separate but equal doctrine, 105, 165; and "separate cities" for African Americans, 19, 150, 208 (n. 30), 227–28 (n. 4); shifting pat-

participation by, in civil rights protests, 137; personality of, 226 (n. 54); and segregated stores, 75, 82

Walnut Street business district, 3, 5, 12, 19–20, 149–52, 155

Walter, Maria, 48

Walters, Arthur, 141–42, 196

Warley v. Buchanan, 164

Washington, Dinah, 150

Washington, Kathleen, 189

Washington, Mathias, 188

Watkins, Hollis, 126

Watts Uprising (1964), 166

Weatherby, Lawrence, 111

Weaver, Robert, 170, 230 (n. 57)

WECC. *See* West End Community Council

Wegenast, Edward, 186

WEST. *See* White Emergency Support Team

West Downtown Renewal Area, 154, 155

West End, 161–64, 167, 168, 183, 184, 186–88, 195

West End and Mid-City Citizens for Desegregation, 193

West End Community Council (WECC), 167, 169, 182–83, 187

What the Negro Wants, 112, 115

White, Walter, 99

White Citizens Council, 117

White Emergency Support Team (WEST), 190, 232 (n. 14)

White employment. *See* Employment of whites

White flight to suburbs, 159–60, 167, 182–84, 195

White liberals: and conservative civil rights organizations, 114; and CORE, 133, 134–35; and desegregation of higher education, 98–99; and desegregation of public schools, 115, 117–19; and gradual view of racial progress, 98–99, 112, 114; hooks on, 114; Hughes on limits of, 112–13; and interracial movement, 105, 107, 109–13, 133; and open housing campaign, 166; and political action, 109–13, 222 (nn. 126, 129); and segregation, 99, 114; and teacher salary equalization, 94; and Wade-Braden case, 115–17; and white supremacy, 112–13, 115

White migration, 17–18, 24

White supremacy, 8, 9, 41, 47, 51, 55, 78, 87, 98, 99, 113–15, 171, 183, 195–96. *See also* Racism and racial discrimination

Wilkins, Roy, 135

Willis, Simon, 108

Wilson, George D., 61–62, 106, 151

Wims, Clara, 138

Winstead-Beckett, Goldie, 2–5, 22, 23, 61, 109, 151, 155, 157

WLOU (radio station), 111

Wolcott, Victoria, 66

Wolters, Raymond, 16

Women. *See* African American women

Woolsey, Frederick, 159

Workforce. *See* Employment *headings*

Works Progress Administration (WPA), 18, 44, 53, 54, 124

World War II, 14, 24–27, 34–35, 75, 79, 113, 126

WPA. *See* Works Progress Administration

Wright, George C.: on civil rights movement, 114; on criminal justice system, 39; on Democratic Party, 87; on desegregation of downtown facilities, 127, 142; on desegregation of higher education, 96, 101; on economic boycott of Louisville businesses, 137; on Kentucky State College, 100; on Ku Klux Klan membership, 86; on police corruption and brutality, 64, 67–68, 215 (n. 49); on "polite racism" and "progressiveness" of Louisville, 40, 46; scholarship on Louisville by, 8, 40

Wright, Gladys, 13

Wright, James, 13, 110

Wyatt, Wilson W., 106, 152

Yater, George, 25, 27

YMCA, 112

Young, C. Milton, 151

Young, J. W. "Boots," 170

Young, Milton, 21, 61

YWCA, 112

Zehnder, Ralph, 186

Zion Baptist Church, 169, 187–88